More Dreams of Mars

Yambu

150 years of Martian dreams,
of stories old and new.

More Dreams of Mars

John Litchen

Yambu

More Dreams of Mars
1st edition
Copyright © John Litchen 2023

!SBN: 978-0-6488801-8-9

Published by Yambu
3 Firestone Court Robina, 4226 QLD.
jlitchen@bigpond.net.au

This one is also for
Bruce Gillespie
and
Dick (Ditmar) Jenssen
who continue to inspire
with their writing and their art

and
for all those who love stories that
involve Mars.

Contents

page:

Foreword

More Dreams of Mars is not a sequel to ***Dreams of Mars — 130 years of stories about Mars:*** It is a companion volume that looks at some of the work published between the years 1876 to 1920, not mentioned in that previous volume, stories long out of print and copyright.

Most of these can be found in National Archival Libraries, and are now available as downloadable PDFs or eBooks thanks to such projects as The Gutenberg Project along with a few publishers that bring back to life forgotten literary works.

It also includes stories that were missed since completing ***Dreams of Mars,*** stories from the 1930s, 40s, and 50s, that I have re-discovered, or discovered for the first time since many of the earlier ones were published before I was born, or before I was old enough to read them or they weren't available in Australia when I was a younger reader.

And it looks at some of the more recent commercially published stories along with self-published eBooks and POD books available on Amazon, and elsewhere that have appeared from mid 2000s to the present time.

In the previous volume I covered books which had been in my collection, mostly stories from the 1950s to 2018, with a few earlier ones that were reprinted in the 1970s. I have subsequently acquired many more Martian stories, old as well as new; enough so that this second volume seems warranted.

My hope is that the stories mentioned here as well as in ***Dreams of Mars*** spark enough interest for readers to want to find them, to enjoy them, to realize how many different dreams of Mars there were, and still are.

The idea of going to Mars, of being on Mars, of colonizing Mars, making Mars a second home for humans, is something people around the world have shared for centuries. It is a dream that will never die, but will keep being modified as we learn more and more about Mars every day.

It is also a dream that will start happening in the very near future.

Millions of books

The advent of self-publishing and print on demand has given millions of authors the opportunity to publish their work and have it on sale with Amazon and other online retailers. In the US alone, self-published books increased by 40% in 2018 with 1.68 million books published. Only 8% of those books were eBooks, but that is still an enormous number. This information is supplied by Bowker who issues ISBNs worldwide. There are no numbers for Kindle eBooks published by Amazon because they have their own identifying numbers, but for anyone who has looked at Amazon's books listed, there are millions of them.

Having the freedom to publish and get their work 'out there', some authors have become overly prolific with series of volumes of continuing stories, often going beyond a trilogy to have four, five, six, with the promise of even more to come. This is particularly noticeable with self-published eBooks.

The proliferation of endless trilogies, is just as noticeable with books published by traditional publishers distributed to bookshops and other retailers. There are far too many that are almost indistinguishable from each other.

Personally, I am not fond of trilogies, and more often than not, won't buy them. But there are exceptions, and those are generally stories published by reputable publishers who have announced at the start that this is volume one of a trilogy. If I am interested in that particular story, or that author's work, I will wait until all of it is published to read the books one after the other without a huge gap in between while waiting for the next one.

Often self-published writers give no indication that the book you start reading is part of a trilogy, and after reading what seems to be a promising story, disappointment and frustration set in when you are left hanging at the end with nothing resolved because there is another volume or two to follow.

I have sometimes selected the first volumes of some already published trilogies with a Martian setting to see how the story begins, and if it captures my interest, then I will follow up and read the other books in the series, but if not, then I won't waste money buying the subsequent books, or the time needed to read them.

Because there are millions of eBooks on Amazon and other retailers, it is impossible to find all of those that specifically relate to Mars, so once again there will be titles missed because I don't know of their existence, or because the price asked is too high, or the synopsis simply doesn't interest me.

Most eBooks have attractive covers and appear interesting, but often fall below expectations. It's hard to tell when purchasing, but once I start reading them, there are some I can't finish because: they are too derivative, are so badly produced they aren't attractive as books, or I get tired of misspelled words and typographical errors… sorry, but these things quickly kill off any desire to read further

On saying that however, I do congratulate everyone who has the perseverance to write and publish a book. It's not easy. It takes time and dedication. But you did it! And that does matter.

Even though the cover art may look professional and attractive I look at who the publisher is and what information, or lack of it is at the start of the book. This can indicate self-publishing, amateur publishing, or vanity publishing. Vanity publishers will publish anything regardless of quality because the author is paying them to do so; they are nothing short of a con to take advantage of unsuspecting writers.

Book lovers are interested in more than the words or the story. They love the way a book looks, the way it feels and smells, as this enhances the reading experience. They do not want heavy, cumbersome books bloated with thick paper, large print and double spacing between each paragraph to make it appear longer, bigger and heavier. It detracts from the enjoyment of reading. Too many amateur as well as self-publishing companies produce inferior and unattractive work which in the long run can only be detrimental to self-publishing.

Unfortunately, it is impossible to tell what the quality of these stories or what the printed books will be like until they are purchased. The covers are almost always attractive, but sometimes the content does not live up to the promise of the cover.

I chose the eBooks or the printed versions mentioned in this volume, firstly because the titles and the covers were attractive, or the synopsis promising; and secondly because the price was reasonable. Of those I didn't choose because the price was ridiculously high for a self-published paperback book, the story may have been very good and beautifully written, but to ask $40 or more for a paperback novel is a bit much when other similar books are $20 or less. And when postage has to be added, then for me it's not worth buying.

Exciting stories

What fascinated me when I was a teenager in the 1950s was reading wonderfully exciting stories of space travel and exploration of the planets in the solar system as well as further beyond. These stories published in the 1940s and the 1950s — long since vanished and mostly forgotten today— always exhibited positivity and excitement combined with a sense of wonder at what the future may bring; something that has stayed with me to the present day.

My biggest annoyance today is that many of the newer stories by today's authors are not doing anything new, but are often derivative, or they attempt to re-invent or re-do what was done long before the author was born.

Have these authors not read any of those early stories?

Are they not aware of what was done before?

Do they not know what tropes or traditions writers of the Golden Age used that were generally agreed upon by their contemporaries as well as their readers, which made explanations unnecessary because everyone knew what the universe the stories were set in was like?

My impression is that many modern writers as well as their readers, have never seen those early stories. They have no idea of what was done before, and not knowing, blindly forge ahead trying to reinvent, usually not as well. Their stories are more than likely to contain ideas garnered from B grade movies, action blockbusters and TV rather than early fiction, and this is why their new stories lack the '*sense of wonder*' that infused those earlier stories. For me, they are less interesting and less memorable overall.

Armchair Fiction is one of a number of publishers, *Wildside Press* is another, using print on demand publishing to bring back some wonderful stories (novels, short novels and novellas) from the early decades of science fiction. Many of those stories were written by well-known authors at the start of their careers, as well as authors no one now remembers.

It is really good for someone like me who grew up during that era to rediscover the excitement I felt back then while reading those stories. I still get that same sense of wonder about the endless possibilities the future could hold.

Those past futures could now be seen as alternative futures to the one we live in. Our present future is equally as interesting although coloured more by negativity than positivity for the future to come.

I have bought some of the *Armchair Fiction* volumes that contain stories about Mars, and there were quite a lot more than I expected.

Many of these early works are surprisingly good, and generally more entertaining than some of the very latest stories, and are well worth rediscovering if you haven't already done so.

My hope is that this present volume will help generate interest in those earlier stories and curious readers will go out and search for them.

Part One
Early Dreams

More Dreams of Mars

Chapter One

Forgotten Gems from Early Days

One of the earliest...

An interesting small book that at first, I thought was written by a modern author in the style of how something like this would have been written in 1876 is *A trip to Mars* by Charles K Landis (*written in 1876 but never published until 2015*). Subtitled: *As described by an eye witness.*

Reading the introduction changed my mind, as did some of the scientific ideas presented within the text itself.

Landis was a Philadelphia attorney who established his law practice before he turned 21. He then went on to invest in real estate when the railroads began to penetrate inland. He is credited with having established or assisted in the development of several small towns, such as Colville (later known as Elwood), Hammonton, Vineland and Sea Isle City. He was a ruthless businessman, but privately he was restless and travelled a lot. He kept diaries and journals of his adventures, all of which are part of the **Vineland Historical and Antiquarian Society's** archives. They published this book which was only discovered in their archives around 2015. I *googled* their name and discovered they are an actual Historical Society, which is what convinced me their claims regarding this book are likely to be true. While writing this book, Landis was tried for the murder of Uri Carruth, a newspaper editor with whom he had been in conflict for some time, and was one of the first people in the USA to be freed on the grounds of temporary insanity.

Our protagonist (*the story is told in the first person*) is travelling in the Tyrol which he believes is the most beautiful part of Europe stretching from Salzburg to the Alps. Exploring some of the wildest parts he is caught out at night during a ferocious thunderstorm while travelling along a rocky path beside a mountain stream, and is struck by lightning and rendered unconscious. Whether he fell into the stream or was pushed into it by an avalanche of rocks and boulders isn't explained. He wakes up in a bed in a medieval castle. He had been found and rescued by an elderly gentleman, a scientist and philosopher to whom the castle belonged. The man was also a member of the Rosicrucian's, a secret society of scientists and other wealthy people who have made many fascinating discoveries which they keep to themselves. He had been out during the storm to conduct experiments with electricity when he saw a body borne along by the rushing stream, rescued the person and took him back to his castle where he mended a fractured skull, broken bones in both arms and legs as well as cracked ribs.

The injured man whom I will refer to as Charles, discovers his rescuer, like other members of this secret society, was almost 400 years old but appeared hale and as hearty as someone in their sixties. After discussions with his rescuer, known as the Count Motzen, Charles decides he wants to become a member of this secret society, and the Count is willing to induct him into it, but this will take time as other members need to be brought there to be a part of the induction. Meanwhile Charles returns to the US where he takes care of business matters before returning to Europe to again visit the Count. Travelling back, he keeps thinking about Mars and recent reports he has read in newspapers regarding the possibility of life on Mars and upon arriving at the Count's castle, he suggests that they might be able to go there. The Count explains that going there would be no problem because he has discovered certain rare minerals in the mountains that are Martian in origin, and by refining this mineral into a metal they can construct a carriage that will take them to Mars because this rare metal will be repelled by the Earth and attracted to Mars.

The Count belies that meteorites are attracted to Earth where they burn up in the atmosphere, because they are made of Earth elements, and likewise meteorites attracted to Mars will be made up of material and elements of Mars.

It is interesting how at a time when air travel by anything other than a hot air balloon was inconceivable, the more technical minded authors had to come up with something that would enable their characters to leave Earth to go to Mars or the Moon or elsewhere. Inevitably, they came up with the idea of anti-gravity. H G Wells had *cavorite* named after his character Professor Cavor, who invented a rare *anti-gravity* metal that was attracted and repelled by sunlight and from which he built a sphere to take his people to the Moon. They could travel wherever they wanted depending on how they exposed this *cavorite* to sunlight. Various other authors had different means of producing the effects of anti-gravity so their travelers could leave Earth and go to Mars and other planets. Some even imagined using the power of electricity which to them seemed a wonderful source of mysterious power. Percy Greg in 1880 had his space ship powered by *Apergy* and *Antapergy* which used repulsion and attraction of sunlight to power his ship. George Griffith in 1901 had his metal airship powered by an electrical repulsive force which in effect was an *anti-gravity* drive. Jules Verne simply shot his characters inside a projectile out of a giant cannon to get them into space. Others, like Edgar Rice Burroughs, used wishful thinking, or teleportation or something like that to get their characters off Earth and onto another planet.

Using metal that was composed of Martian matter and which would be attracted to Mars isn't any more fantastic than any other means and actually seems logical considering the year in which the story was written, 1876.

The ship constructed was cigar shaped so it would float as a boat would on water. It had extremely thick walls padded with wool to keep the heat in as they suspected it would be so cold in outer space that even mercury would freeze. Once they take off, at night so they wouldn't be seen, they ascended so slowly that they had barely got more than a few hundred feet into the air before it dawned and thousands of people could see them. The Count thought that the iron in the nearby mountains hindered their attraction to Mars and prevented them from rising as fast as they wanted. But rise slowly they did, and the higher they got the faster they travelled, until they left the Earth's atmosphere and the stars were revealed in all their glory. Although being attracted by Mars the ship was also attracted by the sun which drew it off into a much more elongated orbit than anticipated.

Charles was concerned that the attractive forces in space would be equal from all directions and they would never go anywhere and would be stuck in space forever. The Count reassured him that he had considered the possibility but decided to take the risk anyway... While their speed increases as Mars draws them closer, they discuss the theory that Mars is geologically older than Earth and that it must have developed life there much sooner and that this life would be more advanced and technologically superior to what is on Earth. *A common theory which comes up in many stories about going to Mars written at the turn of the nineteenth century.* Then, much sooner than expected, they are rushing towards Mars and the Count ejects excess Martian metal plates from the outside of the ship to lessen the attraction and to slow down their descent.

As they descend, they see a large beautiful city and flying boats come up to greet them. Like a feather they land on the roof of a building and a huge crowd comes out to meet them. Unbolting the hatch, Charles and the Count emerge to see the *Marsians* (which is what the author logically calls the inhabitants of Mars), gathered around. They are clean and dressed in toga-like clothes and are definitely human which the Count thinks are Roman in character. The Count gestures to the best dressed person whom he assumes is important, and unable to communicate in each other's language, the Count resorts to pantomime to get across the idea that they have come from the third planet from the sun for a visit. They are taken inside the building which is opulent and constructed of fine marble. The visitors are impressed with the construction of the buildings in the city and fine fixtures they display.

In early Martian stories, authors always had their buildings constructed of lustrous materials like fine marble with fittings made of gold or other precious metals. There is not much mention of fittings or of gold cups and plates here, although it is hinted at… this of course was to impress the reader with how wealthy the Martians were and how little they actually cared for being wealthy, to them it was normal.

At this point the reader is getting the impression that Mars is a utopia, because they are more advanced socially as well as technologically compared to the Earth (of 1876). Very quickly the Count learns the language so they can communicate. The Count is a linguist and speaks many languages, so learning a new one is easy for him.

Early writers of Mars stories always assumed that Mars would be more advanced, a utopia, and used this to make comparisons of Earth cultures and beliefs. This story is no different and the author has his characters see many advances that Earth doesn't have. All the buildings are constructed of marble, and there are gardens and trees surrounding them. The buildings have running water both hot and cold, but unlike Earth buildings they are not connected to a sewerage system as are buildings in cities on Earth. The Count believes this is a vast improvement since the evil miasma that emanates from sewers on Earth is the cause of such horrible diseases like cholera and typhoid. *Excrementitious matter from 'closets' or toilets* is collected in a box filled with chemically treated dried earth and this is taken away daily and disposed of, thus there is none of the foul odors that come up from underground sewers which don't exist on Mars. Animal droppings in the streets are shoveled up and placed in similar boxes along the streets and taken away daily. The streets are hosed down and washed overnight, and this, compared with the murderous systems used in the cities on Earth like Paris, London and New York, the Count believes, raises the *Marsian* civilization beyond that of Earth.

It was this description that convinced me the story really was written in 1876 as the publisher's claim.

Transport is in vehicles drawn by large animals or in flying boats that are filled with a gas lighter than the atmosphere, which makes them float, and drawn along in the air by two large bird-like animals. They have electricity which is carried on lines underground to power lights and other machines and is also used to help improve the cultivation of vegetables and fruits. Using electricity to improve plant growth was a common idea in the late 1800s and this concept also appears in other Martian stories from that era (*see* **Dreams of Mars** *page 25.* **Melbourne and Mars** *by John Fraser 1889*).

Electricity is generated by the ebb and flow of the tides in the nearby ocean which forces water through narrow pipes into generators and pumps. They also have underground atmospheric roads, tubes in which a vehicle floats along at great speed to carry people to and from distant locations around the city. Yet the Count is amazed that they have never heard of steam power, which was the driving force on Earth for trains, metal ships, mining machinery and other heavy industrial equipment. On Mars all transport is drawn along by draught animals on the surface or large flying animals in the air. The top speed of these animal drawn vehicles is an astonishing 30 miles an hour. (*That would have been very fast for someone to comprehend in 1876 when the fastest land vehicles would have been horse drawn carriages which I don't think could have achieved 30 miles per hour.*)

Once the language is understood the Count gives a series of lectures to explain about Earth and its customs and how superior the *Marsian* customs are when compared to those of Earth. The obvious difference is that the *Marsians* treat each other with courtesy and kindness, and are always friendly. But all utopias have something that is wrong and this is intimated when, out and about, Charles and the Count notice there are guards in many places armed with crossbows and spears, swords and knives. They are told this is to protect the citizens from the encroachment of ferociously wild animals.

Travelling about they discover the city is walled off from the wilderness as a form of protection from marauding wild beasts. When asked about these beasts the Count and Charles are taken to an arena where wild caged animals are let loose for the guards to train in methods of killing them. After observing this activity, the Count wants to demonstrate how effective his earth-guns are with their explosive bullets and insists on being let into the area to show the weapon's effectiveness against one of the wildest animals. Reluctantly the *Marsians* allow him to do this. As he enters the arena they immediately release a monstrous beast which rushes towards him. He blows half its head off which doesn't stop it. His second shot penetrates behind the foreleg and into the heart and the beast drops. These beasts have two brains and to kill one either the heart has to be penetrated or the head completely blown off. The *Marsians* could never do this with crossbows and spears, and they are astonished at the effectiveness of the Earth weapon. The Count immediately organizes for them to manufacture copies of his rifles and guns, suitably sized up for *Marsian* use since the *Marsians* are all over 6 feet tall and are very strong compared to Earthmen. Once he finishes training them in the use of these weapons, they go on a hunt to eliminate some of the dangerous animals that constantly threaten the city.

The last part of the story concerns this hunt and their encounters with several different ferocious animals including a large group of flying gorillas that are particularly dangerous. After some very close encounters they eventually make their way back to the city. In the last part of the book the travelers discover the *Marsians* are Christian and that Christ had visited them in the past, just like he had on Earth. They don't find this astonishing because if God had created the whole universe, and had filled it with humans as well as other animals, why would not Christ have visited other humans on other planets if he did so with Earth? They also discover that deformed children are eliminated so they never grow up to spoil the race and that criminals no longer exist because anyone exhibiting such behavior is also eliminated, humanely of course. The end result of this eugenic practice was a near perfect race of beings on Mars.

The story ends abruptly here, which I found disappointing because I did want to know how the two travelers would get back to Earth if their ship was made of Martian metal and was attracted to Mars. How would they make it attractive to Earth so they could return?

On the whole, it is well written and entertaining, and it does give a modern reader an insight into how people at the end of the nineteenth century saw the world around them and what they thought other worlds like Mars would be like.

Often mentioned but practically unknown...

Across the Zodiac by Percy Greg (1880)

This work when originally published in 1880 was subtitled: ***The Story of a Wrecked Record, deciphered, translated and edited by Percy Greg.*** It is often mentioned in various literary texts regarding stories about Mars, but not much detail is given, which is a pity because it is actually a very good story.

Typical of work published during this era, the first chapter sets the scene by explaining how the author came to be in possession of the manuscript he claims to have translated and edited.

An Englishman travelling in America encounters at a function a retired Southern Army Colonel who proceeds to tell him a remarkable story of a shipwreck. This Colonel was sent to Mexico by General Lee just before the loss of the war between the North and the South and in time he became the crew of a steamer that was sailing towards Brisbane (Australia). Conditions on the ship were abysmal. One night while he was sleeping the ship crashed into a coral reef. The crew abandoned it and made their way onto an island. No one knew where they were. The sextant was smashed as was most of everything on the ship. The crew decided to go back on board during the day to see what they could salvage, but the Colonel couldn't stand the stench and the filth on the ship and decided he would not go back. He walked away along the beach to see what else there was on this unknown island. He was half way around the island when there was a sudden brightening of the sky as a huge meteor came tearing into the atmosphere. Flames burned around it but a dark sphere inside the flames momentarily obscured the sun. There was an almighty crash, a massive explosion and the shock wave knocked him off his feet. When he regained consciousness sometime later, he made his way back to the site of his shipwreck to discover his ship, and presumably the crew because they were on board attempting to salvage stuff, were all gone; vanished as if they never existed.

All around him trees were flattened and pieces of metal and concrete were scattered over a wide area. A huge crater marked the point where the meteor, and that's all he could think it was, crashed. On examining what he could see, he found a strange metal box which contained a manuscript, written on a peculiar paper the like of which he had never before seen. It was written in a strange language or some kind of code and was the only surviving artifact in the debris from whatever had crashed onto the island.

The only other thing that survived the crash that destroyed his own shipwreck and devastated half of the island was a small boat used to bring the sailors ashore. For some reason it had been beached well away from the crash site and though partly damaged was still intact enough to allow the Colonel to escape the island. He doesn't go into how long it took to be rescued or how he managed to get back to civilization, because there are far too many similar stories extant. He gives the box and the manuscript to the author (Percy Greg). There is then a brief passage as the author describes the character of the text in the Manuscript and explains it took several years to decipher and translate it. He then mentions that what he has published is only the first part that deals with one voyage to a planet, and that if the response of the public is reasonable, he would consider publishing the other parts. The narrator of the story is never named, and it is told in the first person. The narrator knows perfectly well who he is and never divulges his own name.

The story then begins with *chapter II*, and describes how the narrator uses *Apergy* and *Antapergy*, against the gravitation of the sun and of other celestial objects to power a ship capable of travelling in space. This chapter describes the three feet thick walls filled with concrete to insulate against the cold of space, the motive power and how it is applied to make the ship move, how he will regenerate oxygen and remove carbon dioxide, furnishings like chairs bookshelves, food supplies as well as a fresh garden. The concrete floor is covered with cork and carpet. This is a massive ship one hundred feet in length, fifty in breadth, and about twenty feet in height. The ship he calls *Astronaut* also has windows of special glass that can act as telescopic magnifiers, as well as straight windows. He explains how he would steer the ship and expresses some concern that it wouldn't be ready for the Mars Opposition. He also explains how fast the Earth travels and how this speed is his starting speed and how he will take aim at Mars once he has attained Earth orbit.

There is nothing about orbital mechanics, his means of navigation is to keep his destination in sight through the forward window and aim straight towards it. There is no airlock. A Large window which he entered through is firmly cemented in place to prevent air escaping, so if he wished to exit the ship (*Astronaut*) on arrival he must break this cement to release the seal and then can climb out. To use the ship again he must enter the same way and re-seal the glass window with cement.

Finally, when all is ready, he takes off. The ship rises rapidly and silently. There is not even the sound of wind whistling past. Through his windows he sees trees and buildings rapidly diminishing until within moments he is unable to discern them. He passes through a cloud and marvels at how it looks from above (*something no one was likely to have seen in 1880*) with cavities and hillocks of mist, light reflecting from a thousand broken masses of vapour at different levels until finally he rises way above it and begins to see stars with more and more coming into view as the sky darkens. Within 30 minutes he was surrounded by blackness filled with distant stars and could see the Earth as a globe rapidly receding beneath him. At this point since none of the stars were scintillating, he realized he was outside of the Earth's atmosphere.

Chapter III describes his voyage from Earth to Mars, detailing how the ship works and how he navigates. He has a close encounter with a huge meteor as he passes through a ring of meteors, mentioning that scientists believe there are many rings of meteors circling the sun just as the planets do.

From my point of view, an annoyance with these early novels is that everything is described in minute detail which tends to slow down the narrative, in some cases making it tedious. With this story, although it is slow moving the details are quite fascinating as they open a window into what scientific knowledge was contemporary in 1880. Some of it was reasonably accurate while other parts were pure speculation.

As he gets close to Mars he thinks about the distance he has travelled over the 30 days of the voyage and comes to the conclusion that the Earth is not, as generally accepted, some 95 million miles from the sun but is much less, concluding that the 'solar distance' of the Earth is only 9 million miles, and that accordingly makes everything in the solar system correspondingly closer than previously thought. He estimates his speed as 45,000 miles per hour, and he arrives at Mars sooner than he expected. On the morning of the 39th day he arrives and slowing down prepares to land on Mars.

He compares Mars to Earth and unlike Earth Mars appears to have more land and less ocean. Instead of continents surrounded by oceans he sees a vast land area with several smaller landlocked seas. It takes him a couple of days of slowing down and gradually descending towards Mars and there is much description of how the land and the seas look. Finally, he lands on mesa at the edge of a mountain range and emerging from his space ship he observes the scene before him. Far in the distance is a small town or a cluster of buildings, and between that and where he stands on the mesa, there is a huge area of cultivated land. The seas are predominantly grey rather than blue. The general colour of the land is orange. The vegetation is orange rather than green.

Chapter IV begins with: *I will not attempt to express the intensity of the mingled emotions which overcame me as I realized the complete success of the most stupendous adventure ever proposed or even dreamed by man. I don't think that any personal vanity, unworthy of the highest lessons I had received, had much share in my passionate exultation.* ...and it goes on like this for a couple of paragraphs before he gives us information about the lesser gravity of Mars because of the size of the planet compared to Earth. He discovers the air of Mars is breathable and similar to the air on Earth around a height of 16,000 feet. He observes *the sky is pale green, and the vegetation, mostly small, was of a yellowish colour, the flowers generally red, varied by occasional examples of dull green and white...* The mountain range behind him rises to around 25,000 feet.

Anything Earthly he refers to as Tellurian (Latin meaning Earth), while anything Martian is referred to as Martial. Martial of course has a different connotation today, being warlike. His inhabitants of Mars are not martial in the modern sense.

Descending from the mesa he landed on he soon encounters small animals and as he enters the cultivated area, he comes across a human figure.

The person is described as being shorter than himself by about a third, but with a larger chest area in comparison to an Earthly human like himself. He attempts to communicate with the Martian but neither can understand the other. Finally, he takes the Martian by the hand and starts walking towards the distant buildings of the town beside the sea. They traverse fields of culti-vated fruit and cross several roads before following one into the outskirts of the town where he is immediately surrounded by suspicious natives. There is a minor altercation which is stopped by well-dressed person who is of some importance. This person takes the human visitor by the hand and leads him further into the town and to a large compound where he is taken inside and treated like a valued guest. They manage to communicate in a rudimentary way. While being treated like an honored guest he realizes that he is actually a prisoner.

Chapter V is titled Language, Laws, and Life.

A common practice of authors of fantastic tales at the end of the 19th century and the beginning of the 20th century is they felt the need to explain in great detail what their point of view character was seeing. Often pages of information, (*infodumps in modern terms*), were presented so the reader could understand that the story was taking place somewhere other than on Earth or at some other time in the future rather than the present time when the story was written.

In this story Percy Greg has glass sliding doors that open sideways from the centre rather than opening on hinges. The doors would retract into the walls. There is even the suggestion that electricity is involved though not much is said about it. This would have been astonishingly marvelous in 1880, although every shopping mall has doors exactly like that today and a modern reader could perhaps wonder why a detailed description of these doors appears in this story.

Although treated with courtesy and kindness, when he attempts to leave the compound the first time he finds himself alone, a young child stops him as he is about to release the latch on the door to the world outside. The child indicates that it is dangerous for him to leave and taking his hand leads him back into the residence.

Back in the house he begins his study of the language, and apparently, he manages to learn it very quickly. And here there are pages of examples of Martian language and grammar, with how the verbs are used in the past, present and future tenses, how adjectives and nouns change according to who or what is being referred to, with lists of the declension of verbs.

There is also much discussion and explanation of how the Martians live, and the government they have, which appears Utopian and communistic.

In *chapter VI,* an official visit by the Area Regent follows in which he has to determine if the guest is truly of another planet, how big he is compared to the locals, and how he managed to arrive. The Regent will report back to the Suzerain (The Supreme Ruler) after inspecting the vessel in which the guest arrived and the machinery within. Martian scientists do not believe that other planets have life on them and think this strange large visitor is a demon or an impostor telling lies, which explained his rough treatment on descending from the mountain where he left his space ship. Until the Regent reports back, the guest will for the time being be under the protection of the law, and no one will be able to harm him.

There is also a suggestion of a budding romance between Eveena, the eldest daughter of his host, and himself. Apparently, women are kept hidden, and if outside they wear veils as only the members of their direct household are entitled to see them. The men rule and women are subservient although it is claimed they have equal status to men.

I suspect the author has mixed prevailing communist theory with Arabian culture to arrive at a suitably strange culture to explain the Martian way of life in comparison with 19th century European life. Several times the narrator makes reference to his experience in the Arab World as a mercenary soldier, and I suspect for the author, the culture of Arabia and its people was exotic enough to be used as a model for his Martian civilization. The compound where the human is staying seems modeled on the compounds of tribal rulers in Arab countries.

Another instance of using prevailing scientific thought is that of Eugenics. Children born who are deformed, or whom the doctors perceive to be antagonistic or in some way a threat to the pleasant way of life experienced by others are not allowed to live, except in exceptional circumstances. There are a group of doctors, and our guest's host is one of them, who believe that nature should not be altered, and that these difficult children if brought up in loving families can change and benefit from living in more pleasant conditions. Eugenics and communism were evolving philosophies at the time this novel was composed. This makes the narrator's host an exception because children in general are put in state nurseries shortly after birth and a brought up and educated away from any family connections. The girls, when of age, are sold as brides.

Martians are also it seems, immortal. All diseases can be cured and anyone who chooses not to live because they have lost interest in doing so can ask to be terminated (euthanized). Those who are incurably insane are not allowed to live. Selfishness and personal interest have been bred out of the race over millennia. Of course, there can be accidents and people do die, but in general the population is happy and stable.

All these things contribute to give an impression of a utopian society compared to a Europe of mixed languages and cultures and petty wars between the monarchies and other regimes that prevailed in 1880.

The biggest problem for modern readers is that there is an excessive amount of detail regarding every little thing which slows down the events taking place. Perhaps, when it was written the author thought everything that was different from what Europeans understood in 1880 to be normal had to be explained in wondrous detail to convince the readers of the time that the events taking place were actually happening on Mars.

When the regent arrives to accompany the alien guest to his ship, the vehicles they travel in have three wheels, two at the back and one in front which is used to steer. There is a canopy that can be drawn over to protect them from the sun. The vehicles are made of tubular metal, so light that the weight is negligible. The driving force is electricity.

Electricity was the wonder power discovered in the 19th century, and was used by many authors of that time as a means of powering vehicles, space ships, flying machines, and other inventive and imaginary devices. Everything on Mars is powered by electricity, not only in this story but also in other contemporary stories set on Mars.

Arriving at the foot of the mesa where he landed his ship, the Regent, his associates, as well as the narrator and Eveena, all have to leave the vehicles and climb up to the mesa on foot. At the landing site on top of the mesa the narrator leads the party and helps them enter into his ship where some of them are surprised at the primitiveness of his equipment, though the force he uses to power things (*apergy*) is not electricity but something else, and this impresses them.

Meanwhile Eveena wanders off to look at flowers on the hillside and follows a path down the side of the mesa. She becomes trapped when a log she crossed over a chasm falls away. The human-alien rescues her but not without forcing the Regent to assist. He at first refuses to concern himself with this young female but the narrator threatens to kill him if he doesn't assist, forcing him to do so, and in turn creating an enemy. Once Eveena is rescued the Regent quickly departs and our hero has to carry Eveena down the hillside to where their vehicle was left. She lost her veil and covering so on the way back the canopy is drawn over the vehicle so others will not see her.

Even Esmo, his host, is astonished that his guest went to so much trouble to rescue his daughter, and blames her because she didn't remain where she was but wandered off endangering both their lives. There is much discussion here about how females are regarded on Mars compared to how the narrator would respect women on Earth. There is also the implication that he is treating her as if she was his wife, while he considers he only did what he would have been expected to do on Earth had he been responsible for looking after a woman in his company.

It's at this point that the human guest realizes that all is not what it seems. Although the Martians are technologically well in advance of human civilization their moral code is degenerate as far as he is concerned. Women are oppressed, and the general population believes in certain things, and anyone who contradicts those ideas is either killed or taken away for re-education so they will fall in line with what is expected of them to believe. It now looks more like a dystopia rather than a utopia. Esmo and his family are part of an ancient secret group that believes differently from the general Martian population. So, the benevolent utopia is not so benevolent after all.

Most of what follows in *chapters VII to IX* is what today would be called World Building, and is usually not included in a story in such large amounts, but would be surreptitiously inserted where needed. In the nineteenth century those kinds of details were always included in stories, and no doubt readers back then expected it, or certainly needed it in order to understand the alien environment in which the story takes place.

The author details the climate, the length of the day (*and he gets it right as 24 hours and about 40 minutes, which was well known in 1880 but often is ignored by some modern writers who manage to get the length of day wrong*). He also explains how the day is divided into hours and what hours people work. His explanation of the difference between the Northern and Southern hemisphere's summer and winter is accurate in regards to duration because of the oblong nature of Mars' orbit around the sun. Using that to add credence he then goes on to talk about the temperatures and they are cooler, as expected, for a planet further from the Sun than Earth, (*but not as cold as we now know them to be*), the rainfall, agriculture, mining and automated preparation and refining of metals, work ethics and practices, and the monetary system being based on the value of a particular parcel of land. He talks about the mathematics based on 12 instead of 10 but working much as the decimal system in France. Nothing of note happens in these chapters until the end when the guest is told by Esmo that they are going to visit the Martian ruler who lives about 6000 miles away, which means he will get to see a lot of Mars as he travels that great distance.

He is also warned to accept humbly gifts given, and not to contradict this ruler in any way. He is told the ruler is fascinated by adventure and especially his adventures in travelling alone from Earth to Mars. Esmo also warns him to keep his ship ready for rapid departure should anything untoward happen, but under no circumstances should he reveal he has any plans for departing Mars and returning to Earth.

But before he travels across the planet to see the supreme ruler, he is inducted into the family's secret society, marries Eveena in a ceremony that involves signing a marriage contract for a two-year period. Two chapters are taken to explain in detail what is involved with the wedding, and the last part of these chapters has both newlyweds making an excursion to a fish farm and a water purification plant where the newlyweds discover how the fish are caught and farmed, and how electricity is involved in this process to stun the wild fish so they can be collected and their eggs taken for breeding in the fish farm. They also discover how the water is purified to remove all sediment as well as microscopic bacteria, which is his understanding of how diseases are transmitted, because they are the seeds of diseases and epidemics. He also believes it more likely that diseases are transmitted through water which is ingested into the body rather than by air which only enters the body while breathing. The Martians believe that diseases are caused by self-multiplying germs and laugh at the idea of spontaneous generation, (an idea most likely still prevalent in 1880).

Chapter XII is where the big journey begins with the newly-weds as well as Eveena's father Esmo and his son, Kevima. They travel by boat along a huge river at a leisurely pace so there is time to observe all aspects of the landscape, which of course is described in minute detail.

Before departing on a sea voyage our human visitor and his Martian wife are inducted through a long ceremony into the secret society of which Eveena's father is a member, and is actually the leader. As the narrator goes through the induction, we find out what the society's ideals and philosophy are, why they are a secret society, and how they envision changing Mars into a freer society.

Setting sail to the Northern polar region the human visitor and his Martian wife travel on a ship which when the portholes are closed can sink beneath the surface and become a submarine. It would return to the surface every few days to replenish the air within the boat. During this voyage they are attacked by a sea monster reminiscent of a giant eel. Monsters still exist in the seas of Mars, but not on land where all animals have been domesticated to serve the Martians. The ship/submarine is powered by electricity, and like Jules Verne's Nautilus in 20,000 leagues under the sea, the part of the boat and the propellers which the serpent has attacked are electrified with surges of power to stun the animal and make it let go.

*Jules Verne's book predated **Across the Zodiac** by seven years. The American imprint being published in 1873. It first appeared in French in 1872. It is likely that Percy Greg read Jules Vern's **20,000 Leagues Under the Sea** and used elec-*

tricity to power his undersea vessel as did Verne. He may have remembered that marvelous scene where a giant cephalapod had grabbed the Nautilus wrapping its tentacles around it being repelled by electrical surges sent through the metal hull. But then other writers of the same era also used the wonderful seemingly limitless power of electricity for all kinds of future machines. At this time, the power of electricity must have seemed endless, almost magical, capable of all kinds of marvelous things. Very primitive submarines may have existed at the time these books were written, but they certainly would have been impractical. Using a futuristic undersea vessel was as good an idea as using a space travelling vessel, when no one knew much about what was under the surface of the sea any more than they knew about what was outside of the Earth's atmosphere.

Near the north pole our human visitor participates in a wild animal hunt for fur which is used for clothing as well as other items and is slightly injured, much to the chagrin of his escorts who fear the consequences that would be meted out to them by the Supreme Ruler if anything happened to endanger the life of their alien visitor. But he is okay and the voyage continues.

When they finally arrive at the palace of the Supreme Ruler an audience takes place in which the visitor is interrogated by the Ruler. He responds to the Ruler with politeness and respect but this is obviously not what some of the other regional Lords who are in attendance expect. One in Particular has it in for the visitor in regard to the way he was threatened when Eveena's life was in danger.

The Supreme Ruler reminds the visitor that even if ten women were in danger, he should not have threatened the Regional ruler in the way that he did. That man is among those in the audience chamber and glares malevolently at the visitor letting him know that he will one day get even.

The Supreme Ruler then dismisses the other people and takes the visitor into his private chambers where they can talk more. He also offers the man a house to live in and an estate to generate an income. He informs him that he has selected six other young women to be his wives, six of the best from the nurseries where they were brought up and trained.

Eveena is an exception to the rule where all children are kept in nurseries and never know who their parents are. She lived at home with her parents and was exposed to a very different life from those normally brought up in a nursery.

Reluctantly the visitor accepts the fact he now has seven wives and a major household to manage as well as a large farmed area as part of the estate bequeathed to him by the Supreme Ruler. Walking in his estate with one of his new wives he meets a person who offers to manage the estate for him. This person is a member of the secret society that wants to change Mars and he warns the visitor that an attempt might be made on his life.

There are some people who do not like the disruption he has brought into their lives and their beliefs by the simple fact that he is not of their planet (Mars) but is from somewhere else. One of those people in particular is the Regent from the area where he first landed in his ship. Because of the way the visitor had threatened his life he holds a deep enmity towards him, which is compounded by jealousy at the knowledge of what the Ruler gave the visitor in the way of an estate and number of wives, and compounded when he sees the Supreme Ruler take the visitor into his chambers for a private conversation. He is the person behind the assassination attempts on the visitor. Through the corruption of one of the visitor's new wives he discovers the existence of the secret society that wants to change Mars and manages to convince her to attempt to poison he husband.

The narrator's conversations with the ruler are enlightening. He is the only person on Mars who the Ruler can talk to as an equal. The narrator respects the Ruler but doesn't kowtow as does everyone else on Mars. They can converse in a more natural manner, but even the Ruler can't convince the Visitor to reveal the secrets of the power that is used to operate his space ship. He will never betray his human race in case the superior technology of the Martians could be used to conquer the Earth.

As the story progresses there is jealousy among the wives for the affections of their master, and dislike of Eveena because he always prefers her to any of the others no matter how impartial he tries to be. Plots unfold as the secret society becomes known and there is the feeling of a revolution about to occur across the planet. The visitor is also inducted into a major position within that secret society.

At the end when preparing to flee the planet with his first wife Eveena his party is set upon by the local regent with a number of soldiers who in a battle kill Esmo, the leader of the Secret Society. Eveena is also killed by a discharge from one of the Martian electrical ray guns as she jumps in front of her husband to protect him. The visitor manages to board his ship and takes off. He flies over to the town and his father in law's compound where defenders are battling hoards trying to enter it. He lands on the roof of the house and hands the official medals of power to one of his secret society associates, conferring upon him the position of leader. The visitor had temporarily become the leader of this secret group after Esmo had been killed. But he is about to leave Mars and handing over the leadership is his last action. There is nothing to keep him there after his wife and her father had been killed, so he leaves.

And this is where the story ends.

As mentioned at the beginning the translator of the text (Percy Greg) states there are further manuscripts relating to voyages to Jupiter and other planets, that have yet to be translated, adventures that we will never hear about. We also know that the writer of the manuscripts dies in the crash of his ship when he eventually returns to earth, because this is how the manuscripts were discovered.

Over all this is a surprisingly interesting story, elongated by modern standards, but still engrossing and enjoyable.

Good fun and entertaining

Honeymoon in Space by George Griffith (1901)
This is worth a mention because it has several chapters set on Mars.

Griffith's ideas regarding the planets are consistent with what was considered factual (although speculative) as the world entered the 20th century. Everyone believed other worlds were inhabited, but what forms these inhabitants took and what levels of civilization they had attained was pure speculation and depended entirely on the imaginations of the various authors.

Griffith's story opens with a trans-Atlantic ship carrying passengers from America to England. On board this ship is a beautiful woman who is going to England for an arranged marriage. She is accompanied by a chaperon as young single women never travelled alone. As the ship is only a few days out from America a mysterious airship rapidly approaches and draws alongside. It is a large metal and glass construction that should not be able to fly yet there it is, floating a few feet above the waves and keeping the same speed as the ocean liner. The airship has conning tower, and propellers at the rear to send it forward but how it floats is a mystery.

This is typical of the air ships imagined at the turn of the century. Some had sails and propellers, some were constructed like wooden ships, but as the 20th century neared, the ships became constructed of metal and took a more torpedo like shape. In this story the liner's captain makes a reference to Lord Zeppelin and his bag-like airships that use hydrogen gas to float them, so the idea of an airship that floated was already a reality of sorts.

The ship's captain and crew are astonished. The airship edges closer to the liner, a sliding door opens in the side and a gangplank is dropped to connect the two ships. An English man, Lord Redgrave, walks across the gangplank after asking permission to board. He is looking for the young woman who is going to England to be married. She is the daughter of the scientist who invented the means of driving the airship, but he built it in England. He had worked with the scientist in Canada and met his daughter, fell in love with her, but had to return to England before he could say anything.

Lord Redgrave explains to the captain that a war in Europe is imminent and he asks the captain to allow him to take one of his passengers off the ship, the young woman, Zaidie Rennick. Zaidie and her chaperon accompany Lord Redgrave onto his airship and it pulls away from the ocean liner and rapidly ascends above the cloud layer. He asks her to marry him and she immediately agrees, but first he has to go back to New York and demonstrate the powers his ship has. He is hoping that by showing the world what his ship can do, and that with a fleet of ships such as this, the world could be prevented from entering another war. Of course, the ship was built in England, demonstrating the power that England has.

After some demonstrations in America, Zadie and Lord Redgrave are married and they set off for their honeymoon by taking off into space for a journey around the solar system.

The ship, which he calls the *Astronef,* is powered by what the Lord calls Repulsive power. By increasing the power which is directed at whatever he wants to fly away from, in this case the Earth, the speed of the ship rapidly increases and the ship is pushed away from the Earth. Basically, it is an anti-gravity device. (*A common means of powering an airship, used by authors around this time.*)

Their first stop is the Moon where they discover in a deep crater the remnants of life that once existed on this body. By then it was known that the Moon was airless, so authors took that into account. They are using air-suits, much like a diver's suit, with weighted boots to keep them on the surface due to the lower gravity. They find a swamp deep in a crater where repulsive humanoid creatures are fishing for something to eat. Even though talking about how very cold the Moon is, the author forgets that water in a deep crater would be frozen. Fortunately, they don't stay here long and soon depart for Mars.

Pushing away from the Moon they soon approach Mars as it swings around its orbit towards them. They stop first for a brief look at the two moons circling the planet before heading down towards the surface. They can see lakes and seas, cultivated land and of course canals and cities. The moment they enter the upper atmosphere and descend below some layers of pink clouds they encounter a number of airships rapidly rising up towards them.

The only thing he got right about Mars was the color of the sky, pink. And that I think was only because he was trying to be different and come up with something no other author had imagined regarding Mars. He tests the air and finds it fizzy, like champagne, but breathable. The fizziness he thinks is because it must have extra carbon-dioxide in the air. The air is also thicker than he expected which explains why propeller driven aircraft can fly.

Hovering above the city they watch the Martian airships rise up towards them. While they are wondering about how to approach the Martians, the ships begin to encircle them, obviously trying to trap them. The Martian ships all use propellers to drive them forwards.

They see gun ports opening on the encircling ships and fearing they are about to be fired upon, Lord Redgrave jumps his ship a thousand feet up above the encircling Martian ships, then moves forward to pass over them. An explosion of pink gas fills the space he had occupied a moment before.

The Martian ships start to rise and attempt to follow them. Lord Redgrave immediately uses the *Astronef*, which has a battering ram in front, to dive down on top of one of the leading Martian ships and splits it in half. The Martians shoot more gas bombs at them, not knowing that the Lord's ship is sealed against the atmosphere so it can fly through space. This time they use one of their own explosive guns to blow a Martian ship to pieces. They shoot back up into the higher atmosphere above the clouds where the Martians can't follow them, then almost immediately drop back down on top of another ship, smashing it to pieces. The Martian ships scatter and retreat. Now Lord Redgrave follows one of the ships down to the city they had seen below and when the ship lands Lord Redgrave hovers his ship a few feet above the ground and waits to see what will happen.

Thousands of Martian emerge from the city. They all look the same, humanoid, rather large with huge heads and big chests. There is no obvious difference between male and female and Lord Redgrave and Zadie speculate that years of trying to survive on a slowly dying planet has made them all the same, it also explains their warlike attitude towards strangers. They fought each other for untold generations in order to survive., and presumably, still do.

Someone approaches from the city. This being is dressed in fine clothes and looks important. He goes to the Martian ship and speaks to its commander who has exited and is standing some distance away from his ship. Suddenly the Martian ship turns its guns towards the hovering *Astronef.*

A large number of Martians emerging from the city begin to approach. Lord Redgrave doesn't hesitate. He immediately fires on the Martian ship, obliterating it, and then turns his guns on the approaching hoard of Martians and fires at them, killing hundreds with one hit. The crowd retreats, and the official finally approaches the hovering ship which now lowers itself to the ground.

Lord Redgrave opens the sliding door and lowers the gangplank and allows the Martian to enter. Wondering how they will communicate they are surprised that the Martian Lord speaks crude English.

Lord Redgrave speculates: "*The Martian people have developed along practically the same lines as we are doing, but they have done it faster and got a long way ahead of us. We are finding out that the speech which we call English is the shortest and most convenient. The Martians found it out long ago and killed anybody who spoke anything else. After all, what we call speech is only the translation of thoughts into sounds. These people have been thinking for ages with the same sort of brains as ours, and they've translated their thoughts into the same sounds. What we call English they, I daresay, call Martian…*"

How is that for an explanation? Later authors had Martians speaking English because they learned it from radio and TV broadcasts emitted from Earth over many years. In 1901 there was no widespread radio broadcasts nor any television.

What happens next is that the Martian official thinks Zadie is a marvelous beauty because female appearance has been bred out of the race. He wants her and insists Lord Redgrave give her to him. When Zadie recoils and Lord Redgrave refuses, the Martian reaches out to grab her. Lord Redgrave shoots him in the head, and throws his body out of the *Astronef*.

Sealing the sliding door, he immediately takes the ship at full power away from the surface.

It shoots up into the sky and out into space within seconds, instantly vanishing before the eyes of the watching Martians.

And that's it for Mars.

They then go to Venus where they discover in the very thick atmosphere beneath the cloud layers, angelic humanoid beings that are a cross between human and bird and who can fly. After Venus they go to Saturn and Jupiter where they have more almost life-threatening adventures. Leaving these two planets they find themselves being drawn off-course and discover it is because two dead stars have been approaching each other. They collide and a new star is born, a variable star which as it turns out is heading away from the solar system. They regain control of their ship and finally return to Earth after having watched the miracle of a new star being created.

It's good fun and entertaining, but so ridiculously out of date now.

The Nebula Hypothesis

The Nebula Hypothesis was a popular theory at the end of 1800s and into the early 1900s. It is mentioned on the second page of H G Wells' **War of The Worlds** where he briefly states: *Mars: …if the nebula hypothesis has any truth, is older than our world: and long before the Earth ceased to be molten, life upon its surface must have begun its course. The fact that it is scarcely one seventh of the volume of the Earth must have accelerated its cooling to the temperature at which life could begin.*

He then goes on to suggest that because it is further from the sun than is the Earth it must also be closer to the end of its planetary life cycle, that its resources must have been consumed, and with less sunlight, a thinner atmosphere, and lower temperatures, intelligent life would be forced to evolve rapidly.

Percival Lowell was prominent believer in the Nebula Hypothesis and it is the basic reasoning behind all his work relating to Mars and the books he published. Many other scientists agreed with the hypothesis as did many writers, so a general consensus was that Mars was more advanced in age than Earth and had developed life long before the Earth did, and that if the Martian civilization was not more utopian and advanced than that of Earth, it was possibly a waning civilization struggling to survive a slowly dying planet, or a civilization that has died out as the planet itself became a cold uninhabitable desert world.

Early Martian story concepts

The idea of a utopian society of some kind was an often-used for stories about Mars in which our own level of civilized development could be criticized by comparison. The society in these stories from the end of the 19th century almost always depicted Martians as wise, benevolent beings who looked much like ourselves, but were so much more advanced socially and technologically.

Reading these books today the technology now appears quaint, naive or even risible, but we have to remember the authors extrapolated from scientific discoveries of their time attempting to imagine how it would be in their future.

The other type of story background popular at the beginning of the 20th century was that Mars had once been highly civilized but its civilization had long died as the planet dried up and now the canals built to sustain life were filled with dust, and the cities along them were no more than ruins buried in sand. This variation became popular during the 1930s through to the 1950s, and continued to surface in later stories as well, right up to the present time. It usually featured archaeologists discovering something profound that could affect human civilization.

Another idea was that Mars was inhabited by ferocious warlike beings. After all, Mars was the God of War, so why wouldn't the inhabitants of a planet named after the God of War be extremely warlike rather than benign? **Honeymoon is Space** by George Griffith (1901) has its Martians exactly like that.

Just before the turn of the last century Mars was at its closest to Earth, in opposition for the first time when astronomers had improved telescopes and could see the planet more clearly than ever before.

There was a frenzy of excitement, of new discoveries, and many new ideas of what it was like on Mars. A plethora of articles in scientific journals, newspapers and magazines as well as novels and books about Mars suddenly appeared. The controversy of whether there were canals on Mars or not raged throughout the scientific community with as many claiming to have seen them as there were those who simply couldn't see them at all.

In fact, the more powerful the telescope, the less likely it was that canals would be seen, which is the exact opposite to what one would expect. The smaller image seen in the less powerful telescopes, which often wavered and appeared blurred because of movements within the Earth's atmosphere, enabled some people to see the optical illusion of straight lines across the surface of Mars – *the canals.* The man who first saw the marks on Mars clearly as canals, Percival Lowell, was adamant that they were artificial and had been constructed by intelligent beings on Mars. He imagined all kinds of reasons for their construction and convinced others through his books on the subject to also believe in the existence of the canals. Lowell's drawings of the canals on Mars became more elaborate as time went on.

Those who believed outnumbered those who didn't believe in the canals and couldn't see them no matter how hard they looked.

It wasn't until Lowell died that the idea of canals existing on Mars began to diminish.

Right up until the mid-1960s people still argued about whether the canals on Mars existed or not.

After Mariner 4 that idea was dispelled forever.

Martians are not always nasty

The Great Sacrifice by George C Wallis (1903)

H G Wells in 1897 depicted Martians as horrible invaders with superior intellects that looked down on humans and saw them only as a food supply.

Six years later George C Wallis changed that view, making his Martians spiritually benign and scientifically far in advance of humans. They were so far advanced that they could manipulate gravity and cause the outer planets to re-align.

They sent messages to the beings on Earth (us) who noticed the planetary re-alignment to warn of impending destruction of the planet by a massive interstellar swarm of meteors. The messages made it clear that they moved the outer planets to protect Mars and Earth from destruction by having those planets block the incoming meteors.

They also moved Mars so it would be in the path of the incoming meteors that weren't destroyed by impacting the large outer planets because they knew these meteors would impact the Earth. Everyone on Mars was prepared to die, while astronomers on Earth watched the outer planets destroyed and vaporised as the Martians blocked the worst of the meteors. As the smaller meteors leading the swarm started impacting our atmosphere, people waited in various ways for the end.

When Mars vaporises in the path of the meteors, the astronomers watching realize that the Martians had destroyed their planet and themselves by forming a huge gas cloud that would cause most of the remaining meteors to burn up long before reaching the vicinity of Earth. The biggest meteors had been destroyed by the Martians shifting the major planets, and what was left was destroyed by placing their own planet (Mars) and vaporising it in the path of the rest of the meteors.

The altruistic Martians, whom we never see and are not described, had sacrificed themselves so Earth could be saved. This finally left Earth as the largest planet in a much-reduced solar system.

A beautifully written story that has been brought back to life in a fabulous collection called **Lost Mars – *The Golden Age of The Red Planet***, edited by Mike Ashley (2018).

More Benign Martians

The Certainty of a Future Life in Mars by L P Gratacap (1903)

This is purportedly written by a gentleman, Bradford Torrey Dodd, who died in Christchurch not long after completing this manuscript in 1895, whose papers were delivered to the editor, L P Gratacap, some years after his death.

This story device to set the scene for what follows was common in many novels from the 1880s through to the early 1920s. Edgar Rice Burroughs used a similar device to draw the reader into his Mars stories featuring John Carter. So too did John Frazer, the author of *Mars and Melbourne (1899)*. (*See Dreams of Mars page 26. 2018.*)

Dodd, as a young person, moved to Christchurch New Zealand with his parents. His father wanted to set up an observatory in the nearby mountains (Mount Cook) because the seeing for astronomers was beautifully clear above New Zealand. Dodd's father was fascinated by a new device (radio telegraph) that could send messages over long distances without wires. He adapted it to use magnetic waves recently discovered by Professor Hertz. He believed he could receive messages from the planet Mars and devoted much of his energy, time and money, listening for these messages.

When Dodd's mother died, his father became distraught, and left young Dodd on his own. He eventually came back convinced that his dearly departed wife had gone to the Sun from whence all spiritual energy emanates giving life to everything on the planets. He believed he could somehow contact her using magnetic waves and a device he invented that could receive emanations from the Sun. Although wealthy his father invented various machines that used electricity and which garnered them considerable income. Obsessed with trying to speak to his departed wife he became convinced that there was an evolution of life on the planets with spirits arriving and departing continuously, from Mercury to Venus, from Venus to earth, from Earth to Mars, and so on. He decided that the spirit of his wife had gone to Mars where it was reborn, and wasted no time in trying to send and receive messages from Mars using the device he invented that utilized Magnetic waves.

Father and son experimented with their magnetic telegraph and succeeded in sending and receiving Morse code messages from their observatory and another distant site they had established. After proving it could be done, they then devoted their time to trying to receive messages from Mars which was at that time only 35 million miles from Earth.

Finally, a message arrived. Their machine picked up the magnetic wave signal, but no international code, or Morse code they knew helped them decipher it. Stunned, they were convinced that this was an extra-terrestrial message. They were convinced the message came from Mars.

Taking turns, they monitored the device for further messages but nothing else came. Not long after that Dodd's father became ill, suffering a severe hemorrhage that left him weak and debilitated. They moved from their observatory on Mount Cook back to Christchurch where his father could recuperate with the help of another family called the Dodans, whose daughter fell in love with young Dodd.

Dodd's father knew he was dying and so told his son that no matter where his spirit went, he would endeavor to contact him via magnetic wave emanations. He believed that the deepest memories were not lost to the spirit that departed from the body. Together they studied Morse code until understanding it was at a subconscious level. Hopefully it was Morse code he would use to contact his son. On his dying bed, he reminded his son; "Remember, watch, wait. I will send the message."

It was a year later that a message came. Dodd had almost given up hope. He couldn't monitor the device 24 hours a day and hired someone to help to enable him to sleep, but he was awake when the message came. He could hardly believe it, hardly contain his excitement when he heard the Morse code. "My son," it began, "I am indeed in the red orb of light we have so often looked up to when we were together on Earth…"

The story is then a very long description (narration or telling rather than showing) of what Dodd's father sees and experiences on Mars. How spirits gather there and slowly condense over time into more solid beings who are all young and vibrant. He explains how the society on Mars functions, how he meets many famous people who had previously died and have been reincarnated on the planet, how they spend their time studying and learning new things, how the canals bring water to other parts of the planet, how electricity is used, (electricity being the new wonder power that promises incredible benefits), how the cities are built from a white marble like stone mixed with a coloured stone that becomes fluorescent at night turning the cities into a maze of colour and light, and many other delightful things. Mars of course is a utopia. Everyone is a vegetarian, everyone is happy.

For the modern reader, there is no action except near the end when a comet impacts the major city. The Martian astronomers knew it was coming and our earthly protagonist is sent via a long canal journey to warn the city of its impending disaster so the inhabitants can be evacuated in time to avoid anyone being killed. It is at this point after the city's destruction that Dodd's father encounters the reincarnation of his wife, and the story ends.

Also, back in Christchurch, the son dies of consumption brought on by the many hours spent in the observatory recording the message from his father. Presumably he goes to join his father and his mother on Mars.

For those interested in what people in general thought Mars could be like in the year 1900 or thereabouts, this story is full of fascinating details about ideas regarding Mars as well as what scientific and philosophical concepts were extant in 1900. Many famous scientists and their ideas and discoveries are mentioned to give verisimilitude to the events portrayed in the story. They were of course alive at the time this story was written and their ideas and discoveries were full of wonder and excitement, and much of this does carry over into the narrative.

At 134 pages it isn't a long book. Anyone interested in reading it can search for it on the **Project Gutenburg eBook** site where it can be downloaded for free.

There is an article, *The Planet Mars* by Giovanni Schiaparelli, appended at the end of this story in which he relates his observations and conclusions regarding his discoveries about Mars.

About thirty years earlier (than the publication of this story) he was the first to see lines on Mars which he called *canali* meaning channels. He drew these on his maps of Mars during the oppositions in 1877 and 1882. He observed the melting of the southern ice cap in 1882, 1884, and 1886.

He published this article in French in the magazine **Nature et Arte,** in February 1893. It was translated by Prof. William H Pickering into English for the board of the Smithsonian Institute in 1894 and in October of that year it appeared in *Astronomy and Astrophysics Vol. XIII* numbers 8 and 9.

In this article he was himself calling the lines he observed on Mars canals rather than channels, and speculated much on their width, on how water was channeled along the canals from melting ice caps to the more tropical regions of Mars. He maintained the changes in colour were vegetation growing or cultivated as a result of water brought from the melting ice caps. He claimed to see seas and continents and islands. He also claimed that because the Martian atmosphere was thinner than the Earth's it would be colder and water vapor would freeze and there would be no rain on Mars, but there would be plenty of snow precipitating at the poles during the Martian winter. His observations showed an increase in size of the polar ice caps during the winter months and a significant decrease in their size during the summer months.

Had Schiaparelli been influenced by the ideas of Percival Lowell?

Or alternatively, could Schiaparelli's speculations about canals and life on

Mars have influenced Percival Lowell?

Lowell was also studying Mars from his private observatory over that same time period and had by that time published his first book, ***Mars***, 1895, and was quite adamant about an advanced civilization existing on Mars.

Lowell wrote another two books on the subject which had appeared after Schiaparelli's article was published. ***Mars and its Canals*** and ***Mars as the Abode of Life*** were published in 1906 and 1908 respectively. These books certainly gave many writers inspiration to compose stories set on Mars, and in some stories, much is made of Lowell's speculations, treating them as if they were undisputed facts. ***To Mars via the Moon by Mark Wicks*** (1911) does exactly that. (*See page 59*)

A long lost classic

Gulliver of Mars (1905) (1963) by Edward L Arnold.
*This book was published in hardcover in England in 1905, but nowhere else until Richard A Lupoff was given a dilapidated copy in 1963. He claims he immediately recognized this as something similar to Edgar Rice Burroughs' Martian set of stories and wondered if Burroughs had ever seen and read it since it was published well before his first Mars novel (**A Princess of Mars**, published in book form in 1917 but previously serialized in All Story magazine in 1911).*

*Originally called **Lieut. Gulliver Jones; His Vacation**, Lupoff published the original text in an Ace Science Fiction Classic as **Gulliver of Mars**, and subtitled it, **A long-lost classic of Martian adventure.** Lupoff isn't suggesting that Burroughs copied ideas from this book but, given the similarities, he does think Burroughs may have been influenced by it in his creation of Barsoom. In the Sf and Fantasy field, most writers are fans, and many fans become writers. They read each other and are inspired by each other, so similar ideas and concepts are repeated across the whole field. Ideas are for the taking; it's what each writer does with those similar ideas that makes their work unique while often seeming similar.*

***Gulliver of Mars** is available as one of the Guttenberg Project classic books and can be downloaded free as a PDF. There are also some people who have organized copies to be printed and sold as a POD book through various sites, but* *why pay them when you can download it for free? Second hand copies of the Ace edition can also be found online through ABE Books, and probably other sites. My copy came through ABE books.*

While walking along the sidewalk back to his rented room in a boarding house, Lt Gulliver Jones is almost knocked over as something huge like a bat flops out of the sky and crashes onto the sidewalk right in front of him. A small man bounces up out of whatever it is and falls badly smashing his head on the concrete. Gulliver rushes to aid the strange man with large eyes only to find him unconscious. He calls a taxi and they load the man into it.

What fell with him was a Turkish type of carpet and the taxi driver places this on the roof while they take the man to the hospital. The strange man dies by the time they reach the hospital and after leaving him there Gulliver returns to his abode and takes the carpet inside with him. He throws it onto the floor of his rented room and proceeds to open the window. Studying the carpet, he sees weird designs which show the planets of the solar system as well as other connecting lines between them.

While waiting for the landlady to bring up his evening meal he thinks about the choices he has made, taking a holiday in New York instead of visiting his girl-friend in another state, which brings him to this place, and he wishes he was somewhere else... anywhere else, he wishes he was on Mars.

The carpet immediately stirs, lifts up one side which knocks him over, and before he can recover, he is wrapped up inside it. As he begins to lose consciousness the carpet lifts up and shoots out through the open window, up into the sky and into space.

He doesn't know how long he was unconscious, but wakes up as the carpet is descending. He sees a strange landscape, with a large body of water obscured by mist, and suddenly the carpet crashes down onto the ground and he is thrown up into the air. He lands on top of a crowd of people knocking some over, scattering many of them, but his fall is broken by a young man whom he knocks over as he lands on top of him.

Trying to apologize he discovers the beautiful young man doesn't understand him, nor does he himself understand what the Martian is saying. After the man bandages his finger which he injured in the fall, he places his hands on either side of Gulliver's head and stares intently into his eyes. Gulliver feels thoughts penetrating into his brain, a most uncomfortable sensation, but suddenly he understands what he is saying, and in response he finds himself talking in the same sibilant language. They understand each other which amazes Gulliver and he immediately speculates on how good this system of learning would be on Earth.

Well, you might say getting to Mars on a flying carpet is ridiculous, but is it really any more ridiculous than Edgar Rice Burroughs using astral projection or teleportation to get John Carter to Mars in eleven books set on Mars? Is it any more ridiculous than H G Wells using light from the sun to energize his strange metal called Cavorite which negates gravity and allows him to take his characters to the Moon? Or Roy Lockwood using a mysterious power called Etherium to power an engine that takes his projectile space ship through the Ether on a journey to Mars? What about a spirit from a dying person going to Mars where it is reborn as a new individual? How is that not weird? Or in later stories where the unimaginable power of electricity is used to power space ships going to Mars and other planets? None of these methods is plausible, but the point I'm making is that how the people in the story get to Mars is irrelevant; it's what they do when they get there which makes the story.

The means they use to get to Mars is a device to convince the reader that the people in the stories have travelled to Mars, one way or another, but it is on Mars where the adventure and the story takes place, and this is what enthralled readers of the day. They accepted the means of getting there as easily as we today accept that rocket ships of various kinds will be used to get people to Mars.

Accompanying his new friend towards the distant city further along a canal, which up close he discovers is rundown and in need of repair, Gulliver has a long discussion in which he embarrassingly discovers all the people dressed in yellow robes the same as his friend An, are female slaves who do all the work needed so the other people can live a relaxed indolent life. They were once priestesses but after a war between the sophisticated Hither people of the cities with the Barbarian hoards spread across the countryside, the Thither people, they lost. Most of the Hither cities were destroyed during that war apart from Seth, which is the last one left. The ape-like barbarians leave the people of Seth alone but extract tribute each year in the form of food, manufactured items, clothes and other things. They also take the fairest maiden available for their King, Ar-Hap. The citizens left in the city of Seth over time have become lazy and only do what is needed and only when it is absolutely necessary. They are beautiful people, but a little empty-headed except for the female slaves dressed in yellow robes who do the bulk of the work while the others amuse themselves. No one wants to work or to exert themselves in any way, yet they expect to be fed and have the comforts of living well.

*I suspect the author read HG Wells' **The Time Machine** (1895) where in the far future the human race had evolved into two distinct races: the beautiful Eloi who lived harmless vacuous lives on the surface in a benign climate while* *the Morlocks lived underground with their infernal machines, and periodically came up to prey on the Eloi for food. This concept could have been in the back of his mind when he created the beautiful Hither people living an almost decadent, listless, seemingly happy life in the city Gulliver first sees who were conquered centuries before and are now 'preyed' upon by the wild hairy Thither people from other parts of Mars. It appears they are the same race that diverged into separate lines of evolution rather than a totally different species.*

Still getting over this revelation, Gulliver and An take a small skiff (moored along the canal for anyone to use) and sail along a wide river towards the city. Along the way they encounter a big crowd of people on skiffs surrounding a larger barge-like boat. On this boat is the King of Mars and his daughter. On seeing her Gulliver immediately falls in love with her, and jumps on board the barge to introduce himself to the King and his daughter. Barely finished introducing himself, a huge log coming down the river collides with the barge. It smashes the barge and the Princess gets caught in its branches and is dragged underwater. Gulliver immediately dives in and swims to the tree while the surrounding Martians are at a loss of what to do. He rescues the Princess and carries her back to the barge where her grateful father, King Hath, invites him to come to the palace and stay with them.

An also accompanies him to the palace which appears as run down and moribund as the rest of the city of Seth. She brings him breakfast the next morning and as they head down into the city, she departs, leaving him to fend for himself. Another young Martian female talks to him and tells him Princess Heru wants him to attend the annual meeting where she sees and prophecies the future for the occupants of the city for coming year. Apparently, the message was transmitted mentally. The Princess wants him to sit in the front row where she can see him, so he does that.

The Princess performs an intricate dance before revealing a white sphere, an implement that is over a thousand years old, that she uses to read the prophecy. It all begins well but suddenly the sphere turns dark red and bloody. The audience is stunned. The Princess turns to Gulliver and beseeches him for aid. He jumps up to go to her and just manages to catch her as she faints in his arms. As they leave the area the sphere used for the prophecy is accidentally knocked over, smashing into thousands of glass shards.

The next morning, everything seems normal, except that Gulliver is told he is to be married that evening. Stunned at this revelation, he decides to go to the festive event where all the females place their name in an urn, and all the males select a name from the urn. When that person selected is called out, she then sits with the person who drew her name and they are officially married. Princess Heru informs Gulliver that she has fixed a hair-width string to her name tag so when he feels it, he can draw out her name. She wants to marry him.

Everyone at the festival is drunk and merry as the names are being called out. As a guest, another King from an outlying city is also present and he has his eye on Heru, expecting to take her as his wife, but says nothing as she joyfully joins Gulliver. Suddenly the party is interrupted by several apelike beings, from the outlying provinces who collect tributes, or taxes from the elegant city folk. They have come to select the fairest maiden to take back with them as part of the tributes. The biggest of these ape-like beings comes over and grabs Heru from Gulliver's lap. Gulliver immediately jumps up and fights this monstrous man to get back his bride. He beats him but falls unconscious from the effect of too much wine drunk. No one else there seems to care and the ape-men take Heru and leave.

When Gulliver wakes in the morning he remembers what happened and rushes outside to see the boats in the harbor that the tributes were loaded onto are gone except for one. He rushes down to the docks and sees Heru being carried on board. He attacks the men taking her. His surprise attack allows him to kill two of them but he is outnumbered and another one smashes him on the head with a mallet. He falls off the boat into the water.

Waking up hours later he finds himself floating along a river on top of several bolts of silk and other materials that formed a raft which fell into the water with him when he was knocked unconscious. This silken raft is being carried out by the tide. Stiff and too sore after his battles to swim to a nearby island, he sees a large animal swim past the raft towards the island. He manages to throw a scarf over the animal's horns, and hanging on it drags him ashore. He is left exhausted on the beach while the animal disappears into the scrub.

As night falls, he finds a place under a tree between its enormous roots to sleep, but very little sleep eventuates as the jungle comes alive at night with all manner of creatures large and small hunting and fighting and feasting on each other. In the morning he ventures out of the jungle to the beach and sees a thin spiral of smoke rising into the air. Heading to it he discovers a camp fire with a pot suspended over it. The beautiful aroma coming from the pot reminds of how hungry he was and he immediately takes the pot off the fire and as it cools down, he eats the contents. When finished he looks up to see a girl staring at him. She is a fisherwoman and comes from a village on the other side of the island. She offers him some fish and they cook and eat it together. She tells him of the brutish Thither people who pass the island on their way back to their homeland and he decides he needs a boat to follow them. He cannot return without having rescued Princess Heru. The girl shows him the path through the jungle to her village and he sets off

Finding the village, he is shown how the boats they use are grown and while partly grown are placed in a mold to continue growing, eventually taking on the shape of a boat or a canoe. They are giant gourds. The insides are scraped out, they are cut in half, and seats are fitted to make the craft ready for use. He is given instruction on what to look for on the mainland, an estuary and a river to follow. He must not go too far north or the river he encounters will be the river of the dead from which no one ever returns. Setting off he paddles furiously and on reaching the mainland sees no sign of the estuary. He has gone too far north. He finds a river and paddles into it. The current flowing inland takes hold of him and carries him along. Soon he nears a raft on which a figure sits in a chair. Hailing it he gets no answer and on approaching close and boarding the raft he finds the occupant dead. Then he sees other rafts all drifting in the same direction, each carrying a dead person. He is being carried along the river of the dead, the one he was told to avoid because no one ever returns from this river.

The further along he travels the stronger becomes the current and he makes no headway trying to paddle against it to return. He has no choice but to go on. Travelling through a deep ravine he sees ahead that the river tumbles over into a gaping hole and everything is being carried towards it. His canoe is surrounded by rafts of the dead crowding him, pushing against him. Closer to the looming abyss he sees a rocky ledge and a short sandy beach. Having no choice, he jumps from raft to raft towards the ledge and leaps across the grab it and drag himself up onto the rocks, while the rafts and his canoe plummet over the edge. In the looming darkness she sees the cliffs are of ice and they are filled with frozen bodies of the dead, thousands upon thousands of them. One of them, so close to the edge of the ice that it almost looks as if he is behind a window, appears to be of a king. He is dressed in fine clothes and wears a crown. He can see no way off the sandy beach as darkness falls. The current of the river coming down is too strong to go against, and it plunges over a precipice into the bowels of the world. Scrounging around he finds enough driftwood to light a fire and settles down to wait for dawn and the possibility of discovering a way out of his predicament.

Waking suddenly, he hears a scraping sound, then almost before he can move a body falls on top of him. A hand reaches for his throat. He struggles violently, throwing the attacker off and discovers it is the frozen body of the ancient king. The fire must have melted the thin ice, allowing him to fall out. Moving the body aside, he takes the crown with its embedded jewels and puts it in his back pack.

As dawn begins to lighten the sky Gulliver hears the sound of footsteps echoing up from the precipice. He cautiously approaches and sees a scruffy man scrounging about in the tumbled rocks below the end of the sandy beach. If someone can get down here, then there must be way out as well. He calls out to the man and in terror, the man races away further down the tumbled rocks, Gulliver follows, leaping over the rocks to catch the man. The man believes Gulliver is a spirit, one of the dead entombed in the ice. Finally, Gulliver makes the man understand that he is trapped here. The man, comes down here periodically to scavenge for jewels and other valuable items that may have fallen from the dead sent down this river into oblivion. They are always dressed in their finest clothes and wearing their best jewelry. Together they find enough trinkets to satisfy the scrounger who then leads Gulliver to an almost hidden crack in the ice. It is wide enough to squeeze into and together they make their way up the crack, eventually arriving at the top of the glacier or ice cliff to emerge onto a barren frozen surface.

The man tells him it is a couple of hours walk to a valley where the ice ends and he will see a road heading towards the city where his precious princess is held prisoner. Gulliver gives this man some of the jewels he had collected as payment. Following the instructions, he finds the road and heads towards the place where the Thither warriors come from. Finding a fishing village, he spends a couple of nights there getting to know the land and its people who are quite generous with their hospitality. The fisherman's wife is entrance by Gulliver's story of his search for Princess Heru. They explain how to get to the capital warning him not to take the left-hand road which leads to an old Hither city ruled by evil Queen Yang. Visitors have ventured there, but none ever return. Keep to the straight road with the sea on your right.

But not long after Gulliver sets out on this road it becomes fog shrouded and he can't see anything. Inadvertently he takes the wrong road and finds himself deeper in the forest. He hears the sound of babies wailing and calls to them but gets no answer. Finally, he comes across a broken gateway, an entrance to the old city. Feeling cold and miserable he searches for a dry place to spend the night. He staggers across an amphitheater covered with the skulls of children and bones, to find his way inside another building via a narrow entrance. Inside on a bier he discovers the body of a Queen, finely dressed and covered with jewelry. Queen Yang. On closer inspection he sees the body is nothing more than a skeleton, and taking her crown he also places this in his backpack.

The next morning, he leaves this ruined Hither city and heads back along the right road to arrive at the walled city of Ar-Hap the king who has his beloved Princess Heru captive. Joining the supplicants, the next morning, he enters the city and approaches the king in his court. Everyone believes he is a spirit and they are wary of him. Gulliver demands that the king give him his princess but the king demands Gulliver perform a task before he would consider this. A task that should be easy if he is spirit as she claims. He gives him 5 minutes to do it. The task it to retrieve the crown of the old King who died centuries ago and who was sent down the river of death. Easy, Gulliver thinks.

Stepping outside he waits a few minutes, then takes the crown from his backpack and returns to the king's court. He presents the crown to King Ar-Hap who is astonished, but not willing to relinquish his tribute prize, he demands another task from the spirit. He wants the crown of Queen Yang. Only then will he release Princess Heru. Again, Gulliver steps outside and five minutes later returns to present Queen Yang's golden crown. Suitably astonished, Ar-Hap refuses to consider releasing Princess Heru. "We will discuss it later," he is told. "Right now, there are other pressing matters".

For days a furnace has been raging in the sky, heating up the land. Things are getting worse. Water has dried up in the wells and the river has shrunken until here is only mud left. The King is needed to perform a ceremony that will bring rain. The who population of the city is to participate. Animals have come into the town from the forests in search of water and are lying about in whatever shaded spot they can find. People are collapsing from de-hydration, and in the sky, the malevolent glowing ball that is bigger than the sun seems to be getting bigger and hotter by the minute. The air is filled with the smell of Sulphur and the noise of a roaring blaze gets louder and louder by the minute. The whole city's population is terrified.

Gulliver assumes it is a comet.

No one knew much about comets in 1905, and all kinds of horrible conse-quences were imagined if one managed to come too close. People in particular were terrified of Halley's comet which was due to come close to Earth in that first decade of the 20th century imagining all kinds of dire end-of-the-world conse-quences.

He assumes that the fires burning in a comet as it approaches close to planet would be like the sun, all consuming, burning with incredible heat, intensifying as it gets closer to a planetary surface.

The ball of fire in the sky gets larger and hotter. People and animals begin to die from the intense heat. The king performs his ceremony but nothing seems to happen. Gulliver thinks now would be a good time to steal Heru and to escape in a boat while everyone is otherwise occupied, but he doesn't have the energy. He lies about beside Heru waiting for the end...

Slowly the false sun diminishes in size and the heat starts to lessen. Rous-ing himself, Gulliver convinces Heru that they should leave. They steal a boat and head off up the coast towards the fishing village where he stayed before. The fisherman and his wife help them, hide them while the Thither King's soldiers search everywhere for the missing princess and her suitor.

Once the soldiers leave the fisherman arranges for a small boat to sail across the sea to the Hither city where Princess Heru once lived.

They have hardly returned when thousands of Ar-Hap's soldiers arrive to ransack the city in search of Princess Heru and the spirit-man who stole her. Thousands are slayed. Princess Heru manages to escape in a small boat via a hidden exit in the basement of the palace. As she does this Gulliver fights off some soldiers and leads them further into the palace as a distraction. He goes up many levels finally arriving at the storeroom where found articles are kept. Barricading himself inside he piles up boxes and pieces of wood against the door to keep the soldiers out for a while. In doing this, he discovers the old carpet which brought him here. He wonders whether it would take him home again just as it brought him here, and as the soldiers force their way in through the barricade, Gulliver lies down on the carpet and wishes it would take him home to Earth.

The carpet immediately folds itself over and around him and as he loses consciousness, he feels it shoot up and out through the windows of the palace. The next moment he finds himself ejected onto the sidewalk in front of his lodgings in New York, but of the carpet, there is no sign. Disheveled and filthy, he staggers inside to find his parents and his fiancé commiserating over his disappearance and presumed death.

The story ends here with him happily agreeing to marry his fiancé then next week and promising to write down the adventures he has experienced on Mars.

*Whether this is better than Edgar Rice Burroughs' first Martian story **A Princess of Mars**, I can't say. All I can say is that this is an enjoyable read, quite entertaining and well written.*

Whether it had in some way influenced Burroughs with ideas, I can't say either. Just as today, authors back then were inspired and influenced by their contemporaries, with ideas and concepts being exchanged consciously as well as subconsciously so inevitably similarities would appear in their collective works.

*I can't say which is better than the other because that is entirely subjective on my part. I leave it to readers of both books to make comparisons and to draw conclusions as to how they feel individually about the books mentioned. What I can say however, is that if you come across **Gulliver of Mars**, it is well worth your while to read it.*

A verdant Mars

As with many of the early Martian stories from 1880 through to around 1910, the planet has rivers, lakes and broad seas. It has verdant pastures and large tracts of arable land under irrigation of some kind, jungles and a plethora of strange weird animals and birds and marine life, usually large when compared to similar life forms on Earth. It also had a breathable atmosphere or at least one that was a bit thinner than ours but certainly breathable.

This Edenic view gradually fell away as the century moved on and we encounter a more arid drier planet with either the remnants of old civilizations struggling to survive, or the remains of ancient civilizations that died out after desperately building canals to bring water from the poles to the arid lands. There were many variations and combinations of the above themes, and it was a long time before the reality of Mars became known (in 1965) which displaced those earlier visions with more realistic concepts.

An unusual romance

Zarlah The Martian *by R. Norman Grisewood (1909)*
This is science fiction because the author uses the recent discovery of Radium *(discovered by Pierre and Marie Curie in 1898)* and speculates how it could be used to transmit images across space from Mars to earth. It is also science fantasy in that his Martian civilization is as human as us but they are around fifteen hundred years in advance of Earth in the knowledge and technology. Grisewood also believed in the nebula theory put forward by other scientists including Percival Lowell, briefly mentioning that Earth is like the way Mars was, but because Mars is further away from the sun, and smaller than Earth, it cooled down earlier and life on the planet began sooner and is consequently more advanced than it is on Earth. There is no mention of Mars being a desert planet. It is verdant and green thanks to the abundant canals (*None of the Martians remember why or how they were constructed.*) that bring water from the areas around the poles. He mentions that the sky is very dark blue, almost black, and the stars glitter far more brightly than they do when seen from Earth, and because the air is thinner than Earth's, it allows more solar radiation to penetrate with none of the diffusion that occurs on Earth.

His Mars is warm and benign. The people are happy, there is no separation of races or languages with everyone speaking the same language, and because they discovered radium 600 years earlier than on Earth, they use its emanations for communication as well as for improving their health. No one gets sick and to all intents the Martians live forever, barring accidents.

The story opens with Harold Lansdale arriving in Paris where he once studied, finding accommodation and setting up a small laboratory on the top floor of his building and experimenting in making artificial glass, a substance that would be as clear as glass, almost indestructible, and able to conduct sound. He spends months working on this and comes up with a product that is flexible and clear and that when an electrical current is applied (from batteries) it appears to glow. He sees an image in the glass that is blurred, smudgy, almost human shaped, and thinking it reflects someone, he turns find no one in his room. There is no one outside either because they would not be able to walk on the roof with its steep slant.

Looking up at the skylight he sees the planet Mars is framed in the window and as it passes below the rim the glow disappears. Thinking to refine his device, he melts the glasslike substance and coats strands of super fine wires with it. He then stretches the wires close together across the frame and applies the same electrical current from the batteries. The next night when Mars again crosses his skylight window the instrument glows brilliantly this time and a sharp image of a man appears. The man waves to him. Expecting a weird creature as depicted in fiction of the day he is astonished to find the presumed Martian is as human as he is. Before much else can occur, Mars again drops below the skylight rim and communication ceases.

The next night is cloudy and Harold doesn't think anything will happen, but he switches on the device and suddenly it lights up and his Martian friend appears. There is a humming sound which Harold refines and all of a sudden, he hears a voice. It is his Martian speaking and he speaks in French. *Bon Soir,* he says.

Stunned, Harold answers in English, and the Martian switches to English. He explains that Martians have been studying Earth for the past 600 years and have managed to learn all the major languages. He spoke in French because he was communicating with someone in France. His device had detected the radium emanations and had honed in on its location. *We have watched and waited for someone to invent an instrument that could respond to our projected light waves… Congratulations on inventing it.*

Realizing that the amount of time he can communicate with the Martian is too short, Harold finds another studio apartment on the top floor of a building nearby. It was once used by an artist and half the ceiling is glass exposing the whole apartment to the open sky. Ideal for him to have much longer times communicating. He immediately moves his equipment to the new location and anxiously awaits the next opportunity to converse with his Martian friend.

The Martian tells him his name is Almos. Nobody has any more than one name on Mars he explains. Almos tells him that he is the inventor of the devices he uses to communicate with Harold, the *radiophone* (for sound) and the *radioscope* (for images). After their recent much extended conversation, Harold sees an image of a young woman in his mind. He doesn't want to say anything yet to Almos, but he can't help wondering who she is.

After some discussions over several nights, Almos explains that they have a device to heal people who accidentally die. Using the regenerating properties of the rays that emanate from radium, a person's mind is captured and stored while the body is regenerated and healed. Then the mind is restored. The same light waves and rays used in the radiograph are used in this machine called a *virator*. There may be a way that you can travel to Mars Almos suggests. Instead of sending an image I can use the machine to capture your mind and transfer it here. I will store my mind while you use my body. When you return to Earth the *virator* will restore my mind.

An agreement is made to try the experiment. It involves each person breathing chloroform to render them unconscious to a near death state, to enable the *virator* to transfer the mind into the other body, a process that Almos has automated. If it doesn't work, both of them will probably die.

When everything is set up, Harold locks up his studio so no one will come in while he is in a near death state, and as soon as the machine starts to glow, he breathes in the chloroform while sitting in an armchair beside the device. He blanks out and wakes up and discovers he is inhabiting the body of Almos. He is on Mars.

A moment later, a young man enters and says an old friend is expecting him to attend a concert where the same radium rays are being used in a new device to record and play the music of flowers. The young man thinks he is Almos. They go outside where a high-speed aircar is tethered I have to be back in two hours-time to terminate this experiment he tells the young man who promises to bring him back. If he doesn't get back in time, when Mars is no longer facing the side of Earth where Harold's machine is, the connection would be cut off and his body on Earth would die while he remains trapped on Mars.

They take off and the flying car enters one of the canals that crisscross the planet, and keeping close to the water it increases speed to a phenomenal pace. They travel hundreds of miles in a few minutes and are halfway around the planet. The concert hall has a device similar to the one Harold devised only on huge scale. The music it produces is weird, and ethereal. While he is sitting outside listening, a young woman approaches and sits with him. It is the woman he has seen in his mind while talking to Almos over the radio-phone. She knows him and greets him by name. He is immediately smitten by her and makes a date to see her the next night.

After returning to the Laboratory just in time to be transferred back to his own body on Earth. He decides he must tell Almos about making a date with this girl, since he won't be there to keep it, Almos will have to go in-stead. Of course, the girl Zarlah will expect Almos; she couldn't have known that someone else was temporarily inhabiting Almos' body. Realizing that his love of Zarlah was hopeless he means to discuss it with Almos to see what can be arranged, but there is no time and he has to return to his body on Earth before the connection is severed.

The flying cars are called *aereonoids*, and they work by using a strange metal found under the poles of Mars. There is no snow or ice above the poles. The property of the metal that extends right through Mars from one pole to the other rejects anything that covers it or touches it. It flings it out into space. By using this metal to construct their *aereonoids* it pushes itself away from the martian surface. The amount of the metal they allow to be exposed determines the height above the ground it will rise to. They use electrical power to move the aereonoid forward. Someone once sealed such a vehicle to make it airtight and attempted to go into space to one of the moons. The *aerenoid* with the explorers inside shot up into space and was never seen again.

Waking after a long sleep he becomes aware that his body feels fantastic and suspects the machine's rays have been regenerating him. Knowing this he believes he should tell the world of its power for regeneration, and dis-cussing it with Almos they both agree it is time that Earth people know of the existence of the Martians. However, one more trip to Mars needs to be made so they can work out how to do what they plan.

As it turned out, Zarlah had also seen images of the man from Earth in her mind and she knew immediately who he was when she met him (in the body of Almos) at the concert. She too had fallen in love with the Earthman just as he had fallen in love with her. This next trip would be different. In-stead of Almos mind being stored in the *virator* while Harold occupied his body, he would simultaneously transfer his mind to Earth into the body of Harold in his studio.

Something doesn't go right and Zarlah believes that Harold is still on Earth and cannot come to Mars. She decides to take the fastest *aereonoid* she can find and fly it to the north pole to be ejected into space through which she hopes to travel to Earth to join her beloved Harold. Harold arrives in time to see her depart, and following her as she tears up the long canal to the north pole, he realizes what she is about to attempt. He can't quite catch her but when he sees her *aereonoid* shoot up into space he does the same. Together the two sealed air cars crash onto the moon Phobos which just happened to be passing nearby in its fast orbit as the *aereonoids* were ejected into space. Harold's vehicle springs a leak and as air is hissing out Zarlah comes to his rescue. She takes him on board her ship and then when he has recovered, they use the Phobos to eject them towards Mars by exposing the special metal it is made of. Almost burning up as they re-enter the Martian atmosphere, they manage to slow down enough to make a safe landing by crashing into a lake.

It ends happily with them safe together on Mars, each professing their love for the other.

The story ends with a note from Almos who has exchanged his life on Mars for one on Earth in the body of Harold. He ends by saying he trusts that this narration will prepare the way for the greater developments soon to be announced by scientists (presumably of both planets).

An interesting point with this story is, it demonstrates the folly of speculating about what life on another planet may be like based on limited scientific observations or knowledge, and using one's own planet's life as a base to draw comparisons. There is no way we can predict what alien life would look like or how it would act.

Almos the Martian explains that before the invention of the radioscope they now use to observe life on Earth early speculations were absolutely wrong. Before reading from an old book speculating about life on the third planet, he tells Harold not to be embarrassed about human speculations of what life on Mars is like.

"That this planet is inhabited we have no reason to doubt, as it is known to be enveloped in an atmosphere, and it is now a generally accepted theory that the changes noticed in its colour throughout the year are seasonal effects on vegetable matter existing on its surface… What the inhabitants are like, however, we can only surmise, but a study of conditions under which they live will help us to picture the wild amphibious creatures they must be. Their planet, more than half covered with water, and being so many millions of miles nearer the sun than we are, is almost continually enveloped in heavy clouds of vapor, which, unless they were half fish, must surely suffocate them. They doubtless seek the depths of water when those clouds of thick vapor arise. Upon emerging, however, they have to face such intense heat as none of us could tolerate a minute and live… They are no doubt provided with steel like skin to resist this temperature… They are of a fierce temperament there can be little doubt, as their atmosphere, which is twice the weight of ours, is so overcharged with electricity, owing to the heat and clouds

of vapor, that violent storms are constantly breaking over them, doubtless killing thousands of them at a time and tending to make the nature of survivors as fierce as the elements which surround them... Their year is but half as long as ours, and this —impeding the laws of propagation, thus making impossible the higher order of mankind— would naturally have the effect of rendering their lives a short, reckless, and ferocious existence, full of unrestrained cruelty and passions..."

Looking at this more than a century after it was written I see it as a gentle dig at those who would speculate about what life on Mars would be like, and more generally, what life on any other planet could be like. We only have our own Earth as a prime example, and this inevitably colors any speculation about life elsewhere, no matter how it is couched in scientific detail. By reversing the idea to imagine life on Earth from a Martian observer's perspective (through the use of a telescope) he makes this point quite clear. I think the author is also having a dig at the human tendency to wage wars both small and local as well as larger conflicts. The First World War was not far off when this book was published.

Boys' adventures

Through Space to Mars (1910)
Or the Longest Journey on Record
By Roy Lockwood.

This is #4 in the Great Marvel Series of books for young readers between the ages of 8 to 12. The first of the series published in 1906 features a couple of young boys who were orphans and became friends when the escaped from slave-like employment with harsh masters. They boarded a freight train and headed west, and eventually met with a certain professor Amos Henderson who found them injured in a train wreck and adopted them. Professor Henderson lived with a coloured manservant called Washington White, who stereotypically cooked, washed, served meals and did all the things expected of a housekeeper. This character is a put-off for modern readers with his southern accented Pidgin English and his use of large words to impress but which leave the characters at times bewildered. But considering the time the story was written and published, the author no doubt thought a character like Washington would add 'color' to an adventure yarn. Professor Henderson was an inventor and explorer who built marvelous equipment and machines in his gigantic workshop. The two boys (and Washington) helped him and accompanied him on many adventures.

The first was ***Through Air to the North Pole*** or ***The Wonderful Cruise of the Electric Monarch.*** They travelled in an airship built by the professor. Their second adventure, ***Under the Ocean to the South Pole or The Strange Cruise of the Submarine Wonder.*** (1906), saw them travelling undersea in a submarine invented and built by themselves and the professor. They called their submarine the *Porpoise* and it could travel at unheard of speeds underwater. They were caught in a gigantic sea of seaweed in the Sargasso Sea, fought off a monster with gigantic sucker arms, walked on the bottom of the sea in strange diving suits and almost got sucked down into an immense whirlpool which the professor believed would take them down to the centre of the world. They would need a different kind of vessel to go down there, and that's exactly what they did in the third book, ***Five Thousand Miles Underground*** or ***The Mystery of the Centre of the Earth.*** (1907). They built a craft called the *Flying Mermaid*, and the professor and the boys and Washington along with a friend, Andy, sailed their ship until they came to the whirlpool hollow shaft and then flew the ship down and into a hollow world inside our own Earth.

In their 4th adventure the professor calls the boys back from school (*via a telegram)* and introduces them to a German professor, Santel Rouman, who has discovered a new source of power and has built two machines to use it. He presents them with an unusual proposition. He wants to make the most wonderful journey on record, *a trip through space to the planet Mars!* and he wants them to build the ship to take them there. They immediately agree and over the course of the next few months a 100 meter-long 10 meter in diameter cylindrical projectile ship is constructed in their workshop.

To add a hint of suspense, a strange person is seen creeping around the premises at night and as the ship is nearing completion this mad person attacks the ship with a sledge hammer trying to damage it. Later they find important components for the Mr Rouman's machines missing, and again, once the machines are installed in the cylindrical ship the strange interloper gets into the workshop and damages the machines which delays their departure because the machines need to be repaired. Mr Rouman explains that he has some enemies in Germany who want the secret of his mysterious propulsion force which is probably why some of the components were stolen, and that same person has probably hired the madman seen skulking around to sabotage their attempts to leave the planet.

On the morning of the departure Mr Rouman finds a hatch unlocked which he was certain he had locked, but doesn't think much of it. They board the ship and the first machine which uses the power he calls *Etherium* is used to fly the ship through the atmosphere. When it reaches space, the other machine will power them through the ether that fills all of space between the planets.

The reason he wants to go to Mars is he believes there is a source of power that gives the planet its red colour, and if he can bring some of that back it will make them all very wealthy. They believe Mars is in habited by beings with a superior intelligence; the canals that cover the planet, seen first by Schiaparelli and others is proof of that.

On the voyage they have an encounter with a comet but survive by increasing their speed to fly through the tail instead of impacting the head. The pass an asteroid, and on the voyage the mad man who tried to sabotage them appears and tries again to smash the *Etherium* engine that powers the projectile ship. They stop him but he gets away and they can't find where he is hiding. Eventually they do find him as again he tries to sabotage the ship. Overpowering him they tie him up and leave him in the storeroom while they land the ship on Mars.

Approaching Mars, they pass the moons, Phobos and Deimos, and the descriptions of these are probably the only real scientific facts in the story. They pass Deimos at 10,000 miles out and very soon they pass Phobos before landing on a sandy stretch near a canal. There is water and many canals all around them and in the distance, they see a glittering city. When they open the hatch and step out, they are greeted by a crowd of Martians waiting for them. They can't make out what the Martians are saying and neither can the Martians understand anything they say no matter the language. They eventually communicate by having one of the boys draw geometric shapes in the sand. The Martians respond to this by doing the same.

Before they can do much else, they find themselves floating towards a boat in a nearby canal. They can't stop floating or turn back or do anything. The Martians are using mind power to draw them along. In the boat there is no obvious means of power but it skims along the surface quite fast. Mr Rouman points to a small metal box at the rear of the boat and the Martians open it to show him a red clay-like substance. When he tries to touch it, they slam the box closed. In the buildings in the city the same little metal boxes emit light, and in the kitchen where a meal is being prepared for them the box gives off the heat for the cooking.

Whatever that stuff it, that's what I want Mr Rouman tells them.

The description of the Martians is what most people accepted would be typical: big brains for being highly intelligent, enclosed in a huge head, with spindly arms and legs, enormous eyes, large ears like an elephant and a nose that is long and pointed which can be moved about to sniff out interesting scents. They are no taller than a meter.

Once they learn a little of the language, they come to understand that the Martians believe that if anyone takes some of the red clay that powers everything off planet, Mars will disappear, so it is forbidden for the strange Earth creatures to touch it let alone take any of it away. That doesn't stop Mr Rouman who is determined to get some to take back to Earth. The professor, the boys and Mr Rouman take a walk to an island where they think the red clay is mined but Martian guards stop them.

Later, they steal a boat and head around the lake to the island where they are almost caught in a whirlpool, but manage to escape. Landing on the island they take several boxes they brought with them and commence to dig up some red clay. They are discovered by a guard but they overpower him and make their way back to the boat. They land far away from the city and near to their projectile ship where they immediately go on board and stow away the boxes of clay. They also discover their mad prisoner had escaped.

Suddenly outside they are besieged by a huge crowd of Martians led by the mad saboteur. The Martians point some weapons at them and inside the occupants feel themselves being stuck to the walls of the ship as some electrical current is projected at them by the crowd outside. Professor Henderson manages to reach a control which activates a counter electric field to neutralize the one attacking them. They then fire electric cannons at the Martians which knocks most of them down, but still more are streaming from the city to attack them, so they activate their atmosphere engine and take off, rapidly shooting up into the sky. Within minutes they are passing the moons and heading out into space where the *Etherium* engine will power up and return them to Earth.

I wonder if we'll ever take another trip like this? One of the boys asks once they have got home.

Perhaps, someday, Mr Rouman replies. *I have some ideas regarding other planets…*

The red material they brought back made them all wealthy.

And there were other trips: **Lost on the Moon or In Quest of the field of Diamonds** (1911) was the next one in the series over subsequent years, with the last one, **By Space Ship to Saturn or Exploring the Ringed Planet.** (1935)

There were twenty other adventure books for young readers all written by the same author over the period from 1900 to 1935, with the more science fiction ones published between 1906 to 1935. The name Roy Lockwood was a pseudonym for a number of authors who were given a synopsis by the publisher and asked to write the story.

Pulp fiction begins to evolve

All kinds of Boy's adventure stories were very popular at the turn of the century and many of these stories tended to blend science fiction elements into them to create a sense of mysterious excitement, to create adventures that were more extraordinary than finding lost relics of past civilizations, or flying into adventures in unexplored parts of the world.

As the world became better known, and there was not a lot left to discover by explorers, the adventures morphed into science fiction adventures on other planets or were stories set in a future extrapolated from the scientific, philosophical and sociological developments at the turn of the century. This led us into the pulp fiction era that began with Hugo Gernsback and his various magazines from around 1915 onwards.

Science with action and adventure

To Mars via the Moon: An Astronomical story. Mark Wicks (1911)

Mark Wicks was an amateur astronomer and as such knew quite a lot about the Moon, which is amply demonstrated in the first 60 pages. He was born in 1852 and died in 1935. Presumably he wrote this story over 1909 to 1910 and it was published in 1911. The events taking place in the story occur in 1909 because that was the year Mars was closest to Earth at little over 36 million miles. It would be another fifteen years before a similar close approach occurred. Naturally there was a lot of interest within the scientific community with all kinds of discoveries being made about Mars as well as many stories imagining a trip to Mars as well as what kind of society they would find there. There was no doubt in many people's minds that intelligent life existed on Mars. Yet there were equal numbers who denied the possibility of life on Mars, or that the canals so many had seen even existed. Chief amongst the deniers was Dr. Alfred Russel Wallace who claimed it was too cold for water to exist and that the polar ice caps were most likely frozen carbon dioxide, and that the lines people saw and believed were canals were either natural chasms or simply optical illusions induced by the poor resolution of telescopes. When using higher powered telescopes there are no canals to be seen, and believers couldn't accept this.

This is not a novel as we understand the term today, but rather a combination of scientific facts and speculation based on what was thought to be the science of the day, mixed with action and adventure. The framing device is the lead character, who is an amateur astronomer, (like the author) answering questions and explaining things to his two companions, who also helped him construct the spaceship they use to travel in to Mars.

In an introduction he explains that he has been impressed with ordinary people who want to know of scientific matters but want things explained in simple terms they can understand. This book does exactly that.

The lead character Wilfred Poynders explains that for more than sixty-three years he has been intensely interested in Astronomy and especially for the last thirty years his interest has been focused on Mars. (*This is no doubt true of the author as well as the character of Poynders.*) With Mars making a closer than normal approach to Earth and fascinated by the 'discoveries' of Professor Percival Lowell, he decides to build a spaceship to go to Mars.

The book is in fact dedicated to Professor Percival Lowell AB, LLD.

Mark Wicks was undoubtedly an ardent follower of Percival Lowell's theories about Mars, and this is amply demonstrated during the latter part of the book.

Poynders had been married and had a son Mark, who died before this story begins, and over time he comes to look upon his old school friend, John Claxton, almost as a second son. John's main interest is in mechanical things and especially things that work with the new power of electricity. Since building a space ship was too big a task for only two men, a third person, a Scottish gentleman by the name of M'Allister, is brought in to help them construct the electric powered spaceship. These two gentlemen address Poynders as Professor, which he isn't but he doesn't mind being called that. They constantly ask him questions which he always answers with a long discourse on whatever the subject might be.

There is no explanation of how the ship works but it appears that the electricity somehow has the effect of anti-gravity. The space ship floats slowly upwards and when it reaches sufficient height to be in the thinner part of the atmosphere, they increase the power to the driving machines and the ship goes faster, fast enough to easily escape the Earth's gravity. They head towards the Moon, and over the next 50 or so pages the reader is assailed with detailed descriptions of all the major craters, seas and visible features of the Moon as they pass over the surface at a height of several miles. When asked if they are going to look at the Darkside, the professor explains that since there is no light there, they won't be able to see anything so there is no point in wasting time to look at it. (*A neat way of avoiding trying to describe*

*something about which no one in 1910 knew anything about. The side facing
the Earth had been well studied and mapped with all its features named, but the
dark-side was an absolute mystery.*) This section of the book is accompanied
by drawings of the Moon, and a map showing all the major features which
Poynders elaborated upon in great detail.

Finally, in chapter eight, they leave the Moon behind and head out towards the point Mars will be at in 70 or so days.

Many people also believed that they knew a lot about Mars. Only thirty
years earlier Schiaparelli had discovered long channels on the surface which
he called *Canali* (which meant channels in Italian but which everyone else
translated as canals), and over the time since then Mars had been studied by
thousands of astronomers and other scientists. There were many arguments
about whether the lines seen were natural channels or artificially constructed
canals, which implied a degree of sophisticated civilization on the planet.
A good deal of the time spent travelling to Mars is spent in explaining all
the theories for and against canals on Mars. Every objection to the belief in
canals and Martian civilization is demolished as Poynders explains in detail
what Professor Lowell has supposedly discovered on Mars. About what the
colour changes signified, about the fact that sometimes there are double canals that run for thousands of miles while others are single. There are ample
details regarding experiments Percival Lowell conducted to determine the
width of the canals.

The facts he explains are as accurate as can be regarding how long the
day on Mars is, about the angle of inclination of the planet which determines the seasons, about the orbital mechanics necessary to reach the planet, the habitable land areas of Mars compared to that of Earth, and other
such matters. But what Poynders and his two friends discover on Mars when
they finally land is based entirely on extrapolating ideas Percival Lowell had
been proposing for many years. Here, the story events, while purporting to
be scientific, are clearly imaginative speculations of a utopian society, the
kind everyone on Earth hoped would be their future, which in 1910 seemed
dark indeed with the First World War only a few years ahead. Imagining a
Utopia was usual in stories set on Mars that were written at the end of the
nineteenth century; stories like **Across the Zodiac** by Percy Greg (1880)
and **Melbourne and Mars** by John Fraser (1890 *see Dreams of Mars, page 26.*)
Even Percival Lowell's books **Mars** (1896), **Mars and its Canals** (1906), and
Mars as the Abode of Life (1908) proposed Mars as a utopian planet with
a highly developed civilization technically and ethically far superior to the
civilization on earth.

During the voyage out from Earth the three travelers are training themselves to breathe the lesser atmosphere of Mars. Eventually, Poynders and his companions approach Mars and attempt to land at a certain place but somehow the ship is stopped. No matter how hard they try to push power into the engines, the ship hardly moves, except in one direction. They finally follow the direction that allows movement and they find themselves guided to a complex city where thousands of Martians are waiting for them to land.

They are made welcome on landing and Poynders makes a remarkable discovery. His son Mark who died at a young age has been reborn as a Martian and is the son of the present leader of Mars. The Martians are remarkably like extra tall thin humans, (a common concept in many early books). They have glowing eyes indicating an inner vitality that humans lack. They are vegetarians and after a while the human visitors soon begin to exhibit similar traits. John falls in love with a lovely Martian woman whom he has to give up once they return to Earth because she would be ostracized as a freak on Earth. Accompanied by his new Martian son, Poynders and his companions are given guided tours all over Mars. They travel in air ships, and they travel thousands of miles along the canals. Great detail is presented about how the canals are constructed and how they function, and during this all arguments against an inhabited Mars are demolished through the explanations Poynders gives, or the answers he receives from his Martian companions.

There are some interesting points that later authors also used, one example being that humans expend enormous sums of money on preparations for wars whereas there are no wars on Mars. If the money spent on war preparations was spent on welfare, humans would be much better off, and possibly much more advanced scientifically as well as ethically. There is much made of the social conditions on Earth compared to those on Mars. (…and this hasn't changed even today where there are just as many people who claim spending money on space exploration would be better spent on helping the poor or on developing better means of feeding those who live below the poverty line.)

Another interesting point is that the travelers in this story find Mars to be generally flat with slight undulations, *whilst hills and mountains are very rare.* The author states unequivocally that there are no high mountains anywhere, the highest altitudes rarely approach 2000 feet, and such heights as these are quite exceptional. This immediately brought to mind Arthur C Clarke's statement in his story **The Sands of Mars**, where he states (in italics) *There are no mountains on Mars.* He later apologized for this statement but qualified it by saying *there are no mountains on Mars as we understand them, like the Himalayas or the Andes mountain ranges.* Nobody knew then about the giant volcanoes on Mars that are larger than anything existing on Earth, and perhaps even in the whole solar system. The truth about what Mars is like would not be known until NASA sent its Mariner 4 probe to fly by and take photos in 1965.

Regardless of the fact that there is virtually no action in this story, it is well written and full of fascinating information about Mars. It is really quite interesting to see how much was really known about Mars at the beginning of the 20th century and how little that knowledge changed for the first half of that century, at least as far as writers were concerned.

Scientists were beginning to realize that Mars was not the benign place they envisioned, that its climate was far harsher than expected, and that it was not a place that could easily be inhabited by humans. Writers on the other hand ignored that and kept to ideas promulgated by Percival Lowell and those with similar ideas, until the true face of Mars was revealed in 1965, after which they either changed how they wrote about the planet, or abandoned it for places further afield.

To Mars via the Moon is well worth reading and comparing with other similar stories from roughly the same time period. It is pointless to make comparisons with more modern efforts. Good stories are good regardless of when they were written and published, especially if you keep in mind the context of the time in which the story was written. And this is definitely a good story...

A voice of dissension

It is worthwhile noting that Alfred Russel Wallace disagreed with the findings of Percival Lowell and wrote a book outlining the scientific facts known about Mars and what logical conclusions could be drawn from those facts.

Is Mars Habitable? Alfred Russel Wallace (1907)

The author Mark Wicks would also have read the articles by Alfred Russel Wallace, who was the most famous expert on the geographical distribution of animal species and was considered the father of *Biogeography*; as well as his book *Is Mars Habitable?* (Published in 1907), in which he refutes the findings and imaginings of Professor Percival Lowell, finally stating unequivocally that *Mars in uninhabitable*.

It is well known that Alfred Russel Wallace proposed an independently developed theory of evolution, based on his travels, his collecting, and his observations of animal, plant and insect life in South East Asia, and how it is different from animal, plant and insect species in lands and islands further south, such as New Guinea and Australia, to develop a theory of evolution. His articles in scientific journals prompted Darwin to prematurely publish his own theories on evolution in his book ***On The Origin of Species*** (1859, and later ***The Descent of Man 1887***). Both Darwin and Wallace had travelled widely to the most remote places on this planet and drew their conclusions from their observations and later studies of the specimens they collected.

There is a short preface at the beginning of the book ***Is Mars Habitable?*** in which Wallace states: "*This small volume was commenced as a review article on Professor Percival Lowell's book,* **Mars and its Canals***, with the object of showing the large amount of new and interesting facts contained in this work did not invalidate the conclusion I had reached in 1902, and stated in my book* **Man's Place in the Universe***, that Mars was not habitable.*"

Wallace of course was as interested in Astronomy as much as anyone else, and being of a scientific bent, and since Mars was at its closest approach to Earth in some time and the whole world was fascinated by the red planet, he came up with alternative ideas about how Mars had formed as a planet and how he did not believe the wild enthusiastic imaginings of Percival Lowell.

Wallace explains how the canals and oases described by Percival Lowell as 'non-natural' may have been formed as 'natural' features. To do this required a small volume rather than a simple article.

The eight chapters in this volume are:
1. Early Observers of Mars.
2. Mr. Lowell's Discoveries and Theories.
3. The Climate and Physiography of Mars.
4. Is Animal Life Possible on Mars?
5. Temperature on Mars — Mr. Lowell's Estimate.
6. A new Estimate of the Temperature of Mars.
7. A Suggestion as to the Canals of Mars.
8. Page Summary and Conclusions.

In Chapter one Wallace details the early observations of the planet's ice caps and seas (or what was thought to be seas because of the darker colour), talks about Schiaparelli's discovery of *canali* (Channels) the spots that intersect these canali, and discusses the changes of colour occurring seasonally and what was in general thought about this.

The second chapter details Mr. Lowell's observations, discoveries, which goes into a lot of detail about the so-called canals mapped by Mr. Lowell and his fantastic ideas about the origin of the canals.

Chapter three covers the physiography of Mars and its climate, and talks about there being no permanent water on Mars, no clouds and therefore no rain, no mountains hills or valleys; with a lot about the supposed dimensions of the canals, and whether they are irrigation works and other matters as proposed by Mr. Lowell. He is actually full of praise for the observations made by Mr. Lowell although he doesn't accept Mr. Lowell's conclusions regarding the canals as being the work of intelligent beings.

Chapter four discusses the possibility of plant and animal life on Mars, and what is needed for such life, such as an atmosphere (assumed by Mr. Lowell and others) to be like ours, but with slightly less surface pressure. He also goes into the reasons why water vapour cannot exist on Mars and why it is much colder than suggested by those who believed intelligent beings existed on Mars.

The next two chapters discusses firstly Mr. Lowell's considerations of the temperature on Mars, and secondly what estimates of the real temperature on Mars is. To bolster his arguments, he compares temperatures on Earth at high altitudes where the air is much less thin but still nowhere near the lesser pressure on Mars, how radiation is lost to space (ie. heat) at high altitudes, as well as on the Moon, and he applies these observable results to Mars based on what was actually known about Mars scientifically. He is highly critical of Mr. Lowell's beliefs. He also points out how much lower the temperature is at the poles, much lower than the freezing point of water. And in general, he claims the highest temperature on Mars at any time is still below the freezing point of water.

In chapter seven he proposes an alternate theory of how Mars formed by the accretion of rocky material (unlike the nebular theory of gasses coalescing to form the Sun and the planets), but since Earth and Jupiter had obtained the bulk of the rocky material, what was left to form Mars was not enough to generate a molten centre in the planet. It formed as a cold planet. Later meteor and comet bombardment liquefied the surface turning it molten, and as it slowly cooled (and shrank) against a cold interior, cracks appeared on the surface. Because the surface had been liquefied it tended to be remarkably smooth and remained so as it cooled, resulting in no hills, mountains or large indentations other than a few craters formed by meteor impacts. These impact points are where the cracks first appeared. (The so-called oases suggested by Mr. Lowell). He explains similar linear cracks can be found on Earth and gives many examples, but Earth was affected by weather and erosion by water while Mars was not. It is easier to see the cracks on Mars while it is more difficult on Earth. There is a lot of detail about why water doesn't exist on the surface of Mars, and even if it did, why there would never be enough to fill the canals without it being lost by evaporation across thousands of miles of desert. He also suggests that intelligent beings would not be stupid enough to build such canals in the first place.

The final chapter is a summary of all Mr. Lowell's ideas and Wallace's reasons why those ideas are wrong, and once again goes into independent proofs made by other scientists regarding the low temperature of the Martian surface and the uninhabitability of Mars. His very final sentence unequivocally states: '*Mars, therefore, is not only uninhabited by intelligent being such as Mr. Lowell postulates, but is absolutely UNINHABITABLE.*'

This is a fascinating little book that should be of value to anyone who is interested in the history of what people believed about Mars at the end of the 1800s and into the early 1900s. The fact that there were as many scientists who believed Lowell's theories as there were those who were inclined to believe Wallace is interesting in itself.

Novelists of the time preferred to believe Mr. Lowell and wrote stories based on his ideas, such as the one by Mark Wicks, ***To Mars via The Moon,*** in which he puts forth both arguments for intelligent beings on Mars and their construction of cities and canals and other infrastructure. Wallace's arguments regarding the uninhabitability of Mars and the impossibility of intelligent, or any kind of life on the planet, were often demolished in favor of Mr. Lowell's theories.

In retrospect

Mars as depicted by Wallace is more believable than the Mars suggested by Lowell. At least he tried to stick to what was known scientifically to explain what he thought Mars was like. Lowell on the other hand let his imagination run wild, which in turn influenced many of his contemporaries into believing that they too could see what he saw. And that influenced many writers of fiction who produced best-selling stories set on a very fanciful Mars.

To me it was clear that as far back as the beginning of the 20th century, there was considerable knowledge regarding Mars, but the authors of the day ignored such scientific matters preferring to rely on their imaginations and desires for a better place than Earth was. They continued to maintain the earlier theories and beliefs of how the planets and life evolved, and where necessary, added to their imaginings some scientific observations to create a veneer of credibility. Some kind of Utopia was always suggested as a comparison to their present existence, or as an ideal to which we should attempt to attain in the future. And this went on right up until the mid-1950s where slowly more scientific detail started to appear in stories which were becoming less fanciful and more technically accurate regarding Mars. Even then, the general consensus was that Mars didn't have large mountains or deep valleys and the surface was relatively flat and smooth, having been blasted by sandstorms for millions of years, which would have eroded away any mountainous features.

But knowledge of Mars was still limited and fanciful ideas continued to appear, at least until 1965. After Mariner 4 sent back those grainy close-up images depicting a barren cratered surface; something no one ever expected to exist on Mars. When later photographic images of a stunningly beautiful Mars came back from other robotic devices sent to the planet, writers of stories set on Mars had to change to incorporate this new reality, or they abandoned Mars altogether and set their stories elsewhere in the solar system or the local galaxy.

It would be almost two decades before writers returned to Mars with new stories of exploration and adventure, excitement and mystery, and they haven't stopped writing about Mars since then.

With the advent of self-publishing and eBooks there has been a daunting proliferation of stories about Mars (as well as every other subject). Many of these stories have little regard for scientific facts, and simply use recycled ideas from ages past but there are exceptions and a patient reader will find some very good stories in amongst the mountains of ill conceived books found online.

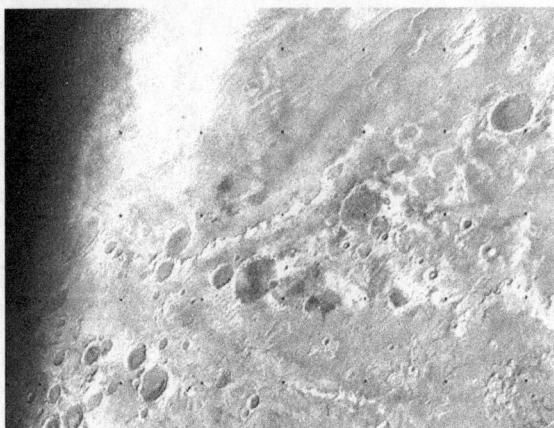

One of the two dozen images of the Martian surface, sent back from Mariner 4 in 1965 which shattered all previous conceptions of what Mars was like.

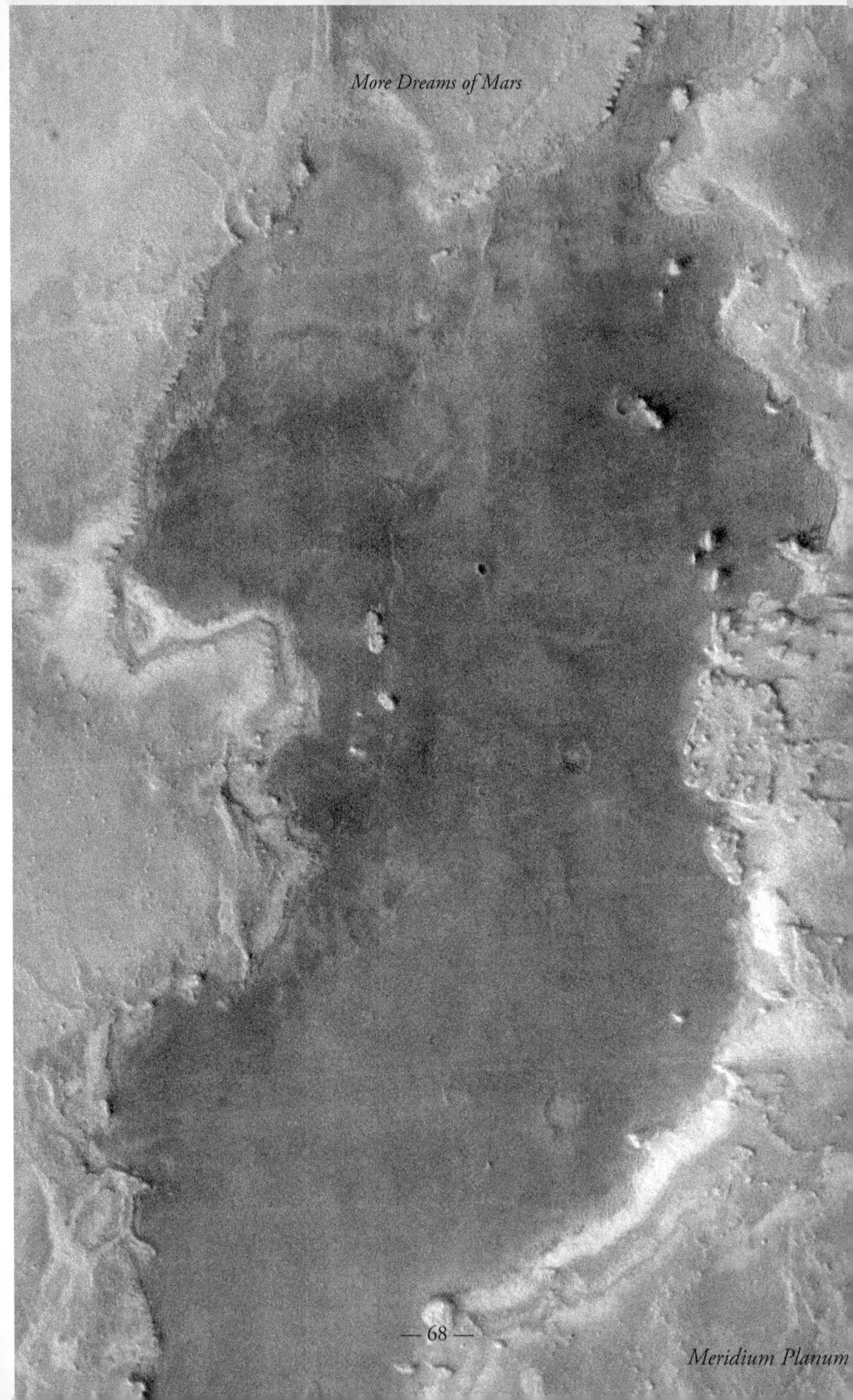

Meridium Planum

Chapter Two

Pulp Fiction Classics

A bridge between the old and the new
Hugo Gernsback and the advent of pulp fiction

Is Hugo Gernsback, the father of science fiction in America?
It could be argued that modern science fiction began when Hugo Gernsback, who immigrated to America in 1904, and started his magazine *Electrical Experimenter,* among others.

Being an inventor, he was particularly interested in stories that used scientific ideas as a basis for the action, and the adventures in the stories he published. He mostly acted as an editor and a promoter of scientific stories using his various magazines for publishing them. He also wrote what is believed to be a seminal science fiction novel ***Ralph 124C 41+: A Romance of the year 2660.***

It first appeared as shorter works in his magazine *Modern Electrics,* then later appeared as a novel in 1925. I remember reading this when I was about fifteen years old and the name stuck in my mind for years. The edition I read in the mid-1950s had been revised and published in 1950.

I never saw his second novel, ***Baron Münchhausen's Scientific Adventures,*** which also first appeared as a series of stories in another of his many magazines, because those magazines were published before I was born, and as a novel it wasn't published until after he died. I only recently discovered this fantastic story, and it brought back many memories of the kind of story I loved as a young teenager in the 1950s.

Baron Münchhausen's Scientific Adventures
by Hugo Gernsback (1915-17 1928, 2006)

Baron Munchhausen was a fictional picaresque character invented by writer *Rudolph Raspe* in 1785 or thereabouts. He wrote outrageous adventures which people loved. Collected under the title of ***Baron Münchhausen's Narrative of his Marvelous Travels.*** Other writers also wrote stories about the infamous *Baron Munchhausen,* and the more fantastic they were, the more popular they became. A number of films were made of his adventures the earliest being by Georges Méliés.at the beginning of the 1900s. In 1942/3 An extravagant colour German film made during the Nazi era titled ***The Adventures of Baron Münchhausen***, was rediscovered and restored in the 1990s. The Terry Gilliam film of the same name and based on the original Rudolph Raspe stories was made in 1988.

None of these films or early stories are in any way related to Hugo Gernsback's updating of the Baron's adventures, putting them into a science fiction context.

Lauded as his second novel, these episodic stories first appeared in his magazine, *Electrical Experimenter*, from 1915 to 1917. They were later collected and reprinted in his new magazine *Amazing Stories* in 1928 with the title ***Baron Münchhausen's New Scientific Adventures*** or with the same title without the word new. *Amazing Stories* was the first magazine devoted entirely to what he first called *scientific fiction*, then *scientifiction*, and finally *science fiction*. This last name stuck and is still used today to identify this specific genre of fiction, a genre that one could almost say Gernsback invented in its American form. The episodes collected as a novel never appeared in book form while Gernsback was alive. (He died in 1967). *Armchair Fiction* produced a beautiful edition in 2017, as part of their 200th double novels celebration as well as the story's 100th anniversary, by reprinting this first, (or one of the first), truly science fiction novels. It is well worth obtaining if you haven't yet read this story.

It is told from the viewpoint of I M Alier, an inventor of a radio device for extreme long-distance communication. He receives a message purportedly from the Baron, whom everyone thought had been dead for over 100 years. The Baron explains that it was thought he was dead, but the embalmer made a mistake and instead of eviscerating him before embalming he simply injected the embalming fluid directly into his veins, causing him to go to sleep and remain preserved but alive until the effect of the fluid wore off more than 100 years later. He had now travelled to the Moon in a ship he had invented and constructed, and was sending this broadcast from there before moving on to Mars. I M Alier reports for the reader the stories radioed to him from the Baron interspersed with activities of his own.

In the original stories the Baron dealt with the Turkish Ottoman Empire and its invasion of Europe, but in Gernsback's version the Baron who has defected from the Prussian Empire has aligned himself with the British and helps them and their allies to defeat the Germans during the First World War. This no doubt had great relevance for readers in America at the time it was published because The First World War had only just ended.

Very quickly the story progresses to the Baron travelling to the Moon with another scientist and his dog and a canary in a special sphere-shaped ship he invented that uses anti-gravity to power it. Much like similar stories from the end of the 19th Century, some form of magnetic or electrical, or other mysterious power often called anti-gravity is used to get the travelers off Earth and into Space. He discovers there is an atmosphere on the Moon, but it is sulfuric and tenuous, extending only twenty feet or so above the surface. The dog is first out of the ship and it coughs and splutters as it breathes the Moon's atmosphere. The Baron is next out and his companion follows, and they too have difficulty breathing the sulfurous atmosphere at first but become used to it. After this, the dog and the canary are not mentioned again.

He wasn't wrong about that. There is an atmosphere on the Moon but it is so tenuous its molecules don't touch or bounce off each other. It is referred to as an exosphere and is virtually indistinguishable to being in the vacuum of space. The principal gases are not sulfuric but are helium, neon and argon. The Moon's exosphere is roughly one trillion times as tenuous as the Earth's atmosphere.

There is also a description of how the Earth looks from the Moon and how the Baron sees it rotating which immediately conjures that magnificent iconic photo taken of the Earth rising over the edge of the Moon by the Apollo 8 astronauts when they orbited the Moon in 1968. What a sight that must have been! It makes you realize that sometimes those early authors actually got something right.

It has now been confirmed there is water on the Moon. Apart from that which is contained within the structure of various rocks, there is also frozen water in deep polar craters the bottoms of which are never exposed to sunlight. Water that has been there for perhaps several billion years...

There are lakes underground in caverns, with fish that are fluorescent as well as some turtle-like creatures, but the Moon on the surface is dead, battered by meteors that fall continuously, impacting the surface making craters.

After accidentally falling into a large crater that extends right through the Moon to the other side, the Baron discovers the Moon is hollow which he suspects happened as the newly formed moon cooled rapidly, suggesting that centrifugal force caused the molten interior to be pushed outwards leaving a hollow centre when it cooled into rock. Emerging on the dark side of the Moon the Baron dives back into the crater so he can fall back down and through once again to emerge on the daylight side where his space ship had landed and where his friend is waiting for him.

Not every speculation can be right, and the hollow Moon, although popular, is incorrect. The Moon once had a molten core which gave it a magnetic field, but since the core has cooled and solidified the magnetic field has disappeared along with any evolving atmosphere which like that of Mars would have been blown away by the solar winds from the sun.

When a meteorite impacts some of their equipment, destroying it, they decide it is too dangerous to stay on the Moon and they depart for Mars.

There is a long discussion here of what Percival Lowell has 'discovered' regarding the Martian Polar regions and the thousands of Canals that criss-cross the planet. The general consensus by scientists at that time was that Mars must be inhabited in order to have so many canals built that are often thousands of miles long, built to fight off the slow death of a planet drying up. The various colours were thought to be irrigated areas of plant life, used to sustain the inhabitants, rather than seas or oceans. The canals traverse these areas so they can't be seas. The actual canals can't be seen from earth either, but what is seen according to Lowell is the vegetation that grows alongside the canals, vegetation that requires irrigation from the canals. He estimated the lines they see from Earth are at least 6 miles wide to be visible from space.

The Baron muses that Mars is smaller than Earth and (like the Moon) started cooling much quicker than did the Earth which still has a molten core and many volcanoes. Civilization would have begun much earlier on Mars than on Earth and the Martians would be much more advanced than the humans, especially when one considers the length and number of the canals used to take water from the polar regions to irrigate the more arid tropical areas.

This theory of planetary evolution was used by many writers at this time, including H G Wells who explains the theory in the first few pages of his book **War of The Worlds.** *(1898).*

In the first two decades of the 20th century, the general populace still believed that there was intelligent life on Mars and that these beings had built the canals to stave off the inevitable death of their planet. This gave writers the opportunity to imagine all kinds of advanced and collapsing societies that inhabited Mars, which disguised as fantasies or entertainments they could use to contrast and comment on the faults of their own societies, cultures and political systems. Some of these books became popular and can still be found today in various forms, while others are long forgotten.

As the Baron's ship comes down to land on Mars it is captured by a number of flying vehicles that use some kind of golden yellow ray that takes hold of the Baron's globular space ship. He is taken to a specific part of the enormous city where the ruler of Mars resides. The cities of Mars which extend along both sides of the enormous canals are built on pillars 500 feet into the air to avoid the continuous dust storms that blow across the surface. The buildings are transparent. The roads are made of metal with millions of tiny holes so when a huge storm comes that reaches high enough to envelope a city the dust left on the surface falls through the holes back down to the ground below. The Martians are at least 9 feet tall, and proportionally larger compared to humans. They wear clothes of woven metal which grounds them against electrical discharges. They also use helmets that can transfer the electrical impulses of thought from one to another so they read each other's minds. The Baron and his associate are given helmets so they can communicate with the Martians.

They are taken on a guided tour of Mars so they see how giant electrical machines emitting yellow rays are used to create the flow of water along the canals; water that wouldn't flow naturally because the Martian terrain is absolutely flat. They attend concerts where strange music is projected from weird electronic tubes controlled by the thoughts of the composer. They are later taken to a gigantic concert hall which seats over 2000 Martians to experience a concert where music is played with colours, with smells, and finally with sound. There is also a spectacle involving precious water that is suspended by anti-gravity and sculpted into shapes floating in the air above the tank that contained it. After the Martians stared at the floating water for some time it was allowed to collapse back into the tank below... and that was the end of the concert.

The Baron and his companion were also taken to an observatory where a giant telescope showed them the Earth. The Martian ruler then used the scope to zoom in on Earth, enlarging it until it filled the centre of the room, floating there in 3 dimensions. He further zoomed in to show the North American continent, and continued to zoom in until it showed the city of New York as seen by an aviator five thousand feet above. Further enlargement allowed the Baron and his companion to see actual people walking along the streets.

The two humans are suitably astonished at this spectacle when they realize they are 60,000 000 miles away and how much the Martians are technologically advanced compared to the human race. Proof of this is adequately shown when the Ruler takes the Baron and his companion to watch a new 'small' canal being constructed. Several giant machines emitting powerful rays literally melt the sand and rock away fusing the sides and base to a glassy impenetrable barrier. The machines don't generate heat but disrupt the molecular structure of the soil and rock, vaporizing it, making it appear to melt into nothing. Once filled with water it will not soak into the thirsty desert beneath. This small canal is only 600 miles long, four miles wide and 12 feet deep. It is perfectly straight.

As Mars gets further away from Earth in its orbit around the sun the communication between Baron Münchhausen and Alier in his home radio station degenerates. Even though the Baron had built a relay station on the Moon to broadcast his recorded messages to Alier, when Mars gets beyond 80,000,000 miles contact is finally lost. Alier is left hoping that once Mars has travelled around the sun and again approaches opposition contact will be regained, but that won't be for at least another Earth year. The reader is also left here —the story ends at this point— wondering if there will be further adventures to be related.

What makes this story interesting is it reads like a modern story even though it was published over 100 years ago (1915 to 1917) when compared to the stories written twenty years before it.

The style of writing had changed considerably as pulp magazines developed, being more concise, and less convoluted, although some of those elements still prevailed. It is dated of course by the use of the terminology used for the extrapolated future scientific equipment regarding radio broadcasts. The relay on the Moon is called a *radiomatic relay*, and Alier is always adjusting his *harmonic ultra-amplifier*, *selenium vapor enforcer* and his *coupled inductance balance.* He also devises an *ampliphone* (a loudspeaker) so he can hear better the signals relayed from the Moon.

Anyone interested in stories about Mars over the last 140 years or more should read this delightful story. It is a bridge between the old-fashioned stories and ideas and ways of writing, and the more modern styles to which we are now accustomed.

The cover prize competition

Not only did Gernsback edit his magazines as well as sometimes contributing stories of his own under various pseudonyms he also ran competitions to encourage new writers. In 1926 he had what he called *The $500 Cover Prize Contest.* (1st prize was $250, 2nd $150, and 3rd $100.) The stories were to be not more than 10,000 words and had to include a scene in the story that was depicted by the cover illustration in their December 1926 edition of *Amazing Stories, The Magazine of Scientifiction.*

The illustration depicted a strange landscape where a number of male and female beings who were basically human in appearance but who had rows of feathers growing backwards from their arms, over their shoulders and from the back of their head, were staring up into the sky where a gigantic sphere-like ship floated. Suspended beneath this ship was an ocean liner, held up by some kind of magnetic attraction.

The third prize winning story was written by a woman and Gernsback was full of praise for her effort. It's a Martian story called ***The Fate of the Poseidonia*** by Mrs. F C Harris, but the byline under the title of the story reads: by Clare Winger Harris. It was published in the June 1927 issue of *Amazing Stories.* The story is set in the future year of 1945.

Even though the author is a woman the story is experienced from a male perspective, as were most stories from that time.

Mr. Gregory is attending a lecture being given by a professor Stearns, Head of the Astronomy Department of Austin College. The lecture is about Mars.

At this meeting Mr. Gregory meets an odd appearing man and for some reason they dislike each other on sight. The man is slightly short in stature with a coppery skin. His legs and arms seemed rather spindly while his chest was larger than expected. He wore a skull cap, which made Gregory think he could have been injured. He called himself Mr. Martell. Reluctantly shaking hands with the stranger Gregory feels uncomfortable touching the man's skin which seemed dry and spongy.

As the lecture proceeds Martell and Gregory find themselves seated beside each other. Martell interrupts the professor a couple of times to correct what he calls erroneous facts regarding the amount of water on Mars, but what puts Gregory off him completely is that when the lights were dimmed so they could study the 'lantern slides' of Mars projected onto a screen, Martell's eyes glowed with a phosphorescent light.

The lecture proceeds and the professor is discussing the loss of water on Mars and his supposition that it is a dying planet (as suggested by Percival Lowell), with its people struggling desperately and vainly for existence, when Martell interrupts and asks, *Just suppose that the Martians were the possessors of an intelligence equal to that of Terrestrials, what might they do to save themselves from total extinction?*

Martell suggests if the situation were reversed and the people of Earth found themselves in a similar situation what would they do? There is some discussion here about the ingenuity of humanity and how they would find a solution eventually, after which the meeting concludes and the guests leave.

Mr. Gregory lives in a hotel apartment and a few days later on returning home he encounters Mr. Martell in the hallway and finds the strange man is living in a nearby apartment on the same floor. They ignore each other apart from the usual cordial greeting if they encounter one another in passing.

We find out that Mr. Gregory is seeing a lovely young lady called Margaret. His relationship with her is gradually becoming estranged and he doesn't understand why until he sees her with a rival, the nefarious Martell, his disliked neighbor. She tells him that aside from appearances Martell is a forceful and interesting character and she is upset that Gregory resents her association with Martell. Gregory is decidedly upset and furious and decides to spy on Martell to see what he is up to. He sneaks along the corridor and peers through the keyhole into Martell's lodgings, and sees him seated in front of a desk on top of which is an odd boxlike contraption. A glowing mist seems to be floating above the box and Martell is staring into it and speaking. Retreating, Gregory immediately goes to tell Margaret what he has seen but she accuses him of jealousy, and rejects his suggestion that there is something wrong with Martell.

In April 1945 there is amazement around the world as every major city on the Pacific Ocean coasts experience a retreat of the water. The whole ocean level has dropped by several feet. What catastrophe could have caused this is speculated in all the newspapers. What catastrophe could cause the disappearance of millions of tons of water overnight? Scientists are baffled. Has the ocean floor cracked and the water drained down into I deep abyssal caverns? As implausible as this seems people in time accepted the idea and went on about their lives.

Not long after this event, Margaret, with whom Gregory had not spoken to for some time, calls him to come over to her apartment. When he gets there, he discovers Martell is extremely sick, almost dying. Margaret explains that Martell wanted to speak to him, but Gregory refuses. He wants nothing to do with the man who stole his girlfriend. While there he sees a news report on the Television which tells of the disappearance of the Pegasus, a transatlantic flying machine, with all its passengers. He is upset because he knows this fantastic machine, has actually been on it.

Heading back to his accommodations he decides to enter the rooms Martell uses and see what he can find. He immediately goes to the box device on the desk and there are five buttons. Pushing one the mist forms above the device and a strange scene, so realistic he finds it hard to believe, appears. A stocky being not unlike Martell appears and walks towards him. The man has coppery skin and is naked, but there are feathers growing out from the backs of his arms, extending all the way up and across his shoulders and onto the back of his head. The being waves at him as he walks towards where Gregory is. Gregory switches off the device and the vision vanishes. He depresses another button and a man similar to Martell appears. From what he sees in the background the man appears to be in Germany. The man is astonished to see someone other than Martell, and again Gregory switches off the device. The device is obviously a means of communication for Martell and his other associates, but who are these strange men, and what are they doing? The third lever switched to another sumptuous apartment but it seemed to be empty. The machine starts buzzing, as if someone was trying to connect with it. The fourth lever revealed a face like that of Martell, but seemingly more menacing. He glared at Gregory who promptly disconnected by switching the lever back. Standing up he glances around the apartment then leaves. Back in his own rooms his telephone is ringing. It is Margaret wanting to tell him that Martell is okay. She tells him Mr. Martell wants him to come over because he has something to tell him, but again Gregory refuses.

Rushing back to Martell's rooms he enters again and switches on the machine, this time using the fifth lever. The mist forms and the image which appears seems to be looking down from a height. He sees hundreds of men that appear to be like Martell working in what looks like a shipyard. There were literally thousands of huge spheres also floating nearby or under construction. All the people had shoulders covered with layers of feathers. The land around consisted of red cliffs cutting down into deep gullies. As he watches the sun, shrunken to half the size of ours sets and the whole place is immediately dark. Moments later he sees a small moon rise and pass rapidly across the sky. Then he sees a great spherical bulk enter the image area. It has a metal band circling the middle and hanging beneath it suspended with some kind of electric or magnetic tethers is the missing airliner, the Pegasus. In the clutches of this unearthly marauder the magnificent Pegasus, looked like a child's toy. As he watches he sees sphere after sphere rising up and eclipsing the tiny moon, all heading towards the bright blue-green star that he suspects is the Earth. Suddenly, he understood what they were doing.

At that instant there is a commotion outside the door and several police officers rush in with Martell leading them. "That man is a spy," he declares and the officers seize him. He tries to explain that Martell is a spy but they won't listen to him. He is handcuffed and dragged out of the room during which activity he loses consciousness with a sharp pain stabbing at his heart.

He wakes two days later to find himself incarcerated in a mental ward. No one believes him when he says he is not mentally insane. 'They all say that!'

He asks if he could speak with Professor Stearns who could vouch for his sanity, and the guard says he would arrange it. Meanwhile he gives him a newspaper which has headlines screaming about a second retreat of the ocean, this time it is the Atlantic. Ships reported great waves that almost caused them to sink. The island of Madeira reported millions of dead fish lying on what used to be the sea bed but which was now exposed. The newspaper continued with the fact that the Poseidonia travelling across the Atlantic had radioed that thousands of giant spheres had filled the sky and they were sucking up the ocean. The captain immediately turned the ship around and headed back towards the US but it was followed by one of those huge spheres. They couldn't escape it and... there the radio message ended.

Again he calls for the guards to release him, he wasn't insane, he could explain what was happening to the oceans, but they ignore his pleas. Get Professor Stearns he asked and that they did.

Finally, when the professor arrives Gregory explains that the Martians have been secretly planning on stealing the Earth's water to replenish their own dried up ocean beds. First it was The Pacific, and now The Atlantic. He tells about the radio television device he saw and how they communicate with each other and with Mars.

"Stupendous," gasped Professor Stearns. "Something must be done to prevent another raid." And he thinks they will have to bring out the tremendous weapons of war that have remained silent and unused for decades. It is the only way to fight them. Then the professor leaves.

This time when the guard gives him the latest newspaper, he sees the passenger list for the Poseidonia and there is his girlfriend Margaret's name along with those of her parents. Completely distraught he settles back into his cell. Shortly after the guard delivers to him a package. Professor Stearns had suggested that he was able to receive mail.

Opening the package, he finds the very same boxlike contraption he had seen and used in Martell's apartment. Inside was a card, *For Gregory in remembrance of Martell.* Feeling like smashing the device, he resists the temptation and placing it on the table he attempts to switch all the levers but nothing happens. He finally manipulates the fifth dial, and slowly a mist begins to appear above the device. It reveals the same aerial view he had seen before but the thousands of spheres had gone and seated on the grassy verge beside a lake were a group of red-skinned white feathered people. One of the figures stands and points up to the sky, and the viewpoint shifts and reveals a great sphere beneath which was the dwarfed massive ocean liner the Poseidon hanging suspended. He was seeing the victory of Martell the Martian, who had filled his world's canals with the waters from Earth's two major oceans.

He closes his eyes, momentarily stunned by the thought that Margaret and all the other passengers on that ocean liner were now dead, frozen by the cold of outer space as the ship was carried between the worlds. But her face appears and she tells him that Martell rescued her before the ship was taken into outer space and that she is the only survivor. "*Do not weep for me,*" she tells him. "*I will take up the thread of life in this strange but beautiful world. I can't talk long but I wanted to tell you that Terra need fear Mars no more. There is sufficient water now...*"

Her face disappeared, replaced by the leering face of Martell. He was minus his skullcap and his feathers stood erect. He grinned malevolently. Gregory reaches to switch off the machine but it switches itself off. Martell had cut off communications forever.

Eventually released from the mental hospital, no one believes his explanation of what happened to the Pegasus and the Poseidonia and are still searching the ocean depths where they were last reported seen. He knows they will never find them. They will never be seen on Earth again.

Gernsback was surprised that the author of this story turned out to be a woman because in his eyes: *as a rule, women do not make good scientifiction writers, because their education and general tendencies on scientific matters are usually limited.* He goes on to praise her as an exception and wishes that she writes more stories for his magazine *Amazing Stories*.

Descendants of Starfarers

A common theme used in early science fiction stories was that humans are the descendants of star-faring beings who colonized or established a base on Earth many thousands of years ago and that the human race descended from these beings, (or were created by these beings), who left for whatever reasons. Their descendants over time retrogressed to a more primitive state before advancing enough to develop towns and cities and states, which perhaps explains why religious concepts regarding God, or a multiplicity of Gods, appear in almost every culture throughout Africa, Europe, Asia, Oceania, and anywhere else where humans have settled. In some African cultures there are references to the Gods having come from certain specific stars. Could this be merely coincidence, or is this a deep-buried racial memory of past events?

Since Schiaparelli first noticed what he called *canali* in 1877, and with Mars being in everyone's consciousness from that time on, humans descending from Martians was another often-used theme in stories published after the turn of the century. When that concept first began, I have no idea, but an early example of it is *The Retreat to Mars* by Cecil B. White, published in Amazing Stories vol. 2. No. 5 in 1927, followed with a sequel *The Return of The Martians* the following year, 1928. Together these two stories make one longer story.

The editor of Amazing Stories claims that Mr. White is an astronomer and scientist and he propounds an entirely new and interesting theory about the origins of mankind in this world. That the author was influenced by Professor Percival Lowell is obvious in the text and also, he adds a footnote recommending that readers read *The Planet Mars, Mars and Its Canals*, and *Mars as the Abode of Life*. (1896, 1906, 1908.) These were all readily available at the time Cecil B White wrote his two Martian stories.

The Retreat to Mars and **The Return of The Martians,** by Cecil B. White (1927 – 1928)

One evening as the narrator, Arnold, is about to open up his observatory to take spectrographic images of a particular star, an older man approaches him. This man, Hargraves of the Smithsonian Institute explains he is here because Arnold had made some remarkable observations of the planet Mars the year before when it had been at its closest to Earth. They establish a rapport by joking about several astronomers who argued with Schiaparelli over the existence of *canali* on Mars. It is implied that Arnold had actually seen them and had reported such in the journals read by scientists.

"I'm an archaeologist and I know nothing about Mars, but I have a big surprise for you," Hargraves tells his host.

It must have been a common idea up until the first decade or two of the 20th century that humankind originated in Asia and spread from there to the rest of the world. Hargraves suggests something else; that humans evolved and spread out to the rest of the world from Central Africa.

I always thought it was common knowledge that humans began in Africa, but then I was born in 1940 and by the time I was old enough to understand such things it was accepted that humans had emerged in Africa, although no one knew with any certainty how far back that beginning was.

Hargraves was on an expedition into Africa with two other associates. One of them died from infections caught in the swamps and the other returned because of the same illness. Hargraves, also afflicted, was recovering slowly, when one of his native bearers brought him an artifact that came from a distant valley where no natives dared to venture. They considered it the Abode of the Dead. The object was made of an advanced metal Hargraves had never seen. It couldn't be scratched or marked and it had some indecipherable inscription cut into it. He was more than intrigued and demanded the native show him the way to this distant valley. As soon as he recovered enough to travel, they set off, through the swamps, across wide savannah, and eventually into the foothills of a mountain range somewhere in the darkest centre of Africa.

On finding the spot where the artifact had originated, Hargraves discovers a metal object buried just under the surface. Using a sharpened stake to poke though the earth he begins to discern the size of the object, a rounded cylinder of enormous size with protruding metal struts that stick up into the air. They dig around it to uncover it and this takes days of careful shoveling and carting away of the earth. Finding a circular indentation Hargreaves thinks it is a door of some kind. There are two holes on either side and he decides this door unscrews. On the second attempt he manages to open it. *It was a left-hand screw rather than right hand. Reading his attempts to unscrew the door reminded me of the H G Wells Martian ships where the door or the hatch was unscrewed from inside.*

Inside he finds a set of 12 keys marked with unfamiliar hieroglyphics, and another bigger door.

It doesn't take him long to figure out which key goes into which hole because each is marked with a symbol corresponding to what is imprinted on the keys. Once inside Hargraves discovers a treasure trove of boxes which contain what he calls books, these books when opened depict scenes in three dimensions even though the surface of the page is flat. The illustrations come with specific hieroglyphics which enables him, as an archaeologist, to decipher the written language. He discovers this is a library and it tells a story.

Millions of years ago, Mars cooled before the Earth did because it was further from the sun, and so life began earlier there. Intelligent life evolved and civilization followed. The Martians are humanoid but around 9 feet tall, and with big chests because of the thinner atmosphere on Mars. As their planet started aging, they began conserving water deep underground in caverns. They also constructed the canals and the pumping stations at the locations Percival Lowell called oases, to shift the water to various heights in order to irrigate the land where the seas had dried up. They didn't try to irrigate the sandy deserts since there wasn't enough water.

Observing the Earth evolve closer to the sun, they decided to set up a colony on that beautiful planet and came to what is now Central Africa. The Martians had to use metal frames to help support them in the much stronger gravity and struggled to survive. Their children, which they hoped would be born and would adapt naturally to the higher gravity and thicker air were born shorted and stockier, and less intelligent. The third generation was even worse; they were nothing more than human shaped animals. Abandoning the colony as a failure, the Martians returned to their home planet. But before leaving, they collected together all the knowledge they had, in volumes of books and set them up as a library in three different locations. One, on a continent that sank into the ocean, another, on a continent that is now buried deep under ice, and the third one in Africa. The library was designed so that an intelligent being would be able to decipher its contents and discover their history. This is the one Hargraves had discovered.

The abandoned descendants of the Martian colonists evolved over time into the various human progenitors we are familiar with, spreading across Africa, and out of Africa North and Eastwards into other parts of the world, eventually to become us.

The story finishes with Hargraves telling the astronomer he can publish this story and is free to study the remaining texts from the Martian library which are now housed at the Smithsonian Institute.

The Return of The Martians, begins with Arnold the astronomer receiving a telegram from Hargraves asking him to come at his earliest opportunity. When he gets to Washington Hargraves explains that they have been studying the encyclopedia the Martians left in the library in Africa and have discovered the instructions on how to build a communication device that uses different principle to radio with which they can at last, talk to the Martians. There is abundant government funding since the US government doesn't want other countries to get hold of this technology. Arnold agrees to help build the device, which then must be transported across country to his private observatory where they will use his telescope to target exact locations on Mars where the receivers have been built.

When communication is finally established, after a number of minor errors, the Martians congratulate the Earthmen on finding the library. They are ecstatic that their descendants have finally made contact with Mars the home planet. They invite the Earthmen to visit Mars. Overjoyed at the prospect Arnold is only too happy to go to Mars. The Martians tell them they can bring two others with them so Arnold decides to bring his wife, and Hargraves brings his associate from the Smithsonian. The Martians tell them a ship will be sent to collect them in fifteen days and will land in the lake near where the observatory is housed.

They packed enough food to last 55 days, clothes, some instruments needed for research and a case of technical books that the Martians wanted so they could study how humans had evolved. The ship, somewhat bullet shaped with stubby wings comes in at tremendous speed and lands on the lake, gliding to a halt beside a small pier where the humans waiting have stacked their luggage. In no time, with the help of a mechanical arm, their luggage is taken on board. The four humans follow and meet one of the crew who shows them their quarters on the ship. It has been pressurized to match the air pressure at sea level on Earth so they can be comfortable throughout the voyage. When they get to Mars, they will have to wear space suits because the pressure on Mars is far to low for humans to use. The four crew members who operate the ship are all giants, 9 feet tall with huge chests but spindly arms and legs, and they have to wear a special armor to help their bodies cope with the higher gravity of Earth. On board the ship they find refrigerators for them to keep their food preserved. The Martians had told them to bring their own food since they may not be able to eat what is grown on Mars. During the journey to Mars Hargraves and his companion, Dr Smythe, study language texts so they will have no trouble communicating once they arrive. Arnold also studies the language but is not as proficient as the other two men. They are given a tour of the ship and how it all works is explained to them. From this point on there is barely a mention of Arnold's wife other than she had gone into the kitchen and prepared a meal for the men which was ready after their inspection of the ship. There is a whole chapter given over explaining how the ship works.

Two weeks later they arrive and fly down through the atmosphere to land on a huge balcony which is part of an enormous building. All around them are other enormous buildings as far as they can see.

There is a description of what they see as they come down from orbit and this matches closely to ideas suggested in the latter two books by Percival Lowell, **Mars and its Canals**, and **Mars as the abode of Life**. There is even a direct quote from Mars and its Canals : —*Whether increasing common sense or increasing necessity was the spur that drove the Martians eminently sagacious state we cannot say, but it is certain that reached it they have, and equally certain that if they had not they must all die. When a planet has attained the age of advancing decrepitude, and the remnant of its water supply resides simply in its polar caps, these can only be effectively tapped for the benefit of the in habitants when arctic and equatorial people are one. Difference of policy on the question of water supply means nothing short of death... they must combine to solidarity or perish—*

Much is made of the perfection of Martians, that none want for anything, and that all are beautiful and of one mind. Those who are born who disagree are eliminated. Sickness is unknown as all diseases have been conquered. The social status of everyone is equal. No one dies except by accident, or unless they feel the effects of old age coming upon them, then they go to an institution where they are painlessly put into the long sleep that knows no awakening.

It all seems wonderful to the human visitors. The Martians ask if they would mind undergoing some medical tests. They agree and Arnold is first. He enters a hospital type room where a group of people are operating weird machines. He stands on a dais and is surrounded by a green glow. Appearing in a mirror in front of him is his reflection and as she watches his clothes then his skin become transparent so his insides can be seen. The Martians the n inform him that there are a couple of things wrong with him that they can fix if he wants. Of course, he agrees and they take him into another room where he is rendered unconscious so they can operate. When he wakes, he feels terrific and when his companions asked why it took so long, he was gone an hour and a half, he explains they operated on him and fixed whatever was wrong. Hargraves is next, and then presumably the others.

After all have been treated and 'cured' they are told *"From now until the end of your stay, you will be shown all that we can show you of this planet, and ample facilities will be given you for each to study that part which interests you most. On your return, you will be accompanied by four other machines (space ships)— the vanguard of our second invasion."*

That's the kicker. The Martians are all lovely and friendly but they will return to Earth.

The final paragraphs have Arnold saying there is no need to talk about the surprise the Earth people will have when the Martians return. They want to organize our woefully muddled world into a world that would begin to approach the idea we had witnessed on Mars.

Arnold and the others are in agreement because they seem totally unconcerned.

Perhaps the world in 1928 was not such a nice place anyway and the author was suggesting that there was room for much improvement, and this is reflected in the attitude the characters exhibit.

Ominously the story ends with Arnold saying; *Let the world rest assured; there will be no sudden upheaval, but a gradual change in which the whole of humanity will benefit in ways the idealists have never dreamed of.*

It seems the world is not much of a better place even today, but none of us would want an alien invasion, benign or otherwise.

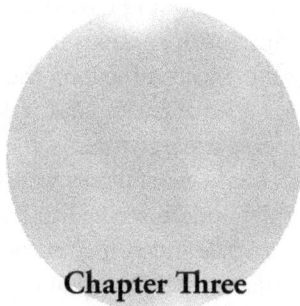

Chapter Three

A Golden Age emerges

Most of the short stories set on Mars during the 1920s through to the end of the 1930s depicted Mars as a hot desert planet, with an atmosphere that was still breathable although somewhat thinner than Earth's. Characters often didn't wear special suits but simply whatever an explorer in a desert country might wear. They carried water bottles and sought the shade of large rocks or what could be found beneath rocky ledges to avoid exposure to the sun. Sometimes concessions were made so that although the temperature wasn't as hot as an equatorial desert on Earth, being more like a high desert such as the Atacama, it was still unbearable because the thin atmosphere allowed too much solar radiation and ultra-violet rays to penetrate.

There was no thought given to what kind of flora and fauna could live in such a dry desert and writers chucked in sparse dried-up scraggy plants and monsters like a giant snake which could grind up silica and gain energy by digesting this material, then it would attack humans who happened to come across it.

If it digested ground up rock, how could it possibly be interested in wet sloppy humans?

Still, the human characters had to have something that threatened them, and why not a giant snake, or some other similar monster, or wild nomadic tribesmen inimical to humans who appeared out of nowhere. They were often tall and thin and copper coloured, or even green and slightly reptilian — weird if there was no water on Mars, but then some rather strange reptiles can be found in deserts on Earth, so why not Mars?

It was Mars, and no one knew anything about the place so writers could imagine whatever they wanted as long as it threatened the survival of their characters. In many cases the story could have been set in a desert on Earth since the action and the characters would have been the same; but by adding space ships, intermittent dust storms, canals desiccated or otherwise, with ancient abandoned cities falling into ruin along the length of them, made it Martian. That meant it was science fiction and it would be snapped up by the editors of such newly popular magazines.

Some stories were good, but in general they were bad if not execrable. But from the 1940s onwards the standard seemed to rise and the longer stories, novelettes and novellas, were of a much higher standard even though they still utilized the same or similar tropes. Many of the more famous authors of the 20th century began their careers during the 1940s and 1950s, which not only makes these two decades a *Golden Age* for science fiction, it also makes it a *Golden Age* for stories with a Martian setting.

Two different views of Mars by the same author

The Ambassador from Mars by Harl Vincent. (1930)

Harl Vincent —Harold Vincent Schoepflin, was born in 1893 and died in 1968— was an engineer, and a writer from the beginning of the 'pulp' era (1920s and 1930s), contributing many short stories to the popular magazines of the time. He wrote a few novels which have been revived in recent years by *Wildside Press* and *Armchair Fiction*. He stopped writing at the end of the 1930s when most pulp magazines vanished as the Second World War commenced. He did write a novel, ***The Doomsday Planet***, which was published by Tower Books (1966) two years before he died.

The Ambassador from Mars, originally published by Experimenter Press in 1930, has been republished by *Armchair Fiction* in its two complete novels series.

Frank Chandler, an architect who runs a successful business in New York is exhausted, unwell. Feeling depressed he wonders why he puts so many hours into his business, often working late into the night. He once loved his work but now he is not so sure. He is missing the fun, the romance, the excitement of living that he desires, and is tired of pampering his exclusive clients. He leaves his office at 10 pm and takes a walk to Central Park where he sits on a bench and lights a cigar. The moment he presses the lighter an enormous spark seems to envelope him and he feels as if he is being sucked up into the air, into space, before losing consciousness.

He wakes up confused, hearing the sound of strange voices speaking an unknown language, and on opening his eyes he finds himself on a bed in a room full of complex medical equipment with people wearing surgical masks fussing about him. As he wakes, they leave and he is alone in the room. Sitting up he manages to get out of the bed and pushes a call button beside the bed. He is astounded at the person who responds; tall, perfect physique, looking like a Greek God with skin the colour of burnished brass, enters the room to attend to his needs. He speaks perfect English.

"I am Ky-lin," he says, "and it is with great happiness that I observe your complete recovery."

Apparently, Chandler had been on the verge of a breakdown (presumably from stress and overwork). He goes on to explain that there is a surprise awaiting. He takes Chandler into another room where an old friend from his school years, Doctor Jack Conway, has been waiting. Chandler had thought Conway was dead since he had been missing for six years and no one knew what had happened to him.

After dressing in his own clothes Chandler and Conway enjoy a meal of strange viands after which his friend reveals that he is in a space flier, and that they are on their way to Uldur, which we call Mars. The flier he explains is as big as an ocean liner and can carry thousands of people but at the moment it only has a skeleton crew, and that they came to Earth to kidnap you at my request. Chandler is mystified and astonished. Jack also explains how Chandler has been modified medically to be able to breathe Mars' atmosphere and to find the lesser gravity perfectly normal. In the control room he sees through the same device that they used to kidnap him, the planet Earth from a great distance which convinces him he is actually on his way to Mars. Travelling at incredible speed they arrive in a few days and descend down to Mars.

The way the ship is described gives the reader the impression of absolute luxury, similar to what one would see in first class on board a major ocean-going liner on Earth, with richly carpeted stairs, writing rooms, a saloon, a sitting room where taps are gold plated; everything reminiscent of extreme wealth. He discovers Ky-lin is a prince, and his father is the king, the leader of the people of Mars.

But they have a problem. Two problems really… Mars is dying, and is no longer able to support the population. Where once many cities thrived and many millions of people lived, there is now only one city and the entire population that's left, lives there. The other problem is there is an implacable enemy, a foul creature that lives in the caves and underground spaces that were once human but have evolved over thousands of years into something grotesque and monstrous, and that these beings have also run out of food and come forth at night to prey on the remaining Martians. They catch them and kill them and take them back underground to eat. No weapon the people have can stop them.

Flying across the surface towards the hidden valley where the remaining city is located Chandler sees how barren and desiccated Mars has become. Once he meets the king who is dying, he has the Martian language implanted into his mind so he can communicate with them and learns that their solution is to migrate to Earth where they hope their superior science would compensate for the inconvenience the migration would cause.

They don't want to just arrive unexpectedly or people might think they were invading. They want to do it diplomatically, to convince humans to allow them to migrate from Mars to Earth. But they have been unable to communicate with Earth, so they kidnapped Chandler at the suggestion of his friend Jack. (It isn't explained how Jack came to be on Mars in the first place…but he has been there long enough to be a suitor for the King's daughter.) The Martians believe with two humans they could convince the earth people of their intentions. They need to implant in Chandler, the details of how to build a machine like the one used to kidnap him, so that they can then communicate directly with people on earth. They officially appoint Chandler as the Martian Ambassador to Earth.

Once Chandler has seen how difficult life on Mars has become, he is willing to go ahead with the plan. He also helps them with solving a means of killing the monstrous beings that attack the city at night which gives them the time they need for him to go back to Earth and to build the device.

He is returned to Earth and he convinces a group of scientists and world leaders to build the communicating device which takes about two years.

Finally, two years later when they make contact and are ready to discuss how they can migrate the remnants of the population to Earth, massive quakes start, volcanoes erupt and Mars begins to break up. They see all this through the communicating device but there is nothing they can do about it other than to watch on helplessly as Mars breaks apart. Great fissures had opened in the crust allowing water from the lakes and remnants of seas to pour into the hot interior creating massive explosions that break the planet apart. They were too late, and Chandler is devastated that all his friends have been lost, that Mars is no more.

This final destruction of Mars takes place in 1942, and Chandler can never forgive himself for failing in his mission, and for the loss of all his friends on Mars.

There is one final short chapter where it is explained that this story has been recreated from notes and diaries and what the teller of the tale remembers Chandler saying to him. He didn't want any of this to be public knowledge until after he was dead.

This well written but relatively simple story was a delight to read and does leave the reader feeling sympathetic towards Frank Chandler as well as the imagined loss of the planet Mars.

Thia of the Drylands by Harl Vincent (1932)

Cliff Barron, has washed up as a pilot because he contracted a disease on Mars that left him crippled. His employer won't or isn't willing to pay for him to go to Mars where he can get special treatment to restore his health and strength.

Disillusioned, he encounters Sykes, a rival company owner, who offers to pay for his medical treatment if he is willing to test a new method of getting to Mars; A method that will get him there in less than an hour using a form of magnetic impulse to shoot a projectile carrying passengers along an invisible magnetic tube that operates the way radio waves are broadcast between a sender and a receiver. Desperate to regain his health he is only too willing to accept. He also wants to get revenge against his former employer who has literally dumped him on the scrapheap.

He goes to Mars and finds himself in the middle of a conflict between the Canal Unions and a tribe of outlawed barbaric Drylanders. They want to kill him and he doesn't know why. He is saved by their beautiful female leader who helps him escape their clutches so he can get the medical treatment promised to him. On the way to the clinic he is accosted by a secret service agent from Earth who wants to know how he got to Mars. He escapes this man and gets inside where he undergoes the treatment which gives him back his health and strength. Leaving the clinic, he is followed by the secret service people whom he believes work for his old boss who wants to know the secret of the magnetic impulse transport. If it comes to fruition his company and all its pilots and space ships will become useless, his company bankrupt.

Barron makes his way back underground to find the man who hired him for the test is inside the projectile killing the Drylanders he promised to take to Earth. He wants to hand them over to the Canal Union authorities for a ransom. Barron prevents Sykes from killing Thia who has just boarded the projectile. He just manages to get into a couch before the projectile shoots off into space, earthbound. Sykes is crushed to death by the force of the acceleration. But the projectile stops halfway and floats freely in space because the sending -receiving station on Earth has been disabled.

Thinking they will drift until they suffocate, a huge space ship suddenly appears and locks onto them. It is his former boss and members of his former crew who have been waiting at the midway point to rescue him.

Suddenly, the tables are turned. Barron finds out it was his former boss who paid for his medical treatment, not Sykes who actually wanted him dead. Sykes apparently stole the plans for the magnetic transport system from a friend of his former boss who were developing the system together. He can't go to Earth or Mars with Thia because they are wanted by the Martian Canal Unions as well as the Earth government, so he is given a ship, he marries his 'princess' and is free to head off toward Jupiter and its inhabited moons.

I can't say this is a remarkable story; it is however, reasonably entertaining and typical of the kind of stories published in Hugo Gernsback's magazines.

It was also reprinted in 1967 in a magazine, *Classic Science Fiction Stories*, which reprinted stories from the early *Amazing Stories* magazine.

A brief jump back ten years gives us a book that is fiction but it isn't a story or a novel:

The Planet Mars and its Inhabitants (1922 - 1956) is a dissertation, an elongated description of Mars, its canals, its society, arts, entertainments, philosophies, and most pointedly religion.

It is a summing up of all that was thought of and speculated about Mars up until the time it was written and published in 1922. It reads like background material for a long novel. Most of this would be hidden somewhere inside a novel rather than explicated directly.

Unfortunately, there is no novel. All we have is this long lecture divided into 21 chapters which discuss population centers, temperature and climate, the elaborate canal system, property, trade and barter, transport, use of cosmic or universal energy, clairvoyant visions, knowledge of God, political system, education and training, music and many other items that are based on Christian religion and *The Word of God*.

It has been credited to James Scott Marshall who says it was written down and edited by J L Kennon and is the revelations of a Martian Spirit called Eros Urides. The dedication is *to the millions of God's children on this earth enthralled in darkness, for whom the solicitude of the Father is now in evidence.*

It was republished in 1956. It is available as one of the **Gutenberg Etext** *PDFs* and can be downloaded free.

Vandals of The Void by M Walsh (James Morgan Walsh) (1931) (*not to be confused with a Jack Vance novel of the same name that was published twenty years later in 1951. It too was a space opera but had nothing to do with Mars.*)

This is a typical space opera from 1931 which has every planet in the solar system populated by human variants. There is space travel between the three main planets, Earth, Mars and Venus, and the space-ways are policed by the (IPG) Interplanetary Guard, who have their own ships but can commandeer any ship at any time if needed. They are responsible for the smooth running of traffic between the inner planets and maintaining law and order.

Something mysterious is attacking space liners and cargo ships travelling between the planets. Icy cold penetrates the ships seeming to freeze all on board putting them into a coma of sorts and when they wake up, nothing appears to be stolen or damaged, and all the people are grouped in the lounge, and no one remembers how they got there. All IPG officials are on alert because ships are being randomly attacked by invisible aliens, from ships that are also invisible.

On his way to Mars, on vacation, Sanders has been alerted and approaches the Captain of the Cosmos on which he is travelling to Mars. He doesn't want to take over the ship but asks the Captain whom he knows to continue as is. They come across an abandoned ship and boarding to examine it find that all the occupants are asleep in the lounge. The ship had been attacked. The crew and the passengers wake up as the ship's temperature rises back to normal. When an IPG ship arrives, Sanders own ship as it happens, they take over and Sanders goes back onto the Cosmos to continue his trip to Mars. Two of the passengers on the Cosmos are Martian Elite, a father and his daughter Jansca, who are highly regarded on Mars. Sanders falls in love with the Martian girl and they pledge themselves to each other in a blood ceremony. To celebrate being betrothed they both partake of a Martian drink that has peculiar properties. When their ship is later attacked and people go into a coma, they are immune because there is something in the Martian drink they had that counteracts the gas used to put people into a coma. They discover the attacking aliens are invisible because they wear cloaks and helmets that cause light to vibrate at a different frequency than what people can see. Confronting the invisible aliens Sanders and Jansca shoot them with ray guns which turns them visible when they die. The aliens are from Mercury and they have attacked Venus and are wanting to attack the other three planets to expand into the solar system.

Collecting the capes and helmets from the dead Mercurians and discovering how they function; Sanders asks the Cosmos to dock at the Martian IPG base in orbit around the planet where they can have the cloaks examined by the scientists there as well as tell the IPG commanders what they have discovered. The ships from Mercury are also invisible, and as they later discover have superior weapons to what the IPG have.

Going down to Mars, Sanders marries his Martian girl in accordance with their customs, becomes an honorary Martian, but hardly has time for a 'honeymoon' before he is requested to return to the orbiting Guard Base. A large number of ships have taken over Venus and are heading towards earth. Everyone is called back on duty. Commandeering the Cosmos, the latest ship and the most modern, which has now had disintegrator weapons added as well as an invisible cloak, Sanders, with his new wife Jansca, leads a force of Guard ships to Venus to battle the invaders from Mercury. He meets with Earth Guard ships ahead of the Martians following and they head for Venus. Travel between the planets of the inner system is quick, only a few days or perhaps a week because of the special engines used. What follows is an encounter with the Warships from Mercury as the Guards fight to reclaim Venus. When they are almost overwhelmed by the alien ships the Martian fleet arrives to save them. The cosmos is destroyed in the process but Sanders, and Jansca who accompanied him into battle, manage to escape. Venus is reclaimed and the invaders are pushed back to their home planet of Mercury.

This would have been an exciting story when it was published in 1931, but by 1940, and certainly in the 1950s, much more was discovered about Mars and the inner planets and that kind of story would not have found a market. However, it is quaint and enjoyable, and the extrapolation of scientific gadgets from what was known in 1930 is also delightfully antediluvian when looked at today.

It's a free download from *Project Guttenberg of Australia*, so if you have nothing else to read it is worth a look at.

Early John Wyndham

The Lost Machine by John B Harris (1932)
This is an interesting story by the author we know as John Wyndham (1903 – 1969).

John Wyndham Parkes Lucas Benyon Harris started his career writing for early American science fiction magazines using various combinations of his names. John Benyon, the name he used for his two longer Martian stories, **Stowaway to Mars** and **Sleepers of Mars,** (see *Dreams of Mars* pages 61 – 65) was sometimes changed to John Benyon Harris or John B Harris. Sometimes he used the name Lucas Parkes, also his real names, and one of the last books he wrote in his career as John Wyndham was a collaboration with himself, *The outward Urge* as by John Wyndham and Lucas Parkes. Before the 2nd World War he wrote science fiction for American Magazines and detective novels for British publications. After the war he wrote the science fiction accredited to John Wyndham, starting with *The Day of the Triffids*.

In the first of his two Martian novels, *Planet plane*, or *Stowaway to Mars,* (1936) a British adventurer is planning to go to Mars, part of a race against international rivals. Each group is building a rocket ship to take them there. The first to arrive and return will win an enormous sum of money put up by an American newspaper publisher. There are attempts at sabotage which the British group foil, and later when they take off and are well on their way to Mars, they discover a young woman has stowed away on board. She tells them she wants to go to Mars to prove the story her father told was true, that he discovered an intelligent machine, which self-destructed before he could show it to anyone. No one believed him and his science career went downhill from that point. That brief background explanation for her presence on the rocket ship was the subject of an earlier story published in *Amazing Stories* in April 1932. (Vol. 7 No. 1.), *The Lost Machine*, told from the viewpoint of the Martian Machine.

This story was probably the genesis of the novel which spends a lot of time on Mars where the machine society is looking after a dying world in which not all the machines are sane. When humans interact with them, all kinds of mayhem occur. Mars as it appears in those two later novels, is a dried-up dying planet where intelligent machines are still maintaining ancient cities alongside giant canals while the native Martians remain in hibernation until the planet can be revived.

The Lost Machine opens with the young woman discovering that their strange intelligent machine has dissolved into a puddle of liquid metal, just at the moment her father brings in his colleagues to see this intelligent machine he had told them about. They are skeptical and castigate him for attempting to fool them. Left embarrassed the father studies the remains and wonders why the machine self-destructed. Sometime later the daughter finds a manuscript left by the machine. It had written down in its own language what had happened to it. It also left enough clues so they could decipher it.

At the end of their journey, approaching the Earth's surface to affect a landing, they are astonished to see so much green, and huge amounts of water. Banuff, the machine's live Martian companion, suggests the planet must be terribly hot because they see smoke erupting from many stacks of rock. They land in a field and because the gravity is too heavy, and the air too thick for Banuff, he stays on board while the machine goes outside to explore. It heads towards the rocks stacks when on looking back it sees their ship explode with a terrible sound.

People come rushing out of the rock stacks and head towards the wrecked ship. But the machine (*which the author regards as masculine*) gets there first and cradling his companion Banuff in his grappling appendages —the machine has 4 pairs of legs to assist it with mobility in the higher gravity of Earth as well as tentacle-like appendages in front beneath an array of lenses which would be the equivalent of eyes that can see in any wavelength day and night— it turns towards the approaching humans and lays Banuff down gently in front of them, thinking that they would know better what to do with a living thing that no longer functions. If it was a machine, he could fix it, or better still it would fix itself, but being a biological creature, it can't be fixed when it stops functioning.

The approaching men are astonished by the box-like machine with so many legs and appendages, and scared of it. When it moves tentatively towards them one of the men fires a gun and a bullet ricochets off the metal of the machine. The machine rapidly retreats into the forest behind the open area where the ship landed. The men fire bullets at it but they all miss.

For a day and a night, the machine travels through the forest discovering that hard paved paths traverse the land and the forest in various places and that the irregular stone outcrops are too symmetrical to natural and therefore must have been constructed. On the second day he saw his first machine, and was delighted. Approaching it he tries to converse but the machine is not only dumb, it is also very primitive and sits on wheels. A young woman is inside the machine and cannot start it. She sees the coffin shaped machine approach and is terrified. But when the machine stops beside her car it leans in and does something that fixes it, and suddenly her car can start again. Quickly she drives off.

He watches the machine with the woman inside dwindle in the distance and sadly wanders off. He stares up at the stars and sees his home, the fourth planet rise in the sky and knows there is no way to go home. Wandering through a field he is attacked by a herd of primitive horned animals, things that had been extinct on Mars for millions of years. When a group of people emerge from a farmhouse to see what was disturbing the cattle, they discover the strange machine, and terrified, they retreat back to the house. But a moment later a man emerges and approaches the machine. He is drunk and thinks the machine is some kind of weird animal. He treats it like a dog and orders it to follow him, and the machine, reading the man's mind, understands and follows.

The man locks the machine in a shed and in the morning decides to take it with him and sell it. He goes to a circus and tries to sell the mechanical animal, telling the man he had constructed it himself, but when the circus owner wants to look inside the machine to see how it works, the machine takes off, rushing into the circus tent and terrifying the animals inside as well as the people watching the show. There is no way the machine will allow someone so primitive to look inside and touch its workings.

When the man and his car are about to leave, he orders the machine to get in. Preferring to accompany the man than to wander off alone the machine complies, and they leave the circus and the panic-stricken people.

Later that evening when the man is drunk, and with his companions they are driving along a road when another car approaches from the other direction. Instead of passing each other the drunk driver veers towards the oncoming car and they crash head on. Their car tips over and the other one runs off the road into a tree. The machine is amazed at the stupidity of the earth machines that crash into each other. When the drunk men get out of their car, they approach the other and find a young woman standing beside it. One of the men grabs her and makes threatening sounds.

To the machine, it was obvious the woman wanted nothing to do with the men. He recognized the woman as the person whose car he earlier fixed. Moving in amongst the drunken men, he shoves them aside while grabbing the woman in his tentacles. Carrying her aloft he rushes off through the countryside. The girl is at first bewildered and frightened, but remembers this machine helped her with her car earlier, so when the she is placed higher up on its back and held firmly while it rushes through the woods, she relaxes.

The machine can read her mind and from that he determines where she lives and how to get there. He takes her home and meets her father who is the first person he meets who isn't afraid of him on sight. He finds these people kind and intelligent and tries to communicate with them. When the man suggests they have others like him come to look at him the machine knows they want to dismantle him to find out how he functions and would want to build replicas. There is no way it will allow this, so it writes some notes for them about what happened.

The story finishes with the intelligent machine realizing it is on a world where everyone is utterly mad, so he decides to terminate himself.

"It dissolved itself with my acids," the Doctor says.

He tells his daughter Joan to burn the manuscript left by the machine because he doesn't wish to be certified.

Before reading Wyndham's two longer Martian stories it would be worthwhile reading this shorter one as a prelude. It would be nice to see this and the two longer stories presented in one volume since they are, together, one long story. But that's wishful thinking on my part.

Continuing his Martian Odyssey

Valley of Dreams by Stanley G. Weinbaum (1934-5)

In 1934 Stanley G. Weinbaum began writing science fiction and published his first story, *A Martian Odyssey.*

This story presented a weird biology for the inhabitants of Mars, something that had never been done before, where the creatures both intelligent or otherwise were neither plant nor animal but some kind of combination of the two. The human protagonist in this story, after surviving the crash landing of his exploratory vessel, met a Martian called Tweel who showed him around and who protected him from a horrible creature able to manipulate minds, to create visions attractive to that mind in question in order to attract it to its death. The story became a cult classic and has been remembered with much fondness since then.

What is rarely, if ever mentioned, is that the author wrote a sequel to *A Martian Odyssey* called *Valley of Dreams*. It was one of the twenty or so stories he wrote in the 18 months after his first story. Unfortunately, his promising career terminated abruptly when he died of lung cancer in 1935.

Valley of Dreams was later collected in a volume of his stories, *A Martian Odyssey and Others*, published in 1949.

Dick Jarvis, the chemist of the famous Ares expedition to Mars is sent out by the captain to recover the film and the photographs he took before he unfortunately crashed in the desert. The captain even suggests he might be lucky enough to encounter Tweel again, and Jarvis remembers how Tweel had saved him from the dream-beast. Leroy the biologist accompanies Jarvis in the last auxiliary craft on the ship. They are to salvage what they can from the other crashed auxiliary and return in time for the Ares to take off for the return to Earth.

They find the crashed ship, recover the films, and in the process explore a bit further away. They discover an enormous ruined city built alongside of a major canal, and on landing they find various life forms and also a group of beings that look like Tweel. When Jarvis suggests he would like to meet Tweel again they others like him, go and fetch him.

Tweel is excited to be reunited with his human friend and takes Jarvis and Leroy on a tour of the ruined city. They are shown a series of murals that depict life on Mars and during their explorations estimate that the city is at least 15,000 years old, older than any civilization on Earth. Tweel and his companions work in the city to maintain the flow of water in the canal. This isn't really explained. But what they discover as they work their way deeper into the city, is a mural that shows a being like Tweel and a human with an elongated nose almost like the beak Tweel has. Jarvis says it looks like Thoth, an Egyptian God, and Tweel gets very excited. Thoth is what his people are called, and yes, they did visit Earth thousands of years ago when Egyptians were nothing more than scattered tribes in a barren land.

Weinbaum isn't the first to suggest Martians influenced early human development, or that Humans descended from Martians forced to abandon their home planet. It was a common idea expressed in many stories, and is still used today over 100 years later. Perhaps the earliest was Garrett P. Serviss who wrote the first sequel to H G Wells' *War of The Worlds*, *Edison's Conquest of Mars*. In his story published in 1898 he suggests that Martians built the pyramids and influenced culture and civilization in the Himalayan regions. (See *Dreams of Mars* pages 40 – 43.)

Leaving the city Jarvis wants to look at a valley he saw while they flew over, that was strangely grey and smudged, different from the rest of the landscape.

As Jarvis and Leroy approach the edge of the drop into the valley, Tweel desperately tries to stop them. This makes Jarvis more curious, more determined to see what is in the valley. Tweel interposes himself between Jarvis and the edge of the valley but Jarvis pushes him aside and looks down into the valley.

What he sees is paradise, a heaven that is irresistible. He can't stop himself from moving down into this paradise even though he realizes that the images in his mind are the same or similar to what the dream-beast he had encountered before had done to him. He can't stop himself. He feels a gentle embrace... and at that point Leroy shoots the creature that had confused Jarvis' mind to reveal that he is caught in the tentacles of a dream-beast. Realizing that the whole valley is filled with these beasts able to manipulate minds they rapidly retreat and finally make their way back to the Ares. Once again Tweel had saved Jarvis.

This story doesn't have the impact of *A Martian Odyssey* and by comparison seems flat, being told in the form of the character retelling to the captain of the Ares what had happened to him. It is an old-fashioned way of telling a story and it lacks impact because of it, and perhaps this is the reason it is not well-known, or is hardly ever mentioned. Still, it is interesting to read it as a companion to his first story which promised the possibility of a brilliant writing career. Regrettably the author died before this promise could be fulfilled.

John W. Campbell Jr's Brain Stealers

The Brain Stealers of Mars by John W. Campbell, Jr. (1936)

Before he became editor of *Astounding Stories,* John W. Campbell, Jr wrote a number of science fiction stories for magazines such as *Thrilling Wonder Stories,* as well as a number of stories under the name of Don A Stuart, perhaps his most famous being **Who Goes There?** published in *Astounding Stories* in 1938, which in 1951 became the basis for an awful film called *The Thing from Another World.* Years later however, people look back on this film with nostalgia. In retrospect it doesn't seem as awful as it did— or is that just me?

They won't look back on this story, originally titled **Imitation**, but retitled by the editor of *Thrilling Wonder Stories* as *The Brain Stealers of Mars.* Campbell plays around with the idea of Martian shape-shifting creatures that can read minds and recreate exact copies of any living thing or being. Two fugitive humans fleeing from Earth authorities after having created a massive explosion during an experiment with Atomic energy, the same energy that powers their space ship, find themselves on Mars.

They encounter the shape-shifting creatures that make copies of each of the two humans so none of them know who the real persons are, except of course the two people, Penton and Blake. They know, but how can they prove it to each other. There are a dozen copies of each person, all claiming to be real. They need to be certain that when they return to Earth, they are in fact the same people who previously left there. Since the shape-shifters can read minds and duplicate anything thought, there must be a solution which neither Penton nor Blake can reveal.

It's an amusing story with some silly ideas about Mars, one of which is that the Martians are centaurs, but at least a third of them are shape-shifted duplicates, and the real centaurs don't care, because if the copy is as perfect as the original, what does it matter since they are both the same, both real?

Campbell went on to use the shape-shifting alien with terrifying effect in a story that is still highly suspenseful and scary even today. **Frozen Hell** was its working title and it was set in Antarctica. When it was published in *Astounding Stories* in 1938 it became **Who Goes There?**

Do read the story and don't bother with the films: the original directed by Howard Hawks, and a remake directed by John Carpenter, which at least was set in Antarctica. Years later a prequel to the remake was also made and it finishes where the remake begins. I would like to see a re-telling of the story made without the ridiculously exaggerated alien effects Carpenter created that do nothing but distract the audience from the real horror: an alien that can shapeshift and be anything it wants to be with no way it can be told apart from the original.

H G Wells turns again to Mars

Star Begotten by H G Wells (1937)

In 1937, H G Wells returned with another Martian story, **Star Begotten.** This short novel is both a comedy on pseudo-scientific thinking as well as a commentary on the possibility of an impending world war.

Published in 1937 it also questions the validity of psycho-analysis, complex systems of self-deception, blindness, humiliating and restraining things, the menace of dictators like Hitler, and evasions and conformities to social pressures… it appears very much like Wells was ahead of his time in suggesting such things. Or could it be that human nature doesn't ever really change no matter what century we live in?

This is not an action story, but rather a story told through conversations between learned gentlemen at their Gentleman's Club.

At a scientific discussion one night Someone suggests that cosmic rays are bombarding us at all times and that these are responsible for mutations that are the foundation of evolution. Joseph Davis, the viewpoint character, a bestselling writer of popular histories, has just discovered his wife is pregnant and he begins to have concerns regarding the outcome.

As the discussion proceeds at the club another person suggests that the cosmic rays may be coming from Mars and that the Martians, having been defeated in their earlier attempt to conquer Earth because the gravity was too strong for them and they had no immunity to earthly viruses, as related by one H G Wells, are now trying to create mutations of themselves that would be able to live on Earth. They would look like people but be somehow different. He further suggests that there may already be a substantial number of people already turned into Human-Martian hybrids.

Joseph Davis immediately thinks his wife, who has been somewhat indifferent to him of late may be a Martian and their future son will also be one. Returning home, he studies his wife and becomes convinced she is a Martian. He confronts their doctor regarding her condition and in time convinces the doctor that Martians are bombarding the Earth with cosmic rays to induce mutations in human offspring that would be Martian and could live easily on Earth.

The rest of the story is with a group of people, convinced Martians are altering the genetic nature of humanity by bombarding Earth with cosmic rays, and they discuss how long it has been going on and how the Martians might recognize each other while remaining hidden from Humans.

They make assumptions that Martians are cleverer than humans, are further along the evolutionary scale because their planet cooled earlier than did the Earth and thus evolution began there sooner and life developed earlier, and that they are further along the evolutionary scale than the people on Earth. They also begin to assume that the way to recognize Martians in the human population was to look for the geniuses, the super smart kids, of which there seemed to be an ever increasing number all over the world, which then brings up the thought that the invasion is already well under way and there is nothing they can do about it.

Returning home one night, totally disillusioned, he tears up the manuscript of the latest book he was working on and throws it in the bin. His wife is stunned. She says there was such good writing in it. No matter, he replies, nothing to the writing that will come. Pointing to his son he declares he is tearing up the past to make way for him. Him, and his kind — in their turn.

It has taken him years to rid himself of old prejudices and outmoded ideas. Undecided whether to ask his wife if she is a Martian, she preempts him and suggests that he himself may have become Martianized.

In that instant his doubts disappear and he has an epiphany. He is a Martian, and so is his wife, and the future belongs to their children and all the other children born who will be Martians.

H G Wells was never short of ideas, and this slight novel is resplendent with them. As always, the quality of his writing sets an example for others to emulate.

Early Jack Williamson

Nonstop to Mars by Jack Williamson (1939)

A story of interest to people who are curious about Jack Williamson's early fiction. He was amongst a few well-known writers who in the 1930s were at the start of their careers and who regularly produced short stories and novelettes for the science fiction pulp magazines like *Astounding*, and *Amazing Stories* amongst others.

This is a novelette in which an early flying hero 'Lucky Leith' is caught in a weird tornado-like storm as he is flying over Antarctica.

Well aware that the weather has been getting increasingly bizarre with incredible auroras and electrical storms, he takes his chances to fly and is caught by the edge of a massive tornado and his plane is damaged. Being a good pilot, he manages to land on a remote pacific island. Here, he discovers a young female astronomer who is studying Mars and has seen a strange meteor impact on that planet. It was she who originally discovered the celestial object entering the solar system and she originally thought it would impact Earth, but it hit Mars instead. But from that moment on the weather has been getting worse and worse.

She is monitoring the Earth's weather and atmosphere and in particular, the incredible vortex tornado which stretches all the way up into space. This storm seems to travel all around the world, coming back to where it was 24 hours earlier. She concludes that the storm is in a fixed spot and as the world rotates the storm appears to be travelling along the same line of latitude, always over the same spots. In 24 hours, it will return to pass over the island where she has her observatory and weather station to wreak further if not total destruction. She makes a remarkable discovery: not only does the vortex storm stretch up into space but it continues to extend all the way to Mars.

She was alone on the island because one of her team accidentally broke his leg when the tornado storm passed over the island a couple of days earlier, and the other male member flew him off the island using their new rocket ship. She tells Lucky that flying gasoline driven airplanes is old fashioned and he should learn to fly rockets. Her company builds and flies rockets.

Through her astronomical observations she concludes that an alien space ship had landed on Mars, it wasn't a comet or a meteor that impacted the planet. The aliens have used advanced science to create a vortex that is sucking up Earth's atmosphere and transporting it to Mars. Her and her team are hoping to fly a rocket to Mars so they can stop the aliens before it is too late for Earth's inhabitants, but the rocket under construction may not be ready before all Earth's atmosphere is gone.

When her team member returns in his rocket ship to get her there is no room for Lucky so he is left on the island. He has no choice but to try and fix his damaged plane, which he does before the vortex returns, so he can fly away from the path of the massive tornado, which is more severe each time it passes over the island.

Lucky concludes that if the vortex is sucking up Earth's atmosphere it will be full of air, and if there is air then he can fly his plane in it. He decides he has no choice but to go to Mars and try to stop the aliens from sucking up any more atmosphere.

Flying into the vortex he is sucked along it with incredible speed.

He emerges from the vortex and crash lands on Mars not far from the alien construction that is generating the massive vortex. Without seeing any of the aliens he manages to get close to the generator and contrives a bomb made of gasoline and compressed oxygen which explodes and destroys the vortex generating machine.

Stranded on Mars, he is happy to have saved the Earth from having its atmosphere stolen and is resigned to be a '*Robinson Crusoe*' when he sees the familiar exhaust of a rocket ship arriving. Who else should be piloting it other than the girl he met on that remote Pacific island? She has come to rescue him.

How did she know he had flown his plane to Mars? How could she have known he survived the storm?

At what point did she fall in love with him before leaving him stranded on the island with the massive storm about to hit?

There is no mention of how long it took her to get to Mars, and presumably she would have taken off while the vortex was still active, and while Lucky was still in transit to Mars inside the vortex.

This is typical of the stories published in early pulp magazines where a long preamble sets up the premise of the story and introduces the main characters. A short section with action and setbacks as the protagonist attempts to solve the problem, then right at the end, sometimes in the very last paragraph or two, an abrupt finish that seems ridiculous in hindsight. All that aside, it was still an enjoyable story that would have appealed to teenage boys back in the 1940s. It was published the year before I was born so I never saw it until only recently.

What was interesting to me was to see how much Williamson had improved as a writer from when he wrote this in 1939 to the point where he wrote **Beachhead** (see page 220 – *Dreams of Mars*) in 1992 with 53 years of writing experience in between the two stories.

Teal Ridge

Chapter Four

And the Golden Age continues

WestPoint 3000 AD, by Manly Wade Wellman (1940)

A Mars invasion story. In the year 3000 New York (and presumably every other major city) is very different, having soared to great heights, being built on top of the older city whose inhabitants now never see the light of day. They live underground in tunnels and abandoned covered over streets. Over the centuries they have become vitamin deficient, stunted and pale, while those who live above in the city are strong and healthy. They consider the underground inhabitants as inferior, or as slaves to do the dirty work that keeps the city running. Over the years Garr Devlin's father has stolen from the people above medicines and vitamins and other foods unobtainable below to keep his son strong and healthy like those who live above. He wanted his son to have a better life than to grovel about underground.

In 2389 the World League was formed and the capitol is now Saint Louis where the President and the Governing Body reside. In 2775 there was a war between Earth and Mars and the Martians were defeated. Peace has been maintained ever since, but not all Martians were happy with that and over the years a rebellious faction had evolved. They want to retake Mars as well as to attack and conquer the Earth. Many Martians have come to Earth to train at human schools and amongst those a number of rebels are working in secret to foment a revolution. They have infiltrated the Underways where the poorest people live and have established worldwide connections to spring into action when the leaders of the rebellion are ready.

The story opens with the attempted arrest of Garr Devlin's father John. Both are arrested and John Devlin protests that his son is innocent, that he was the one who stole. It falls on deaf ears, and in the elevator taking them to the surface there is a scuffle. John is killed. Garr in a fury kills one of the policemen escorting them in the lift and on reaching the surface he attacks those waiting for them. He is overpowered and arrested and taken to a court where he is sentenced to WestPoint military school not only as punishment, but for his extraordinary ability and his rebelliousness. These are qualities they need.

At WestPoint Garr discovers there are many Martian students as well as a large female contingent. The Martians. Because they have soft bodies and tentacles, wear an environment suit which gives them a more humanoid shape, with their tentacles hidden apart from two that are used as arms. At night, in private, they take off their suits so they can be more comfortable. They also have the ability to read minds, communicate with each other mentally, and no one can keep a secret from them. Garr however is a rare person whose mind they cannot read, and this quality more than any other is important to those who run the military school. Garr is recruited as a spy, after getting into trouble by talking to one of the female cadets. Knowing the Martians can't read his mind, he is placed in quarters used by the Martian students so he can find out what they are planning. He pretends to sympathize with their ideals and they readily accept him. He quickly finds out the Martians are ready to start their takeover of Earth and simultaneously of Mars, in a few days' time. Reporting back to the Commander he discovers the girl he spoke to is his daughter, and they have a feisty relationship. (We know that this will inevitably lead to romance, and it does as she saves him, and later he saves her, from dangerous situations.)

There is plenty of action and double crossing between the characters as Garr discovers the plot by the Martians includes recruiting people of the underway to stop working to paralyze the city so the Martians can take over. The Martians thought that because Garr is from the Underways he would hate those who live above and would join their rebellion, but they don't realize he is first of all loyal to the human race in preference to the Martians; he will fight for, not against, humanity. At the same time back on Mars the rebels are coordinating their attempt to overthrow the Government. There is a lot of fighting in the Underways of New York until the revolution and the attempted takeover of the Earth is thwarted.

The Martians on Mars are warned by the Earth government and they too defeat the rebellion about to take place there, but this is only mentioned in passing. The story is really about what happens on Earth and how Garr and his female cadet together save the World.

All in all, a fast moving, well written story, that stands out from many other stories published in the early 1940s.

What I love about these early stories is the extrapolated future that includes such things as pneumatic travel in tubes underground connecting cities, (*something now being talked about and possibly under construction in the US*) air cars, (*which may still happen*) locks that can only be opened by using light beams, electric guns that fire bullets that heat and melt their target on impact. The bullets can be thrown by hand with a similar effect on impact though not with the same energy output as they would have if fired from a gun. and ray-guns that can be used for cutting and welding metal as well as killing enemies, yet at the same time everything seems so old-fashioned.

This novel has been revived in a double issue from *Armchair Fiction* who deserve praise for bringing to light many stories that would otherwise be forgotten. It is paired with **Holy City of Mars** by Ralph Milne Farley.

Some shorter stories

The teacher from Mars by Eando Binder (1941) (1932)
One of the few stories that depict a Martian as being benevolent rather than hideous, cruel, terrifying, nasty or whatever else the authors during that time imagined Martians were like.
Told in the first person from the Martian's viewpoint it is unusual.
The Martian is a teacher who arrives to teach a teenage class of 'high' school students the rudiments of interplanetary history as well as the Martian language which currently is used by the scientific community throughout the solar system.
The kids don't like him and immediately make his job difficult in the extreme. Their attitude towards him is obnoxious and downright nasty. They claim Martians are cowards and never stand up for themselves. They are rebellious in class and throw things at the teacher. That he accepts this continuous hazing without complaining only shows his good nature, and presumably the good nature of all Martians compared to the human teens who bully him throughout his first term of teaching.
The point is made that belligerent humans had spread throughout the solar system, and they treat everyone they encounter elsewhere such as Martians as inferior. Seen from the viewpoint of the Martian teacher humans certainly are not nice people. As much as his pride won't allow it, he wants to return to Mars.

When the students accuse him of murdering a human somewhere near the school, of having strangled him with his tentacles (Martians have tentacles instead of arms) they gang up on him and almost beat him to death. Finally, it is discovered that some other human strangled the victim with a rope and the Martian teacher really is innocent. The kids back off and leave him alone.

At a school assembly shortly after, the principal announces that during a battle in space between pirates and the space patrol, the Martian teacher's son was killed protecting the patrol ship's captain, who just happened to be the father of the gang leader whose gang has been harassing the teacher since he arrived. The teacher is presented with a special medal for the bravery of his son. Suddenly the attitude of the gang leader (and his followers) changes when it is realized the Teacher's son was a hero and that he saved the captain of the patrol ship. Before the teacher can do anything else the gang leader insists that the teacher stay on, as do all his cohorts and so the story finishes on a positive note.

When asked to select one of his best for a collection titled ***My Best Science Fiction Story***, a collection of 12 stories edited by Leo Margulies and Oscar J Friend and published by pocket books in 1941, Eando Binder said this story was written in 1932, that it virtually wrote itself and it was one of which he felt was his best. He thought presenting the story from a Martian viewpoint was unique because it showed the thoughts and feelings of an alien being, as well as showing (racial) discrimination and intolerance.

The author also lamented that by 1941 nothing in that regard had changed. (*He would be horrified to know that nothing has really changed for the better since he expressed those thoughts in 1941, and we are now in the year 2020*).

Other authors asked to select their best story for this 1941 collection were Isaac Asimov, Robert Bloch, John W Campbell Jr., Edmond Hamilton, Henry Kuttner, Murray Leinster, Fletcher Pratt, John Taine, A E Van Vogt, Manly Wade Wellman, and Jack Williamson; the best of the best from 1930 to 1940. Of course, all these authors went on to write better and better stories as they honed their skills during the Golden Age of SF

The secret Sense by Isaac Asimov (1941)
This well written short story by Isaac Asimov was published when I was one year old.

I grew up reading Asimov along with Clarke and Bradbury; they were my favorites when I was in my early teens, so it was a delight to discover this early story from Asimov. It postulates that the Martians have senses that are different from humans. The human arrogantly considers that the Martian's blindness to colour, and inability to taste flavors or smell scents, is a disability, but the Martian assures the human that one doesn't miss what one never had. To the Martian human music is indistinguishable from random noise, he can barely discern any difference between the notes. He can never see the colors of a sunset or a field of flowers. But the Martian asks can the human feel or sense the current passing through a copper wire? Can he see the beauty of applied magnetism?

The human response is that every race has its attributes.

The Martian implies that one shouldn't look down upon another because what they perceive is different from their own.

The human convinces the Martian to allow him the chance of experiencing what the Martian does, and he is told that there is a way in which this could happen but the effect would only last for five minutes. Desperate to find out the human insists it should be done.

The Martian brings in a machine like a complex harp that uses electrical currents when played but the human hears nothing, sees nothing. The Martian calls for a master musician to come and play the machine and for a doctor to inoculate the human with a substance that will open the cortical cells in his brain to be receptive. The side effect is that it will only last five minutes and can never be reactivated. This is done and the human at last can perceive the beauty the Martians see and feel and sense. It is so incredible he can barely come to grips with it when suddenly it fades and is gone. His five minutes are up. Suddenly there was nothing, he was blind to all the Martians could experience.

For the rest of his life he would feel the incredible loss of something he only experienced for a mere five minutes, something the Martians experience all their lives. To them he was blind, and would always be blind, something the human finally understands.

The Martians are Coming by Robert W Lowndes (1941)

A simple story with an unexpected surprise ending. From my recollection, it was common for magazine stories in the 1940s and 50s of various genres to have a twist at the end, something totally unexpected. This no longer seems fashionable.

In *The Martians are Coming*, two reporters set out to prove they can talk to Martians by building a device that enables them to mentally communicate with the inhabitants of Mars who appear to be like huge spiders. During the conversations with the two humans the Martians claim to have survived a war on their dying planet by eliminating all mammals. But they have no water, and many of them have never had a bath as long as they have lived. They seem very nice at first which leads the two humans to invite the Martians they are speaking with to come to Earth where there is plenty of water. They are given the coordinates for an area that is particularly swampy and uninhabited. They were waiting for such an invitation, and naturally assumed the humans meant for all of them to come.

Suddenly the Martians are on their way; the whole lot, in two thousand ships each with a thousand Martians on board. The two humans realize their horrible mistake when the Martians tell them how many are coming, and that they are bringing their weapons as well. When asked why bring weapons, they answer with 'it's a long-established tradition'.

Thinking that thousands of horrible spider-like beings are going to over-run the Earth, the two humans contact the armed forces, and immediately the swampy landing site is sealed off. Barbed wire fences are quickly built all around, and various regiments of the armed forces surround the area with heavy guns trained to fire on anything they want to target in the swamp. Nobody likes giant spiders, and the thought of thousands of them swarming out of so many space ships was terrifying.

The Martians are contacted again by the two reporters who are told the ships are above the Earth and about to land. Everyone tenses up waiting for the ships, but they see nothing. They expect to hear a lot of noise as the two thousand ships land but they hear nothing. We have landed, the reporters are told. Still no one sees anything.

The Martians frantically contact the humans to tell them they are being attacked by flying monsters twice their height with six legs and long blood sucking snouts. Thousands of them are attacking and all the Martian's weapons are of no avail to fight these monsters off. In no time at all contact is lost, and still the humans see nothing.

They didn't land on Earth, one of the humans suggests.

Yes, they did, the other says.

He aims his flashlight on a clump of swarming mosquitoes about a hundred yards into the swamp, and beneath the knot of swarming insects they see what looks like thousands of tiny cylinders, no bigger than cigarettes, scattered across the damp ground; the Martian space ships that contained the whole Martian Race.

The Martians are being wiped out by the mosquitoes and gnats that infest the swamp.

Holy City of Mars by Ralph Milne Farley (1942)

This is a sequel to *City of Lost Souls* (1941) and the events that occurred in that story are briefly woven into the text during the first chapter.

There is nothing remarkable about this story. It is typical of the pulp novels published in the magazines of the time; a swashbuckling adventure wherein the hero, Earthman Don Warren, returns to the ancient City of Lost Souls in search of his love, Esta, the princess, or daughter of the tribal king that rules this part of Mars.

Mars is depicted as an arid desert world with water brought into civilized areas by man-made canals. The only mention of animal life is a slith which is a large lizard of some sort and is used as a beast of burden in much the same way as are camels in the deserts of Earth.

There is also an encounter with a buzzard like creature, also a reptile that looks like pterodactyl. No other mention is made of other animals, plants, or what kind of ecology exists. We are to imagine it is like the worst desert areas on Earth. It is also very hot during the day and very cold at night. And of course, the atmosphere is perfectly breathable.

There is a secret well that supplies water to the Lost City which makes it an enviable oasis in the vast desert. The Martian army wants to control the city, other tribesmen want it as well, (why, isn't explained) and in the middle is Don Warren playing both sides against each other. There is treachery, misguided love, macho fighting between two of the principal characters, betrayals and reignited friendships amidst constant action that leaves the reader breathless.

Is it worth reading? Perhaps... It's not the best example of a Mars story from this era. The writing is rough but acceptable, but overall it doesn't compare to other Mars stories from that decade, especially if you are a fan of Leigh Brackett's wonderful and evocative Mars stories.

The Cave by P Schuyler Miller (1943)

Originally published in *Astounding Science Fiction* in January 1943, this story has been anthologized a few times in the 1950s or 60s, but is largely unknown to modern readers.

It is a simple story. A human mine worker is travelling across Mars and is caught in a bad sandstorm. A number of native Martians of various species are also caught in the sandstorm and use a particular cave as a refuge until the storm passes. The miner abandons his vehicle as sand clogs the engine intakes. It gets stuck and very quickly looks as if it will be buried. Pushing blindly through the swirling sand to find a spot out of the wind beside a cliff face the human finds the entrance to a cave and crawls inside.

Typical human, he doesn't think any Martian native is anything more than an animal even though some of them wear primitive clothes and that they can communicate with each other. They are what is left of earlier Martians who millions of years in the past built cities long before the planet started dying.

He doesn't understand that all species on Mars however much they may fight or hunt each other will always help each other to fight against the harsh nature of the planet. Animosities are put aside in order for all of them to survive. Hence there is a ritual when they enter the cave to avoid the vicious sandstorm. Certain words are spoken and agreed upon so both predator and prey together can safely weather the storm.

The human doesn't know this when he enters the cave and discovers the others in there. He doesn't speak the words necessary for them to accept him. They can't decide whether he is intelligent, or even alive by their standards. When he takes out a water bottle and takes a few sips he commits a grave offence without realizing it.

He is attacked by the most monstrous of the predator Martians and fights back by shooting it and wounding it. One of the other Martians wields a knife and kills the big predator and the human realizes that perhaps they are intelligent after all. He is grateful to the Martian with the knife for saving him and is about to thank it when it stabs him in the abdomen, killing him.

Over millions of years as the planet died and dried up water has become the most precious thing of all, and anyone entering an abode with water always shares it with the others there. The human didn't do this, so he was considered not alive, not intelligent, and perhaps even an evil agent of the ancient gods that ruled Mars. He has to be eliminated for the safety of the others.

I take it that the message of this story is that we shouldn't insult the customs or culture of those we know nothing much about. It may be far more complex than we can understand. We should make an effort to blend in rather than assume superiority, to understand rather than denigrate, or the consequences can be very bad.

This is a beautifully rendered story and the author makes it clear from the beginning that the human character is not a likable person. It doesn't come as a surprise that the ending is violent and the human doesn't survive. The human got what he deserved.

Mars as envisioned by Robert Moore Williams

Robert Moore Williams (1907 – 1977) was a prolific writer across two decades, the 1940s and the 1950s. Among his many science fiction stories, he wrote a number set on Mars. The earlier ones were written in the 1940s but a collection of his Martian stories published in book form in 1970 contained stories that ranged from 1941 to 1952. He was prolific enough to use other house names, like many authors during that era, and one of the names he used was E.K. Jarvis.

You Can't Escape from Mars was another story using the house name E K Jarvis, (See page 68 *Dreams of Mars*) but this one was authored by another writer, Paul W Fairman. Different writers used the same house name.

Most of Robert Moore Williams' stories are entertaining and enjoyable to read, although in the long run they aren't memorable. They were typical of the plethora of stories written and published over those two decades, of which so many were published using pseudonyms so no one reading them knew who wrote what.

The Red Death of Mars, by Robert Moore Williams (1940)

Teams of archaeologists are exploring the ancient sand and dust covered ruined cities of Mars. One team discovers a city that appears not to be abandoned but preserved, ready for occupation at some time in the future. When this team fails to report back a rescue team is sent down. The rescue team finds all three previous team members are dead with no apparent cause, but each has an agonized expression on their face. Their ship is totally inert, with no radioactive emissions from the ship's uranium fission drive, which they consider to be impossible.

The rescue team finds several giant ruby crystals scattered around the inert first ship and takes one of them inside their own ship to examine it. However, one of the men drops it and it shatters into minuscule fragments that immediately dissolve into a red gas. As they explore the abandoned city one of them discovers a room buried deep and sealed by a massive foot thick steel door. In front of it are heaps of ruby crystals. Ignoring the crystals which they think are massive jewels, they force entrance to the buried room and discover a number of sarcophagi with Martians in them in a state of (suspended animation) frozen sleep. They open one and extricate the Martian who in time wakes up and isn't surprised at all to be woken by large aliens, but on seeing a red ruby crystal near the door— it had rolled in accidentally as the earthmen entered— he immediately withdraws a knife from his belt and slashes his own throat. The stunned humans retreat back to their ship.

Back on board they try to radio the base but their radio is dead, and very quickly they discover their atomic engines are also dead. The ship is inert just like the other one. They too will have to be rescued when the home base figures out they can't be contacted. Meanwhile they discover one of the crew is dead and the captain has been attacked by a floating ball of red gas. They manage to get the gas away from the captain but he is almost done for. Barricading themselves in the galley where the walls are the thickest, they try to figure out what to do. The ship is now surrounded by red glowing spheres of gas. It appears that the red crystals are a cocoon stage and that the gas ball is the adult living creature. They live on radiation and energy given off by both mechanical and living beings. They latch on and suck the energy out, killing Martians and Humans and rendering machinery like ship's engines inert.

One of the guys suggests that the Martians may know how to defeat them but probably didn't have time to do it before they were overwhelmed and retreated into frozen sleep. He wants to go back and revive another one so they can ask it. He slips out of the ship at night and keeping close to the sand he crawls across to the city where the sleeping Martians lie. He gets one and revives it and throwing it over his shoulders he makes his way back to the ship. They are almost caught by a large gas sphere, but one of the crew ejects a smoke screen which hides them and they get back inside.

The problem then is that they cannot communicate with the Martian because their languages are so different. Slowly the gas balls eat into the metal of the walls and begin seeping into the galley where the survivors are hanging on. When the captain asks one of the crew for some water, and the crewman passes him a bottle, the Martian goes berserk. Leaping up and down and wildly gesturing he indicates that he wants the bottle of water. When they finally understand what he wants they give it to him and he immediately starts splashing water on the gas balls seeping through the walls. They immediately sizzle and retreat.

That's the answer. That's what will destroy the red gas balls, the red death of Mars.

Water— Something Mars has not had for millennia.

When the rescue team arrives to rescue the rescuers of the first group, they are amazed to see a group of (revived) Martians cavorting and dancing with joy amongst the group of smiling surviving Humans. Mars and the Martians can be revived, and the red death defeated because the Humans have plenty of water.

An enjoyable story and worth the trouble to find a copy (online) if you like the kind of fiction published during that era, the 1940s and 50s.

Death Desert by Robert Moore Williams (1941)
This time Williams has a different Martian setting. Still a desert world,

very hot during the day and down to freezing point (of water) at night, but no mention of canals or ancient cities.

There is a human colony, Mars City, from where Red Kelly hired someone called Knuckles Roker to take him and his fiancé out into the desert in an insulated, air-conditioned desert buggy. Kelly had saved the life of a desert tribesman and in return the tribesman had given him a map to an ancient temple where Martian diamonds were to be found, and told him to help himself. Having done just that, on the way back to Mars City Roker steals the money belt with the priceless diamonds and abandons Kelly and his fiancé in the desert, fully expecting them to die of thirst in the harsh desert heat.

Kelly however, knows there is a waterhole in a deep gully within a day's walking from where they were left. Leading his fiancé, they struggle across the desert, rapidly dehydrating as they succumb to the relentless heat. The sun is fierce because there is only a thin atmosphere which does nothing to dilute its strength.

This was a common trope in the 1940s, along with the thin Martian atmosphere being breathable.

As they travel along a canyon Kelly sees the tracks of desert camels and realizes there are some desert tribesmen out there somewhere. They too are probably heading towards the same water hole. He doesn't tell his fiancé because he doesn't want to frighten her, but he knows these wild desert tribesmen are brigands, ruthless bandits with a strict severe code of honor and conduct. They are always ready to kill intruders without question if they take offence.

They arrive at the water hole to find it dry, desiccated, with not the slightest sign of water. There are camel footprints there as well but no sign of the tribesmen. Exhausted, on the verge of hallucinating, Kelly comes up with an idea when he sees a desert monkey. They have a superb sense of smell and can detect water deep underground. He decides to trap one, and using his shoelaces to make a noose, he lays it on the sand and covers it so the monkey can't see it, and then he waits.

Curiosity eventually gets the better of the little monkey and it comes closer to see what this strange being is doing, lying so still on the sand. The instant it steps on the spot where the noose is buried, Kelly pulls the string and leaps up. He has caught it. Once he calms the creature down, he starts feeding it salt tablets. The salt tablets make it thirsty and then Kelly lets it loose. He still has the noose around its neck and hanging onto the shoelace he made it from he lets the monkey lead him along the base of the canyon. The monkey sniffs the floor and cracks in rocks until eventually it finds a spot and starts digging. Immediately Kelly joins it and they furiously dig deeper and deeper and they find water. It seeps into the hole and partially fills it.

Unable to contain his excitement, Kelly leaps up and down yelling and screaming about how lucky they are and together they start drinking the beautiful water. No longer thirsty they are about to fill a couple of water containers they had when the tribe of desert warriors appear, lances pointing down at the two humans. The noise Kelly made had attracted them.

Kelly has been on Mars for some time because he has no trouble conversing and understanding the tribesmen. He tells them he has found water, and suddenly the tribesmen seem more friendly. They fill their water bottles from the water in the hole. The leader then tells Kelly they have been tracking him since he stole the diamonds from their temple, and they want them back. When Kelly explains they had been stolen from him by the man from whom they had hired the desert buggy, and he had left them in the desert to die, they decide not to kill him. They ask how he knew about the diamonds and he explained he had saved the life of one of their tribesmen and he had given him a map and told him to help himself to some diamonds as payment. Where is this map? They ask him. When Kelly tells them it's in the desert buggy with Roker. They decide they will take Kelly and his fiancé with them to track down this Roper.

Travelling through the night they come across the desert buggy with Roper asleep inside. *You can borrow my lance if you want to kill him while he sleeps* the leader says, but Kelly doesn't want to do that. He will take him down but first he wants to retrieve the money belt with the diamonds.

A vicious fight ensues as Roper wakes ups and Kelly attacks him. They fall out of the buggy and continue the fight on the sand. The Martians enjoy the fight immensely, amazed that so much damage can be done with fists. They have always used lances and never considered fighting with fists. Once Roper is knocked out and is unconscious, Kelly hands the money belt to the leader of the Martians. He also retrieves the map from inside the buggy and hands it to the leader who verifies that it actually was drawn and signed by one of their own. He hands back the diamonds and says *they are yours. Our obligation is complete.*

But just as Kelly was feeling happy, the leader says there is now nothing to stop us from taking them back and killing you. Furiously Kelly castigates them for not being honest and questions their code regarding obligations for saving a life. Laughing the leader says he was only testing him. The diamonds are yours because you also saved our lives by finding water and showing us. With the water hole dry few of us, if any, would have got back alive, but you saved us, and so the diamonds are yours.

The story finishes with Kelly, his fiancé and the little monkey inside the rover, with Roper still unconscious but tied securely on the floor, heading back to Mars City, where Kelly will be a wealthy man and can marry his fiancé.

When Two Worlds Meet by Robert Moore Williams (1970) (Curtis Books Modern Library Editions.)

Six of his better Martian stories were collected in a single volume taking the name of the lead story. The other stories in the volume are not in the order they were written and published, but in order to create a timeline, and to give the collection the feeling of a novel with six chapters. None of the stories link with each other as a fix-up novel would, but they do give an impression of the early exploration of Mars by unwanted humans and their gradual communication and acceptance by Martians. I might add that the humans in the stories are generally devious characters with their own self-interest at heart, while the Martians, as nasty as some are, come across as better beings than do the human protagonists.

The stories in the volume are: *When Two Worlds Meet* (1950) *Amazing Stories*, *Aurochs Came Walking* (1954) *The Magazine of Fantasy and Science Fiction*, *On Pain of Death* (1941) *Astounding Stories*, *The Sound of Bugles* (1949) *Startling Stories*, *The Final Frontier* (1950) *Super Science Stories*, *When The Spoilers Came* (1952) *Planet Stories*.

The two earlier stories mentioned above, *Red Death of Mars* (1940) and *Death Desert* (1941) have no connection with the stories in this collection and the Mars depicted in these two stories is totally different from Mars depicted in the collected stories, with the only similarity being the planet is a desert world.

One of the themes that runs through the collected stories is that the Martians utilize, when necessary, long lost science of their forebears. The planet is generally in ruins with desert tribes existing as nomads or as remnant populations in cities falling into ruin alongside old canals that no longer function. Tribal leaders with the help of priests control ancient knowledge and power which Earthmen —who are not wanted on Mars and who are generally forbidden to stay in any Martian city— wish to have. A couple of the stories involve a human surreptitiously working to understand and obtain ancient technology, especially regarding anti-gravity and a new form of a star drive that would make rocket ships redundant, and other humans trying to get that knowledge by whatever means they can.

The final story involves a human trader who helps the Martians obtain the trace minerals needed to restore viability of the land for agriculture, and whose son leads a band of brigands wanting to take over the trace mineral business over the whole planet being thwarted by an old Martian leader and other elders who use mental power to change the way the humans think, and by inference, the future of Martian and Human relations.

There is a strict moral code here that is not easily understood by Humans, although the protagonist in this story accepts this code which enables him to operate amongst them as a trader. A similar moral code is implied throughout the six stories. The use of mental power also appears in the story **On Pain of Death** as a dying Martian helps his human friend fight against another group of piratical humans. Mental power is also how the Martian priests and elite warriors access some of the ancient technology.

The stories don't do for Mars what Leigh Brackett did with her stories set on Mars, but they nevertheless create an alternative vision of Mars that is sustained across the six stories in the collection in which the Martians come across as better beings when compared to the Humans, with the relationship between both gradually improving as the stories progress.

The stories are felt from the perspective of the Martians with usually one human protagonist living amongst them. There is not much about what humans have actually done on Mars or what their base is like since every story takes place in a Martian locale.

The human race was on Mars on sufferance. They had crossed space but were not the rulers of the Red planet. Nor were they ever likely to be. There was a languid trade between the two worlds; that is if the Earth people had something to trade that the Martians wanted, then they would trade, otherwise they weren't interested.

Beginning with the first story, **When Two Worlds Meet**, the Martians are antagonistic towards humans, but by the last story, **When the Spoilers Came**, this has changed to a more accepting, almost congenial state.

There are some excellent descriptions of Mars and Martian cities that produce in the reader a sense of place, a visualization of what Mars is like.

In **The Sound of Bugles** we find: *A garden spot, a city of bright crystal domes of rose and amethyst and coral and blue sky, a city of winding walks that curved around the low domes in eye-delighting variety. A flower garden, where bloomed in carefully tended plots every exotic flower that had ever put forth blossoms into the thin air of this ancient planet.*

Running along each walk were streams of bright clear water, irrigating the flowers, adding freshness and beauty to a spot already so beautiful that an artist would go mad trying to catch the color tones and the balanced symmetry of dissymmetry expressed in changing curve and shifting straight lines. Beyond the city was the main canal going off to the low hills which once had formed the shed from which this city drew its water.

The reservoir was still there, the hills were there, all open to the sky from which no rain had fallen for a hundred centuries...

There are other places less beautiful, such as the holy city of Sudar where, *beyond the city lay the desert with its fretwork of canals and its pathetic patches of green growth, pathetic because where once grain had grown as far as they eye could reach now only a few patches were under cultivation.*

The soil no longer contained the trace minerals necessary for grain to be life giving… which leads into the final story. **When the Spoilers Came**, about a trader who helps the Martians with the trace elements needed to produce healthy grain.

In the first story there is an incredible fortress, built into the sides of and the lava tubes within an extinct volcano, where different classes of people live on different levels within this massive artificial as well as natural edifice. This idea is later developed in much more detail in the novel **King of The Fourth Planet**, published by *Ace Books* in 1962

King of The Fourth Planet. (1962)

Once again Robert Moore Williams has portrayed humans as being greedy, ego-driven nasty people, with the leader of the group in a ship being a megalomaniac. I suspect the author had communist ideals underlying his way of thinking because capitalism is portrayed as being vile, with each individual out to get the better of those above with higher status while simultaneously trying to keep those beneath where they belong, as virtual slaves. The exception is the lead character John Rolf who was once the head of a huge space faring company out to exploit the riches of other planets like Mars, but who had a change of heart. Abandoning his previous life and his family, he came to Mars where he could live a secluded life away from Earth's rampant corruption. He wanted nothing more to do than meditate and pursue an invention that would enable him to read minds which he hoped would help better mankind.

On Mars there is a gigantic mountain called *Suzusilmar* which is higher than Everest and which has *breathable air synthesized by ancient scientific wizardry, of which neither men nor Martians remember anything (and I immediately thought of one of Mars' giant volcanoes when I read this, but Volcanoes like Olympus Mons had not been discovered when this was written). There are seven levels, each with its own distinctive architecture, buildings and parks. On each level Martians live, each level wits own customs and inventions, each level different, with only an intangible something called The Law being the same for all levels. At the four sides of the mountain great flights of steps, narrowing at the top, lead upward from the desert reaching to the highest level where a spire is a lance aimed at the depths of space.*

The lowest is the desert and is inhabited by wild primitive tribesmen similar to those found elsewhere on Mars and who are featured in earlier stories collected in the volume titled **When Two Worlds Meet**. The various levels are carved into and built around this giant mountain which extends beyond the upper levels of the atmosphere.

The first level has no electricity or powered machines. The second level has a degree more of development, and so does the third level. The fourth level, where John Rolf has established himself is devoted to science and the development of ideas and inventions, while the fifth level has superior science and medical people able to heal and cure most ailments of physical injuries. There is little mentioned regarding the two higher levels initially because all the action begins and takes place on levels four and five.

Supposedly, the whole mountain is ruled by a fabled person referred to as *The King of Mars*, who holds the destiny of all those who live on the various levels in his hands. No one talks about him. John Rolf is portrayed on the cover of the Ace edition as mad looking man with a shock of white hair standing on end while electrodes plugged into his temples are connected to a strange device. This is the invention he has constructed which enables him to free his mind, allowing it to roam away from his body to insert itself into the minds of other people so he can see, feel, and hear what they are thinking. Unfortunately, it doesn't work the way he wants and he finds his mental image, his consciousness, trapped inside the maelstrom of other human minds. Unless his consciousness, his inner self can be brought back into his own body it will die and he will be trapped forever in the mind of someone else. He is taken by a Martian friend up to the fifth level where another friend is a doctor who can help him.

A spaceship has landed on the desert below. A spaceship from the predatory company he once led, filled with 200 mercenary crewmen who are searching for him and for whatever he has been developing on Mars. The implication is that this company is the defacto ruler of Earth after perhaps subjugating other smaller commercial companies, and can do whatever it likes or wants. Hardesty, the leader of this group on the ship finds out Rolf has developed a mind reading device and he wants it. He wants it so he can know who is trying to take his place and so he can thwart these higher up to eventually become the leader of the Company and of the world.

Rolf discovers this because he accidentally entered the mind of Hardesty which showed him how corrupt and eager for total control over others Hardesty was beneath his veneer of politeness and civility. In order to convince Rolf he should hand over the device he has brought along Rolf's daughter, abandoned on Earth, but who is now a personal secretary (a sex slave) to Hardesty.

Father and daughter reconcile and are happy to see each other. She refuses to go back to the ship. Her lover, who is also a crewman on the ship defects from the ship to stay with her and her father. Hardesty is furious that she stays and kidnaps her, locking her inside the ship as a hostage to convince Rolf to hand over the mind reading device.

Hardesty and the crew also believe that untold treasures are hidden on the higher levels and they want this for themselves. Meanwhile, using the device to try and find out what the ship's crew are intending, Rolf loses control and is trapped not only in the mind of Hardesty, but he keeps transferring to others nearby, such as his daughter, then her lover. He can't get back to his own body. The daughter's lover takes the unconscious body of Rolf up to the doctors on level five and they try desperately to get Rolf's consciousness, his *I-self*, to reunite with his body. If they can't achieve this the body will die. With their medical devices they impart energy into the comatose body to keep it alive, but the *I-self* is trapped elsewhere and can't return.

In the meantime, Hardesty has organized the crew along with many desert tribesmen to attack the mountain. With the promise of untold treasures, they force their way up from the first level to the second, and then the third, but are held back at the fourth level where barricades block the stairways and the fourth level inhabitants are fighting back.

Eventually the doctors on level five manage to get Rolf's *I-self* to return to its own body. They inform him that they have been summoned to the seventh level and should leave immediately. It is a long climb to the top. Rolf knows it is only a matter of time before Hardesty and his evil crew breach level four and make their way higher, so there is a feeling of desperation as Rolf, his daughter and her lover, and the Martian doctors head up the thousands of steps to level seven.

Throughout the story there is a bedraggled beggar, with a stooped posture and deformed hands and legs, who uses a staff to support himself who hobbles around and seems to go from level to level at will. Others won't go up a level as the Law forbids it but the beggar can go where he likes. Rolf on occasion has helped the beggar and regards him almost as a friend. As Rolf and his group make their way up the stairs, the beggar follows them. When Rolf wants to help him, his Martian doctor says to leave him, that he will be fine. They need to get to the top as soon as they can while the battle below at level four continues. Hardesty uses a helicopter to drop hand grenades on the defending Martians and finally a breech is made and the mercenary humans push through.

When Rolf reaches the fabled seventh level, he finds inside the spire Martians from various levels seated on a wide circle around a dais where a chair rests in front of a huge abacus like device. Each Martian seated in the tiers encircling the throne also has a smaller similar device. Finally, Rolf who is told to remain silent, will see the fabled King of Mars. Seated silently for some time Rolf hears the faltering footsteps of the beggar who is the last to arrive. The beggar makes his way to the chair on the dais and sits down. Stunned to realize that the beggar he befriended is the *King of Mars* Rolf waits to see what happens. The King reaches forward and starts to touch various beads on the abacus and the others seated around do the same. A musical symphony, improvised spontaneously fills the spire with incredible sound and harmony and energy.

It is interrupted by Hardesty and his bandit crew who finally reach the seventh level and force their way into the spire. They demand that Rolf hand dover the mind reading device and threaten to shoot any Martian who moves. They are contemptuous of whatever is happening and of the '*primitive goons*' seated in the circle.

It appears that the Martians of the upper levels can read minds, and they explain what is happening to Rolf and ask him to remain calm. The beggar is the most powerful of them all and is only this way because of an accident while he was manipulating the power, they all can control to a degree. When Hardesty tries to shoot the beggar or King, his weapon misfires. Others try to shoot the Martian '*goons*' but their weapons don't work either.

The king orders the humans to return to level one, but before they leave, he tells them to look outside the tower. They see their spaceship without its engines operating, rising up into the air. As they watch it accelerates more rapidly and disappears up through the atmosphere into space.

I have sent it back to where it came from, the king tells them. *And you and your crew will go down to level one where you will obey The Law, and if you work hard enough you will be allowed to progress to the next level.*

John Rolf is stunned that the beggar, the *King of Mars* can manipulate the energies of space and can control it down to individual atoms. He knows it will be many years before he can approach this ability and can move up to a higher level, but is content to return to level four with his daughter and her lover as citizens of Mars.

There are moments of evocative description that lifts this story above the mundane. *Suzusilmar* is like a great dream that has its roots in core of Mars and its top in a metal spire pointing to the depths of vast space. Who dreamed this mighty dream? Who carved the terraces in this vast mountain?

No human, and no Martian — except perhaps a blind beggar known to some very few as *The King of the Red Planet* — can rightly say that he knows.

It's actually an entertaining story if you keep in mind the time it was written, and the feelings then of how big business was beginning to control not only the environment but the government as well. I suspect it was a comment on the US as it was evolving in the decade of the 1950s with the depression over, and the Second World War over, and big business beginning to dominate as it expanded at a rapid pace.

Chapter Five

The Golden Age — in full bloom

The 1950s was the decade in which I discovered science fiction, 1952 to be precise – at 12 years of age. It was a decade replete with stories about Mars, not that I noticed that in particular at that time. I was simply entranced with science fiction and read everything I could get my hands on. Even so, there were books I missed, such as those by Sir Patrick Moore, a British Astronomer, and Captain W E Johns, the author of the *Biggles* books which numbered well over 100 by 1950.

The style of writing had changed in general for the better, but still, in some magazines, stories were published that seemed out of place by then, stories in which the writing style even then seemed old-fashioned, rather than contemporary.

City of the Dead by G. M. Martin (1950)
This novella is probably best forgotten.
Published in *Amazing Stories* in 1950, it doesn't represent the type of writing that was becoming the standard in the 1950s but harks back to the way stories were written and told in the 1920s. There were so many better stories in the 1950s from authors like Arthur C Clarke, Isaac Asimov, E. C. Tubb among others, (see chapter four, page 119, **Dreams of Mars**) that I am surprised this one was actually published, unless it was a reprint from an earlier age because there weren't enough stories to fill the magazine. *Amazing Stories* often used reprints from decades earlier.

It concerns a lost city on Mars called Launn, so far into the desert that human settlers and even the local natives think it is a legend. An explorer named Granger found it years before, and told everyone it was filled with the bodies of Martians that are frozen in stasis, neither alive nor dead. His ambition was to return to the lost city and revive these ancient Martians that had been frozen in stasis for more than fifteen thousand years. A team from Earth sets out to find the city and to see if they can revive its inhabitants who had been rendered immobile in the midst of whatever they had been doing. The team leader is convinced some kind of energy, and advanced science was the cause and if they could discover it, then Earth could benefit immensely.

For me, the story doesn't gel, with stereotypical characters that are not convincing and who don't engender any feelings one way or the other. The insect creatures the team encounters in the lost city are risible and are probably only there to generate tension in the plot. A kind of adulterous affair between one of the female characters and an expedition member other than her husband is just silly, and needless to say she is betrayed part way through the story. I didn't find out whether she returned to her husband or not since I gave up reading it at this point.

I presume they found the source of the energy that immobilized the Martian population and brought them back to life, and in doing so gained new advanced scientific knowledge for Earth. That was the whole point of the story wasn't it?

Martian Nightmare by Bryce Walton (1951)

This short novel is interesting only as a comparison with other Martian stories that were published around the same time. It has been revived and published by *Armchair Fiction*.

Personally, I feel it is a rushed and truncated first draft, more or less typical of the stories published in the pulp magazines of the day. It may have been edited to fit the magazine's length requirements, by having chunks chopped out, but I can't be sure of that. It does seem disjointed, and some of the sentences seem incomplete, but that could be a style common to the hard adventure stories people preferred in the 1950s. To me it seems more like a hangover from the type of writing popular in the late 1930s and 1940s, rather than what was becoming more common in the 1950s.

When compared to the Martian stories of Arthur C Clarke, Isaac Asimov, Cyril Judd or E C Tubb, it is not in the same league. There is no feeling of being on Mars, or even of getting there. We have to accept that it is on Mars because the story tells us that that's where it takes place. It is all action from the second chapter, when they arrive and crash onto the surface.

The three soldiers are sent to Mars to spy on the activities of a renegade group of warring people exiled there one hundred years previously. These people, called Oligarchs were the cause of an atomic war that virtually wiped out Earth's population until they were exiled to Mars. Over the intervening 100 years the Earth has evolved into a peaceful place where everyone lives happily and without conflict because their brains have been modified to remove any memories of violence or warlike thoughts and intentions. They also live long lives, because the three people being sent to Mars were once, 100 years ago, members of the military force that defeated the Oligarchs. Their old personalities have been re-implanted in their brains for this mission.

Approaching Mars, they are attacked by three advanced spaceships that immediately come up from the surface and start firing at them. They retaliate even though their ship is damaged and manage to destroy the Martian ships. But they crash land on Mars. They find themselves beside a lake surrounded by wild forests, and in the middle of a battle between human military forces and Martian natives. Two of them are wounded and the third (Danton, the viewpoint character) pretends to be dead.

The bodies he is hiding amongst are collected, loaded onto wagons which are then taken to a huge factory like complex. Tossed onto conveyor belts the bodies go into the factory where a number of 'brainwashed almost robotic' workers sort the bodies into various categories. They are dismembered and the various parts, arms, legs, heads, hearts, livers, kidneys, and so on are stored in refrigerated enclosures.

Danton jumps off the conveyor and starts climbing up to a higher level. He is spotted and is forced to shoot the guards that try to capture him. There are too many of them and he runs out of bullets. They capture him but instead of killing him they take him to see someone who turns out to be a female Oligarch who is also much older than 100 years. All of the Oligarchs exiled on Mars are those original ones from Earth and they are desirous of returning and re-establishing their power over the population once again. She also tells him they have remained young and vigorous by using the body parts salvaged from the dead which are revived for use as rejuvenating spare parts for all the Oligarchs.

When Danton tells them, he is part of the rebellion (outside of this complex where the Oligarch's live), they don't believe him. They suspect he has come from Earth. To Danton's surprise his two other companions, both of whom are wounded, are brought in, and they admit they all came from earth. They also say they want to join the Oligarchs because they are sick of the peaceful society on Earth.

Danton won't have a bar of it and manages to get a gun and shoots the female Oligarch as well as one of his companions. The other one, who was blinded after they crash landed, he takes with him, and they go down to the basement of the complex where the atomic power station exists. They manage to sabotage it and as the building complex starts to fall apart, the Oligarchs who are dependent on its power to keep them young and alive start to die. Stanton manages to escape but his blind friend dies as the power station is destroyed.

Suddenly (*with no showing how he found a space ship or managed to return to Earth alone*), Danton is back on Earth where he relays to the Chief of the World Government what had happened and they no longer need worry about the threat from Mars, he also asks to be reinstated to his peaceful self. He no longer wants to be a soldier.

The final paragraph has Danton waking up as someone called Burton, the same person he was at the opening of the story, with no recollection of ever being Danton the soldier.

The Crystal Crypt by Philip K Dick (1954)
This first appeared in *Planet Stories* in 1954.

It opens with a group of Terrans, the last of them, leaving Mars bound for Terra (Earth) as the threat of a war between Mars and Terra is imminent. The passengers consider themselves lucky to have made it onto the last passenger ship leaving the planet. Suddenly they are ordered to remain in their seats as Martian fighter ships have ordered the passenger liner to land on Deimos where there is a Martian check point.

A black clad Province Leiter leading several soldiers enter the ship and proceed to examine everyone. They tell them the greatest city on Mars has been destroyed and three people, two men and a woman, are suspected of blowing up the city. They use a Martian lie detector and proceed to ask everyone individually if they had anything to do with blowing up and destroying the city. One by one the lie detector assures the Leiter that the person asked is telling the truth when they deny destroying the city. Puzzled, the Leiter and the soldiers leave the ship and it takes off from Deimos to continue the journey.

One of the passengers is sitting next to a young woman and he strikes up a conversation. Heading to the lounge for drinks the woman suggests they sit at a table where a salesman is already seated. Another man joins them and the passenger with the woman starts asking questions about their work. He mentions they'll be quite a few hours on the journey to Terra so they might as well pass the time getting to know each other.

Like his later novel ***Martian Time Slip,*** Dick has people travelling from Earth to Mars or Mars to Earth in a matter of hours, like a long-distance flight across a continent or around the world. He also likes characters who are salesmen, hence this suspicious man wanting to know what kind of salesman the other person at the table is. The man is happy to oblige and brings out his carrying case to show office supplies and an object like a crystal sphere with a miniature city inside.

After some back and forth he elicits a story from the salesman who, though at first is reluctant to give details, is convinced that all Terrans can be trusted and so tells the story of how they infiltrated the city pretending to be a priest and two peasants going there to perform a marriage ceremony. They plant three devices that triangulate to cover the whole city, and after they leave and head into the nearby hills, they trigger the devices planted and with a massive explosion of light the city disappears. They barely escape a senior Leiter and a group of soldiers combing the bush for suspicious people. They locate their hidden aircar and quickly return to catch the last ship leaving Mars for Terra.

Feeling safe and somewhat proud of what he has done, he explains that the city hasn't been destroyed, it has been shrunk to a size small enough to be encompassed inside the crystal he has in his sample case. (No explanation for how this could be done. It's simply stated as a fact.)

The passenger then reveals that he is a senior Martian investigator and he suspected that the city hadn't been blown up —mentioning something about loss of mass and an anomaly in the gravity where the city once was. He calls to a group of men drinking at the bar and they all turn out to be Martians disguised as Terrans. The three are stunned at this horrid turn.

The Martian investigator orders the passenger ship to be turned around so the three criminals can be taken back to Mars. They are told, *you have a very interesting process. Mars will benefit a great deal from it. Perhaps it will even turn the tide in our favor. When we return to Marsport I will begin work on it at once.*

This is not one of Dick's better stories. It's well written but quite ordinary compared to his later work both short and long, and once read is easily forgotten. Nevertheless, Fans of Philip K Dick will want to read this if they can find a copy of it.

Old fashioned fun for younger readers in the 1950s

Kings of Space (1954) **Return to Mars** (1955) **Now to the Stars** (1956) by Captain W E Johns.

W E Johns was born in 1893. He was a bomber pilot with the Royal Flying Corps and was shot down and captured in Europe on September 16th 1918. After the 1st World War he remained a pilot with the Royal Air Force until he retired to become a full-time writer of fiction, mostly aimed at teenage boys who loved reading exciting adventurous stories. During the first half of the 20th century, he was one of the most popular writers of fiction for younger readers surpassing everyone except for Enid Blyton. He produced over 200 books of which 101 were about airman Biggles. But Biggles also appeared in several Gimlet stories (another one of his popular characters) while similarly Gimlet appeared in some Biggles stories so the real number of Biggles stories is not a definite 101, but could be several more.

In the 1950s and 60s he started a new series of science fiction stories all featuring Tiger Clinton (an aeronautical engineer) and his son Rex and their interplanetary adventures with an eccentric scientist, Professor Brane, who discovered a new propulsive force that uses cosmic rays, and his butler/assistant who helps him build a flying saucer shaped space craft with which to explore the Moon and nearby planets.

The Kings of Space kicks off the series. On a deer hunting expedition in the Scottish Highlands Group Captain Timothy Clinton, RAF retired, 'Tiger' and his son Rex find themselves lost in the mountains after it gets dark and a fog descends. After stumbling about for hours in fog shrouded darkness they discover a remote Castle in a valley, and when let in they meet Professor Brane, who only let them in when he heard (over the intercom) that Tiger was an aeronautical engineer. He thought he could use this person's help with his 'flying saucer'.

Much of this book is spent with the professor explaining about flying saucer sightings and his belief they are alien craft, with discussions about the solar system and especially with the Moon and Mars. Also hinted at is the Cold War between Russia and America and the possibility of total annihilation of the world. (This was a big concern with many novelists in the 1950s for obvious reasons; the world was almost on the brink of an atomic war during that decade.) There are spies (in the last chapter) who want to steal the space ship and want the professor to reveal its plans. There are no plans; they are all in his head, and on several occasions, he has stated that he would rather die than reveal how his ship works, so his way of getting rid of the armed spies at the end of the story is to give them the ship which he has set on remote control, and he shoots them straight up into space while leaving the door into the ship open. There is no airlock on this first space ship and the spies quickly die once the ship gets above the Earth's atmosphere.

The first two thirds of the book cover working and testing the ship, and even when they do this at night there are reports in the local papers of flying saucer sightings much to the annoyance of Professor Brane who doesn't want to attract attention. The information Professor Brane gives to his new crew mates is in line with what was known about the solar system in the 1950s, but because Captain W E Johns grew up before the first world War and later fought in that War, his ideas regarding whether there is life on the other planets in the solar system is by today's standards, old fashioned, typical of what was thought at an earlier time.

Up to this point the story is more or less science fiction, but from the moment they arrive on the Moon it becomes adventure fantasy with absolutely no scientific base. W E Johns obviously holds to the ideas that were promulgated by earlier scientists and pseudo-scientists, that the planets in the solar system followed the same evolutionary path and that Venus (and the Moon) were more like Earth was during the age of the dinosaurs, and that Mars is what Earth will become like in the far future.

When Professor Brane and his companions arrive at the Moon, they discover remnants of life hanging on in deep valleys, giant worms that live underground, hardy cactus-like plants that grow on the inside slops of the crater they have landed in, and some kind of turtle lizard thing that comes out and ferociously feeds on the giant worms when the sun shines into the crater. "A Glyptodon," the professor exclaims in wonderment.

There is a trace of atmosphere left but not enough for them to breathe so they must use their space suits (which are called Cosmosuits) when they exit the ship. Because the space ship doesn't have a proper airlock, they must allow the air to escape so they can open the door. The many craters on the moon are filled with mud so the professor decides that the moon must once have been more like the Earth, but was now a dying world with only a few remnants of life hanging on. They make a hasty retreat when the glyptodons that appear look as if they might attack them.

Travelling on to Venus, they discover a perpetually cloud covered very humid tropical world of fetid swamps, filled with monsters exactly like those found during the age of the dinosaurs. They can breathe the air so they don't need to wear their cosmosuits. It is dark and hot and gloomy because of the immense cloud cover above. Venturing out into the swamp they see several brontosauri feeding in the shallows. While they watch, a Megalosaurus attacks one of the feeding brontosaurs ripping it apart with such ferocity the observers are stunned. Suddenly the air is filled with wild barking sounds and a large group of hairy bipeds attack the Megalosaurus, hurling rocks at it, bashing it with clubs, and ripping off shreds of flesh with their teeth. The professor is stunned to discover these leaping bipeds are primitive humans. When the bipeds see the observers, they immediately attack them, forcing the human visitors to make a rapid retreat to their space ship.

The implication is that Venus is at an earlier stage of its evolution, like the Earth was millions of years earlier. (Obviously W E Johns forgot that human bipeds never co-existed with dinosaurs; that millions of years separated the time they existed on Earth — a common mistake by many people. Also, all of the creatures they see are exactly like those that existed on Earth in the remote past.)

They just manage to get off the planet. Their space ship could barely find enough cosmic rays to use since they were absorbed by Venus' massively thick clouds, and it struggles to gain altitude. Just when it looks as if the ship will fall back down it emerges from the dense cloud cover and once back in space it returns to normal. They fly back to Earth and Scotland to prepare for the trip to Mars.

Before landing on Mars they land on Phobos and discover a small village in a crater. The stone dwellings are deserted and there is one desiccated corpse of a Martian. It appears to be human except that it is much taller than humans from Earth. They have no idea how long it could have been there. The professor surmises that Phobos must once have had a thin atmosphere but it has been dragged away by the nearby Mars' greater gravity, leaving it airless.

And Mars, they discover when they finally land in the middle of an abandoned town, is old and dying, all desert with the only green reedy plants growing along the sides of many canals used to bring water from the polar regions. The atmosphere is thin but breathable, so they don't need to wear space suits. There are no mountains since the constantly moving sand has worn them down into nothing more than humps. They discover after walking around the town that it is occupied by people that look like us only taller, but they are all diseased, blind, dying or dead. Most of the dwellings are deserted, but they did find corpses in some of them. The few remaining Martians either can't see them or they are so listless they can't interact with the visitors from Earth. While they are there (in the second last chapter of the book) massive clouds of pink poisonous mosquitoes rise up from the canals to feed on the remaining few Martian people. The clouds are so massive that they blot out the sky, but very soon there will be nothing left for them to feed on. The Professor realizes that the massive clouds we see from Earth obscuring the planet are not dust storms but swarming insects.

Perhaps the author was prescient in using mosquitoes. It has recently come to light that the tiny mosquito is the worst predator of humans in existence, on average killing almost a million people annually through the horrible diseases it transmits when biting. No one likes mosquitoes, but no effort expended by humans has been able to eradicate them. Using mosquitoes on Mars may at first seem ridiculous but in hindsight, wasn't a bad idea after all, assuming that there was a breathable atmosphere for humans and a viable climate that could support mosquito breeding, and in his story Mars has the canals which are the breeding spots for the huge hordes of mosquitoes that decimate the Planet's population, forcing them to migrate to the asteroid belt..

The professor decides they will return to Earth where he will develop a kind of insecticide to either kill the mosquitoes or force them to devour each other until they become extinct.

When the clouds of mosquitoes fly towards them the professor and his companions race back to their ship and just get back inside before the mosquitoes darken the sky above them, clogging their rocket exhausts.

Leaving Mars, the professor vows to return as soon as possible to save the Martians.

Return to Mars. (1955)

It takes about a year before Professor Brane, Tiger and his son Rex, along with the ever-present butler assistant-engineer Judkins, and a doctor, an old associate from the war, Squadron Leader Clarence Paul MD. Known as Toby have built a new improved version of their flying saucer shaped space ship (Spacemaster II), after having lost the first one in getting rid of a couple of spies who wanted to know its secrets. During that time, he has also developed an insecticide that he hopes will eliminate the mosquitoes on Mars by either directly killing them or by genetically altering them to turn cannibalistic so they feed on themselves.

Stopping once more on Phobos when they arrive in their new ship, they discover marks on the surface that indicate other space ships had landed. Several more bodies (Martians) have been placed in the abandoned dwellings. Landing once more in the same town they visited the year before; they find only one person is left, barely alive. They take him on board and try to give him medical help. They also take off and travelling along the weed choked nearby canal they spray the surface for several miles with the newly developed genetic insecticide.

Unfortunately, the insecticide works differently than the Professor expected. It rapidly causes the mosquitoes to increase in size, overnight, until they are almost a foot long. Other things eat them and they too grow enormously large. Suddenly within a day or two there are, giant ants a yard long, various other hideous animals such as bats, and rodents that have grown extraordinarily large as well as a massive growth of trees and reeds and other bushes along the canal. It is turning into a wild jungle as they watch. The professor is even attacked by a giant beautiful butterfly that acts more like an eagle, swooping down to grab at him.

From this moment on, the story is more science fantasy than science fiction, but in the 1950s little distinction was made between the two genres, and the more fantastic the adventure could be the more likely it would find an audience with the young teenage boys for whom W E Johns was writing. I don't think W E Johns could really imagine anything alien. His idea of alien, was to make the smallest earthly insects into giant versions of themselves, or to have co-existing with some variation of humans, ancient extinct animals that once dominated the Earth, such as dinosaurs in all their magnificent varieties. All the animals and insects in his stories are simply giant versions of what exists or existed on Earth.

W E Johns subscribed to the common belief at the end of the 19th century that all the planets, planetoids, asteroids, and moons were inhabited by beings that looked like us, and that were of varying sizes depending upon the gravity of the world they lived on, and that each and every world had an atmosphere that was breathable, although often thinner with less pressure than that of the Earth. Only a very few places had an atmosphere so thin as to require the Professor and his team to don their *'cosmosuits.'* He also believed that space was full of various gas molecules and that planets got their atmospheres by attracting oxygen molecules along with other rare gases that were spread throughout the cosmos.

Writing these SF stories in the 1950s his ideas were certainly old fashioned when compared to his contemporaries such as Arthur C Clarke, John Brunner, Kenneth Bulmer, John Russell Fern, Isaac Asimov, Robert Heinlein, Murray Leinster, Chad Oliver and many other writers of science fiction who tended to base their stories on the science of the day extrapolated into the future. W E Johns simply transposed the kind of adventures he was used to writing for his 100 and more Biggles books to a new set of characters with the location being in space and on various planets and asteroids or moons.

Biggles was a character from the first World War and the times between that and the second World War. His readers had grown up and were not interested as much in Biggles anymore, and the younger generation of children who had grown up during the second World War and the 1940s were not the same as these young readers who devoured his early books. Science fiction was something they were excited about, as was I — albeit not until the early 1950s when I became a teenager. They were more familiar with the ideas that customarily permeated science fiction and didn't find W E Johns space adventure stories to be scientific enough to generate a sense of wonder. His 10 SF books were not as popular as his earlier Biggles books, and it has been said that readers found these stories pessimistic, probably brought on by the madness of the Cold War between Russia and America with its threat of impending nuclear destruction, and his prophetic concerns about polluting the environment.

As an aside: I never saw any of these 10 SF books during the 1950s when I was devouring almost every SF story I could find. I have only discovered them recently, and have read the first four of them to see how they compare with material written by his contemporaries. I mention them here in case some readers are not aware that they existed and who may be curious about them. They can be found in second hand bookshops along with most of his other output, so there is a lot of reading for those interested in the books of W E Johns.

The Martian they rescued begins to recover and they find his name is Vargo. He communicated telepathically through Rex, the youngest and the most perceptive of the Spacemaster crew. From him they find out that the Martians abandoned their home planet as the mosquitoes were killing them off. They migrated to the many different planetoids and mini worlds that occupy the asteroid belt, but soon they will have to leave them as the atmospheres of those small worlds are leaking away into space.

They had considered moving to Earth but changed their minds when it was discovered a large asteroid was going to impact that planet if three months' time, most likely killing everyone and everything on the surface. Vargo also tells them that the solar system today is the result of an experiment that went wrong millions of years in the past. At that time there was another planet between Mars and Jupiter and the Martian scientists were conducting atom smashing experiments there and it got out of control. A massive explosion shattered the planet, the remnants of which are now the asteroid belt.

The destruction of the planet threw so much debris into the system that the sun was blocked out. Earth was plunged into an ice age and moved closer to the Sun and gained the Moon. When the sun reappeared, the ice melted and water filled the holes made in Earth's crust by the debris bombardment creating the seas. Jupiter, the most beautiful planet, was set on fire and it still burns today. Saturn gathered some of the debris into orbit around itself and those are the rings. Mars' atmosphere was blasted away and the planet turned into a desert. The canals were dug to bring water from the poles but Mars was basically unlivable and they moved to the asteroid belt. They still come back to Mars to grow food in the sub-tropical areas, but the mosquitoes keep them from re-occupying the planet.

The Professor explains that he can get rid of the mosquitoes and can help with making Mars habitable again. Vargo guides the Spacemaster II and its screw to asteroid belt where they will meet the rest of the Martians.

But before they can depart, Tiger is kidnapped by a rogue Martian who wants him to guide them to Earth and show them where they can land. He wants to steal as much as he can before the planet is destroyed. The others in the Spacemaster II head off for the asteroid belt but on the way their ship is controlled mentally by the rogue Martian who tows the ship (with his more powerful one) towards Jupiter where it is captured by that massive planet's gravity. Unable to escape because their ship simply isn't powerful enough, they become resigned to falling into the huge burning planet. But just before all hope is lost, they are rescued by two Martian flying saucers the crews of which mentally tow the Spacemaster II to safety.

On Ceres, which is where the Martians mostly live, they find out that they won't help get rid of the asteroid that will impact Earth. That is a problem for your planet to solve, the Professor is told. But he convinces them if they help blow up the threatening asteroid, he will get rid of the mosquitos on Mars and start the restoration of the planet to make it livable again. Reluctantly they agree.

Before they take off to do that some of the Martian scientists want to collect wood, a rare commodity in the small worlds. There is only one small world where trees and vines and other plants grow insanely wild and can actually be seen fighting each other. Rex and Toby accompany the scientists. The only place they can land is a fused area of metallic rock on which nothing grows. Everywhere else is covered by writhing, madly moving jungle trees and vines, all fighting each other to gain height, to reach as much sunlight as they can. Stepping out Rex and toby are attacked by thick vines that wriggle across the bare fused ground to wrap around them, strangling them. The scientists quickly chop off the vines and the trapped visitors are freed as the vines fall off them to wriggle and writhe with dying spasms. As soon as the scientists chop down the needed tree branches, they gather them and bring them back to their ship.

Why use axes? Did not circular saws and chainsaws exist in the 1950s? I think this side adventure was added to fill out the story as well as to show the author's attempt to describe another different world. He does mention it reminded him of what a jungle on Earth would look like if speeded up so we could see how the plants grow, fight, and interact with each other.

Almost as soon as they return from collecting the wood, they take off to look at the rouge asteroid, this time with Rex and Toby back in the Spacemaster II. On the way they stop at the kidnapper's home (mini) world where they rescue Tiger, much to Rex's relief, and capture the rogue Martian.

The asteroid threatening Earth is destroyed by the Martian's bomb but not without a couple of mishaps occurring that almost kills them. However, they escape and head back to Earth. On the way home they find their ship is slowly disintegrating and have to be transferred to the Martian flying Saucer accompanying them.

This is quite a good scene where the Professor and his crew have to pull themselves along a cable stretched between their airlock and that of the Martian flying Saucer accompanying them, while the Spacemaster II is falling apart around them. The Martians had told the Professor while on Ceres that his ship's metal wouldn't stand up to the constant radiation bombarding it in space, but he didn't take much notice until his ship began disintegrating as they approached The Earth.

They land back at the Professor's Castle in the remote Scottish Glen. The Martians take off and as the crew approach the castle a couple of reporters accost them, wanting to know what had just happened. When he tells them they've just been brought home in a Martian Flying Saucer. The reporter believes him so the Professor tells him they have saved the Earth from destruction by a giant wandering meteor. When the reporter asks "what proof can I give?" in his newspaper story, the Professor tells him to say "you have had a message from Mars."

The next book in the series takes our intrepid team back to Mars not in an improved Spacemaster ship, but in a Martian ship called Tavona, for the Professor to carry out his agreement with the Martians, before the team ventures further out into the solar system for more adventures and discoveries.

Now to the Stars (1956)
Begins with the professor, Tiger and his son Rex heading back to Mars, but this time in a Martian flying saucer (Tavona) rather than one the professor might have constructed. He knew then that earthly metals used in his original Spacemaster were corroded or destroyed by metal fatigue caused by the radiation in space. The Martian ships use a different metal found only on Mars. Rex brings a cute kitten with him as a gift to his new 'girlfriend' but it escapes into the wild along a nearby canal before they leave for Minos where the majority of the Martians live.

The rest of the story concerns adventures in and around the asteroid belt and the other planets of the solar system, with the crew returning to Mars on their way back to Earth in the last chapter. There they find that their escaped kitten has eaten some Martian animals that had been infected by the professor's insecticide and had become an enormous monster of a cat. It preyed on the Martians trying to rebuild their planet as the professor's terraforming began to improve conditions. Tiger was forced to shoot the gigantic cat to remove the menace. After that they return to Scotland and home.

In each of the subsequent space adventures, our intrepid heroes, after a three-month gap on Earth (in Scotland where the professor lives), return to Mars to check on how the 'terraforming' is progressing before heading off into outer space for more adventures. They use the Tavona, a Martian space ship with other Martians as crew members in all the subsequent stories, and so they are all connected as a very long narrative.

A major concern that runs through the background of most of them is the threat of nuclear power and the possible annihilation of Earth by nations willing to wage war against each other. (W E Johns was not alone in this; many authors from the 1950s and 60s used this very threat as the basis of some remarkable stories.) He often refers to the Martians who experimented with atomic power on the fifth planet which was subsequently destroyed, blasted into the fragments that now are the asteroid belt, as a warning to readers about that same possibility happening on Earth.

Humans polluting the environment in which they live is also another background concern. It may have been these concerns that put off younger readers because the ten books in W E Johns' space adventures were not as popular as his earlier **Biggles** books, or perhaps it was because his earlier readers had now become adult and were no longer interested in those kind of adventure stories.

Sadly, most of the stories are dated because of silly ideas regarding the planets, planetoids and asteroids, which in retrospect probably didn't even seem plausible even in the mid-1950s and early-1960s when these books were written. But still, they are worth looking at because at the very least they do retain a certain nostalgic charm.

The other books in the series are: *To Outer Space* (1957), *The Edge of Beyond* (1958), *The Death Rays of Ardilla* (1959), *To Worlds Unknown* (1960), *The Quest for the Perfect Planet* (1961), *Worlds of Wonder* (1962), and *The Man Who Vanished into Space* (1963).

All these space adventure stories were originally published by *Hodder and Staunton*, and all of them have beautiful cover art reminiscent of the that era. The five that were later published in paperback were not as impressive.

Captain W E Johns died in 1968.

An Anthropologist on Mars

Artifact by Chad Oliver (1956)

Chad Oliver was renowned for his gentle stories that focused on alien contact, or first contact, from an anthropological viewpoint. He was in real life a professor of Anthropology at a Texas University.

Dr Dixon Sanders was an anthropologist (just like the author) at a university in Texas. He didn't know Man had landed on Mars. He also didn't know what had been found there, until he was called from Washington and asked to go there to look at something. He ended up being flown to a special base somewhere in New Mexico where a general in charge of the space program showed him an artifact and asked him to identify it, or to tell them how old it could be.

The artifact was a stone tool with one side chipped away to make a cutting edge, a typical Neolithic tool. Without knowing where it was found or anything else about the site, he could not determine its age. It appeared to be recently made but it could also be thousands of years old. When he was told it had been found on Mars he was astounded. That meant there was or there had been intelligent life on Mars.

He was asked to go to Mars to see if they could find more and he readily accepted. He also was asked to recommend another anthropologist to accompany him so they could properly excavate the site and look for other tools and indications of life.

Typical of the stories written about Mars in the 1950s, not much was really known about the planet. It was assumed that it was slightly cooler than Earth, but not as cold as Antarctica except at the poles, and that there was oxygen in the air although the air pressure was low enough that the humans on the surface had to wear an air pressure suit. It was also expected that there was plant life like one would find in desert areas, stunted, hardy plants. He does mention that there were no canals, that they were a figment of human imagination, which is about the only real thing in this story.

Landing near where the artifact had been found the two anthropologists set up a series of excavation sites but find nothing of interest. There is a fair amount of detail regarding how an archaeological dig is performed and after six or seven hours a chipped spear head or perhaps a knife is found. And after ten days with nothing more than a couple of broken stone scrapers and a charred bone they decide they should look elsewhere. They spend the next month sinking test pits in many different locations and find quite a few artifacts but no ruins or any signs of habitation. Everything they have found is typical of the Neolithic implements found on Earth.

Unsure of whether what they have found is ancient or recently abandoned, they ask themselves if you were looking for life on Earth where would you go? *Go where the water is,* was the answer.

Using a helicopter, they head for the nearest polar region. They pass over swamps and ice drifts, snow covered dunes, and eventually land near the ice on a mossy strip of cold land. There is a nearby frozen lake and Sanders decides he will cut a hole in the ice and see if he can catch a fish. They catch a fish like a golden trout and see also a black slick shape slide away by the lake's edge into the scrub.

This is where life is Sanders decides.

Three days later they discover a humanoid being is watching them. He is a few hundred yards away from the helicopter. Knowing there must be others, family members at least somewhere nearby Sanders takes the fish and offers it to the fur-clad being who accepts it and communication begins.

The being looks exactly like one of Earth's primitive human ancestors. Sanders concludes the man is not frightened because he has never seen humans before. They exchange names and with gestures he indicates that he would like to see the helicopter up close. His name is Narn and Sanders leads him across to the helicopter and introduces him to the other team members. They get him to enter the helicopter and they take him for a spin above the land. Narn's astonishment is only momentary and shortly after he indicates that he would like to fly the helicopter. He had been watching intently every move the pilot had made. Reluctantly they allow him to sit in the co-pilot's seat and then he flies the machine, a bit roughly at first but when he gets a better feel for the controls, he flies it like it was something he had done all his life.

Returning back to where they met him, he takes Sanders to where he lives in a cave under the ice. Sanders meets Narn's family and discovers a series of beautiful cave paintings that are far more detailed than anything found in Neolithic caves on Earth. Narn learns the rudiments of English almost instantly. Sanders stays a couple of days here in the cave with Narn and his family, but reluctantly has to leave. The people waiting for him with the helicopter will be wanting to return to their space ship for the return to Earth.

Sanders looks into Narn's eyes and sees a wordless hope. Sanders feels a kinship with Narn and a new race of humans on Mars, and the story ends here as the helicopter lands to take him back to his ship, but Sanders knows that a new chapter had begun as he and Narn look up into the sky full of stars in an ocean of loneliness.

If you are a fan of Chad Oliver's writing, then this early story will only enhance your appreciation of him and his later work.

The threat of Atomic War

It's interesting that stories published in the 1950s often used an atomic war as a means of propelling the story forward.

The 1950s was the decade of the cold war between Russia and America in which each seriously threatened the other with atomic weapons, (bombs and missiles — launched from land-based silos as well as from atomic powered submarines patrolling enemy coastlines). An atomic war seemed inevitable and the so-called Doomsday Clock showed one minute to midnight indicating the absolute seriousness of the threat. People built useless bomb shelters in their backyards and kids in schools were taught to duck beneath their desks in the class room and close their eyes. No one knew how devastating an atomic explosion was or could be. The Cuban missile crisis could have been the start of such a war but it was narrowly averted and the world took a different path than that of Mutually Assured Destruction.

Planet of Exile by Edmond Hamilton (1958)

In this short novel, an atomic war forces humankind to abandon Earth in favor of Mars.

The story opens with a man running wildly in panic through a forest at night until he remembers who he is, Kenneth Farrow. He was to sleep for 6 months to test a gas that induces artificial aestivation or hibernation. Scientists had the idea that if there was an atomic war there would be too many people to support in the bomb shelters, so if they could have them hibernate until the radiation levels outside the shelters subsided, they didn't need to worry too much about feeding them.

Farrow, a physicist working for the Defense Scientific Commission, is unmarried and with no family dependents. He agrees to the hibernation experiment and is placed in a small hermetically sealed bomb shelter, and on breathing the gas in the shelter he falls asleep. He was to be woken up by his colleagues after 6 months. Inside the shelter there are cans of food, dried food, and various weapons, rifles and guns, and ammunition for them.

Something went wrong. An atomic war happened. Millions were killed, and the whole of the North American continent became irradiated and unlivable.

When an earthquake breaks open the hermetically sealed bomb shelter

Farrow wakes up and has no immediate recollection of who he is or why he is locked up in what to him resembles a tomb. In panic he runs down the cliff into a forested landscape terrified that something awful has happened. He discovers an old highway that is cracked and overgrown with huge trees growing, trees that take a hundred years to reach such heights, and slowly it occurs to him that he has been asleep for a very long time.

He returns to the shelter and opens a can of food, and after eating he grabs a loaded rifle and some ammunition before setting off through the wilderness to search for signs of civilization, but there are none. Several hours later he hears an enormous sound and looking up he sees a rocket ship passing overhead to land some distance away.

He rushes towards it hoping that he will be rescued. He approaches cautiously not sure whether the occupants of the ship are human or not, but getting closer he sees they are human, and that they also speak English. Abandoning his caution, he calls out to them and approaches. One of them immediately points a weapon at him and discharges a bolt of energy. It misses him but involuntarily he brings up the rifle and fires a shot at the man, wounding him in the shoulder. The others immediately start firing their energy weapons at him and he turns and runs off into the bush.

The moment he enters the bush he encounters a young woman who insists he follow her if he wants to be safe. He can barely keep up with her as they flee from the people of the rocket ship. She tells him they are Martians, but he insists they are humans and they speak English (as does she).

Safe for the moment, she explains they were humans who went to Mars in the days before the War.

Farrow knew about the rocket ships going to Mars. They had discovered several oases where plants grew and water could be found on the otherwise barren planet where it would be possible to establish a colony. After the war had devastated the country a group of survivors in the South knew it was only a matter of time before the poisonous radiation drifted down to kill them all so they used as many rocket ships as they could and took as many people as possible and established a colony on Mars.

Periodically they return to gather materials, minerals and ores unavailable on Mars, but whenever they see survivors like her, they shoot to kill them. Her people survived the poisonous radiation because they lived high in the mountains, and when the radiation had eventually diminished, they came down from the mountains to live on land that was now a forested wilderness, evolving into the various tribes that now exist, and which the Martians try to kill whenever they see them.

Thinking they are safe for the moment they are suddenly surrounded, and the leader of the Martian group insists on not killing them.

"He has a new projectile weapon and we need to find out how that is possible," he tells his men. *"Don't kill the girl either, I have a use for her."*

Surrounded they are captured and taken back to the space ship.

"How could they have found us?" the girl, Jen asks.

Suddenly Farrow sees a hideous creature, hairy with six limbs, arms and legs, with huge eyes that stare hypnotically at him. He feels tendrils of thought in his mind and he knows instantly that this creature is a Martian and it can read minds, that's how they were found.

The ship takes off for Mars and with Farrow and Jen as prisoners locked in a cabin. The Martian creature is also there trying to extract information from Farrow. The Martian humans want to know how he survived more than a hundred years. They want the formula for the hibernation gas and will use the native Martian creature to get it from Farrow's mind.

But during the journey, Farrow discovers that the Martian is also a prisoner, and has been forced to help the humans who occupy Mars.

It tells them that the rulers of the humans on Mars want to keep the population ignorant of the fact that Earth is safe, and that there is no more radiation. They want to maintain their power and control. If the population could know the truth they would want to return to Earth and leave Mars to its true inhabitants. It also tells them that the Martian rulers want to dose Jen with extreme radiation to make her sick and dying. They want to show her to the general population as proof that Earth is not a safe place yet to live, to maintain their power and control.

The real Martians would like to see the Earthmen gone, so it is willing to help Farrow and Jen escape so they can tell the settlers the truth, that Earth is safe and people can live there. The moment the ship lands (in a compound well away from the human settlement) the creature causes a mental block with the guards and helps Farrow and Jenn escape in a stolen rover. They head towards a distant hidden valley where the last of the true Martians are living peacefully.

The crew of the space ship as well as extra men from the distant city give chase and almost catch them but not before the creature with Farrow and Jen enter a crevice that leads to a hidden valley where the last Martians live. They don't want any violence and refuse to help the escaped earth people. However, when it is explained that the ruthless humans on Mars will drop bombs on the hidden valley to kill every living thing, they agree to use their mental powers to stop this from happening.

With the help of the native Martians Farrow and Jen go to the city where they force the leaders to reveal the truth of the Earth situation; the truth that it is safe for humans to return to their own planet and no longer need to remain exiled on Mars.

And the story ends with the possibility of everyone going home and being happy.

There is however a doubt in the mind of Farrow who wonders if in time Humans have learnt anything, or will they simply repeat the same mistakes as before. Jen's final words are that she hopes not, that surely, we have learned something.

"*I hope to God you are right,*" Farrow says, and that's the end of the story.

Santa Cruz

Chapter Six

Sir Patrick Moore and Mars

Science Fiction and Patrick Moore

The Maurice Gray series of stories by Patrick Moore began in 1955 with *Mission to Mars.* This was followed by *The Domes of Mars* (1956), *The voices of Mars* (1957), *Peril on Mars* (1958), and *Raiders of Mars* (1959).

Starting in 1952 Patrick Moore wrote science fiction novels geared towards younger readers. Today these would be called young adult books, but half a century ago were considered to be children's books, or juveniles.

There were his five (Maurice Gray) Mars books, five Robin North books, six Scot Saunders books, two Gregory Quest books, plus a number of unrelated individual novels.

Sir Patrick also wrote over 100 books on astronomy, the Moon, Mars and The Solar System, The Universe, Black Holes in space, and even speculative science books such as *The Next Fifty Years in Space* (1974), again for younger readers as well as for the general adult reader.

He was a Fellow of The British Astronomical Association from 1945, and he presented the longest running science show on TV, *The Sky At Night,* which began in April 1957 and continued on the BBC until he died in 2012. In all those years and more than 700 episodes he only ever missed presenting one episode due to illness.

He was Knighted in 2002 and is now Sir Patrick Moore, CBE, FRS, DSc (Hon), FRAS. Some of his non-fiction books were written concurrently with his science fiction novels, but after his last science fiction novel was published in 1980, he concentrated entirely on non-fiction.

Sir Patrick was a member of the British Interplanetary Society and would have known other contemporary science fiction authors such as Arthur C Clarke who had already by that time published *The Sands of Mars.* (1951).

He did however, 50 years later, rewrite or revise his early story *Mission to Mars* (1955) —in light of the new knowledge gained about Mars from the various flybys from 1964 onwards, the rovers on the surface and satellites in orbit that monitor the planet — and retitled it *Voyage to Mars* (2003).

Whether he revised any of his other early fiction I have no idea, but it is interesting to compare the first version with the 50 year later revised version of the same story.

Mission to Mars / Voyage to Mars. (1955 /2003)

In the first of the five books featuring him, Maurice Gray is a 16-year-old teenager whose parents are killed in a motor accident, and whose guardian shortly after dies. Maurice's only other relative, his uncle Professor Leslie Yorke, works at the Woomera Rocket range in Australia so Maurice is sent to Australia. In Moore's future scenario England and Australia who run the Woomera Rocket Research Centre have joined forces with the Europeans and the Americans to use Woomera for building and launching their space ships to the Moon and to Mars.

In the 1950s this would seem a logical extrapolation.

Everybody is so busy hardly anyone takes any notice of him. Any time he mentions his uncle the subject is changed. He makes friends with Bruce Talbot who is only a couple of years older than him but who seems to know his way around and is involved in secret and confidential research. Bruce takes him under his wing, and shows him around.

Very quickly Maurice finds out that his uncle had been to the Moon and was now on an expedition to Mars, only no one has heard anything from that expedition once it landed. They don't know what has happened and they are in the process of preparing another expedition to go to Mars to find out, or alternatively to rescue the original expedition's members.

Maurice, who is an expert in using Morse Code and whose training is in radio communication (he studied this at school in England — *remember; this was written less than 10 years after the end of the 2nd World War in which Morse Code communications played a pivotal part*) and to help pass the time they allow him to assist with monitoring the radio bandwidth they use to communicate with Mars and with the space ship when it was on its way.

He has a good ear and after several hours of monitoring he hears a faint signal. He calls to the others there and together they receive a message from Mars telling them that the original ship had crashed on landing and was unable to be repaired. The co-ordinates of the crash site are given and they are told they could survive on their supplies of oxygen for another eight to nine months… then the message is covered up by static and random noise.

It is suddenly imperative that the rescue mission departs as soon as possible because the transit to Mars will take about 6 to 7 months. But the new space ship *Ares* has a problem. It needs a crew of four to operate it and if they are to rescue the four already on Mars the *Ares* will be too heavy to take off.

The *Ares* has to be modified to reduce its weight, so some things are taken out. If they use three instead of four in the crew, they may be just able to bring back the stranded crew already on Mars. However, the three selected to go are collectively too heavy which means someone would have to remain on Mars. Maurice suggests that he is lighter than the radioman selected and that he could replace him. He knows as much about radio and Morse Code as the other. Eventually it is agreed and Maurice is on the crew of the rescue ship. There is a brief period of intense training to bring Maurice up to the level of the other crew members, and then finally the *Ares* blasts off for Mars.

The *Ares* is a two-stage rocket with the initial stage using chemical propulsion to lift the ship up above the atmosphere. Once this stage drops off the second stage, an atomic powered rocket, ignites and blasts the *Ares* up to escape velocity (7 miles per second), and into orbit where it then is inserted into a trajectory that will take it to Mars.

As is usual on such a lengthy trip —and especially in movies of such voyages— something must happen and usually it is something like a meteorite striking and holing the ship which has to be suddenly repaired. In this case it is the radar equipment which they need for navigation and precise control during landing and takeoff, which is mounted on the outside of the hull that is damaged. Bruce and Maurice go outside to see if they can repair it.

It is unrepairable, and as they are about to return Bruce's tether comes loose and he drifts away from the ship. Maurice immediately goes to the rescue, even though Bruce tells him not to do it. He undoes his tether and uses the hard space suit's motor to guide himself across to where Bruce is rapidly disappearing. Bruce's motor doesn't work which is why he was unable to come back. They make it back after some tense moments, and of course Bruce and Maurice become firm friends forever.

The rest of the voyage to Mars is unremarkable. As they get further away from Earth their radio signals become weaker until the only way left for them to communicate is via Morse Code. But no matter how close they get to Mars they cannot pick up any radio signals of any kind other than intense static.

They also have trouble landing. There is something in the atmosphere that upsets radio and radar and anything else of that nature. Unable to see how close they are, they land too hard and their ship is slightly damaged. Not only that they also can't send messages of any kind back to Woomera control nor can they receive any in return. They are as stranded as the first crew. They determine that they are about 100 miles away if the coordinates given to them at Woomera are correct.

It turns out that there is a layer in the atmosphere, called the violet layer, that is highly magnetic. Its magnetism waxes and wanes, and sometimes almost disappears for a few moments. It is only during those moments that messages can get through. They try to contact the first mission but are unable to get through at first. Meanwhile they explore their surroundings and this time Maurice gets stuck in a collapsing sand dune and is rescued by Bruce and their other team mate David Mellor.

They know they haven't much time to rescue the first explorers and set out to find them. They carry all the spare oxygen bottles they can because the others would be very close to running out by this time. They estimate it will take them three days and two nights to walk the 100 miles. As they get closer the violet layer clears slightly and they are able to get a message through, to be told the crew waiting for them only have two days of oxygen left. They hardly have time to sleep and they force themselves to keep walking.

They make it just in time. Maurice gets to meet his uncle. They find out that the radar equipment on this first ship the Hermes, is intact even though the rest of the ship is too damaged to fly. They cannibalize the equipment and with the help of the exhausted crew from the Hermes, they make their way back to the *Ares*. They immediately replace their radar with that from the Hermes and all climb on board. They take off and for a few moments the tension rises as they wonder whether they will get through the Violet Layer and whether they will gain the proper escape velocity. They do, and at last they are on their way back to Earth and the Woomera Rocket base.

The final chapter is a summary as they are safely back at Woomera. They discuss what allowed them to actually rescue the lost crew of the Hermes when the position given was wrong. They had help in finding them but they wouldn't explain what that help was. The final conclusion is that Maurice will stay at Woomera and continue his training so he can take part in future missions rather than go back to school in England.

In a brief introduction to the revised volume now called **Voyage to Mars**, Sir Patrick explains that he thought it was a good story then and still thinks so today (2003) so he decided to rewrite it to bring it up to date with what has been discovered about Mars over the intervening 50 years.

When he wrote the original the Russians had not even put their first sputnik into space and the Americans had done even less. No one knew any real facts about Mars and basically could make up anything they wanted as long as it sounded reasonably possible. Most who wrote about Mars in the

1940s and 1950s followed certain suppositions. They all thought there was some kind of plant life on Mars and perhaps even primitive animals. They all believed it had a breathable or almost breathable atmosphere even though it was much less that the air pressure at sea level on Earth. They all assumed Mars was colder because it was further away from the sun, but no one suspected just how very cold it really was.

As a consequence, most stories about Mars written during that time exhibit the same faults. But does that necessarily make them bad? Unreadable? Or even ridiculous? Not at all. A modern reader can overlook the common misconceptions as long as the story is internally consistent and the characters are believable or sympathetic in some way.

The first thing that is obvious on reading the revised version is that the opening paragraphs of almost every chapter have had their sentences rearranged, not changed but slightly rearranged. Whether it reads better this way is doubtful, but obviously the author must have thought it would read a bit smoother. Other noticeable differences are with some of the vernacular, expressions that may be well understood in 1950 but in 2003 would unintelligible to a modern young reader.

For example, on page 38 of the original is the expression pluck. *Gray —if you've pluck enough to come with us!—* is changed to, Gray — *if you've courage enough to come with us!*

Another example is on page 68 in the original Maurice says, "*Phoof, I was dead away, and no mistake.*" Whereas in the revised edition he says, "*Phew, I was well gone, and no mistake.*"

All in, another expression used in the original appears as *exhausted* in the revised story.

Blast-off is changed from the original to *lift-off* in the revised story. *Going outside the space ship* is called an *EVA* in the revised story, and electronic monitoring devices and cathode tubes, used in the original story are referred to as computers in the revised version. They were something that never existed back in 1955.

In the original he describes the Martian sky as being deep blue with a hint of purple close to the horizon whereas in the revised version the sky is yellowish pink with a touch of mauve on the horizon.

It is interesting to note that in the original, Mellor is remembering that on Earth they speculated about whether the sky would be blue or white and of course it is dark blue, but Maurice says he doesn't care if it is pink with green spots as long as they could get out of the mess they find themselves in… Little did Patrick Moore realize it would be discovered years later that the sky actually is a pinkish colour.

In the original, Maurice sees something flying in the air some distance away but is not really sure on later reflection. In the revised story what he sees is a dust storm forming.

In the original there is quite a bit about moss like vegetation creating some of the green colour they see from space as they approach, and on the surface, there is quite a lot of scraggly vegetation. In the revised version the green colour is a result of mineral degradation or changes producing greenish coloured dust that blows away sometimes exposing darker rock underneath. Mars is dryer than they expected and there is no plant life anywhere. This is mentioned several times in the new text.

In the original, Mellor finds fossilized bones which he deduces are from a humanoid being.

In the revised he finds some bones but doesn't say what they are.

There are no changes to the temperatures encountered on Mars which in both versions ranged from 50 Fahrenheit during the heat of the day to minus 70 Fahrenheit during the night. Mars is really much colder than that. It was known as far back as 1929 that the temperature range near the equator was from +7 Celsius during the day to -90 Celsius during the night, far too cold to be sleeping out even in a space suit. Far more accurate temperatures have been measured all over the planet since then with atmospheric probes, and the rovers moving about on the surface. Mars is definitely a hostile planet, but one does not get that impression in either versions of the story. And as for the atmosphere, in the original it is mainly nitrogen, with oxygen, (certainly unbreathable) but only ten percent of the pressure at sea level on Earth. In the new version it is more realistic being mainly carbon dioxide.

There is a whole chapter deleted from the original. In it, Maurice and the others are sleeping on their trek to rescue the Hermes crew, when they are attacked by a slug-like vicious dog. Maurice shoots it and the others wake and fire shots at more that are lurking in the bushes. As Dawn approaches and they are continuing on their trek Maurice sees a flying bat-like creature that appears to be of hominid shape. It flies over them a couple of times and a bit later they see it attacked by the same slug-like dogs they shot at during the night. They race up and shoot the predators thus saving the hominid which flies away.

As they get further to their destination, they think they are lost. They keep trying to contact the Hermes but get no response. They are at the spot given in the coordinates in the message received at Woomera, but the Hermes isn't there. Time is running out; if they don't find them in the next few hours, they will be dead from lack of oxygen. It's at this moment that the bat-like hominid reappears. It flies over them and lands in front. It screeches at them and flaps back up into the air then lands further on, and screeches at them again. It does this a couple of times before they realize it is trying to get them to follow it. Maurice decides to call it Horace. They follow it in a different direction and just when they think it will be too late for the Hermes' crew, they see the wrecked space ship in the distance. They make it just in time to replenish the other team's oxygen and save them. Horace flaps away and is not seen again.

In the revised story there is no mention anywhere of life on Mars and Bruce decides to use a laser beam to bounce a Morse Code message off the surface of Deimos in the hope the Hermes' crew will see it. They do and they respond in kind. This is how they find the Hermes' location and save the crew. The crew also helps them by dismantling their intact radar guidance system and they transport this back to the *Ares* which enables all of them to escape from Mars.

In the original the bones they find are brought back to Earth and a paleontologist examines them and concludes the shoulder had a structure that allowed for wings of some kind. In the revised version the bones are looked upon as being more advanced than expected, and they wonder whether there was once an advanced Martian civilization.

Essentially though, the story is exactly the same in both books and even the modern revised version still feels like something written in the 1950s.

For myself, I preferred the original version even if in some parts it seemed quaint. It does have a sense of excitement that would have appealed to me when I was fifteen back in 1955. It still appealed to me today. The minor changes to the revised version do not make it any better or more readable, it just seems a bit old fashioned but with a few modern terms put into it. Why bother to revise it unless it is substantially different or more in line with what was known about Mars in 2002?

As for the following books, some things mentioned in the original version, Mission to Mars, are expanded or become pivotal parts of the following stories, which is perhaps why the other stories in the series were not revised or rewritten; they would end up as very different stories altogether. The most important element from the first story is that there are small scraggly plants growing in many areas. This was natural assumption —even by astronomers— because we know on Earth even in the most inhospitable desert areas hardy plants exist. For example, in parts of the Atacama Desert where it has never rained in recorded history a very hardy plant survives from the moisture that condenses out of the air during the night. It is not enough moisture to wet the ground, but it is enough for these particular plants. So why not something similar on Mars? Patrick Moore was not the only person to consider this, many authors of science fiction adventure stories also thought the same —right up until the mid-1960s when the first photographs of the Martian surface were sent back to Earth from Mariner 4 as it passed by the planet to show nothing but a barren cratered surface with no canals and no indication of plant life of any kind. Later flybys and rovers on the surface have subsequently confirmed this many times over. It doesn't mean Mars is not beautiful or enigmatic, it simply means it is not like what people had thought it was or would be.

The Domes of Mars (1956)

Takes place almost five years later. Maurice is now in his twenties and working at Woomera Rocket range as a qualified radar and radio operator. He has been selected to return to Mars to become part of a small permanent colony that has been established in the intervening five years. His two companions from his earlier rescue mission to Mars, Bruce Talbott, and Professor Mellor, already went back to Mars two years earlier and he is looking forward to reuniting with them soon. He wanted to go with them when they left but his uncle thought he was too young to make up his mind and wouldn't let him go. Most of the twenty-five people already there he knows because they trained and prepared for the voyage to Mars at Woomera.

On this voyage out there are five and the only odd one is a Romanian named Miroff who is an astronomer and who remains aloof from the other four members of the crew. He has no function on the voyage out other than to take photos of the stars. The leader of the expedition is a Dane, Alex Haller who is an engineer and pilot, and the rest of the crew are from England, Scotland and America.

Very quickly during the voyage out Miroff gets on everyone's nerves. He is irritating and hardly speaks to anyone unless it is to complain.

The only excitement this time on the voyage out is a meteorite hits the ship while almost everyone is asleep, passing through, blasting a hole in both sides of the hull. There is some loss of air but Maurice wakes up from a bad dream to realize the pressure has dropped so much it is difficult to breath. He rouses everyone and the two holes are soon repaired. Then about two thirds of the way they receive a radio message warning them not to come to Mars. "Lowell to E.5. Do not proceed. There is danger. You cannot help us. Return to Earth. Repeat, return to Earth"

But it's not possible to return. The ship must follow the trajectory. To alter it in any way would use up too much fuel rendering the ship unable to land. They have no choice but to proceed. Before they can get any clarification of the danger warned against, the signal is lost in the background static and solar radiation noise that ruins most radio broadcasts from Mars. They keep trying to contact the Mars base but no signal gets through the magnetic cloud layer in the Martian atmosphere.

Miroff insists they turn back so they can warn Earth, but is voted down by the others who all want to continue. They have friends on Mars and want to help them if it is possible. Miroff has no choice but to accept the decision and keeps out of everyone's way for the rest of the voyage to Mars. Arriving at Mars they experience problems coming down through the Violet Layer which upsets their guidance systems but they manage to land. Since the first two landings on Mars just over four years earlier the newer ships have been modified and improved so the magnetic effect of the layer isn't so pronounced. They land a few miles away from the Lowell base and will have to trek across the desert to get there.

Even on the surface they can't contact the base so they still have no idea of what the danger or the problem is. Maurice's two friends, Bruce and David, are there at the Lowell Dome. The Lowell Dome is actually a series of four domes that are inter-connected with tunnels. There are air locks at each end of each tunnel as well as elsewhere in the dome that lead outside. There is another dome, the Pickering Dome, a small single dome, which was built near where the first expedition's ship crashed. This is a much smaller dome and is the location of biological experiments involving plant hydroponics. There are four scientists over there. There was a cable strung between them so messages could be sent either way but this was damaged and no longer works.

Checking their gear Miroff decides he will remain behind since he doesn't want to trek to Lowell to find the base destroyed and have to come back again. The other four are happy to leave him there.

Leaving the ship, they soon find the cable that connects Lowell base with Pickering, but it is damaged and broken. They follow the cable and find the base, and immediately they see why the message wanted them to not to come. One of the four domes is completely destroyed while another is deflated with a huge tear in the higher part that formed the roof.

Catching up with his friends from the rescue mission four years earlier Maurice is told by Mellor that the air purification plant which uses atomic motors blew up destroying all their air purification equipment and set fire to the second dome. The only way to stop the fire was to cause a tear in the dome so the oxygen atmosphere was vented and that immediately snuffed out the fire. They only have enough oxygen stored to last them a few months unless they can repair the damaged equipment which doesn't look likely at that moment. The explosion also destroyed their link to Pickering dome and no one knows what is going on there where four botanists are experimenting with growing plants hydroponically.

Extra oxygen is brought over from their ship as well as Miroff who at first seems tame, but Bruce confides in Maurice that he doesn't trust him. The two of them go outside and inspect the ship the colonists came in at the landing spot near Lowell and discover that it has been refueled. Before they can inform Commander Jackson of their suspicions Miroff and three others sneak out and head for the ship. Unable to stop them in time, the deserters take off, and Maurice and the commander are injured from the exhaust blowing them over before they could get far enough away from the ship. The commander's helmet is damaged and unless he can get some oxygen he will suffocate. Maurice takes off his helmet, and holding his breath, switches it with the commander's helmet. People rush out from the dome to grab them but before they get there Maurice collapses and buries his face in the scraggly knobby plants covering the ground around the base. He imagines he is getting little whiffs of oxygen and this keeps him alive until he is rescued.

In reality, taking off or having a damaged helmet would probably be a death sentence on Mars. But in the 1950s Mars was still considered to be warmer than it really is, as well as having a higher atmospheric pressure (though much less than Earth's) than it actually does, even if it was unbreathable.

This business with Miroff, I suspect, was based on the existing cold war between Russian controlled Eastern Europe and America with Western Europe during the 1950s. Perhaps needing a villain for an act of treachery Patrick Moore decided to make him a Romanian malcontent. It no doubt added a touch of reality as readers of the time were well aware of the ongoing conflict of ideas and interests between the Russians and the Americans.

Stealing the ship that could have been used to take some of the colonists back to Earth has left all of them stranded and it is now absolutely imperative that they repair the oxygen producing machinery as soon as possible.

Maurice and Bruce set out to see what has happened to Pickering dome. On the way in a dust car, a vehicle with treads designed to traverse sand and dust more easily than a wheeled vehicle. On the way they pass a few plants that are much taller than expected. Similar to the knobby stunted plants around the base, these giant plants have large pods all over them. Maurice wonders what they are since he has never seen anything like that before. After almost burying themselves in a soft dust drift which took some trouble to extricate themselves, they are forced to abandon the dust car and continue of foot. They find the terrain they are passing through is covered with rows and rows of these massive plants festooned with large pods. It is obvious the arrangement is artificial and the two men wonder who or what could have planted this dense forest.

When they arrive at Pickering, they are welcomed by the people there, and inside the dome they discover that the forest plants, some of which are growing inside, have been cultivated and planted. The pods when burst give off oxygen and they don't need a machine to produce it. As soon as the pods burst the plant dies and a new one starts growing. Professor Charles Whitton is the biologist in charge of developing Martian plants into something useful. These giant ones are the same as the stunted knobby scrub that grows everywhere.

The four people at Pickering had no idea of what had happened at Lowell and were wondering why no one had come over before. Maurice explained but was also excited to know that they no longer needed machinery to extract oxygen. With these plants they would never have to worry about it again. Whitton suggests that with enough of these growing over the whole planet —they do spread very rapidly— they could soon start adding oxygen to the Martian atmosphere and in time could do away with pressure suits and oxygen masks. Lowell can throw its atomic purifiers onto the scrap heap and never have to worry about oxygen again.

The problem is they simply can't trek the 100 miles back to Lowell and carry the plants. They wouldn't live that long and once they die, they don't produce oxygen. Lowell is still in as much danger as ever regarding its oxygen supplies. Maurice suggests they get everyone at Lowel to come over here to Pickering, which will be crowded, but there would be abundant oxygen because of the plants. They try to send a radio message but the Violet Layer's magnetic field prevents radio communication. Not even Morse Code gets through.

Since Pickering was built beside the crashed original ship from the first expedition, Maurice suggests that if there is enough fuel, he may be able to get the ship to lift up enough into the atmosphere to jump over to Lowell 100 miles away. It's worth a try.

Maurice and Bruce blast off but the Violet Layer causes problems and they go higher than expected and run out of enough fuel to land properly. The ship comes down much further away than Maurice hoped and there is just enough thrust left to partially brake, but the ship still crashes and Bruce is injured. The problem as always is oxygen. Is there enough to last until someone from Lowell can get to them? Maurice goes out alone to see if he can get up on a high dune from where he can send a radio message to call for help. He does and keeps sending so the rescue dust car will have a direction to aim for. Very soon after they are rescued, just in time.

At the end, everyone has trekked across the 100 miles to the small Pickering Dome which was designed for five people and not thirty. But quickly they build a larger dome nearby and having a forest of oxygen producing plants all around means they will never need the atomic air purifying plant again. Staring across the Martian plains covered with these plants Maurice finally considers himself to be man of Mars.

All plants produce oxygen as a by-product of converting Carbon dioxide into a food source; it's how we got the oxygen in our atmosphere.

Moore wasn't the first to use that idea transposed to Mars. Arthur C Clarke did it in 1951 with The Sands of Mars, wherein he has a plant that has pods filled with oxygen that the colonists can extract. The plants Clarke describes, are like the forests of giant kelp that grow in the ocean along the coast of California and other places. Anchored to the sea floor, the bulk of the kelp floats upwards with hundreds of pods filled with air to make it buoyant. He transposed this idea to a similar plant he has on Mars, among others.

Without a doubt Patrick Moore would have read this book since they were contemporaries and also knew each other. Whether he was influenced by the idea of oxygen producing plants as a result is moot. He could simply have had the same logical thoughts that led Clarke to come up with the idea, so he too came up with a similar concept for oxygen producing plants that could save the colony and be effective eventually in changing the Martian atmosphere to something more amenable to humans.

The Voices of Mars (1957)

The story opens with Maurice, Bruce Talbott and David Hellor in an area covered with the oxygen pod plants that had been developed 10 years earlier. There are now almost 200 people on Mars and the two locations where bases had been established have grown considerably, so much so that those on Mars think of them as cities. Maurice Bruce and David are in an area about 100 miles from Lowell which is closer than Pickering, searching for a likely spot to establish another 'city' to house the expanding population. They have established a small dome inside which they can relax without wearing their pressure suits. When anyone is outside the main domes for any length of time it is mandatory to report back twice a day via radio to reassure the base that they are all right. Two tears previously a small dome being set in a different location blew up killing everyone inside, and no one knew about it until much later. Nobody wants something like that to happen again.

Maurice is some distance away deep in the forest of cultivated plants that are rapidly spreading across many desert areas. Heading back, he hears a rustling noise in the canopy of the plants and stops to investigate. He sees something strange and he calls Bruce to come and have a look. Bruce appears and they capture together an insect like creature reminiscent of a dragon fly only much larger. David is amazed and immediately starts speculating about how a 'whacking great' dragonfly could get to Mats. He makes an analogy with Earth and how insects soon appeared not long after plants developed suggesting that on Mars there weren't anything like insects here until we developed the oxygen pod plants. That is quite silly and wouldn't even be considered today… and not in this story, or the second one, Domes of Mars, is there any mention of the slug-dog like predator or the winged bat-like hominid creature —which implies a well-developed ecology because where there is one there must be others— they rescued and which later helped them find the way to the wrecked ship and his uncle. It was part of the climax to Mission to Mars, the first story in the series. It's as if those things never happened, which seems odd when they begin to speculate about how this insect like creature is living in the forest the human settlers planted and let run wild. When David asks were there others Maurice says he didn't see any.

Before they can do much else, when they contact the radio base on Deimos the operator warns them to evacuate the area immediately because they are in urgent danger. The danger is that something has sparked a fire in the forest of oxygen pod bearing plants and as each pod explodes it also bursts into flames and with the heat spreading rapidly as the plants burn and shrivel, they are likely to be trapped. They can't survive the fire since their plastic suits and the dome itself would melt.

They stuff the insect creature into an empty oxygen tank and grab what they need. They take the dust-car they arrived in and head through the forest towards more open desert, but they are cut off and have to retreat back to the dome. On the way back, the car is wrecked and they abandon it. Making their way on foot Maurice remembers a clear spot where no plants grow and suggests they dig a hole in which to escape the fire. But the ground is as hard as rock and they barely scratch the surface. The closer the fire gets the harder they dig. A softer spot allows them to penetrate a short distance down but a hard-brittle surface is encountered. Desperately they keep digging. If they can't escape the heat generated by the burning oxygen they will die. Suddenly the hard surface breaks and Maurice tumbles down into a massive hole. He calls out that he is okay and the other two jump in after him.

The fire roars by overhead and they are safe deep inside what appears to be a cave. The only problem is they are 20 feet down and it is very dark. They can't see a way to get back up. By the time they manage to get back onto the surface the fire has spent itself, and all they can do is wait beside the melted dome until they are rescued. A helicopter from Lowell is on its way.

Despite its tension and excitement, I have my doubts that a fire, like a bush-fire or massive grass-fire would burn on Mars as it would on Earth. There is no oxygen in the Martian atmosphere. Even if the pods on the plants are full of oxygen, would not the flames be extinguished the moment the pod burst and the gas dissipates? Logical or not, likely or not, it makes a good opening to a story and gets the reader involved from the very beginning.

In the helicopter the pilot informs them that two emissaries from the United Nations are at Lowell and they are there to assess the viability of the Mars experiment. It is costing millions of pounds, dollars and whatever other currency, and the United Nations Council wants to close it down and take everyone back to Earth. The problem with that is those settlers who have been on Mars the longest will die if they return to the much heavier gravity of Earth. A couple of senior Mars colonists returned a while back and they died shortly after landing of heart failure. After years of living in a gravity field one third that of Earth, the body's muscles have wasted away. Especially the heart muscles. They can't pump enough blood through the body against the higher gravity and collapse. The longer someone has been on Mars the less likely they would be to survive a return to Earth. To close the colony down would in effect murder a third of them, those that have been there the longest. And at this point in the story the colony has existed for just on fifteen years. Only those who arrived most recently on Mars would survive being returned to live on Earth, the other would not have a chance.

This doesn't bother the representative, Ensor. He is vying for leadership of the UN and thinks that by saving the taxpayers the millions it costs to maintain the Mars colony, he will be elected leader. That's all he cares about. He won't listen to any other arguments. His excuse to come to Mars was to find out the real facts and report back to the UN.

Since the meeting he wanted with the whole colony has been postponed until later in the day he decides to go out with his assistant to look at the damage done by the fire. While there he radios back that his assistant Zarev has disappeared. Maurice, Bruce and David go back with the camp commander Jackson flying the helicopter to help look for the missing person, while Ensor pointedly stays beside the wrecked dome.

Maurice suspects he fell into the hole that saved them during the fire, so they go there and climb down. The discover further back an opening that is a narrow tube leader deeper underground and they follow that. They are crawling through a lava tube. Further in Maurice discovers a pile of bones that look as if they belong to a lizard like creature, but they don't have time to collect them, they need to rescue the envoy. They find he has fallen down a deeper hole. It seems that the floor under him had collapsed and down he went. Jackson is seriously injured when he too falls into the hole as the edge crumbles. The others rescue the unconscious Jackson first, then they retrieve Zarev who immediately heads back to join Ensor.

When they make their way out of the lava tube and the large cave, they discover Ensor and Zarev have taken one of the helicopters and flown back to Lowell. When they try to start the other helicopter, they find it has been sabotaged. It takes several hours to fix it enough to fly. They take off and head back, but their temporary repairs don't last and they are forced down with still forty or so miles to go. Another helicopter is sent from Lowell to collect them. By the time they get back to Lowell Ensor and his assistant Zarev have already commandeered a rocket and have departed for Earth. Apart from being a liar, he is also a saboteur, and if he gets back to Earth and tells a story that convinces the UN committee to close down the colony, there is nothing the colonists can do except return which for probably half of them would mean certain death.

The only solution is to send people from Mars to counteract whatever Ensor is doing.

They decide to send two ships, the only two they have left. The first one will have a crew of three who have been the least amount of time on Mars and would therefore survive the greater gravity of Earth, while the crew in the second ship would orbit Earth without landing but be able to talk to the UN Council via radio to put their case forward. In the second ship are Maurice, David and Bruce.

They take off okay and when the make contact with Mars to report a successful takeoff they are told the first ship had mechanical problems and couldn't takeoff. It's up to them to orbit Earth and convince the UN Council not to abandon the Mars Colony. Of course, there is no going back once on a trajectory to Earth. They have to go all the way, orbit the planet, and hope for the best. After that they can return to Mars. The whole voyage there and back would take almost a year.

In Earth orbit they contact Woomera Control and ask if they can broadcast their side of the story but permission is denied. The assembly is going to hold the meeting in private with only council members to vote and only Ensor's report for them to consider.

Mellor decides their only option is to land even if it is likely to kill him. The two younger men may withstand the Earth's gravity long enough to make a presentation at the meeting. As they land the meeting is in progress and the men are taken out of the ship into waiting ambulances. Mellor is so white he appears dead and is taken immediately to hospital. Maurice and Bruce have great difficulty in moving even an arm let alone stand up. They are taken to the General Assembly meeting and ushered in. By the time they arrive Maurice is able to lift his arms and his head isn't hurting too much although his heart is pounding away desperately trying to pump blood around his system against the greater force of Earth's gravity. Carried inside by two helpers each they are placed on chairs near the meeting table. Ensor is furious and doesn't want them heard, but the adjudicator of the meeting allows it. He wants to hear voices of Mars.

Maurice struggles to stand up, and holding the table for support he addresses the assembly. His uncle holds a microphone in front of him so all can hear. He tells them how the trips to Mars began, the rescue mission, and the establishment of the colony. He explains how Whitten developed plants that can produce oxygen which in a few hundred years will make the atmosphere breathable for humans, and he maintains that within fifty years the colony would be independent of Earth, and of the costs to maintain it. He tells of the duplicity of Ensor and how he sabotaged the helicopter to prevent them getting back to stop him leaving, and how the workers around the rockets were lied to so Ensor and Zarev could leave. Ensor lied when he said the Martians attacked him and Zarev. Zarev wandered off and got lost and it was Maurice himself, Bruce and David now in the hospital, who found him in the cave system and rescued him. He explains how the lesser gravity has made the muscles of those on Mars atrophy to the extent that after a few years there no one can return safely to Earth. The heart simply hasn't the strength to pump blood around the body because of the greater gravity, it pumps so hard it collapses. forcing the two hundred to return will be like murdering forty or fifty of them, the ones who had been there the longest. Earth's much greater gravity will kill them, make no mistake about that. He himself is an example of how impossible it would be to return.

While he was struggling to tell his story, Bruce had already slipped into unconsciousness and as Maurice finally concludes his plea, he too collapses. They are both immediately taken to hospital.

What Maurice nor the assembly knew was that Yorke, Maurice's uncle and the first man on Mars, had arranged for an outside broadcast and the whole of Australia heard Maurice's speech, and shortly thereafter the rest of the world. There was no way the public would allow them to close down the colony if it means murdering half the people up there in the process.

Maurice wakes up on board a space ship orbiting Earth. The only way to cure them or help them was to get the three of them into a gravity free environment. The doctor tells them when he is sure they are all right they can leave for Mars, and that when they do, he will accompany them. And the assembly...? They wisely decided not to bring the colonists back to Earth.

Maurice knows they can never return to Earth again. He looks out at the planet below them and understands that Mars is where he belongs and when he thinks of Mars he is thinking of home.

It is interesting to note that there is not one female character in any of these stories. All the characters are men, and presumably all the 200 or so people on Mars are also men. Also interesting is that in my secondhand copy of **Mission to Mars** it has the name Margaret Waller – and her address in Middlesex inscribed in red ink inside the front cover, and a note inside the back cover in the same handwriting which says, *this is a jolly good book.*

I couldn't agree more!

In the revised version of the first book Patrick Moore substituted one male radio operator at the Woomera Rocket base control room with a female character, but she only appears in the early part of the book. Perhaps when these stories were written in the early to mid-1950s there were not many women involved in the sciences, (especially in Britain) and since the stories were aimed at teenage boys, possibly the author presumed they wouldn't be interested in female protagonists in any case. This doesn't make the stories bad or sexist or anything else; they are still enjoyable stories. Some of the speculative science is a bit old fashioned because nothing much was really known about Mars, or about space travel at that time, but as always, there was a lot of speculation. The language used in some scenes is rather quaint and old-fashioned, and this does give the three books a certain charm.

Comparing them to Arthur C Clarke's **The Sands of Mars,** and to his contemporary E C Tubb who wrote five or six novels with Mars featuring prominently, Moore's three books are definitely written for the younger reader, and I would suggest the British reader rather than an American reader. There is a simplicity about them that is endearing. Although Clarke's story did have teenage protagonists, a teenage boy on the ship going to Mars and a teenage girl, the only girl on Mars, and inevitably they fall in love, they were subsidiary to the main character and the story about the development of the Martian colony and its means of gaining independence from Earth.

On the other hand, Tubb's novels of Mars have a gritty noir feeling and sense of moribund maturity because they were aimed at an adult American audience rather than young adult readers. Tubb was also a British author but he knew the major market for his work was in the US.

The first three of Patrick Moore's five Mars books can be considered as one story (divided into three parts) and are complete as a story.

Part one: rescuing an ill-fated first mission, part two: returning to Mars to establish a colony, and part three: fighting to save the colony from being shut down, concluding with a positive resolution for the future continuation of the Mars colony. Maurice, Bruce, and David are the three people featured across the three books, and as well in the two subsequent books that continue the story of the settlement of Mars.

I suspect the fourth and fifth books were created as a response to the popularity of the first three.

Peril on Mars (1958) begins ten years after the conclusion of the near disastrous Earth trip in Voices of Mars, with Maurice and Bruce on Deimos where a radio station has been established for long distance communication with Earth as well as short distance communication with Mars. They receive a message that an inbound ship from Earth has on board a passenger as well as the usual supplies. They are anxious for news of Earth because there is political upheaval and serious threats of war, but as in all the other stories radio communication is never very certain because of the solar radiation as well as the magnetic Violet Layer in Mars' atmosphere.

When the supply ship 'lands' on Deimos they discover the passenger is a 17-year-old boy who is small for his age and only looks about thirteen. Richard Rawn is about the same age as was Maurice when he first came to Mars on the rescue mission. (***Mission to Mars)***

I suspect Patrick Moore introduced this new character so his focus could remain on someone young, since Maurice and Bruce are now twenty years older than they were at the beginning. The following two books have Rick as the feature character with all the others from the earlier three books taking subsidiary roles. All of these Mars books are written for younger readers.

There is some talk about the possibility of a war on Earth and although the ship's pilot would rather remain on Mars, (he has come back to stay in the fifth and final book) he has an obligation to return to Earth because his crew has family there and would want to be with them in case of war. Moments after we meet Rick, an emergency call from comes from David Mellor asking Maurice and Bruce to take the shuttle and fly down to a new base called Huygens Dome which is on the other side of the planet from Lowell, the first and main base on Mars. Something has gone wrong and no one knows what because radio communication is currently impossible.

They have no choice but to take the newcomer Richard, (they call him Rick) with them. Either that or he has to return to Earth with the supply ship since they can't leave him alone on Deimos. Of course, he agrees to go with them down to Mars.

The rest of the story is an exciting adventure and if this was a stand-alone novel it would be a terrific read. But it is part of an ongoing series and it introduces something here that simply doesn't fit with the earlier novels.

Although it mentions the experiments from the second book that created the oxygen producing plants and the fact that they spread very rapidly, and that if not careful a disastrous fire could result because of the oxygen in the leaves and pods, he has added life forms that simply couldn't exist. Although these vicious life forms are an integral part of this story, needed for the drama and excitement of the experience young Rick has, they are jarring from my perspective.

The author comes up with the theory that on Earth, when plants invaded the land, animals soon followed, and the implication is that because of the plants, animals spontaneously came into existence. He postulates that because on Mars Professor Whitten had developed these oxygen producing plants from the original small stunted versions that grew in some parts of Mars, allowing them to proliferate has also allowed animals or in this case large insects to appear. He claims that evolution on Mars is proceeding far more rapidly than it did on Earth and what took millions of years on Earth only takes weeks or months on Mars. The idea itself is ridiculous, but perhaps no more so than any other ideas prominent in SF stories during the 1950s.

The shuttle crashes in the desert about 40 miles from Huygens Dome which is in the middle of a large forest of the oxygen plants. Rick, Maurice and Bruce have no choice but to walk through the forest to the dome. Via their suit radios they have made contact, and the three people are there warn them to be very careful traversing the forest.

Rick encounters one of the dragonfly type creatures and is amazed but while he watches another more vicious flying thing with a sharp snout and lots of teeth rips it in half and starts toward the three men. It doesn't fly very fast and they manage to escape it only to stumble upon a nest of these 'vile' creatures who immediately launch an attack. Bruce is bitten on the leg near his ankle and quickly succumbs to poisons infection. Rick and Maurice manage to carry Bruce and escape the slow flying predators. They make their way across a cleared space to Huygens Dome where two people are waiting to help them inside.

Rick immediately treats Bruce's ankle and extracts the poison. He has had medical training and although not a qualified doctor yet, he has completed most of the training and is able to treat Bruce.

Unfortunately, they are trapped at Huygens. The other member of the team there took one of the two helicopters to fly back to Lowell for help. The other helicopter there is damaged and won't fly properly.

The rest of the story concerns the battle for survival of the inhabitants of Huygens as they try to survive against an ever-increasing onslaught of the flying predators. It appears they are developing a rudimentary form of intelligence and they are coordinating their attacks in response to what the dome's inhabitants try to do to prevent them from entering. They manage to partially fix the damaged helicopter and Rick flies it up above the dome as high as it can go so he can radio a message for help that might get through to Howell, as well as to warn them that they should be careful of the oxygen plants near their dome because they will be full of the developing predator insects.

Forced to go outside to get some oxygen plants to replenish the dome's supply the insect predators hide eggs in the plants and they hatch out within minutes of being inside the dome. They attack in such a controlled and vicious way that the remaining people in the dome are forced to put on their pressure suits and exit the dome. Apart from all that there is the very sudden appearance of large lizard like things that remind them of dinosaurs, which leads the scientists in the dome to speculate more about the rapidity of Martian evolution. The whole idea is just so improbable that in my view it ruins the story, but I have no doubt that in 1958 teenage boys in England would have devoured this story with unbridled enthusiasm. It is an exciting read, a thrilling adventure, and everything happens at such a pace it is difficult to put the book down.

Rick, after sending the message for help is returning down to the dome when a dust storm blows him way off course and he crashes into the desert. Those left in the dome think he is lost. Oddly coincidental, he crashes not far from where the other helicopter was forced down and the occupant of that vehicle joins him. Together they send a message using their search lights aimed at Phobos where a manned radio station has been built. The occupants of that station see the SOS and notify Howell which sends someone to rescue them. Together they fly back to Huygens where they rescue the remaining occupants. The forest is then sterilized and all the insects killed. All the forests will to be sterilized over the next few months to prevent further evolutionary developments. All they want are the plants, not the insects and animals that spontaneously developed. The main point of this story is that Rick proves he is adaptable to changes in circumstances and that he is reliable and with his medical training, more than very useful.

In my view, the spontaneous development of insects and animals is an anomaly. Surely the author could have come up with a better idea, although perhaps it wouldn't have been as exciting.

Another anomaly is from the first story in the series where Maurice and Bruce save a huge bat-like hominid flying creature from a bunch of predatory dog-like slugs, and this creature appears intelligent and leads them to the people they want to rescue. This implies a Martian evolution that is quite different from anything mentioned in the following books. In the second book these life forms are entirely forgotten and the author maintains the only life around is the small moss-like plants that give off oxygen which are what are later developed into the large oxygen bearing plants that grow into the forests, and which saves them as a colony by guaranteeing an abundant and continuous supply of oxygen.

It is in the third book that the idea of spontaneous generation of insects is suggested, although not directly. I got the feeling that somehow a small dragonfly could have accidentally been transported from Earth on a supply ship. And why a dragonfly? These creatures need water, rivers and lakes, none of which exist on Mars, not even in Patrick Moore's books. Mars is a dust bowl of rock, sand dunes and super-fine dust. No water anywhere. Would it not have been better to imagine an insect akin to a cockroach rather than a dragonfly? That would seem more likely to be accidentally transported to Mars than a dragonfly. Those things would probably survive anywhere. (But not on Mars as we know it today.) There is also a slight hint that the dragon-fly creature could harbour a rudimentary intelligence.

It's in the fourth book where the idea of spontaneously generated life takes precedence and is the basis of the whole story with the sudden appearance of vicious predatory insects as well as large lizards like dinosaurs. Fortunately, the action in the story is so intense it overshadows the silly idea of spontaneous generation of life that mimics Earth's early development.

The fifth book takes a different idea and this turns out to be a fitting finale to a good overall sequence of stories.

Raiders of Mars (1959)

Mars is now a sanctuary. Over the twenty years since the first habitats were constructed at Lowell Base the population has grown considerably. There are several more habitats scattered across Mars, and since the Seven-day War on Earth during which atomic lithium bombs devastated all major cities, several thousand people have come to Mars to avoid further conflicts on Earth and to find a stable environment in which to live.

The war has been over for six years as the story opens. Maurice and Bruce are on their way to Deimos radio base for a routine check when the intercept part of a strange message, something about suspicions aroused, situation requires watching. Unable to make sense of it they call Deimos to let them know they are just about to arrive. Ferrier, the man who wants to remain alone on Deimos welcomes them when they arrive but during the process of discussing activities and the possibility that they might visit another scientist, Werner Kronstein at Newton Base near the North Pole, Ferrier suddenly attacks Bruce and Maurice knocking them down and when they wake up, they find themselves tied up.

Nothing has been heard from Newton Base for several months, other than a report that says experiments still proceeding, everything is normal, no one has any idea of what is happening there.

After a routine flight check of the nearby forest of oxygen plants to check if there was any more animal or insect development, (of which there is none) Rick, along with Yang Cheng and Pierre DuBois, both relative newcomers who arrived after the recent war, are joking about whether there are any real Martians or not as they return to Lowell city where they are asked to go the Newton Dome to see what they can find out. Bruce and Maurice were going to go there on their way back from Deimos. "*That is unwise,*" Yang informs them, "*has Kronstein been told?*"

Apparently Kronstein doesn't tolerate interference with his work.

Something is going on at Newton and they need to find out what it is. They organize to take two helicopters, with Yang and Dubois in one while Rick, is in the other with Norman Knight. The flight is initially uneventful until Yang calls them and says he can see ruins of an ancient Martian city.

As they fly over the area Yang's helicopter suddenly goes into a spin and dives down into the ground. The tail of the helicopter is broken in the crash and the two men crawl out as the other helicopter lands. While Yang insists that he had no control over the helicopter, the others decide to walk over to the nearby Martian ruins to examine them.

At the ruins they uncover a door which they somehow trigger to open. Rick and Knight, and Dubois tentatively enter into a long tunnel sloping downwards. They go a short distance in and suddenly the door behind them closes trapping them inside the ancient ruins. They race back but cannot open it. They realize that Yang must have closed the door, that he knew about the ruins and had been here before. There's no way out, they are trapped, and all they can do is venture further into the ruins to search for another way out. They go deeper and deeper, until they find a central area where several tunnels lead off. They choose to take one that appears to be going up rather than down.

But before going too far their torch batteries fail and they are left to grope along in total darkness. Finally, they see a glimmer of light and they make their way towards it. It is another door but the light comes from a crack in the metal and rock above it. The crack is just narrow enough for Rick, the skinniest and smallest of them to squeeze through, only to do that he has to take off his clothes and pressure suit. He will have to hold his breath because the Martian atmosphere can't be breathed. One of them takes Rick's helmet so he can give it to him the moment the door opens.

They succeed in escaping and back at the crashed helicopter they find the radio has been smashed deliberately and they can't call for help. They can't fix the smashed undercarriage but they contrive a way to repair the tail strut using the soft Martian metal from inside the tunnel where they saw a large hangar with many ancient machines.

They manage to take off but whenever they land the whole thing will collapse and won't be able to take off again. Their only choice is to continue on to Newton Base since Lowell is too far behind them and don't have enough fuel. On the way they receive a distress call. Reluctantly they divert to help save the victim of a crashed helicopter who is trapped in the machine only to find it is Yang. His legs are trapped in the wreckage. They debate whether to leave Yang to die there or to try and rescue him. Yang understands that since he left them to die, he could expect nothing else in return. However, they do rescue him and all fly to Newton. It's Yang who tells them what is going on. Kronstein and Ferrier were the two scientists on Earth who created the lithium bombs which were given to the various World leaders who in turn used them to destroy their enemies thinking they had an advantage. Millions of people died during those seven days of war and Kronstein and Ferrier are wanted as war criminals. People on Earth believe that they died since no one has seen them since the war. But they disguised themselves as refugees and came to Mars. On Mars they have been developing an atomic lithium bomb which they plan to use on Lowell, to destroy it, so they can have complete control of the planet. They tried on earth and it didn't work, so now they will settle for Mars instead. There are people in Lowell city who could recognize them and they don' t want that to happen. The bomb is now ready and they are about to use it.

When they land at Newton Kronstein welcomes them as if everything is normal except, they find when they go to bed in the quarters given to them, they are locked in.

Back on Deimos Ferrier has put Maurice and Bruce into a small shuttle with no fuel for landing and no space suits so they can't escape, and sent the rocket into a decaying orbit around Mars. They will be able to watch the destruction of Lowell City before they suffocate and burn up on entry into the Martian atmosphere.

In Newton, in the middle of the night, the locked door opens and Yang enters. He explains that for saving his life he is obliged to save theirs by allowing them to escape. The rocket outside is fueled up and they can get in and take off, giving them time to warn the others of the impending destruction of Lowell. He has fueled a sand-car and left it by the airlock for them to use to get to the rocket. Rick and Norman escape but Dubois doesn't make it. They warn David Mellor and insist he evacuate the base which is what starts to happen.

They continue on to Deimos in the rocket and confront Ferrier and his couple of assistants who immediately take them prisoner. They are about to be executed when Mellor arrives to save the day. Once they know what happened to Maurice and Bruce, Rick and Knight with Mellor set out to catch the rocket in orbit in which Maurice and Bruce are trapped.

When they find them, the problem is then how to get them out of the doomed shuttle. The air lock has been damaged so once it opens all the air will be let out into space, and the two in the ship have no space suits. How they solve this is as thrilling and nail biting as anything imagined by Hollywood filmmakers, and is a highlight of the story.

Once out they head back down to Mars and Lowell City which has now been evacuated. The search then goes on for the helicopter in which Kronstein will deliver the bomb. He doesn't know his plan has been compromised. With helicopters flying patrols around the area of Lowell City as far out as twenty miles they eventually find Kronstein's helicopter and force it down by dropping another helicopter on top of it so it crashes. Kronstein is killed, the bomb doesn't go off, and Mars is saved.

This whole story is a nail-biting finish to the 4 other novels, even though the idea of two megalomaniacs trying to control a whole world is somewhat dated these days, but it was a popular trope in stories and films right through the 1950s and on into the 1960s. It fits into this story and in the context does seem appropriate.

There are no female characters mentioned in any of the stories. Only once are women and children mentioned, and that is in the final book where a brief sentence refers to them being in one of the other dome cities, and presumably they came to Mars after the Seven-day War on earth as refugees seeking a better life.

My feeling is that this irrevocably dates the books to the 1950s when women stayed at home, were rarely seen in any workplace, and only boys had exciting adventures. Girls were never mentioned. Apart from that, the stories are enjoyable if we consider the time in which they were written and published.

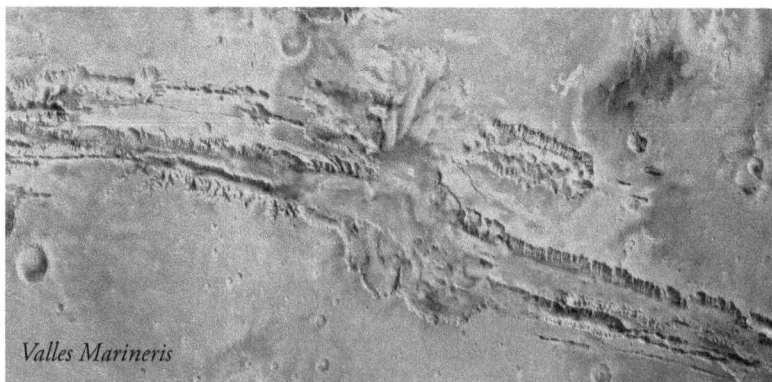

Valles Marineris

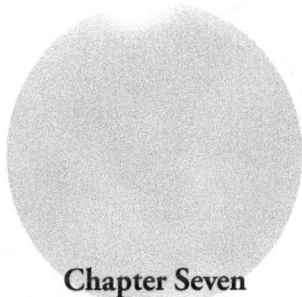

Chapter Seven

The end of the Golden Age

As 1960 rolled on no one knew that in five years, their perceptions of Mars would be forever changed. NASA had successfully launched its **Mariner 4** probe which took 7 months to get to Mars, arriving in July 1965, after which, on seeing the images sent back to Earth, no one would ever look at Mars in the same way that they had previously. (See chapter seven, The new reality of Mars – *Dreams of Mars* page 165.) But until that event, writers continued as usual, imagining whatever they wanted as long as it seemed reasonably logical based on what was generally thought to be true about Mars.

Lost Race of Mars by Robert Silverberg
Aged 25 in 1960, Robert Silverberg already had published several novels before this one. His first novel, *Revolt on Alpha C*, was published in hardcover in 1955, and then in Paperback in 1960. *The 13th Immortal* was published in 1957, *Starman's Quest* in 1958.
He was a student at school when he sold his first short stories.
Revolt on Alpha C was accepted in 1953, (while he was still a school student) but not paid for nor published until two years later. His career as a science fiction writer began with the sale of that novel. And what a prolific writer he became! There were times when his stories filled whole magazines, but because of his prolificity, many of them were published using pseudonyms. In 1956 he published 54 short stories apart from also working on novels for young adult readers (once known as juveniles). 1957 was even better with 85 short stories published, 66 in 1958 and 43 in 1959. After that his short story output diminished but his production of novels increased both under his own name as well as a combined name, Robert Randall, used with co-author Randall Garret.

Like his contemporaries, the only way to make a living as a writer was to produce vast quantities of stories to fill the voracious appetites of the readers of popular pulp magazines.

As pulp magazines began to wane, the popularity of short novels, (often with two published back to back as with Ace novels) increased. Payment was better so writers concentrated more on writing novels than short stories. There were a couple of years over the next ten when Silverberg only produced one short story, spending his working time writing novels.

Lost Race of Mars was first published in hardcover by *John C Winston Company* in 1960.

It was illustrated with line drawings by Leonard Kessler. It was aimed at teenage readers between the ages of 12 to 16 so was classified as a juvenile. It was later published as a paperback, with the same illustrations, by *Scholastic Book Services* in 1964 — and this is the copy I have.

Jim and Sally Chambers, brother and sister, travel to Mars with their parents who are both scientists, and who have won a grant to research life on Mars for one (Earth) year. The children are excited. They have heard the stories of the lost race of Mars and can't wait to go searching for them.

Mars doesn't turn out to be as friendly as they expected. Their parents struggle to get enough equipment allocated to them for their research, which the colonists consider a waste of time. They see no practical benefits from such research. Jim and Sally are ostracized at school and no one wants to be friends. The whole family is considered to be a burden, using up oxygen and resources that could be used better elsewhere. The kids are taken on a tour of an old cave where ancient Martians once lived and they see paintings and drawings that show them what the Martians looked like. They also see a couple of dead mummified remains that are so desiccated they cannot see any features other than they had spindly legs and arms with a rather large head. They are laughed at by everyone when they express a desire to look for other caves where some of the old Martians might still live. "They've been extinct for tens of thousands of years," they are told.

Mars is described as mostly desert, with no mountains left since they have been worn down over millions of years by endless sandstorms. The water that once existed as lakes and seas had dried up and the few plants that struggle to survive, do so because they have enormous root systems that go far beneath the surface to find remnants of water. The sky is described as deep blue, rather like it appears at a very high altitude on Earth. Animals that are brought to Jim and Sally's parents on the promise of extra food vouchers are small rodent-like creatures no bigger than mice, and one tortoise thing. The only other animals ever seen resemble a cross between a spider and a crab, and there are many of them scuttling around out in the desert. Then one day a miner turns up with something that looks like a cat with two kittens. One of the kittens is immediately adopted by the children who miss their cat back on Earth, while the cat and the other kitten are examined by their parents.

No one has seen any animals like this on Mars before and suddenly the other children at the school all want to be friends with Jim and Sally. Still, they scoff when Jim and Sally again say they want to go in search of the old Martians. No one believes they exist. Even a few of the original settlers who once claimed to have seen them no longer believe in their existence.

One morning Jim and Sally contrive to borrow a sand crawler vehicle so they can go exploring. They pretended to borrow it for their father whom they say wants to go exploring in the nearby caves for other specimens to study. They take their new pet cat with them as they head out into the desert. Several hours out a sandstorm blows up and they are blown away, becoming lost. When the storm clears, they have no idea where they are. While stepping out to look around, their new cat leaps out and runs towards a large outcrop of rock. It disappears at the base. Jim and Sally chase after it. They don't want it to be lost or they would have a lot of explaining to do when they get back. They crawl down into a low cave entrance where similar steps are carved into the rack as were seen in their earlier exploration. But unlike that place standing right in front of them and holding their new pet is an old Martian. The old Martian is described as looking like a grey gnome, with spindly legs and a large head. He is smiling up at them, because they are so much taller. The old Martian asks them to come on down, not to be afraid.

Astonished that they can understand his English, they soon learn that communication with Martians is telepathic. Language doesn't matter. The Martian thanks them for looking after their animal (also a pet to them) and goes on to explain how they live, what kind of plants they use for food, for lighting the caves, for producing oxygen, storing water and so on. They are also told that they fear Earthmen and so remain hidden, that no Earthman can ever find out where they live. All entrances to their underground habitats are mentally hidden and cannot be seen by any humans passing by.

Worried because they are lost, and knowing that the colonists will be searching for them, they explain they must return. The Martian offers to guide them back to their dome. When he does that and sees other sand crawlers approaching, he disappears, leaving the children to convince their parents and the other colonists of what they discovered.

No one believes them. Even their father at first doesn't believe them, but he is eventually convinced. He wants to go back out with them to get samples of the plants the Martians use in their habitats; they would be beneficial to humans. He thinks if they could plant them all over Mars, they could help regenerate the lost atmosphere. To make Mars more livable again.

The Martians will not allow us to see them if there are adults with us, the children explain, so they would have to go out alone. The manager of the colony finally agrees to allow the children to go out once more, but they have to bring back samples, take photographs of the Martians and of their habitats, in order to convince him they are telling the truth.

The children go back out into the desert, and once again they encounter the old Martians who allow them to take photos, plant samples, and seeds, with which the children finally convince the colonists that the Old Martian Race is still alive and surviving, even though they will never be allowed to see them. Proof that Old Martians still exist is big news on Earth and the government allows the family an indefinite grant to stay on Mars to continue their research. And suddenly, they have all the equipment they need for their research, as well as the promise that whatever else they may need will be shipped up from Earth. The children however make one final request. They ask that their cat, left back on Earth, can be shipped up to them, since their new catlike pet has returned to its rightful owners, the Martians.

As one would expect, looking at it almost 60 years after it was first published, it isn't up to the standard or the depth of the works Silverberg produced later in his career, but for 14 to 16-year-old readers who may have read it in 1964 it would have been entrancing. I never saw it back then, (I was 24 years old in 1964) but having recently read it (in 2019), I found it enjoyable, and wished that I had seen it and read it way back then.

The Secret Martians by Jack Sharkey (1960)

Earth has a well-established colony on Mars; a small city settled inside a large crater.

Common with most stories written with a Martian setting in the late 1950s and early 1960s, it was assumed that although thin the atmosphere was basically the same as on Earth, equivalent to that around the height of Mount Everest. Climbers had attained Everest's peak without using oxygen, though it wasn't as common then as now. People also lived and had done for many generations at great height in the Andes of South America. With proper acclimatization living and breathing the Martian atmosphere was not seen as a problem.

Another common assumption was that Mars was mostly desert, and like deserts on Earth it would be hot during the day, with temperatures dropping down to zero and below at night, except for Mars the authors exaggerated the coldness at night making it equivalent to temperatures found in Antarctica, or even colder. At least that part was almost right, but they were way off with how hot the daytime temperature would reach.

And practically every author agreed that there would be some form of native Martian life, and what they depicted was as varied as their individual imaginations could conjure. Most authors also had Mars riddled with caves and lava tubes which sometimes had free running water deep underground, and which almost always harbored some kind of native life.

In this story *Marsport* had been established in 2014 by Tri-Planet Refining Corporation as a mining site. Uranium is what they wanted and Mars had plenty. (In the 1960s uranium was used for both atomic weapons as well as power stations, and many authors used it as a key plot point in many ways.) Mars also had plenty of iron and huge smelters were set up to extract oxygen from the iron oxide. These smelters surrounded the original encampment which grew into a city and apart from the melted iron producing enough heat to keep the city warm during the freezing nights it also flooded the crater with oxygen which increased the pressure of the air within the crater enabling the city's inhabitants to walk and breath freely without additional equipment. The runoff from the smelters was allowed to flow through the city as rivers of molten iron. It flowed to a site where it was made into iron ingots and processed into various products.

The story opens with the World's controlling AI brain selecting Jery Delvin as the only person to investigate how 15 boy scouts on a return trip from Mars could vanish while in transit from Mars to earth. He is called in by the head of security and told he is heading for Mars to investigate the disappearance of the 15 boys.

Delvin was chosen because he has an uncanny ability to detect falsehoods from truths. He is given a special Amnesty disc to carry which allows him to go anywhere, to do anything, to demand whatever he needs to help his investigation. He is literally above the law. On board the ship to Mars he encounters a beautiful girl, the sister of one of the missing boys who beguiles him and steals his Amnesty disc as the ship lands and passengers disembark.

Complications almost immediately occur as Delvin is arrested for carrying a banned deadly weapon, a disrupter, a kind of handgun that disrupts the atoms holding matter together so it literally falls apart. Only security forces can carry weapons like this. However, he proves his credentials by having the security people contact the head, Baxter on Earth who hired Delvin, so he is released.

Almost immediately he is drugged in a Bar, tied up and imprisoned in a subterranean cell. He escapes and finds a native Martian arguing with the bar owner and a group of other people. The native crystalline beings were thought to be unintelligent and are ignored by most people. He is surprised to see one having a conversation and more surprised to find that it is him they are discussing. On the table between the two is Delvin's disrupter weapon. Suddenly he is spotted by one of the others in the bar and the crystalline being grabs the disruptor and shoots at those in the bar, killing all of them. Delvin takes this opportunity to escape and running through the dark city he again encounters the weird Martian who indicates to him that he should follow. Delvin is reluctant to trust the Martian but changes his mind when a mob of people creeping along the street suddenly attack him as soon as they know he is aware of them. The Martian kills them with Devlin's disrupter then hands it back to him.

The story is nonstop action from this point on, with no time allowed for the reader to think about what is happening. You just have to go along for the ride, and an exciting ride it is too.

Devlin doesn't follow the crystal Martian at first and is captured again by the security forces who imprison him on Baxter's orders. He is subsequently rescued by the crystal Martian who blows a hole through the cell wall with another disrupter weapon. The Martian takes him into the caves that via lava tubes crisscross the whole area and he discovers the girl is hiding in a room deep under the surface. It is warmer down there and the air is thicker so they can breathe it.

Once down there Devlin learns how to communicate with the Martian who understands some English. He asks questions and the Martian nods yes or no, or both, meaning undetermined. Devlin figures out what is going on by interpreting the responses to his questions then asking for confirmation. Eventually the Martian leads Devlin and the girl deeper underground to where the 15 boys are being kept as prisoners by another race of Martians who no one can see because they live partly in another dimension. Only Devlin can see them, and what he sees is more like an abstract image than something solid. These are the secret Martians, who it turns out manipulated the Brain (AI) on Earth to select Devlin. It was them who kidnapped the 15 boy scouts and are holding them prisoner in a weird cage that exists in more than three dimensions.

There are all kinds of shenanigans, twists, cliffhangers and other stuff going on with Baxter, the head of Earth Security, who is now on Mars and who wants to control the three worlds, (Earth, Moon, and Mars), his security forces on Mars, the crystal Martians as well as the Secret Martians underground. He also knows about the ancient Martians and their weird inter-dimensional metal and wants to destroy them. Devlin and his amnesty disc are the means he will use. The secret Martians don't want that to happen or they will be trapped in the other dimension unable to exist anywhere else. They need Devlin to bring down Baxter, the security chief and would-be-world-ruler. After much action this is achieved in the end, and needless to say the girl also falls in love with Devlin and all ends happily as the boys are freed and can return to Earth.

Even though this was published in 1960 and knowledge of Mars was limited at that time, it is still a credible story, and certainly enjoyable to read. *Armchair Fiction* are to be commended for bringing back into print many fine stories from a bygone era that would otherwise have been forgotten.

The Tomorrow People Judith Merril (1960)
The teaser on the cover says: *Back from Mars… with a secret too terrible to remember!*
The back cover is no better: *Something on Mars was killing people!*

With blurbs like that any Mars aficionado would be bursting with anticipation…but would soon be disappointed. Yes, a Russian two-man expedition went to Mars and never returned, followed later by a two-man American team of which only one man came back, and he couldn't remember what had happened on Mars, or at the very least wouldn't say anything about it.

When questioned by his superiors, and later by a psychiatrist as well as other friends all Johnny Wendt would say was, he couldn't remember and that they should check the ship's logbook. Checking the logbook only showed that for the crucial period Wendt's partner disappeared, those pages were torn out and couldn't be found anywhere.

Having come back from Mars alone, Wendt is notorious and is recognized wherever he goes on earth. Everyone wants to know what happened. Unable to cope, Wendt loses himself in alcohol and self-pity. Even his girlfriend, a famous dancer with whom he is in love can't get him to stop feeling sorry for himself and to stop drinking. The bulk of the story is concerned with how Wendt copes back on Earth.

Meanwhile on the Moon, some of the spore samples Wendt brought back are being tested and cultivated in an enclosed environment, with unusual developments.

The story is set in 1975 to 1977 and although modern in aspects compared to when it was published in 1960, reading it today it appears old fashioned and lacking in any sense of wonder. The only thing that makes it a science fiction novel is there are thriving research and mining colonies on the Moon where thousands of people live and work, both Russian as well as American and European. There are regular shuttle flights to and from an orbiting station around the Earth.

This massive station is 12,000 miles above the surface. Supply ships which also bring passengers travel from earth to the big station in orbit. None of this could remotely have occurred in 1977. In 1960 the Russians were way ahead of the Americans as far as the space race was concerned even though it was in its infancy, but any story involving a large established colony or colonies on the Moon should have been set at least half a century ahead, not a mere 15 to 17 years.

The bulk of the story follows Wendt as he copes with his alcoholism, his love affair with the world-famous dancer, and all the people both official and unofficial, political and scientific, who want to know what happened to him on Mars.

It doesn't read like a science fiction story. It is a mainstream story with SF elements forming part of the background. I suppose that in itself was unusual for the 1960s and Judith Merril may have been the first, or very close to it, to create what these days —half a century later— is a common hybrid. Science and science fiction have become so much a part of mainstream life —especially as a result of TV and Cinema— that almost every thriller author includes extrapolated science or science fictional elements in their stories and readers hardly notice. In 1960 it would have been unusual.

Readers of SF were regarded as strange and almost all of them never read anything that wasn't science fiction. They would have been disappointed with this book which was clearly a mainstream novel. Mainstream readers would not have wanted to read this book either, because the cover blurbs clearly labeled it as science fiction, which was something they would never look at let alone read.

Wendt is already back from Mars before the story opens and the reader doesn't find out what really happened until the very last couple of chapters. Mars once had an ancient civilization but all that remains are very old ruins. The Martians adapted as their planet died, dried up, became colder and so on until they became a single identity with all the spores and cells over the whole planet being part of a single planetary being. The Earth people who went to Mars were absorbed into this group mind and the cells Wendt brought back from Mars which the scientists have been growing on the Moon are able to be telepathically in contact with the mind on Mars once they have developed enough.

The story finishes with Wendt going back to the Moon to join with his pregnant girlfriend and with a similarly pregnant Russian woman from the other base in telepathic communication with the spores on the Moon as well as those on Mars.

The story is convoluted and takes a while to develop. For the most part it seems flat, especially when compared to **Outpost Mars,**1951, revised and republished in 1952, (See page 111 **Dreams of Mars**) which she wrote in collaboration with her husband Cyril Kornbluth using the name Cyril Judd. It was later republished as **Mars Child.** This story had all the excitement and sense of wonder that people in the 1950s expected, which is entirely lacking in **The Tomorrow People.**

The Memory of Mars Raymond F Jones (1961)

Although this delightful novelette isn't about Mars as such, there is a strong feeling of Mars that permeates the story. I suspect this may very well be his only story in which Mars is mentioned.

Raymond F Jones is a good writer and his most famous work would have to be **This Island Earth** which was made into spectacular colour film for its time, (1954) which has become an SF classic movie. I remember reading quite a few of his stories in various magazines back in the mid-1950s through to the mid-1960s. I particularly liked his novel **This Island Earth** (1952) which as with most books differs from the subsequent film. His output diminished from the mid-1960s onwards, even though he kept producing novels and stories for another decade.

The Memory of Mars opens with Mel Hastings waiting in a hospital for the outcome of an operation to save his wife after an accident. She dies and he is distraught. The last thing she said to him before the operation was "*as soon as I'm well, we'll go to Mars for a vacation again, and then you'll remember...*" Mel has no recollection of ever having been to Mars even though his wife kept talking about how wonderful the place was. He is terrified of space travel, so there is no way he would ever have gone to Mars.

The doctor who performed the operation wants Mel to come into his office. He informs him that his wife does not appear to be human. Mel is stunned. Her organs are totally different and deeper down than the skin and her blood is green. She has no heart, and he has no idea of how she could have been alive.

There is something very strange here. Mel doesn't believe him and insists on seeing the body of his wife again. When the doctor takes him down to the mortuary, he is convinced it can't be his wife and insists on a fingerprint test. This proves the body, as weird as it is, is that of his wife.

Back home he once again suffers from a recurring nightmare; that he is lost in space and is being pursued by strange things and just as they catch up with him, he wakes up.

Preparing the disposition of his wife's things he discovers a box of photographs of her on Mars at famous tourist spots, the ancient ruins, the spectacular chasms and so on. She looks so happy in the pictures. He is not in any of them which perhaps explains why he has no memory of her going to Mars.

He visits his wife's parents in the country and goes in search of old medical records that proves his wife was as human as he is, and finding such medical reports from high school and other sources he goes back to the hospital to show the doctor who operated on his wife that she had been perfectly normal. He now suspects that something must have happened to her on their trip to Mars which he can't remember.

The hospital doctor sends Mel to a psychiatrist who specializes in memory recovery and using the latest equipment Mel is retrogressed through the last nightmare he had to discover the deeper reason behind his fear of space travel.

They did go to Mars.

He recalls the excitement of boarding the massive liner that takes literally thousands of tourists at a time to Mars, the greatest holiday destination for the rich and famous. Three days out the liner mysteriously has a rendezvous with an almost invisible black ship. All the passengers are asked to board to continue their journey to Mars, but Mel refuses and hides in an escape pod. He gets into a space suit and exits the liner to see what is going on. He is chased by robots and captured and taken on board the black ship where his injected with something that knocks him unconscious.

When he comes to, he is back home and has no recollection of ever having been in space or having gone to Mars.

He decides he must find out what happened on the Mars liner so attempts to buy a ticket even though he can't afford it, only to be told he must wait ten years before being allowed on another trip. He contrives to get an old friend to buy a ticket which he pays for, and then takes his friend's place on the Mars liner. Exactly as before, three days out, the ship encounters the strange black ship and all the passengers are taken on board. He goes with them this time. A steward takes him aside and asks him to accompany him to a private office.

Inside the office he is astounded to meet the owner of the space liner that does the Mars tourist run. This man tells Mel he had been to Mars before and that his wife was an android. All the passengers are replaced with androids who make the trip to Mars and return to Earth. The original passengers have been resettled on another planet where they happily live. The aliens who do this are intergalactic and they have decided humans are too violent to be allowed into anywhere but local space.

They had considered destroying Earth altogether, but changed their minds, hoping that humans would perhaps evolve into better beings as time went on. Mel's memory had been wiped deliberately so he wouldn't know any of this, and it is unfortunate that he now knows the truth.

If your wife had not had that accident none of this would have come to light.

Mel is elated that his wife is still alive. He insists on going wherever she is to join her.

You are already there with her and quite happy too, he is told.

When Mel jumps up and threatens the alien he is shot in the stomach and as he collapses, he sees green blood oozing out of his abdomen. In that final instant he realizes that he too had been replaced, that he too was an android.

At the time **The Memory of Mars** was published in 1961, Jones was at the peak of his writing skills and this is a superbly told story that does not allow the reader to even think about any implausibility it may contain.

Even though it is not directly about Mars there is a strong sense of Mars that permeates the story, and as such it is well worthwhile looking for it and taking time to read it.

Other 1960s stories about Mars can be found **Dreams of Mars.** *pages 135 to 165.*

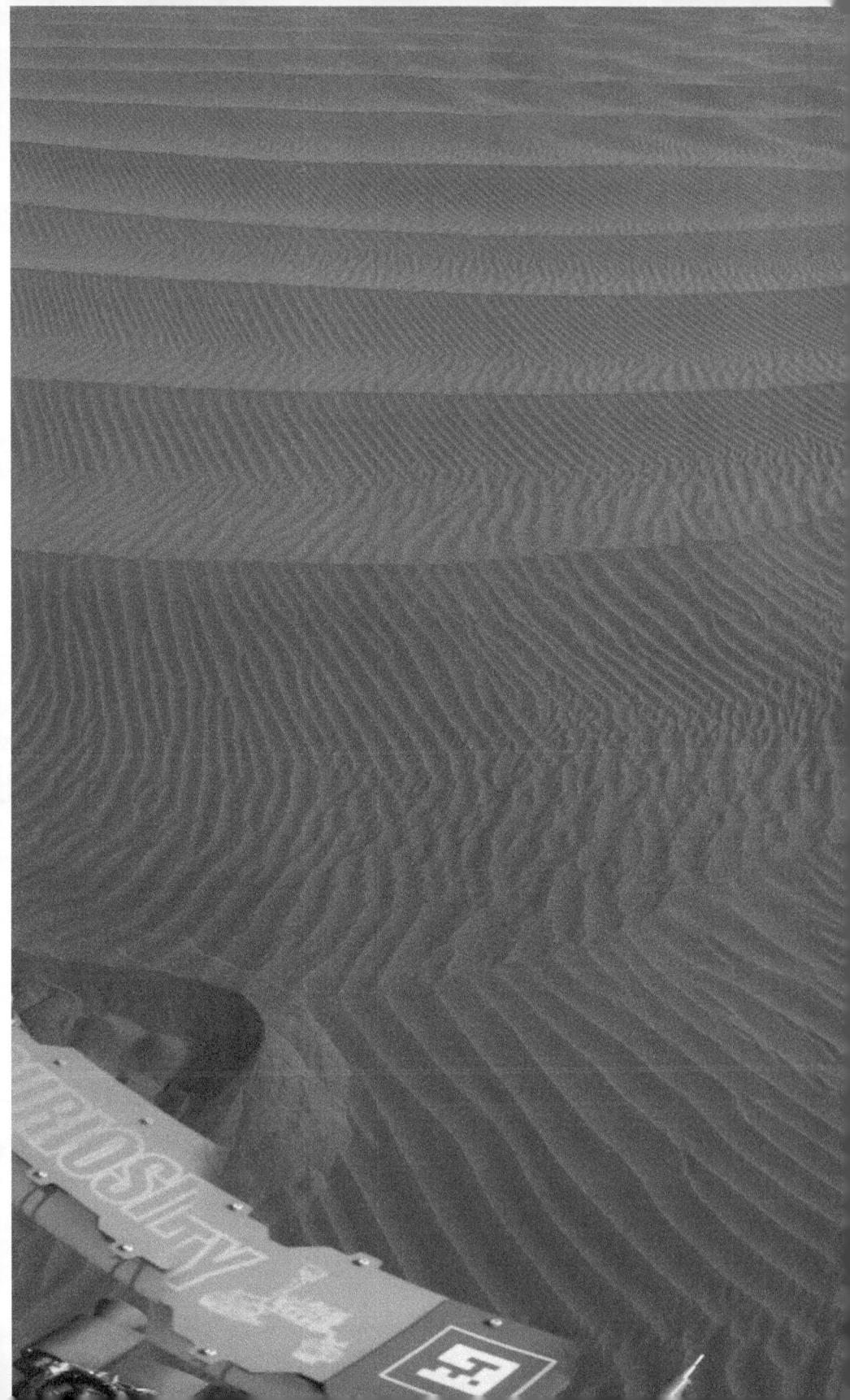

Part Two

After Mariner 4

More Dreams of Mars

Chapter Eight

A few more from the 1970's, 80's and 90's

There were few novels written about Mars in the1970s.

There was Ludek Pesek's *The Earth is Near* published in German in 1970 but not translated and published in English until 1973. Then later in the 70s there were some more; *Man Plus* by Frederick Pohl, (1976), *The Martian Inca* by Ian Watson (1977), *In the Hall of the Martian Kings* by John Varley (1977) and *The Far Call* by Gordon Dixon (1978). (See *Dreams of Mars* pages 179, 182,185,188.)

So it came as a surprise to discover this forgotten book, *Mars 314* by British author F J Pinchin (1970), which predates Ludek Pesek.

Mars 314 by F (Frank) J Pinchin (1970)

Since both *Mars 314* and *The Earth is Near* deal with a voyage out to Mars and the subsequent exploration of the planet before they return to Earth, it seems logical to make some comparisons.

The voyage from Earth to Mars was a typical plot in many earlier stories usually with this journey occupying a fair percentage of the book. Arthur C Clarke did this with his first published novel *The Sands of Mars* (1951) with the first third of the book being about the journey to Mars.

In 1951, no one really knew much about Mars, but by 1970, the first two Mariner probes had been to Mars and sent back photographs of the surface that blew away many preconceived ideas of what was there. F J Pinchin and Ludek Pesek did have an idea of what Mars was like because they had seen the photos, but their resulting stories were very different. Pesek crafted a grim realistic story that depicted the surface as harsh and inimical to human exploration. His crew men struggled to explore even nearby areas without accidents occurring along with the loss of one life. Pinchin's explorations of Mars were dangerous but not in the same realistic category as Pesek's people who struggled to set up a temporary base for exploration. Pesek's descriptions of the Martian terrain were far more realistic than what Pinchin imagined.

Pinchin's Mars is a more benign place even though his characters suffer accidents on the surface. It is however not as realistic as one would think. He clearly states at the very beginning of the book that he is indebted for facts about Mars to **Project Mars** by Willy Ley and Wernher von Braun, **Exploring the Planets** by V A Firsoff, **Space** by Patrick Moore (who also wrote many SF novels for young adult readers among his books on astronomy), and he also mentions Clarke, and Asimov among others who have inspired him.

His Mars also exhibits ideas once current among scientists as well as writers of fiction that there would be some plant life on the surface, and that the temperatures would not be as cold as we now know them to be. He has his astronauts dealing with a daytime temperature of around -10 Celsius to -40 or -50 Celsius overnight. His atmosphere is only 50% carbon dioxide with presumably the other half being oxygen, although this isn't mentioned. The pressure at the surface is higher than in reality, at 10% that of Earth's sea level air pressure. His plant life is mostly moss or some type of lichen, and there is water in the form of thin mists that freeze onto the surface at night, similar to what happens in the Atacama desert where mist from the Pacific Ocean settles and freezes overnight which is enough to sustain some plant life even though most of the desert is barren. I suspect this would seem logical to authors speculating about Mars since they often used the Atacama or Gobi deserts as examples of Mars-like terrain on Earth. All they had to do was imagine Mars to be a bit colder and drier with thinner air.

Like many of his predecessors, he was also of the opinion that the north polar ice cap would be water ice. His Martian sky is a deep blue, consistent with the way the Earth's sky appears from on top of the Andes. He erroneously assumed that it would appear so because his atmospheric pressure on the surface of Mars was similar to that at the top of the Andes Mountains. In fact, the atmospheric pressure is much less than that and the sky isn't blue, but rather a pinkish colour. Ludek got closer, with his sky being brown because of the suspended fine sand and dust.

Pinchin pays homage to Arthur C Clarke on page 42, with the ship in orbit around Mars and the first observations are noted; he states '...*down there all I can see seems to be desert — red sands and scrub stretching as far as I can see. There are no oceans — nothing but wilderness — the Sands of Mars. I guess some of you have read a book of that name...*' And on page 51 after a complete survey has been made with photographs, maps, surface temperatures measured, cloud formation… '*Their work confirmed that there are no mountains on Mars.*' Although I think this again refers to Clarke who famously stated that in italics in his novel ***The Sands of Mars***, and later apologized to readers after the discovery of a row of massive volcanoes with Olympus Mons being the biggest volcano in the whole solar system, big enough that Mt Everest looks like mere foothill beside it. Pinchin attributes the lack of mountains as a fact deduced from a complete lack of shadows observed by astronomers as far back as the early 1900s. His crew assiduously looked for volcanoes but observed none. In fact, when Pinchin wrote this and published it in 1970 Olympus Mons had not yet been discovered.

At least he got some things right. The length of the Martian day is 24 hours, 39 minutes, 35.3 seconds long, and to compensate he has is explorers set their watches back at midnight by 39 minutes, 35.3 seconds.

Set in 1981, the basic story line is of a race to Mars. The Americans have completed a ship in orbit around the Moon and they blast off on a long trajectory to arrive at Mars in 330 days. Meanwhile a Russian ship has also set off using a plasma rocket rather than a chemical rocket, so it can travel faster and will overtake them about half way to arrive in Mars orbit first.

The cold war rivalry between the USA and the Soviets is extrapolated into this story. The Russians want to get to Mars before Russia and the Western nations unite as one; they want this to be the last glorious achievement their nation makes before it becomes part of a worldwide government. They lost the moon race to the Americans and they don't want to lose this race to Mars.

The Americans initially worried that the ships would crash as the long orbits needed to get to Mars would intersect, but the Russians pass them as close as half a kilometer before leaving them behind. Until this point is reached there is little communication between the Russians and the Americans. The Russians gloat about stepping foot on Mars first and planting a soviet flag rather than the united world flag. The Americans are despondent, but their mood improves when the Russians radio them as they move into orbit to ask for help. Their lander rockets won't fire; the electronic parts have corroded and they do not carry spares, so they have been waiting in orbit until the Americans arrived.

This boosts the American's morale. They come to an agreement with the Russians that three of their crew will join three of the Americans in the American lander, and that they will take with them the Russian surface rover, as well as the American hover jet. One of the Russians is a woman, their doctor, and it is essential that she be in the group to explore the surface. The other two members of the Russian crew as well as the two American crew will remain in orbit to maintain their ships.

A base is set up and the six people on the surface begin exploration. They are fascinated by massive splits in the terrain that extend sometimes as far as the eye can see which is, they deduce, what observers on Earth saw and thought were canals. There is no water in them.

To get around they use rocket packs (developed for a war in Asia) when outside of the rover which makes one of the characters imagine he is a *Starship Trooper,* (an obvious reference to Heinlein). Meanwhile the other two have gone off in the hover jet to explore in a different direction. They find a strange rock-like cairn and on closer examination discover it is artificial. They trigger it to open and they discover tunnels and caves leading under the surface which they begin to explore. They have discovered the remains of an ancient Martian civilization. While these two are beneath the surface contact is lost with the base and they can't be warned that a severe dust storm is headed their way.

The other two which includes the doctor who is beginning to fall in love with her American partner in the rover head back towards base but divert to where the hover jet went to see what they can do to rescue their fellow team mates.

When the guys come up from under the surface, they discover the sand storm and there is nothing they can do but wait it out and hope their oxygen doesn't run out first. After a difficult trip the two in the rover manage to find the sand covered hover jet and the two inert people huddled in the lee of a huge rock. Their oxygen has just run out. Fortunately, they are saved, taken back into the rover which is pressurized so they can remove their lightweight space suits and breathe again.

Later further explorations are made back to the tunnels under the surface as well as to the north polar ice cap. One of the explorers there is trapped in a minor avalanche of rock in a cave and breaks a leg. The doctor takes him back to the base where preparations are being made to return to orbit for the return journey back to Earth. They must leave at a specific time or they will arrive in Earth orbit when the Earth isn't there. It is critical that they depart precisely on time.

During the testing phases of the two space ships in orbit something goes wrong with the Russian ship and the captain tries to control it as it falls down into Mars' gravity well. He had remained on board while sending his crew mate over to the American ship. The Russian ship crashes somewhere near the alien cairn and the doctor and her American friend take the rover to see if the captain is still alive. They have a time limit because the American crew need to blasts off at a precise time in order to rendezvous with their orbiting mother ship for the return to Earth. If they don't make it, they will be left on Mars. On the way to the crash site they have trouble with the bearings on one of the six wheels of the rover. They finally arrive at the crash site to discover the ship's Captain is dead. But now their time is running out and, on the way back to base the faulty bearing seizes up and they are stuck.

The only solution is to uncouple the wheel and its opposite and travel back on four instead of six wheels. To do this takes time and they realize they will not get back in time to be lifted up into orbit for the return home. The American driving the rover is the captain of their expedition and he orders the others to take off whether they get back or not, they are not wait or they will miss the precise time to leave Mars orbit for the journey home.

They are still 50 kilometers out from base when they see the lander blasting off to orbit and rendezvous with the waiting mother ship.

There is enough food left in the base to last them for years and they don't seem to mind being together and alone. Someone will come for them soon once what they have discovered becomes known on Earth. And sure enough, as the American ship reaches the halfway point to Earth, they are informed that a Russian Federation ship is already on its way to Mars, so they won't be alone for very long.

This is an enjoyable old-fashioned story typical of many similar efforts produced during the years between 1945 to 1965. It was not labeled as SF but simply published in a hardcover edition similar to other books that libraries had on their shelves. As far as I am aware it did not go into a paperback edition which is perhaps why it never reached a wider market.

Badge of Infamy by Lester del Rey (1973)

The original copyright cites 1957 by *Renown Publications* and later, 1963 by *Galaxy Corporation*. In one variation or another this story has been published 3 times. It may originally have been published under a pseudonym since Lester del Rey often used other names early in his career, although from the 1960s on he mostly used the name Lester del Rey.

In this future world there is still a Congress and a President, but the country is ruled by the Medical Lobby and Spacemen's Lobby, the two controlling groups that determine what rules and laws the government will enact. There is brief mention of other countries, and a plague that began in China and spread rapidly to the rest of the world including Africa. It killed billions of people leaving the USA almost intact, which is how the whole world is ruled by the one government controlled by the Medical Lobby. They are the government and they have one very strict rule: no medical service, or operation can be conducted outside of a hospital.

Dr. Daniel Feldman is a pariah, an outcast. He saved the life of a friend while at a huge party in Canada at a hunting lodge to celebrate his wedding to Cristina Ryan, the daughter of the Lobby President. His best friend, Baxter, accidentally shot himself handling a weapon he nothing about, and lay dying on the grass outside the lodge. There was no way to get him to a hospital in time to save his life. Feldman had to save him. His wife tried to stop him. Even Baxter tried to tell him not to do it, but he went ahead and performed an emergency operation and removed the bullet, something he should not have done outside of a hospital. As a consequence, he was arrested and charged with malpractice and kicked out of the Medical Lobby.

He can't get a job since no one hires a pariah. He is a bum, surviving on handouts and scrounging scraps for food. One night in a cheap flophouse he sees someone else in there dying. He recognizes the symptoms of space stomach, and knows that without help the man will die. He can't help. He gets the flophouse attendant to call an official doctor who arrives in time to pronounce the man dead. He takes whatever money the man had as his and the Lobby's fee, and leaves.

Feldman in desperation takes the dead man's boots. It's cold outside and he needs a decent pair of boots to protect his feet. Slipping away before the authorities come for the body, he discovers something hidden in boots as he puts them on. It is the dead man's ID and his Spaceman's Lobby membership ticket.

Assuming the dead man's identity, he goes to the spaceport and boards the shuttle taking the crew and passengers up into orbit where the ship listed on the ticket is waiting, Boarding the ship in orbit, he sees his ex-wife about to board the ship. She was responsible for reporting him to her Medical Lobby over his infraction of the strict Lobby rules. She is being sent to Mars to the southern outpost, Southport, to set up a new hospital. Previously the only hospital on the planet was in the northern hemisphere. Feldman quickly slips down into the bowels of the ship where he is supposed to be a tubeman, one of those who maintain the rocket tubes the ship uses. Their job is to clean the rocket tubes after the burn that sends them on to Mars. They take the damaged lining out, repair it and replace it before the next burn. It is hot and dangerous work.

The large ships that go between Earth and Mars do not land, they orbit the planet and a shuttle comes up from Mars to take passengers down just as it does when the ship is in Earth orbit.

Somehow, the other tubemen discover he is impersonating an old friend and accuse him of murdering him to steal his savings. When he tries to explain what happened they don't believe him and take him to the captain who orders his pay to be forfeited. His ex-wife is there also boarding the shuttle to go down and she tells the captain Feldman is a disgraced doctor, a pariah.

The captain orders the men to take him down to Mars and leave him there, but don't kill him.

They beat the shit out of him and leave him for dead, but someone left him an extra oxygen bottle so he would have a chance when he wakes up. He manages to get into the Southport station where a tiny restaurant is still open. He can't afford the food but asks if he can sit awhile and the attendant allows it. Hardly there for more than a minute, a couple of men appear and ask if he is the doctor who just came down. He tries to tell them he is a pariah but they don't care. There are no doctors on Mars other than at the official hospitals and they often can't afford to pay for treatment. They are happy to have any doctor who can help them.

Feldman is still a doctor even if he is a pariah and is obliged to help them if he can. They take him in a sand buggy to a small settlement well away from Southport where he discovers people are dying from what appears to be a normal disease that shouldn't kill them. Some of them also have black spots on their skin as well as a small lump on their neck at the base of the head. Many people have this small lump. Mars is a harsh place, dry, almost devoid of air, but plants and a few small insects had survived and adapted. It wasn't completely lifeless. However, earth plants wouldn't grow and had to be modified to survive. Most of the food eaten on Mars and in the space ships and a good part of the Earth is synthetic, and humans have been modified to enable them to eat it. Once modified, they can no longer digest natural food. Feldman discovers that the people on Mars have all been modified to eat synthetic food. Most earth diseases which humans are normally immune to don't exist on Mars, but something does affect people. It makes them get a severe headache with uncontrollable movement of the limbs. When this dies down, they find a small lump at the back of the neck.

What Feldman first works out is that humans on Mars, because they have been modified to eat synthetic food, no longer have an immune system that can fight off normally benign diseases like a common cold or measles. If these diseases are brought to Mars by people arriving from Earth, then the locals are unlikely to be immune and quickly die if they catch it. But too many people are dying of things that should not affect them. But the doctor is more concerned with the black spots and he sets up a small laboratory where he can do research into the matter. He discovers a Martian bacterium inhabiting the black spots, but his equipment is too crude to do much more. He is convinced a Martian virus or something similar could have something to do with the headaches people get at some point, after which it becomes dormant and only years later manifests in ways to kill the infected person.

All the while he is doing this the local Medical Lobby, run by his ex-wife is trying to stop him doing his illegal research. They claim there is no Martian disease, it's something from Earth and it is all under control. In the final stage an infected person goes berserk and starts running and jumping violently until they die in agony. The only thing people can do is to shoot them to put them out of their agony. But it is happening to too many people, becoming an epidemic. The Medical Lobby claims it is the result of hysteria, that there is no discernible cause.

Feldman believes otherwise. He believes that somewhere there is a Martian virus that has laid dormant for millions of years and that when an archaeological team first examined an ancient crumbled ruin, they must have released the virus. They were the first to be affected fifteen years later. And now the disease is manifesting itself in the majority of the population. Very few are immune. Feldman discovers only people who have not had their body altered to be able to digest synthetic food are immune. The Medical Lobby is finally concerned that this disease could be transmitted to Earth where the majority of the remaining population have been modified to digest synthetic food.

When the Lobby sets a trap and captures Feldman, they sentence him to death by ejecting him and his equipment from a starship. They put him into a spacesuit with one hour of air, to enable him to contemplate his crimes. The local Martians who live in settlements outside of the two major spaceports start a revolt against the Medical Lobby. Earth sends rockets with atomic bombs which orbit the planet and threaten to destroy the whole planet if the rebels don't stop. But unfortunately, the disease has already been unwittingly transmitted to Earth and the leader of the Medical Lobby as well as (his daughter) Feldman's ex-wife have been infected, among others. They have experienced the violent headaches and the subsequent development of the small node at the back of the neck. One of the reasons she was sent to Mars was to find a cure. Now they know Feldman has found a cure, but the Lobby wants him dead for doing illegal research. While waiting to be ejected, he discovers the captain of the ship and his wife also have contracted the Martian disease and Feldman tells the captain to change back to Earth normal. Earth normal people are not able to be infected. He doesn't tell this to anyone else.

He and his equipment are ejected into space. After the ship leaves, he is hardly there for the allotted hour when he spots a small lifeboat approaching. The pilot doesn't seem to have much control, but manages to get close enough to throw him a rope which is used to haul him in. The pilot is his ex-wife. Astounded to be rescued by her, she explains that she too has the disease and that his (Feldman's) research is the only hope they have. Feldman takes over piloting the lifeboat and takes it back down to Mars and makes a rough landing near a remote settlement.

What Feldman eventually discovers is that a particular weed which the settlers had adopted to replace tobacco, and which has calming effects, but tastes horrible until you get used to it, stops the virus from incubating and kills it. None of the people who smoke this bracky have contracted the disease, and those who have and who smoke the bracky no longer have the disease. There is a point made earlier about the doctor adapting to smoke bracky because he ran out of tobacco, of which there is none on Mars, so the doctor is also immune to the disease.

Knowing they have a cure, the locals band together to force the Medical Lobby people to leave, and they demand that Earth land the rockets threatening the planet so they can be modified by the Martians for their own use. In return they will supply the cure to Earth in exchange for their independence. Earth finally agrees and Mars becomes independent.

The locals want to make Feldman the President but he refuses, suggesting that one of the locals, his friend Jake should be the President. All Feldman wants to do is his research and he is happy. His ex-wife departs for Earth with the last of the Medical Lobby. Finally, while still recognizing Earth as the mother planet, Mars is now free, independent, and can pursue its own destiny.

This is not as good as his other two Martian stories, *Police your planet*, and *Marooned on Mars*, (see *Dreams of Mars* pages 114 and135). Nevertheless, it is an enjoyable afternoon's read, and should be on any Mars enthusiast's list of books.

Controversial

Jesus on Mars by Philip Jose Farmer (1979)

Philip Jose Farmer often wrote stories that were controversial. Some of his stories were refused publication at first because the subject matter was considered too hideous, bordering on pornographic, or offensive. His very first story, a novella, *The Lovers*, shocked the world of science fiction as it dealt with a love affair between a human male and an alien parasitic insect that took the form of a woman. He was the first to introduce sex and all the emotions this induced into science fiction. This story won a Hugo Award for Farmer in 1953 under the category of Best New Artist or Writer.

Jesus on Mars was probably as controversial as anything else he wrote, and I have no idea how I missed this when it was published in 1979. There weren't too many novels, or even short stories for that matter, dealing with Mars in the 1970s. The stunning revelation that Mars was so different from what anyone had previously thought turned writers off the subject of Mars, making them search further afield for story locations or brought them back to Earth. (See chapter eight, page 177 *Dreams of Mars*.)

Religion is always a sticky subject, and those few novels that deal with religion generally deal with Christianity. This one deals with Judaism which makes it unusual, and different.

A four-person international expedition to Mars arrives after four months in transit and lands in Vallis Marineris. The four crew members are the captain Richard Orme, Madeline Danton, Nadir Shirazi, and Avram Bronski. Orme is African American and nominally a Fundamentalist Christian. Danton is French Canadian and agnostic, Shirazi is a moderate Muslim, and Bronski is Jewish, as well as being religious scholar who has studied ancient texts as well as ancient Greek. He can read and understand that language, but can barely speak it.

What brought them to Mars was the discovery by the satellites observing Mars of what appeared to be a partially buried space ship. The robot rover dispatched to take pictures discovered nearby, a cave entrance where a metal door just visible inside has an inscription on it of two letters from the Greek alphabet, Tau and Omega.

Orme and Bronski suit up and get into the lander while Danton and Shirazi stay on the ship in orbit around Mars. Landing on the surface as close as possible they both exit the vehicle and make their way towards the partly hidden door with the Greek letters inscribed on it.

The two members of the team in orbit are monitoring every move the others on the surface make while simultaneously sending this information, telemetric data and visual data, back to Earth where NASA and the rest of the world is anxiously watching. They look at the buried space ship and are amazed at the size of it. They wonder how no one on Earth had seen this before, unless it had been buried and only recently has been partially uncovered. They approach the inscribed door which they see is in a tunnel rather than a cave and while trying to open it they are stunned when it bursts open and a number of space-suited figures emerge to take them captive. Not all of the figures are human. One of them is an alien humanoid being.

This is a fantastic beginning to a story that is guaranteed to capture the reader's interest. You absolutely have to read on to find out who these humans are, and what they are doing on Mars.

The two Earthmen are dragged inside and the entrance is sealed behind them. They are taken to a luxurious apartment and left there. That gives Bronski the linguist and scholar time to understand the Greek symbols on the door were not from the Greek alphabet but were universal mathematical symbols. It seems very few of the Martian humans could speak Greek. Of the several Martians who began to interrogate them, one of them was a humanoid alien from a race called the Krsh, and the questions they asked were in ancient Greek and Aramaic. They were not the common languages of the people on Mars but scholars had studied them and preserved them and these two languages were what they used to initially communicate with the visiting humans.

Outside of the apartment the space underground was enormous, at least 35 miles away from where they were held, they could see the edge of the underground dome walls rising up. They could see farmland cultivated, double lane roads, scattered residences, villages, trees and forests, rivers, a lake, and high above, too high to see the roof was suspended a glowing orb that represented the sun. It faded at night to be no brighter than the moon. There didn't seem to be any traffic other than horse-drawn wagons, but there were bicycles, and occasionally they saw small car-like vehicles that moved silently along the roads.

The big discovery that stunned them when the questions were being asked regarding Earth history after 50 AD, was that the people on Mars were orthodox Jews. How was that possible?

The Martians also told them they had been up to the orbiting ship and had brought its occupants down and they were being held in another apartment. Whoever the Martians were, they were certainly more advanced than Earth people. But what was more astonishing to the human visitors was they were told Jesus whom they called Iesus ho Christos, was alive and living in the sun above, and that at the end of the month he would descend and walk amongst them.

This information causes an upset amongst Bronski the scholar and Orme the African American, especially when the Martians want to know how a brown man, (Bronski tells them he is Black even though his skin is brown, which is somewhat confusing to them) a gentile, can be a worshiper of Jesus and not be a Jew. Shirazi the Muslim is upset because the Martians have never heard of Mohammed nor of the religion he founded, and Danton the agnostic can't reconcile her beliefs with what they claim is a fact, that Jesus is still alive and living on Mars. There is much discussion amongst the Earth crew regarding their religious beliefs and what they are being told and asked to believe by their captors. I'm sure this is meant to highlight the enormous differences within the various religious sects on Earth and Farmer certainly delights in throwing 'curve-balls' at the reader, to make us think in ways we may not have considered, especially when what we are asked to accept is an extrapolated version of what Jewish life might have been like if extended 2000 years into the future from the time of Christ. We are shown a benevolent, peace loving society that follows strict rules of behavior and decorum in which there is now overt disagreements, no wars, with no one wanting for the necessities of life; a world that is Edenic.

The visitors are not allowed to communicate with Earth and this is also a concern, because NASA and the whole world will be wondering what had happened, having seen their astronauts being captured and taken underground. They are told that once they understand the language used here, Krsh, and how life on Mars is, they will be allowed to contact their people on Earth. There is also a hint that Jesus will return to Earth to fulfill the predictions made in the bible, which is upsetting to them because they see this as an invasion. They also learn that the Krsh left their planet because their sun was failing and that they travelled to other star systems in search of a world to live on. They discovered a warlike world where they were immediately attacked and although damaged, they managed to escape and travel to the star system where the Earth and Mars exist. They landed on Earth in what is now Israel and helped many tribes people with medical and other benefits. They took many on board their ship and after returning some, made their way into Orbit when they were attacked by the nasty beings they had battled before. They had been followed. In a battle that ensued they destroyed the alien followers but their ship sustained considerable damage and crashed landed on Mars. They hollowed out a huge space in which they could grow and cultivate crops, build houses and establish a community. Among the people of that community was Jesus and one of his disciples. The Krsh didn't believe that Jesus was the son of God until he performed a miracle and ascended into the sphere, really an atomic furnace, that they used to simulate the sun. Over time the Krsh and the humans became one society as they expanded underground into Mars.

The big question that underlies the thoughts of the visitors as they learn the language is how is it possible that Jesus is still alive and living on Mars after 2000 years?

The visitors are allowed to wander freely once they understand the Krsh language and Bronski meets a lovely young woman who is fascinated by his blackness and his curly hair. He is the only black person ever seen on Mars. Inevitably they fall in love but cannot consummate it unless he converts to Judaism and they marry. He is reluctant to convert as he is not certain that Jesus really does live. He makes an attempt to escape but that is expected and his Martian interrogator is waiting for him. The other crew members have their problems in accepting that the culture is similar to what it was at the time Christ lived on Earth. One of the things they discover is that the people on Mars live for hundreds of years and that the Erath visitors can be treated but Martians won't do it yet because they are not ready. Eventually they want to return to Earth and treat the whole world's population, but won't do it unless it is free, and no one profits, and that the treatment is made for everyone, rich, poor, ruling, criminals, everyone equally. The Martians have other scientific advances, including anti-gravity enabling floating vessels for transport although they are rarely used, and superior medicine which they use to treat Madeline Danton when they discover she has developed cancer. They cure her and all of them so it will never occur again.

The visitors are allowed to create a holographic video report which will be broadcast to Earth, but only after Jesus has descended from his Golden sun in the sky above. On the day he is to descend the whole Martian population from this and other connecting caverns arrive to witness the event. There are almost one million of them. A floating boat is used to ferry the Earth visitors over the heads of the crowd to a raised stone dais where Jesus is expected to descend. When he does descend, he is the epitome of all historical images depicting him, although slightly shorter and stockier than what the visitors expected. He floats down and demonstrates a miracle by raising Bronski up from where he is seated and floats him across to so he can be close and see for himself that Jesus really is alive. Bronski is convinced of the reality of Jesus but somewhere in the back of his mind there are doubts. He still can't understand how it could be possible and feels that somewhere in all this a fraud has been perpetuated.

The more time he spends with Jesus the more he is convinced that Jesus is real, and later, during one of many conversations, Jesus offers him some explanations. One explanation given is that when the Krsh left their star system in search of another, in one they encountered energy beings that could live inside a star. One of these beings managed to find its way into the power source a fusion generator in the Krsh ship and stayed there. It could manifest itself as one of them, but eventually it had to return to the power source which was its food. On Earth it found the person called Jesus and occupied his body. It absorbed this person's beliefs and moral code, in effect becoming this person, becoming Jesus. When the ship crashed on Mars Jesus was one of those on board. The energy being had no recourse but to live in the artificial sun, a fusion generator, that floated in the cavern dug out under the surface. Jesus's real body couldn't survive the fusion power but the energy being could recreate the body exactly whenever it wanted to descend down to the floor of the cavern and interact with the people there. A true Christian would find much of this confronting, especially the idea that Jesus was a normal human, only adopted as the son of God, and that he is married and has a wife (on Mars). He acts and thinks, as we would believe Jesus to act and think, but he is also very much a normal person, and he wants to return to earth to cure it of all its problems.

At the end of the book, the Krsh, and Jesus return to Earth along with the astronauts, and they are not given permission to land in Israel. There are riots and confrontations in many parts of the world, highlighting the problems that Farmer believe existed in 1979, and solving these seems insurmountable. Eventually the ship lands and the Martian Jews return to the ancestral homeland. Bronski once again has doubts about the veracity of Jesus and thinks he will shoot him with a laser to find out if he can truly survive, and in the procession as they leave the ship someone throws a hand grenade at Jesus. Without thinking or pausing, Bronski throws himself in front, catching the hand grenade and clutching it against his body to protect Jesus. Momentarily, before the grenade explodes, he wonders at the irony of he who was about to shoot Jesus with a laser trying to protect the life of the one he was going to kill.

A miracle is performed and Bronski is restored to life by Jesus and Bronski finally believes that Jesus is real. It doesn't matter whether the person is an alien energy being inhabiting a human body, the end result is what you see. Jesus, alive, and returning to Earth as prophesied in biblical texts, and once the world accepts this, it will never be the same again.

This is an absorbing book and one Mars enthusiasts should read if they can find it. When it was published in 1979 there was a waning interest in Mars and most writers moved on to stories about pollution on Earth, overpopulation, psychological problems of dystopian societies and other more prosaic subjects as the new wave of science fiction smothered old ideas of space opera, and adventures on other planets. Perhaps it didn't sell as well as it would have some years earlier, but whatever the reason, it seems to have disappeared. I never saw it in 1979 or shortly thereafter, and it was only because of an obscure reference I came across that I discovered it existed. I managed to find a second hand copy and don't regret for one moment having read it 40 years after it was originally published.

The Mars of Lin Carter

Once Mariner IV had sent back those grainy pictures which showed Mars to be a barren cratered planet, the old-fashioned style of stories set on Mars that many authors continued to produce practically disappeared. As more probes and eventually rovers visited the planet sending back more detailed images, the Mars that many had previously imagined ceased to exist. The new Mars was beautiful and fascinating, strangely Earth-like at times, but nothing like anyone had ever imagined. Many writers who would perhaps have used Mars as a setting for a story, didn't; they switched to other kinds of stories, in other solar systems or at home on Earth. No one quite knew what to do with Mars. It would take a decade or more, before newer authors started to rethink how they could use Mars as it was now being known. Some retrogressed to the kind of story that had been written 50 years earlier regarding voyages to Mars and initial explorations, but they did it with much more knowledge about rocketry and space ships and probes, and conditions on Mars than those earlier authors had. These stories were technically more accurate, but detailed and fascinating as they were, they didn't seem to have that sense of wonder which imbued the early stories when no one really knew anything at all about Mars or the other planets in the solar system.

There was one author. Lin Carter, who bridged the divide between the early adventure stories set on Mars that were more fantasy than science fiction and the new more technical stories from the decade or so after Mariner IV and the subsequent discoveries made on Mars. Lin Carter was not the most famous among his contemporaries, but a respectable author none the less. He wrote and published four short novels set on Mars. Three of them were published in the 1970s with the fourth appearing in 1984.

Carter was a writer of heroic fantasy rather than science fiction and as such was prolific, having written 12 Conan the Barbarian novels along with many other heroic fantasy series of his own creation. He also edited volumes of Flashing Swords, The Year's Best Fantasy, Weird Tales, among others. He did write a couple of series that were more science fiction than fantasy and one of those series is a group of four novels set on Mars.

His Mars stories have the same basic setting, which include accurate descriptions of the Martian terrain as can be clearly seen from photos and images sent back from that planet, and he uses both the scientific names given to certain features as well as his Martian native names. He also adds speculation regarding long cracks in the surface that are deep enough to have made human observers think they were canals. (A suggestion made by Alfred Russell Wallace – a contemporary of Charles Darwin, and who was also a biologist who suggested the theory of evolution about the same time as Darwin. He also wrote a book which argued against the Canals of Mars that Percival Lowell was convinced were real, arguing that as the planet cooled, large cracks would appear in the shrinking surface, cracks which could appear straight and very long and could be mistaken for something artificial instead of natural. He also suggested that because of its distance from the sun Mars would be far colder that anyone at that time imagined it to be. And he was right about that.)

Along these deep cracks in Carter's stories a moss-like plant thrives along with other kinds of succulents that have roots going deep down (as much a mile or more) where scant water can be found far beneath the surface. He has his natives and Earthsiders who live out in the desert use small portable stills each morning to extract water from these succulents, because there is no water anywhere on the surface of Mars. And because there are plants, there are also those things that live in amongst them, insects and small animals, and consequently larger animals that prey upon those smaller ones. Carter's animals on Mars are more reptilian except for the people who live there. His Martian men and women are basically human looking but with subtle differences that came from a different evolutionary base; something feline, rather than simian as human ancestors were. This is odd because there are no other mammalian type animals mentioned, and there should be if the natives are descended from something feline originally. Every animal he mentions is of reptilian origin no matter what it looks like. The Martians, he reminds us several times over the four novels, evolved and became civilized while the Earth was still in the Pleistocene Age, many millions of years before humans first appeared.

He further suggests that as Mars cooled and started to lose its atmosphere, the oceans dried up, the people became savages and retrogressed into small tribal groups barely able to survive, with some living in the lowlands along the shores of what were once ancient seas, while others retreated into the mountainous areas. The planet didn't lose all of its oxygen and although the atmospheric pressure is less than what it once was, it still contains some oxygen (contrary to the fact that it is 99 percent carbon dioxide) and the pressure is not as low as the scientists have found. In order to have people and some kind of ecosystem, Carter has had to maintain an atmospheric pressure that equates to what we would encounter at the top of Mountain ranges like the Andes. He also has made the temperatures not as cold as the rovers have measured. His temperatures during the day are reasonable for humans to endure and overnight humans sleep in a kind of pressure suit that maintains a comfortable temperature. For most humans to wander around on the surface of Mars, they will at least need a respirator, but more often than not, also pressure suit of some kind as well. There is surgery available to alter the way in which the lungs can absorb oxygen as well as the blood being able to use it so a respirator isn't needed, but it is expensive, and most humans can't afford it so they live in a controlled environment, like pressurized domes and habitats. Each character mentioned in the four novels who is an Earthsider spending considerable time outside of the colonies, has had surgery to enable them to use the little oxygen in the atmosphere more efficiently.

Altering humans to suit the environment was suggested by other authors in the 1970s, Frederick Pohl and Later, Kevin J Anderson, both of whom had fantastic visions of how this could be done, and both wrote complete novels regarding this idea and the consequences to those who were altered. But Lin Carter just hints at it as a way of explaining how his human protagonists can survive out in the vast deserts of Mars like the natives can.

Some of the Martians live in the remnants of ancient cities that are millions of years old and have had newer buildings built on top of them burying more ancient parts, but even these are extremely ancient, older than the entire history of the human race.

I would say that the moment I started reading these stories what popped into my mind were earlier, stories written by Leigh Brackett whose ancient and present Mars was far more exciting, and almost always full of that Sense of Wonder which seems to be lacking in the stories of Lin Carter. His stories are simpler, more straight-forward quest stories, in which a protagonist, (human) of dubious character sets out or is forced to participate in an adventure that takes him across a vast area of Mars in search of something. After encountering and overcoming a number of obstacles the search is concluded and the protagonist, as a result of what had happened along the way, is not the same person as he was before he began.

Carter always begins these stories in the middle of some action, or confrontation that draws the reader in while at the same time imparting essential background details to explain the situation or show us something about Mars. As it progresses enough interest is generated to keep the reader going until the end. Once started, these stories are hard to put down. The tendency is to keep reading to find out how it all ends, and this is a mark of an author who knows how to plot and pace a story. He has written more than 80 novels as well as numerous short stories and has edited multiple volumes of short stories as well as works of non-fiction related to science fiction and Fantasy.

The Man who Loved Mars (1973)

Ivo Tengren is enjoying a coffee in a piazza in Venice when he is approached by three strangers who ask after him. Tengren is wary of anyone who approaches him because he is a *persona non grata*. He was previously on Mars and was sent back to Earth as punishment for being a traitor to humankind because of his involvement with the native Martians. At this point we don't find out what caused him to become a traitor in the eyes of the humans colonizing Mars. His movements and activities are under constant surveillance by Earth authorities, and to be approached by three strangers in a public place is unusual, especially since they wish to confirm who he is.

They wish to take him back to Mars to assist them with an archaeological discovery, the ancient city of Ilionis. In these first few pages we find out much about Tengen and Mars, how he was in love with a beautiful Martian called Yakla and that she died in a battle between Martians and human colonists. We find that there are 9 tribes of Martians, savage descendants of an earlier more civilized race, but they don't occupy all of Mars and there is still much to be discovered. The three people who approached Tengren are an archaeologist, his niece, and a pilot. There are also a couple of burly bodyguards. They have a ship and are willing to take him back to Mars if he would help them find the ancient city of Ilionis.

Ilionis was once the capital city of a mighty empire as well as the gateway to the Gods, but it is now a dead ruin that no one believes exists anymore. It was dead and lost long before humans appeared on Earth. But the archaeologist is convinced he has found it, and they need someone like Tengren to assist them in exploring it, since Tengren has lived on Mars for years and can speak both the high and the low languages of the people. He agrees to go to Mars with these people because he is desperate to return.

In many ways, the kind of adventure that takes place in Carter's Martian novels is reminiscent of Westerns, with Humans (cowboys) traversing desert county occupied by noble savage tribes (Indians), who are under stress because humans are taking over their land, so they hate them and they fight against them at every opportunity.

As they begin their journey out into the desert wilderness, and the rocky uplands they encounter a wild tribe of warriors who are about to kill them. These are High clan warriors whose territory they have entered.

It turns out that Tengren had been accepted into the low clans and had fought with them against other human occupiers, and that he had been initiated into the four of the clans as a Holy Sovereign. But whether members of the high clans would accept this is uncertain. To prove it as they question him, he reveals the sigils embedded or tattooed into his chest, and from his backpack he removes a special cloak, which the now wide-eyed tribesmen recognize, and an iron crown that dates back to far ancient times and has been handed down from chief priest to chief priest for thousands of generations. This crown, all Martians know, and these wild tribesmen are in awe as Tengren places it on his head. It magnifies his thoughts and allows him to project thoughts into the minds of other people.

He projects into their minds; I am the Lord of Lords! I am the Prince of Princes. Nine nations rider in thunder at my heels, and nine banners go before me when I ride to war. Behold me in my power, and fear me. For the Timeless Ones watch over my path, and this world is my domain…

The tribe they'd encountered fall at his feet and pledge to follow him wherever he leads.

And so the quest begins.

To travel across the deserts, they use Slidars which are large reptiles that are used as pack animals or ridden as camels and horses are on Earth. The deserts are composed of fine sand or dust with the consistency of talcum powder. This dust if breathed in causes problems with the lungs and can be fatal, so dust storms are always avoided. The dust is always a problem anyway, as it penetrates everywhere. To keep warm and to be protected from the insidious dust humans wear special thermal suits.

There is a lot of details describing how Tengren became what he is to the Martians, and the reasons why they accept him. Martian history and mythology are revealed, and much of what we learn here is carried over into the subsequent novels. In fact, in the third novel references are made to specific incidents in this novel as well as the next one.

This particular tribal group, The Moon Dragons, are still living in an ancient city. Most other tribes have long abandoned any cities and live as nomads in the deserts and mountains. At this point in the story a description of the Martians is given, whereas in later stories only small hints of their appearance is necessary. Native Martians are taller and thinner than humans, but they have larger chests to accommodate extra oxygen storage cells needed to enable them to breathe the thinner atmosphere. Their heads and the backs of their hands don't have hair but are covered with a fine rust coloured silken fur which is an efficient insulation against heat loss. Their eyes are larger than ours with wider pupils to make use of the lesser light that bathes Mars compared to Earth. It is these slight differences combined with a certain gliding grace along with the copper hue of their skin that makes us think of cats. But in every other essential, they are as human as those who come from Earth. Carter makes a point of emphasizing how earthlike the Martians are in every aspect apart from their slight difference in appearance. This is necessary or else he couldn't tell the kind of stories that he does. He needs similar emotions and similar motives in order to justify the interactions that humans have with Martians. He lets his imagination roam when he has the odd large predator appear, with no explanation as to what these large predators would live on if there were no other smaller animals in the surrounding environment. Sandcats for example, which hide buried in the sand and leap out to attack anything that passes. If the deserts are barren, then what would be there for them to eat, if no human or Martian happened to be passing by? He does give a suggestion that along the wide, very deep cracks that observers from Earth first thought were canals, are inhabited by mosses and a rubbery kind of succulent that sends roots deep down (for miles) to obtain water, and that people extract water from these plants by distilling the chubby leaves. There is also a hint of some bio-diversity in amongst the plants and mosses, but Carter spends little time describing any of this. His main concern is to keep his story moving along at a good pace.

He does bring up several contrasting ideas regarding the origin of both Martians and Humans, to explain why they are very similar to each other, and concludes the various suggestions by saying that the truth is no one really knows.

The archaeologist discovers an inscription in this ancient still occupied city which he translates as here stands Farad (the name of the city) that guards the road to Ilionis, the Gateway to the Gods.

Having entered the city of Farad, they are required to attend a feast in their honor. The humans are aware of how much the Martians hate them, but the archaeologist can't understand why they love Tengren so much, being that he too is human.

Carter takes time here to reiterate the story of how the ancient High Priest (a person with similar power to the Pope and who keeps the nine nations from warring with each other) was taken into custody, for his own protection, by colonial authorities, and how he was being tortured to reveal hidden secrets. The captors were only after treasure, gold and jewels, which they were sure existed, but the drugs they gave him to make him reveal those secrets were killing him. Tengren, killed a guard and escaped with the old priest, who later died but before dying transferred his power through the crystals embedded in the iron crown which are attuned only to the one chosen by the high Priest to be his successor. At first, he wasn't accepted by the Martians, especially the priests, but the warriors concluded that the High Priest with millions of years of memories embedded in his mind knew what he was doing when he selected Tengren as his successor, and the fact that Tengren had killed some of his own kind to protect the High Priest convinced them he was on their side since he was being hunted by his own kind for being a traitor. Once Tengren had been captured by the Human authorities on Mars he was tried as a traitor and sent back to Earth where he was forbidden to return to Mars. The Martian tribesmen all thought he had been killed. But now, he would unite all of them and together they will fight to the last man to get rid of the Human occupiers.

The journey continues and they make their way to the fabled city of Ilionis. There are impediments along the way, but they finally get there and here Tengren discovers the truth of who the timeless ones are. They are aliens of humanoid appearance but of reptilian origin, and they have been in suspended animation for millions of years deep beneath the ancient and fabled city of Ilionis. And these aliens wield power beyond comprehension. Having awoken them, the intruders are now judged.

There are other betrayals and situations that complicate the story giving it a lot of depth and tension which keeps the reader on tenterhooks until the very end.

The Valley where Time Stood Still. (1974)

The story opens with M'Cord riding his slidar out in the desert where he has been prospecting when it lets out a wail. It has smelled something dead or dying. Slidars are lizards as big as a camel that in the wild are carrion feeders. He has been three months out in the desert heading towards the uplands of Eos to do some scouting around Mare Erythraeum, but he was in no hurry to get there.

Slidars have an uncanny sense of smell for something that is dead. So, M'Cord lets his run free and soon he comes upon a Martian warrior trapped with a broken leg underneath a dead slidar. The Martian looks on the verge of death. He is dehydrated with one leg underneath the carcass of the slider. They have a tendency to keep going until suddenly they just drop dead. If this happens while you are riding one, it can be dangerous. The slidar looked to have been dead for several days.

No one lived out in the desert. There are no camping places, and the nearest settlement was 1000 miles away, so he was surprised when he came across the trapped warrior. The Martian was lying on his back and had been trying to push the dead animal off his broken leg with his good leg, but had been unable to do so. He watched M'Cord approach and with his free hand he held a weapon pointed towards him. Martians hate humans which they call *F'yargh*. But no matter how much hatred there is between Martians and Humans, for those who wander in the wild places of the planet there is a code of conduct, a man helps another in need, regardless of blood, feuds or clan-wars, none of which are important when it comes to surviving.

M'Cord gets off his slidar and approaches the injured man. He keeps his hands where they can be clearly seen. He stops and unbuckles his gun belt and lets his weapons drop to the sand. He slowly approaches the trapped warrior and kneels beside him. He takes a canteen of water he has strapped to his side - he knows that if he offered water to the trapped man, it would put the man under an obligation to him - and tells the trapped man he found it in the desert, that it belongs to no one, and he will leave it here in case anyone passing may need it. By denying ownership of the water M'Cord makes it possible for the dying man to accept it without obligation. After a while M'Cord helps get the carcass off the warrior. He then proceeds to strap up the broken leg, setting it so the bones could knit.

When they finally get to talking, the warrior tells him his name is Thaklar, and has trouble pronouncing M'Cord and calls him Gort. M'Cord gives him some stew in which he places a pain killer and some medicine he hopes will help the healing of the bones. With Thaklar on the slidar and Gort walking beside him they travel the distance to where a wide crack in the surface allowed the growth of the blue coloured plants to survive. The Martian didn't give his clan's name, but M'Cord could clearly see he was from the High Clans rather than the Low Clans and was some 3000 miles away from his territory.

Here we learn something more about Mars, the customs of its people, and are presented with a mystery which promises to be intriguing. Who is Thaklar and what is he doing so far away from his customary territory?

As the two get to know each other in the second chapter they grudgingly begin to become friends. They come to an agreement about which direction to travel and begin their arduous journey together. As Thaklar begins to heal M'Cord is unexpectedly attacked by a vicious sandcat. Its claws rip through M'Cord's thermal suit and tear open his leg from the waist to the knee. They manage to kill it but the damage is done. Now it's Thaklar's turn to help Gort. Remembering how Gort had helped him he returns the gesture by offering him some of his own water. *Share my water, Brother*, he says, and the two are irrevocably bound together as brothers.

Thaklar reveals he is heir to the lost greatness of Ancient Mars, knowing the way or the road to the fabled Valley where time stands still, the Martian equivalent of the Garden of Eden. The secret way and a map are passed from generation to generation but Thaklar foolishly fell in love with a dancer who managed to get the secret and the map from him before disappearing. He was outcast and is now searching for this woman, Zerilda, so he can reclaim the map and take revenge. He knows he can never return to his people but the least he could do is to kill the woman who stole the secret thus stopping it from being passed on to anyone else.

When M'Cord's slidar drops dead unexpectedly, it is left for Thaklar to carry Gort, and he struggles towards the ruins of an ancient city where they both collapse in the shade of a wall and sip the last of the water left in Thaklar's canteen.

They are there, almost dead when a bunch of bandits arrive. Amongst them is the very woman Thaklar has been searching for, Zerilda. Also with them is an archeologist Karl Nordgen, and his sister Inga, who have been taken hostage. Chastar the bandit leader and his associate, a stunted priest called Phuun, are using them to help find the way to the hidden valley, as delineated in the map Zerilda stole from Thaklar. Everyone wants to discover the lost Eden of Mars, although most believe it is nothing more than a myth.

The next third of the book is about their journey to find the location of the lost valley, and for this the bandits keep Thaklar and Gort alive. There is a section on the map that is blank, and what should go there is only in the memory of Thaklar, so they need him to guide them to last part of the way to the hidden valley, and he refuses to help if they kill Gort. They all then go together.

The descriptions of the terrain they cross matches photos taken by satellites encircling Mars so the reader knows the places depicted actually exist and can follow the journey on a detailed map of Mars if so desired. For the most part, Carter's descriptions of the different Martian locations are accurate, but he has taken some 'licence' to make the planet more habitable for his characters while still maintaining a feeling of authenticity regarding the landscape.

From above, the hidden valley looks just like another chasm in a mountainous area full of chasms and badly broken terrain. But there are steps carved into the side of the cleft that leads down so they know this is the one, even though looking down it looks like any other jagged chasm. They discover more than half way down, there is a barrier that reflects an image of the chasm back up. The barrier is amorphous and they can continue down the steps right through it, and once underneath a fantastic sight opens up. The air is thick with moisture, and rich in oxygen, there are trees and flowers and grass and running water.

Thaklar warns the bandits that they can turn back if they want, but to continue was dangerous. The valley will fulfill their desires whatever they may be. To drink of the fountain of youth, to live forever, to be healed of all wounds, all is possible, but it all comes with consequences. Each will get what they deserve. But of course, warnings are ignored and Chaster insists on going down into the hidden valley.

The last part of the story is more fantasy than science fiction, but is nicely written since Carter was predominantly a writer of fantasy rather than science fiction, and we see how each of the bandits, the nasty priest, the dancer, the archaeologist all get what they desired and deserved but it is not what they expected. After experiencing some of the marvels of this valley where time stands still, where ancient life forms exist together in harmony, we get to see what happens when this harmony is disturbed.

Understanding the situation, M'Cord and Thaklar try to remain apart from the others and Thaklar insists they should leave the valley. M'Cord who has fallen for Inga wants to rescue her. And Zerilda has also changed for the better, having lost her memory of what she did or once was. Thaklar rescues her and the four of them leave the valley and climb back up the stairs along the side of the mountain. Emerging from the veil that hides the secret valley below they are shocked at the coldness and the thinness of the atmosphere. It takes a while for them to readjust to the real Mars before they can continue the long climb back up out of the hidden valley.

At the top they part ways with Thaklar, with Zerilda, heading back to his own lands, and M'Cord and Inga heading toward Lacus Solis, the nearest human settlement where he intends to marry the Inga.

The City Outside of the World. (1977)

Another familiar plot; Ryker is a loner who spends a lot of time out in the desert, and when he comes into a settlement or a town he stays in the 'native quarter' because the police don't go in there. He is a dubious character who is a smuggler, a gun runner and was wanted for air-car theft among other things. He has arrived at an ancient town called Yeolarn which is older by a million years more than any ancient city on Earth that archaeologists have discovered. While looking for somewhere to stay he feels that he is being hunted. His first mistake is to think it is the police that are looking for him.

He does his best to avoid any watchers, entering the oldest part of the old city to evade them (his second mistake) and ends up in a club that he knows well, (his third mistake) where he sees a particularly strange but beautiful dancer performing a naked dance. She wears only a mask that covers her eyes. She is accompanied by an old man who played a small drum to which she danced, and a young boy who goes around collecting tips after her performance has ended. Everyone in the club was entranced, including Ryker. But as the dancer leaves the room Ryker catches a glimpse of her eyes. They were golden, in a face seemingly cat-like, which meant she was not a Martian. She was not an Earthsider either, which meant she was of an unknown race or perhaps from an unknown world.

His fourth mistake is, having left the club he sees the dancer and her companions leaving and walking down a dark narrow street, he decides to follow them. At this point he becomes aware that there are many hidden people out and about and they seem to be following the dancer's group. Through narrower, even darker streets, the hidden crowd seems to be herding the dancer's group towards a blocked off street where there is no way out. He hears whispers echoing along the narrow alleyways, *Zhaggua*, a rarely used word that means Devil in old Martian. Ryker slips into the small square and hides within a dark doorway as a crowd appears and blocks the way out. These people are now chanting and yelling *Zhaggua, Zhaggua*. With the dancer and her companions cowering against a high wall some of the crowd begin throwing stones at the three trapped people. Very quickly they turn into a mob. Ryker steps from cover and starts firing his energy pistols to stop them. He kills some and forces the others to retreat. But there is no way out of the square other than the path they followed in, and the mob is back there regrouping for another attack.

As all this was going on we also get some back story about Ryker having found a very ancient temple lost in the desert along the shore of what was an ancient sea. He took a number of small artifacts and sold them on the black market, all but one small thing, which for some reason he felt compelled to keep. He wears this on a cord around his neck. This gives us a reason to understand why he is being hunted.

While the mob regroups, Ryker breaks into a building through a window and the dancer and her two companions follow him inside. They go down to the cellar because most cellars have a grate that leads to an old unused sewer system. They prise up the grate and descend into the sewer, closing the grate to forestall being discovered too soon. It won't take long for the mob to find the broken window and know where they went. They follow the sewer to the edge of the city heading to a trading store that Ryker knows well. He obtains four slidars from an old friend who runs the store and with enough supplies they make their way out into the desert.

The middle part of the story is again a chase story as Ryker and his three companions head towards the barren area of the North Pole. They could have gone in a number of directions but for some reason they go that way because it is the more unlikely choice. Ryker of course becomes fascinated by the strange beautiful dancer with the golden eyes. They have a run in with some dangerous native predators, but survive that. No Martian story by Carter is complete without at least one such event.

Taking refuge in an old ruin to avoid a sand storm they encounter a caravan, of the usual odd Martian mix and things begin to get complicated. Valarda, the strange girl with the golden eyes, agrees to dance for the members of the caravan in order to pay for them allowing the group to travel with them. Ryker has a run in with one of the guards and after a fight is accepted by them and will take part in guarding the caravan in payment for being allowed to travel with them.

Camping for the night in another old city, which for some strange reason caused a strong emotional response from the dancer and her friends, Valarda dances for the men of the caravan, much wine is drunk and Ryker finally goes to sleep, only to wake up unexpectedly in the middle of the night. He quietly sneaks out and sees a small group of warriors sneaking up the stairs towards where he was sleeping. He instantly disappears. He knows these are the men who have really been following him, and they have finally caught up with him. The leader of the caravan kept delaying their departure using a number of excuses to keep them there.

In the morning the caravan is in an uproar having discovered a band of wild warriors had ridden into their camp during the night without being discovered, and they had with them a captive, an old man with white hair. The caravan had been waiting for them.

That night Ryker had trouble sleeping, because he was afraid. Something odd was going on.

The word *Zhaggua* is whispered by the members of the caravan, and Ryker knows they are referring to the girl and her companions, though not to him. Him they hate because he is human, *F'yargh*.

The caravan moves on and ascends out of the desert up into the hills that marked the edge of an ancient continent. A small party ascends the mountain first, Zalarda and her two companions with Ryker and Zarouk the leader of the Warriors who had joined them and the old priest. Camping for the night Ryker wakes in the morning to find the girl and her companions gone, his hands are bound behind his back and the small artifact he kept in a bag on a strap around his neck has vanished with them. He has been betrayed by those he tried to help. Not only were they gone, they had taken all the food and drink along with their sleeping gear as well.

They had left him there to die.

Zarouk, the leader of warriors that had joined the caravan laughed at him. No one can trust a *Zhaggua*. But he too was bound, along with the old priest, bound and left for dead, just as Ryker was.

Eventually they free themselves, vowing to take revenge on the girl and her two companions.

The last part of the book opens with Ryker sustaining injuries from being whipped by Zarouk's men. The old human captive with white hair tends to Ryker's wounds. He is an archaeologist who had been searching for petroglyphs amongst the ruins when Zarouk's men captured him. They want him to help them identify the way into the mythological city that sits outside of this world. A myth to all but Zarouk who believes it. He also knows that the artifact stolen from around Ryker's neck by the dancer, was the key to open the door to this mythological city. Using a means of mind control generated by drugs the old priest with Zaruok puts Ryker into a trance in which he replicates the artifact he had once had around his neck. Now they have a copy of the key. They decide to keep him alive in case the key doesn't work and they need to make another, since how it appears is embedded in the deep recesses of Ryker's mind.

Following the tracks of the missing dancer and her companions, they enter the wild shadowed area close to the north pole where they discover a huge carving of an insect-like thing, which they call the Sphinx of Mars. It appears to be solid rock, and search as they do, they can't find an entrance. The next morning someone accidentally triggered something and an entrance was revealed. The men enter warily and follow a path through a black tunnel into a wide room where an obvious circular section of the back wall appears to be a door of some kind. There were no hinges to indicate how it could open, but in the very centre of the blank smooth wall was a place where the key that Ryker had recreated could be placed. Zarouk got the priest to put it the replica there to see what would happen. They had to reposition it and then a shimmer went across the circular door and it melted into a spangled, glittering mist. Beyond it they saw a golden light. A wind blew onto their faces, perfumed and, strange to them, moist. The door to outside was open.

The rest of the story takes place in a Mars that only existed millions of years in the past when it had a thicker atmosphere, and a rich bio-diversity of plant and animal life. The golden eyed people live in a walled city which is guarded by stone robots and the warriors of Zarouk can make no headway against them no matter what they try.

The dancer is their spiritual leader and forbids any harm being done to the warriors attacking them, but some of her retinue are more warlike and want to fight these intruders. A number of battles ensue, and eventually the warriors find a way into the walled city. Meanwhile inside the city a small revolution takes place and the golden eyed dancer is removed from her position of leadership. She is made a prisoner and along with Ryker who has been captured, they are taken deep down into the bowels of the city where they are told they will be judged by the ancient Gods, and if forgiven, will be released, otherwise they will die there.

There are skeletons chained at the edge of a massive pit that appears bottomless. These skeletons are removed and Ryker and Zalarda are chained in their place. Ryker was put there first, and Zalarda a day or so later. The old retainer is also chained up and the young boy throws himself down into the pit.

Once the boy hits the bottom almost instantly something happens. A huge glowing thing rises up out of the pit. Light pours out into the room and the warriors fall to their knees in awe as something frighteningly weird rises up out of the pit. Whatever it is, it talks to them telepathically.

It tells them it is a child of the stars, and that it has wandered the universe since the very beginning, searching for another like itself, searching thousands of stars, but finally tuning to nurturing the life it found on Mars. Upset that people were warring with each other it decides to teach them all a lesson. It brings back the already slaughtered ones who then tear apart the others who are still fighting. Finally, when it is over, the child of the stars directs the already dead to leave and they walk off into the wilderness. It heals the wounded and decrees the vanquished shall live here with the victors and it tells them it will seal the door so no one can escape to the future. Its ruling for Zalarda is that she now becomes an ordinary citizen and the role of the priesthood has been given to the boy who sacrificed himself but who had been brought back to life. Zalarda is now free to wed Ryker, but all of them must live out their lives in this rebuilt city.

I felt this last part simply didn't fit with any of the earlier sections being far too fantasy-like, even more so than the hidden valley in the previous novel.

The first novel finishes with the lead character fighting with the Martians as their leader, fighting to get rid of the human presence on Mars. The next two resort to fantasy endings (which don't really fit the part of the story previously told to that point) in which there is a complete turnaround of the main character who ends up falling in love with a beautiful Martian woman and presumably living happily after that.

Down to a Sunless Sea (1984)

There is a seven-year gap before Lin Carter wrote this fourth Mars story.

It opens with Brandt, a fugitive from the nearest human colony, after having stabbed someone to death in a bar room brawl, out in the desert and looking for somewhere to hide from a rapidly approaching dust storm. He finds the ruins of an ancient settlement, of which there are many scattered around the deserts along what used to be ancient shorelines when Mars had seas, and on entering he immediately see a naked woman spread-eagled and staked onto the ground. She is almost dead from dehydration and exposure, so he naturally helps her, offering her water and releases her from the cords binding her to 4 stakes. She begs him to release her sister who is also bound as she was. By the time Brandt has released the other woman the storm is upon them and they retreat into a basement where there is some protection from the storm.

We find out the women had been set out to die because they had been lovers, which is anathema to the native tribesmen. He tells them he isn't going anywhere near civilized places for at least a month, so if they are okay with that, with being out in the desert country for that time, then they are welcome to accompany him. They tell him they will cook and clean for him, but they will not open their legs for him, which is fine by Brandt, even though he is attracted to the one he released first who is called Zuarra.

The next day Brandt continues on his way with the two women and there is an incident as they are descending down an escarpment where a ferocious serpentine-like creature with three sets of short legs that they call a rock dragon attacks them. Brandt at first is helpless to stop the attack since his slider stumbled and his arm is strapped. He tosses one of his guns to the sister to shoot at the attacking rock dragon but she cowers against the rocks by the ledge they are using to descend into the valley below and doesn't do anything. Finally, Brandt releases his arm and manages to shoot the rock dragon. From that point on Zuarra is not too happy with her sister, Suoli, and wants no more to do with her.

Down on the sandy plain below Brandt spots two strangers who appear to be having trouble so he goes to help, with the women tagging along. No matter who it might be, no one goes off and leaves someone who might be in trouble. It is an unwritten code that everyone helps everyone else, out in the desert if they are in trouble.

They encounter an old Earthsider archaeologist who is being guided by a local warrior. They are in trouble, their slidars having been attacked by a sand cat, another ferocious creature that lives in the desert. The native guide is a wiry typical outcast, while the Earthman is a couple of decades older than Brandt. He is an archaeologist out collecting and looking for fossils. The native guide eyes the new arrivals with suspicion. But they join forces and head back towards the escarpment that marks the edge of an ancient continent once bathed by the sea that covered what is now nothing but a vast desert. They are searching for a cave where they can spend the night relatively safe from sand cats or other predators.

Before settling down for the night the native guide Agila, tries to make a pass at Zuarra, but Brandt stops him with a vicious punch to his face. Agila slinks away leaving them alone for the night. Zuarra begins to look at Brandt differently. She doesn't understand why he stopped Agila, and Brandt tells her it is because she is a woman. Brandt is very respectful of women. This leaves Zuarra wondering…

The next morning, they notice they are being watched by two riders partly hidden at the top of the ridge. They follow them as they move along the old sea floor. Brandt notices that Agila is acting nervous when he sees the riders. Brandt confronts Agila and finds out he has stolen something from the chief of the warrior band that is following them, an ancient bowl made of Martian gold that has ancient writing on it. That means that because they have associated with this thief, they are now as guilty as he is in the eyes of the warriors following them.

They are being followed discretely all day, and they decide that during the night they will leave their tents and sneak off, while the warriors think they are sleeping for the night. Using the golden bowl which has a map on it, the Archaeologist figures out where there should be a gap or a narrow cave, as indicated on the map in the bowl. But it is hard to see since a million years of wind erosion may have hidden it. The group know it is only a matter of time before the warriors find a way down the escarpment, so sneaking off in the dark is their only advantage.

They find the ancient cave and go inside. The floor is paved and way down inside they discover a metal door. Using their energy guns as cutting tools, they burn through the hinges and get the door open. It leads to a series of steps going down deep into the darkness. They leave their gear by the door and with some food and their water bottles they head off down the steps, along with the stolen bowl in the hope that the bandits, when they recover it, will not continue the chase. There are thousands of steps going down seemingly endlessly, but they keep going. After some time, the air they breathe becomes moister and the temperature rises, forcing them to take off their clothes which they carry with them as they continue to descend. Finally, after hours, the Stygian blackness dissipates and further down they see a golden glow. They emerge into a lush forest of giant mushrooms and other fungi. Pushing through that, they discover an enormous sea. The light that permeates the world within Mars is coming from the sea. (Some sort of fluorescent algae). The Martians are having trouble breathing the moist humid air but the two Earthsiders have no problem at all. They grew up breathing thicker more humid air on Earth.

Too exhausted to do much else, they end up falling asleep on the beach by the endless sea.

When they wake up, they spend time examining the mushroom forest and see many wonderful things. The Martians are more astonished than the Earthsiders because they have never imagined anything like this could exist, living entirely on the surface where it is barren and rocky, or replete with endless deserts with not a drop of water in sight. They can't get over their amazement with the sight of the sea, which like the Dead Sea is so salty they can practically walk on it. Agila switches his amorous approaches to Suoli who doesn't seem to mind at all.

The next day they are woken by the bandit warriors who have been following them. As they try to resist the bandits they are attacked and captured by a bunch of young children riding flying insects that look like gigantic dragonflies. They are carried over the water to a boat that they hadn't noticed and dropped on board. The boat sets off across the sea pulled by the large dragonflies, while the children with golden eyes are trying to converse with them. The language they use is so ancient, no one knows it.

Brandt and the archaeologist start to learn the ancient language and manage to pick it up quickly. The others don't try. Brand and the leader of the bandits agree to a truce while they are in this strange world.

After travelling for many hours they come to a city floating on the water beside a beach. There they cause a sensation. No one in this world has ever imagined there was something outside of their world and that these strangers have come from another world. Brandt, his party, and the bandits are treated as guests and given quarters to spend their time in.

During this time, Brandt and Zuarra have become lovers and discover in each other true affection and respect. These new Martians are like innocent children living in a Garden of Eden. Brandt is worried that he has brought the serpent into the garden and that soon, something awful is going to happen.

Sure enough, it does. Agila, greedy and somewhat nasty, has attacked the chief of these people and stolen the jewels he had around his neck on a number of chains. Agila has stabbed him to death. Suoli had one of the power guns stolen from Brandt by the bandits when they overpowered them in the mushroom forest, while Agila had the other. The innocent people crowding in to see what had happened all wailed with the horror of it. They joined hands and their eyes went blank. Agila started to choke. He collapsed in a heap and died, killed by the mental power of the gentle Martians. In a panic Suoli started to aim the power gun at them and she too collapsed in a heap and choked to death. Both of them killed by the gentle Martians that lived in this lost place.

They told the other visitors they had to leave. They would be taken back to where they had been captured and would be left there.

After burying Agila and Suoli, the others are taken to the ship and it takes them back to where they had stood when they first saw the glowing sea. They gather their equipment and head back towards the steps leading up to the surface of the world. The leader of the bandits tells Brandt that he no longer has a feud with him. The thief (of the ancient golden bowl) has paid for his crime, and Brandt and his friends had not known of it when they became involved with Agila. He hands brandt back the weapons he'd taken when he captured them in the forest.

When they finally get to the surface again, they each go their separate ways, and Brandt tells the archaeologist he is going to Sun Lake City and will marry Zuarra.

In each of the three novels after *The Man Who Loved Mars*, the lead character, in the course of the story, finds love and becomes a changed person. Only in that first published novel does the lead become something entirely different.

In a note at the end of the fourth book, Lin Carter explains that he was inspired by Leigh Brackett, (whose stories he read in the SF magazines when he was a teenager) and the planetary romances by people like Edgar Rice Burroughs. He says he even tried to write his four stories in a similar style to the way Leigh Brackett had done hers.

And just to be clear, his first published Martian story is chronologically the fourth, and takes place after the other three. Also, they are not a series, but a loose sequence with Mars as the only common setting. There are no characters that carry over from one story to another, or plots that carry over, as one would find in a series. Each story is set in one quarter of Mars and since the four quarters have been covered, there will be no more Martian stories. (He said that when it was published in 1984).

I for one, enjoyed them, even though they seemed a bit dated by today's standards. I think anyone who likes the old style of planetary romance, the kind of SF that was written during the first half of the last century will enjoy these.

As we get into the 1990's more realistic depictions of what Mars could be like began to appear along with obvious political ideas reflecting the way the world was in the 1990s. Mick Farren came up with a story that depicts the ideas and angst of that decade almost perfectly, translating it into action on Mars.

Mars — The Red Planet by Mick Farren (1990)
The story opens with a superstar reporter Lech Hammond and his videographer arriving on Mars to follow up the rumors that the Soviets had found something alien near Olympus Mons and that they were covering it up, keeping it secret.

At the same time as they arrive, Casey, the Marshal from the American settlements is investigating a series of brutal murders of prostitutes. He has been invited to the Russian sector to help investigate a similar brutal murder that had taken place. His Russian counterpart Irina, believes it is the same killer. The KGB however don't want the Americans in their sector, and they make it hard for Casey as well as for Hammond's news team, kicking them out before they can do any investigating.

Mars is occupied by both Americans and Russians along with Cubans who basically work for the Russians. There are also numbers of crazy people who live like bandits in the areas near Olympus Mons and they prey on travelers or other small groups that go there for whatever reasons. The common idea is that these wild bandits known as *Macheteros* have gone a bit crazy because of the isolation and harshness of the Martian environment.

The story is told from several viewpoints which all come together as the story evolves. Hammond and his steam decide to follow up on the rumors that the Russians are hiding an alien artifact near Olympus Mons where they have a secret base which everyone knows exists but no one has seen. Casey determines that the serial killer who murders and dismembers prostitutes is an American serviceman, but can't pursue his investigation because the American Marine base has been shut off for security reasons and they won't allow him access. He discovers that a covert mission which has his suspect as a member has set off for Olympus Mons to find out what the Russians are up to. He decides to follow them to keep track of his suspect. Meanwhile the KGB has cracked down on people it doesn't like in the Russian sector, taking control, and sending Irina (not arrested) but with a group of political prisoners to a slave base they have near the Olympus Mons installation. When Casey hears about the accident the transport with them has, and how they are force-marched to an independent settlement where they can wait for another transport, he decides to go and rescue Irina with whom he has formed a romantic association.

In the background it is noted that pieces of this alien artifact near Olympus Mons have been taken away and various people have acquired these pieces which begin to affect their minds making them do violent or crazy things. We have seen how the serial killer seems to be possessed by an alien entity. We also can assume that the crazy people (*Macheteros*) who live wild out in the territory near Olympus Mons may have been affected by this alien artifact, so our expectations are that this artifact is somehow alive and evil. We now suspect that the KGB leaders in the Russian sector have been affected by this alien entity which makes them ultra-paranoid. The closer the news team gets to Olympus Mons and the secret Russian base they too begin to have strange effects happening to their minds the longer they remain in that area. While they are refueling and stocking up on oxygen at an independent privately-owned base, an attempt is made to murder a prostitute by one of the covert American team and now everyone knows who the serial killer is, but the covert team continue their mission regardless.

Casey manages to rescue Irina and has the Russians after him, while he and Irina go after the serial killer, whose covert team is heading for the Russian base. Hammond and his news group also head for the Russian base looking to reveal to the world, the truth of what the Russians are hiding there.

Everything falls apart when they all get to the base. While the American covert team sends in its super weaponized man the other two, the serial killer and a female analyst, the serial killer murders her, strips her suit off and begins to dismember her. Casey and Irina arrive and Casey catches the killer in the act. They both shoot each other and die. (A big disappointment because I liked Casey and felt that he should have survived.) Irina is devastated. Meanwhile entering the base, the super weaponized marine, the last of a group called *Rambos*, has penetrated the base and killed a couple of defenders but discovers that the Russians weren't really trying to keep people out, they were trying to keep people in. Everyone inside the base has been affected or infected by the alien artifact, and most have murdered each other. The few survivors only survive because they remain hyped up on drugs to keep them awake. Their minds are taken over if they sleep. The news team gets inside and they want to broadcast to the world what is going on. The world should know about this artifact. Outside the Russians have sent a fleet of MIG fighters to the base. The Americans have also sent an air strike unit and there is a stand-off between the two forces. Inside the base the true nature of the artifact is revealed and those people inside eventually decide that they must eject the artifact into interstellar space where it can do no harm.

After some arguments and confrontation, it is decided that the artifact will be cut into smaller segments and rail-gunned into a Martian orbit where sails will be attached so the pieces can be sent off into interstellar space. It is thought that with the artifact gone the effect it had on humans will also be gone. Unfortunately, this may not be the case...

Once this is done, the story is finished, except for one final note, a scene from the viewpoint of the artifact which is alive and has been for millions of years. It is happy to have escaped Mars and it will in time reassemble itself as it comes together somewhere in interstellar space. But the twist is that it is also happy to have gotten rid of the mind parasites that occupied it for so long, (perhaps implying that these parasites were the reason it crashed onto Mars in the first place) leaving them with those short-lived creatures on the Red Planet.

There was also *The Stone Canal* by Ken Macleod (1996)

I Remember I had a copy of this book in 1997 and read the first two chapters before setting it aside. At the time I didn't like it, but thought I would come back to it later. I must have forgotten about it because I never saw it again. A couple of months ago, 24 years later, I suddenly remembered it and of course couldn't find it anywhere. I searched for it on *ABE BOOKS* and bought a second-hand copy.

Once again, I started to read it but found it hard going. I don't know if it is the tone the author uses or the way he writes, but I simply couldn't identify with any of the characters or with the two settings; one at some indeterminate time in the future on Mars and the other, a little ahead of the present time in Scotland. The socialist anarchic background he uses for the Scottish chapters also didn't appeal to me. I managed to read 104 pages this time, up to chapter 8 before putting it aside.

I simply didn't care that Dee Model — a clone belonging to a wealthy person who used her as a sex slave — has suddenly become self-aware after a mysterious phone call activates hidden programming. She seeks to gain independence as an individual, while trying to determine what her relationship is to Jon Wilde who could be the mysterious stranger who walks into the settlement from out of the Martian desert. He seemed to think Dee was familiar when he saw her in a bar.

Later Dee discovers some ancient photos which show her as the wife of Jon Wilde. Are they both clones of the original couple in the photo? Jon Wilde supposedly died a century earlier and how he could possibly exist at this point in the story has yet to be explained unless he is a clone. Is Jon Wilde the anarchist who is disrupting the political scene in the alternate chapters set in Scotland? I thought those chapters were a distraction and interrupted the flow of the story set on Mars. No doubt they will have something to do with what happens on Mars further into the story, but I doubt now if I will read any more of it to find out.

As I've mentioned elsewhere, there are some books you can't read no matter what. Unfortunately for me this book falls into that category. I did try because it comes recommended by his contemporaries Peter F Hamilton and Iain Banks. Even *New Scientist* said '*Macleod's ideas are always interesting and his descriptive prose is elegant, deceptively simple and extremely vivid.*'

I do like those authors, but somehow, I find Macleod to be too downbeat for me. Having tried to read him twice, I don't anticipate trying a third time. That is not to say others could find his socialist-anarchic background, or his extrapolated futures absolutely fascinating. By all means, if you haven't read him, please give his stories a try.

More Dreams of Mars

Part Three

Onwards into the new millennium

Beyond 2000

Chapter Nine

A new Golden Age

From the year 2000 and on, there have been no end to stories about Mars, and every year, as we get closer to an actual trip to the Red Planet, more and more stories appear. Some are very good, but others are not worth reading or spending money to buy them. The trouble is, you don't know this until you purchase them and start reading.

Whether they are purchased as eBooks or as printed books is up to the readers and their preferences. I don't like eBooks and prefer a printed book. Always, the printed version is a lot more expensive than the electronic one, especially when postage is added to the cost, which means that sometimes a book that appears promising is far too expensive for me to buy.

The majority of these stories are self published so the quality of the finished product is also quite variable, but can be especially poor when printed as a paperback rather than as an electronic download. However, that is a risk I am willing to take most of the time unless there is no other option other than an eBook.

Now that we are well into the new millennium, even traditional publishers are no longer printing large quantities of stock for distribution. They are listing their books, as they have always done, on websites and in journals, only now they are often print on demand, unless the author is famous and lots of sales are guaranteed. If you see a book listed on your favourite book shop's website and order it, the book will be delivered in a few days, printed and sent to you. These publisher's POD books are indistinguishable from any book you would buy if you walked into a bookshop and saw it on the shelf.

For writers, the advent of self-publishing and POD has been a boon, giving them opportunities they might never have had. It has also caused the beginning of a new *Golden Age*, not only for writers of stories about Mars, or writers of science fiction and fantasy, but for all writers regardless of the genre. There are more books published now than there has ever been before, and this trend looks set to continue.

Destination Mars by Dave Tyson (2000)

(*An often used title used on a number of books both fictional and non-fictional about going to Mars and the lead-up to the voyage*).

This story has moments of excitement which proves the author can write action scenes; but overall, the story is confusing and disjointed.

In an alliance with the Egyptians, as a result of a strange artifact made of an alien metal alloy discovered beneath a pyramid, some of this metal was stolen by an American military person and was taken back to the US where it is used in the construction of a space ship to take a crew to Mars.

This space ship has two elements to it, a civilian scientific mission and a secret military mission. The story moves ahead in disjointed fragments which made it hard for this reader to make sense of it. There is a saboteur on board the ship who is destroying necessary equipment. The suspicion is that it is one of the Egyptian crew who is sabotaging the mission. One of the women on board, is pregnant, but it isn't clear who the father is. He lover from years before is the captain of the military aspect of the mission, and he is married to the woman who stole him away from her. There is obviously tension between the two women. But it is a large crew and the rival woman stays in the military part of the ship. The rest of the crew is multi-national with British and French members.

Their mission almost becomes a disaster when they do a flyby of Venus to gain a gravity boost to slingshot them to Mars. Some rather strange things are discovered on Venus as they skim its atmosphere. By this time their ship is not in the best condition and there is a dispute about whether they should slingshot to mars or return to Earth. However, with the book almost finished they go on to Mars where the real saboteur is revealed, as they discover the origin of the strange metal they found under the pyramid in Egypt. They go to the Cydonia region where the final disaster takes place and the real villains are revealed. By far the shortest part of the story is the actual mission to Mars, their arrival, and what happens to them when they make landings in two different places. Most of it concerns the lead up to the journey and how the crew is determined. What is not clear is what the military are up to and their reasons for doing what they do. It was supposed to be a secret, but some detail regarding the military reasoning should be revealed to the readers for this aspect of the story to make sense. What is the purpose to release several missiles down through the atmosphere of Venus, and why do they need atomic weapons and high explosives on Mars?

The story finishes abruptly with a few loose ends that give the impression there will be a sequel, but I am not aware that any sequel was written.

Alan Bean, the pilot of the lunar module for Apollo 12 gives the book a good recommendation, and in retrospect it is obvious he has contributed sufficient information to make the scenes in space and on the Moon credible.

But because the background detail regarding the world political systems in this imagined near future is sparse and confusing, and because there are forward jumps of several years apart in the lead up to the mission to Mars, it was hard for me to visualize the characters and to believe in their motivations for what they do.

UNFS1
United Nations Frontier Service 1
The story of Mars Colony
John A Wells (2001)

Six young men and women, all young, very fit and highly educated are selected by the United Nations to take on the challenge of establishing a colony on Mars. Their job is to construct the base and the facilities that would be used by subsequent colonists to be sent to Mars in three years' time. The three men and three women are from diverse backgrounds from around the world.

There are already colonies on the Moon in 2008 and there is a space station orbiting Mars from which materials are ferried down to the surface. Anti-matter was produced in a laboratory in 1996 and 98 and shortly after a space ship drive using anti-matter was developed. There is a space station orbiting Earth built in 2004 as well.

There is a timeline at the beginning of the story which details the developments that lead to the moment the story opens with the six people selected to go up into orbit and then onto the Moon before being sent to Mars. The timeline covers a period from 1996 to 2008, which makes me think we are in an alternate timeline, or else the author really had no idea of what developments had already taken place regarding shuttles, the history of space development from the 1960s until the present time, 2020. If he had set his timeline to begin from 2010 to 2040 then the developments suggested would be more acceptable. But to have the events in the story taking place ten years ago rather than twenty or more years in the future is a bit odd.

There is also a list of the six characters with details about each one such as height, where they come from, general appearance and scientific degrees and other pertinent facts. This saves the author from inserting these details into the story itself as it evolves, which means for me as a reader the characters do not come alive. It is difficult to picture them as individuals without having to refer back to the list of characteristics and accomplishments of each person listed at the start.

It is published by *Minerva Press,* a well-known vanity publishing house. (*You pay them to print books for you and then it is up to you to sell them as best you can. They don't distribute or do anything else.*)

This is the first book the author has written at the age of 63 — he was born in 1937, which makes him 83 now in 2020, and still writing. It was inspired by a series of articles published in *The Daily Express* in 1999.

It reads like an adventure written for younger readers, like the kind of space action story published in magazines of the 1940s and 50s.

Having finished their training, they set off for Mars from the Moon, and begin the construction of the colony base. Apart from an accident, everything goes fine and the domes and other accommodations are quickly constructed. One of the women, Jane Obotto is Nigerian and also has a degree in witch-doctoring. She uses her skills at mentally manipulating atoms to fix a broken leg and so from this point on the story veers away from science fiction into science fantasy. Jane teaches the others how to be witch doctors, and in no time they are using telekinesis to levitate objects used in the construction of the base and manipulation of atoms to heal injuries.

There is no mention of whether they use space suits or atmospheric suits when out on the surface, no mention of whether the atmosphere is breathable or of its low pressure that would require some kind of suit, no mention of how cold Mars really is, no mention of the hard radiation that bathes the surface. In other words, everything about Mars is like what people in the 1950s thought they knew with none of what is known today. Everything in the story appears to be extrapolated from ideas extant during that era ignoring all the information gained over the last four decades. This is an old-fashioned Mars, (minus the canals thankfully).

The colonists use their 'dousing' skills to search Mars for mineral deposits around which they plan to establish mining centers, as well as to look for evidence of ancient visitations by extra-solar aliens. This they do because they are shown on the Moon, during their training, an alien humanoid body in what appears to be a cryogenic preservation capsule millions of years old. This is top secret. Searching for evidence of aliens on Mars as part of their mission, they find remnants of a crashed ship scattered widely across the planet and they collect these things, using telekinesis to bring them back to their base. Through careful study they discover a number of star systems from which these alien visitors could have come.

Their boss tells them that (they have now been over three years on Mars) that they are building generation ships, around the Moon and Mars, with the intention of sending humans to nearby star systems in search of these ancient aliens. Meanwhile, the first lot of colonists arrive to occupy the base already established, and the six original colonists set about training them for the tasks they would need to do to survive, and that includes teaching the medical doctors the art of being a witch doctor. The story finishes with the six original Mars colonists selecting a generation ship to take on a voyage to the first likely star system the aliens may have come from. Each of the three women is pregnant.

Strangely enough, the story is quite enjoyable if a little flat. If I had come across this when I was in my teenage years during the 1950s I probably would have enjoyed it much more, but it wasn't written then, it was written between 2000 to 2001.

I have no idea of how successful this story may have been, but it was reprinted in 2015, and then followed up by the next story in the series, *The First Generation Ship*, then *The Fleet Goes Out* (2016), *Mars Colony, Human and Senti* (2016), and *Hotab, Interstellar Diplomat,* (2017)

Each book is called *United Nations Frontier Service – UNFS* followed by a number, 1 to 5, with the subtitle beneath it. They come in matching covers and are quite attractive. I have not been able to obtain the following stories so can't comment on what they are like.

Phobos (2003) by Ty Drago.

This is hard to put down once you start reading. It is an old-fashioned story like the kind encountered in the 1950s and early 1960s, but updated with more modern technology. It is a police procedural set on Mars, and Phobos where most of the action takes place.

Mars has been colonized for over two hundred years and a large population exists on the planet. A private corporation controls all activities on the planet. Martians mostly work as miners supplying Earth with raw materials. Earth humans look down upon Martian humans considering them to be less than themselves and rather dull witted, but Martians have other ideas. They want to be more independent. There are even groups, gangs, in densely populated urban domes who act like terrorists against the corporation that controls them and the planet. The story opens with a Martian commissioned officer, Lt Mike Brogue, the only one in the police force, foiling a terrorist plot that threatens to blow up one of the major population centers. He is a tactical analyst and wants nothing more than to do his job. Suddenly famous for foiling this terrorist threat he does all he can to avoid publicity and asks to be sent off-planet. His superiors send him to Phobos where a mystery that has caused the death of a number of scientists working there needs to be solved.

The rest of this nail-biting story takes place on this small Martian Moon.

Arriving on Phobos Brogue immediately places the whole scientific station under Martial Law. This puts off many of the inhabitants who are unwilling to cooperate with any investigation. Brogue is also not popular with the peacekeeping squad whose commander was one of those killed out on Phobos. They are a tight-knitted group and the loss of their commander has hit them hard. Brogue, being a Martian, is intensely disliked by a couple of the team members, who do something nasty to him the first night. Brogue survives, and does not hint much about what happened, but he does demote one of the team members involved in the incident. He makes a few mistakes which gets another of the team killed, but gradually he wins their confidence, because they see he is capable of doing his job, and is not just a stupid Martian.

Something out in the dust lakes of Phobos is killing anyone who goes out there. It is incredibly fast and can track them through the lakes of dust. Initially they think a vicious life form has been discovered and this would be monumental. Life has yet to be discovered elsewhere in the solar system. What few glimpses of it they have had has shown it is impervious to their weapons and almost immediately grows a replacement to whatever part of it has been damaged.

It seems that the peacekeeper group had been hired by the owner of the scientific station. He wanted them to come in and kill the monster that had killed several of his scientists, but the monster killed some of the peace team members which is why Brogue has been sent to investigate. During his investigation he is shown around the station so he can see what research is being done and why it is important to keep the station operating. He suspects something is being covered up, that he is not being shown everything. He also realizes that the monster is not what it seems to be (something which the reader is aware of long before Brogue) and that it can be controlled. There is an aborted terrorist attack on the station that goes wrong and this is linked back to the attack he foiled on Mars before being sent to Phobos, another person is killed, and brogue himself is kidnapped, drugged and thrown outside (in space suit) for the monster to kill, but he outwits it and survives, which is when he realizes it isn't what it seems. There are attempts to thwart his investigation. He threatens to close down the whole station, people rebel and want to leave, and there is a spectacular final confrontation which is totally unexpected but makes sense considering what has previously happened.

He finally gains the respect of his peace keeping team and the mystery of the monster that kills people is solved.

Overall, a bloody good story, with all loose ends tied up and explained. The science is pretty much up to date and the speculative science seems logical in the context of the story. Being published commercially by Tor Books, the reader knows a certain standard has been met or they would not have accepted it for publication. This story exceeds that standard by a long shot.

Banner of Souls by Liz Williams (2005)

Having read *Phosphorous - A Winterstrike Story*, (2018) I looked for and found this book from which is also a *Winterstrike Story*.

Far into the future after Earth has been devastated by climate change and the seas have risen so the geography is totally different, a Martian warrior 'Dreams of War' is sent to Earth by the Martian Matriarch to guard and protect an unusual young girl who seems to be growing and aging at a rapidly increased rate. This girl is being looked after in a fortress by her co-joined grandmothers and a genetically altered human amphibian woman called a Kappa. An assassination attempt is been made on her life and in the process of escaping this attempt the castle in which she lives is destroyed by strange fire.

Earth is ruled by the Martian Matriarchy. There are no males other than wild remnants and the idea of men has been long forgotten. Children are cloned and grown artificially both on Earth and on Mars. The Martians believe that life began on Mars and that they colonized the Earth. Yet there are some that believe it was the other way around. It happened so far in the past that no one knows. There are only legends. What we do know is that at some time in the remote past Mars had been terraformed. It is still a cold desert world even though humans and other things can survive there.

At the far edges of the solar system there is a group of women who are experimenting with modifying humans both genetically and with additional mechanical modifications and they were instrumental in bringing to the solar system aliens known as Kami. A modified warrior is sent from this place called Nightshade, to Earth to kill or if unable to capture the unusual girl.

Nightshade, Mars and Earth are connected via a kind of wormhole which allows fast travel between these places. The other science involved is almost magical with shape-shifting armor inhabited by the ghost of its previous warrior owner able to act almost independently of the warrior it protects, and alien technology controlled mentally rather than physically referred to as ghost technology.

After the assassination attempt on the girl, Lunae, Dreams of War takes her, along with her Kappa on a ship to escape the ruined city of Fragrant Harbour once known as Hong Kong to the remote islands of what was once Northern Japan. There is another assassination attempt organized by the Nightshade warrior Yskatarina Lye but it fails when Lunae time shifts the assassin to a strange future place. But they are betrayed by the ship's captain who allows the mysterious warrior from Nightshade to board the ship. The ship's captain is also a Martian and she obeys the Matriarch who has been killed and her place and position taken by a kami possessed corpse of the previous Matriarch. It's not the person who is obeyed but the position of the Matriarch that is obeyed. This warrior Yskatarina decides to capture Lunae and take her to Nightshade since trying to assassinate her has twice failed. It seems Lunae is the key to changing the future.

Strange things happen at sea and Lunae and her Kappa go missing during an attack on the ship by a monstrous climate changing machine that emerges from the depths. Lunae time shifts into the far future, to the same place she sent her earlier assassin. She does not yet have control of her ability to time-shift. Here she encounters a future version of herself who explains what she needs to do to prevent an alien invasion by the Kami. She has to prevent the 'flood' which she failed to do before, but this time must succeed.

Dreams of War is taken back to Mars for failing to protect Lunae. The Matriarch who is not the same as the one who sent her to earth to protect Lunae wants to punish her so she is stripped of her armor and subjected to a hunt in which she is not expected to survive. But she does. She knows the Martian terrain better than anyone else and manages to use it to eliminate those who are hunting her.

Lunae and her Kappa also find themselves on Mars after having time shifted from the future back to the present. They encounter another warrior who knows Dreams of War and she takes them to the tower where the matriarch and her warriors and servants live. And it is here where Lunae fulfills her destiny.

This is a story of mystery and intrigue and wild action with all the relevant background details inserted into the story unobtrusively for the reader to build a fascinating picture of a very different Mars Earth relationship, while at the same time being totally absorbed by the action and characters involved. It engenders s sense of wonder similar to that created by writers a century ago who wrote about Mars, while at the same time infusing the story with logically extrapolated science and a more modern understanding about Mars. It is so different from mainstream ideas regarding Mars and its colonization that it is, dare I say it, unique.

I have yet to read **Winterstrike** itself at this moment in time.

More Missions to Mars

There are perhaps more than 100 books bearing the title *Mission to Mars* in both fiction and non-fiction categories, which have been published over the last fifty years or more. I have already outlined some of them in my book *Dreams of Mars — 130 years of stories about Mars.* (2018)

Since titles can't be copyrighted it sometimes occurs that authors use the same title that has been used before because it is the most apt for the work they have produced. *Mission to Mars* seems to be very popular, perhaps because it is the most precise title that can be used when writing a story about going to Mars.

What is remarkable about the two books here is that they have been written and published by (young adults) young people still at school or perhaps someone who has recently left school.

With the advent of self-publishing and the ability of anyone anywhere being able to upload a digital book file and have it published as an EBook or a print on demand title, the market place has become overloaded with titles in every possible category. It appears that almost everyone young and old wants to write a book.

Anyone who manages to write a book and go through the processes to have it published should consider that a great achievement, and deservedly, they should be proud of their accomplishment.

However, the results are not always as good as one would expect.

No matter how attractive the cover looks, and some of them have beautifully designed covers, the interior can be quite disappointing. Pages of text where every paragraph has been separated with a double space (making the book twice as long as it needs to be), is a standard word processing default for office documents and other similar pieces of writing. But a book, a novella or a novel, is a much longer document than an office memo and should be formatted accordingly.

It only takes a few seconds to alter the default so the document produced will appear more like the text in a book. Especially if that word processor is being used to create the layout for the book, rather than a dedicated program designed for doing magazine and book layouts.

Another common fault is relying on the word processor to correct spelling mistakes, or grammar. That part of the program works fine and generally, most words if spelled wrong, will be identified and corrected automatically, or at least underlined so the author can see them. What a word processor spell-correct program won't do is to indicate homonyms, or whether they are correct in the context of the sentence if the word is spelled correctly.

The author needs to proof-read the text to find, replace or correct these words, or have an outside reader look over the text before uploading it to a publisher. In other words, the text should proof-read, edited at least line by line as well as structurally so it makes sense. Too may authors fail to do this, thinking that what they have produced is error free, and in their haste to see it published online or in print, they rush the final product into publication.

Even the best authors make mistakes, use wrong words, or present confusing structure or plots, all of which an editor will find and have the author correct.

We all make mistakes. We all can't often see them because we are too close to the work. We are so used to making certain spelling errors that we don't see them as errors, or assuming certain words mean something in particular when in fact they mean something else entirely. This is why an outside editor is needed, or at least highly recommended.

Mission to Mars by La Rina A. Seward (2008).

This is a short book, (a novella) that tells the story of a young boy whose father worked at NASA and who wants to be an astronaut and go to Mars when he grows up. He achieves this and is one of the two astronauts who participate in the first mission to Mars. The author consistently calls the two astronauts astronomers. Using advanced medical procedures that allow them to basically hibernate throughout the months the voyage takes, the two arrive and spend a few days exploring near their landing site before they discover alien life forms that are definitely threatening. Their interaction with these life forms causes one of them to be killed and the President (of the US) calls the mission off and the space ship returns to Earth. That's about it.

It shows promise and could be developed into a reasonable story. Unfortunately, it has some disconcerting annoyances that spoil it for me; many pages double spaced between paragraphs, then other pages where this doesn't occur. It is inconsistent throughout the book.

And then there are far too many words used incorrectly or out of context which spoils the reading experience because it breaks immersion in the story. It makes you stop while you consider that the word in the sentence doesn't make sense. It seems to me that the author is very young by the way ideas are expressed as well as sometimes using words that mean something entirely different to what was intended.

Almost every page, especially after page 40, has simple errors that could and should have been corrected before publication.

Some examples are:

Page 40. Lance Carter show slow progress as well. Should be shows not show.

Page 41. My body is so soar …instead of my body is so sore.

Page 42. It's not the same with out you… should be without you.

Page 44. …an energetic Kevin tear open some astronaut food… tears open would be correct.

Page 45. She puts her head down and tried to keep clam… tries to keep calm should be used. Then the next sentence: She clinches her tissue… should this not be She clenches her tissue?

Page 49. Kevin re assures should be Kevin reassures…

Page 50. In case you haven't notice, should be haven't noticed, and further down the same page we find, What's the real reason you wanted to be apart of this mission? Should obviously be, to be a part of this mission.

Page 59 Kevin looses up for a minute. What does that mean? Loosens up or something else?

Page 61. There are confusing sentences: Then several more extra terrestrial burst out of the pond, should be extra terrestrials because there are several… (The robot) Marsha begins to fire. Kevin halts her to stop. …another extra terrestrial burst out of the pond… should be bursts because this time it is one rather than several.

Page 64. Lance and Kevin breathe heavily as they try to re cooperate from the startle. This obviously should be, recuperate… and what does the startle mean? Being startled? Shocked?

Page 70. I've allowed myself to be influence by… influenced should be used. A few lines further down Kevin reaps a smile as he listens to his partner boasts… (boast) (partner's boast) What does reaps a smile mean?

Page 71, Lance with his mouth open appears to be chilling on what he saw. Kevin tends to Lance and grabs a plastic bag to help him breath (breathe.)

Page 74. The secretary of Defense is trying to ration. Shouldn't this be he is trying to be rational?

If all the unnecessary double spacing was taken out, this book would probably be around 70 pages instead of 96.

There is no information about the author anywhere in the book which is disappointing, but from the many simple mistakes, the colloquialisms used, and the general way of expressing things, I suspect the author is quite young.

The cover also doesn't make sense. It shows a space shuttle on a cracked desert-like surface, with a deep blue sky above in which we see Earth floating just above the horizon. This is reminiscent of the photos taken of Earth from the surface of the Moon. Even in 2008 everyone knew the sky of Mars was (and is) pinkish coloured not blue; also, a space shuttle could not travel to the Moon let alone Mars. It was not designed for that purpose.

But, credit where it's due, the author did manage to write a story and have it published. We can only hope that better things will come from this young author in the future.

Mission to Mars by Morgan Sinnock. (2008)
This has no publication information at all. No copyright date, no publication date, nothing at all. It does have an ISBN on the back cover. The cover has a space suited astronaut silhouetted against a yellowish-brown sky while standing on a rocky ledge which looks like one of the photos of the Martian surface sent back by one of NASA's rovers. There is some information about the author at the end of the book where it says he is attending the Notre Dame Academy Elementary School and he thanks his family and teachers for their inspiration and their assistance. The book has 258 pages and is double-spaced throughout which makes the book twice as big as it needs to be. Having others go over the story for structure, spelling, proof-reading has paid off. There are no mistakes or words used out of context and because of that this book is much easier to read.

This is a one man one mission story about Tony Rodriguez who makes the arduous journey to Mars to accomplish his lifelong dream of discovering extraterrestrial intelligence.

The first half of the story concerns the family life of the character who is working at NASA as an engineer. He asks his boss if he can become an astronaut, and is immediately promoted to that position. He is then told, a new space-craft has finally been built and he will be the astronaut who takes it to Mars. Departure is set for the following week.

No training, just like that he is given the job, and leaves for Mars.

But before he leaves, he has an encounter with an old school enemy who is extremely jealous of his promotion and decides she doesn't want him to go to Mars. She sabotages the shuttle which blows up after catching on fire only a short distance from the Earth, but Tony manages to get into an escape pod, in which he then continues on to Mars instead of returning to Earth.

Landing on Mars he discovers footprints nearby and follows them. He is captured by an alien and his memory is wiped. The alien makes him a slave inside one of the many colonies they have established beneath the Martian surface. He remains a slave there for twelve years while everyone back on Earth thinks he died in space. When a photo he has with him triggers a return of his memory he attempts to escape with the help of another unhappy alien resident. There is a chase and a fight in which his alien captor is killed. After that he escapes with his new alien friend in a flying saucer and returns to Earth to the astonishment of everyone who thought he was dead. There is a big press conference and he is reunited with his family, all of whom thought he was dead and who are now ecstatic to have him back...

It's very childish, but at least it is an easy read and would certainly appeal to 8 to 12-year-old readers who would most likely find it exciting and adventurous.

Both these young authors deserve credit for what they have achieved, like other authors who started their career while still at school.

Robert Silverberg springs to mind: his first short stories were published professionally while he was still in his last years at school. His first novel was written and accepted while still at school, although it wasn't published until two years later after he had finished school.

I suspect these two young authors will go on to achieve success as writers in years to come.

The Mars Company by Joseph Roberts (2008)

The back-cover blurb said: *a colony expedition to Mars finds something no one expected.* That sounded interesting.

The story opens with a huge colony ship built in orbit around the Moon departing for Mars, where it will be used as an orbiting space-port until a proper facility is established on Phobos and a colony base on Mars' surface. All the 484 people on the ship, the crew and the passengers, are married couples without children. Once the colony on Mars is established it is hoped that the couples will have more children so a new generation will be born on Mars and humanity will begin expanding into the solar system.

The ship, the *Herbert George Wells,* simply called the *Wells,* is like a city. It has everything needed for a large number of people to survive. There are atomic power stations, numerous shuttles, workshops, hangar space for the shuttles, fuel supplies, living and recreation areas, the ability to process raw materials found in space and manufacture things they may need, like extra fuel, small planes for planetary surveys, and so on. The idea is that these colonists will establish and build a city on Mars which will be ready for a second wave of colonists in a year's time.

At this point it seemed intriguing.

The departure is smooth and everything is fine for a few days as they build up speed. Several days into the transit a course correction is needed so the pilots swing the ship around to make a short burn to slow the ship enough to correct its trajectory to Mars. Suddenly there is a burst of radiation they didn't expect. Terminating the burn so they can see what could be causing the radiation burst, they discover something massive and totally black obscuring the star field, and they are heading straight towards it. No one knows what it is. Nothing has been detected in this area before. They are travelling too fast to change course, so they brace for impact. Then they hit, and almost everyone blacks out. The ship is violently shaken. Alarm bells indicate considerable damage to some areas. Those still conscious suffer severe motion sickness, which passes as soon as the violent vibrations finish. They are blind as all systems in the ship have gone off-line. As things slowly come back online, they discover they are near a planet that looks like Earth, orbiting a fainter F class star.

They have no idea where they are. There is no sign of Mars, or the Earth and the Moon.

Before they can do anything, the ship is bombarded with meteorites and other orbiting matter and more damage is sustained, but they get through this and head for the earth-like planet where they go into orbit around it.

After a while they work out that they have come through a wormhole and the F class star they see is *Xi Pegasi* and they are 51 light years from the solar system. They discover the planet they orbit has a breathable atmosphere, that 75 percent of the surface is covered with shallow oceans, and that they have no choice but to establish a colony there, which would be easier than doing it on Mars. But not everyone wants to do that. Some want to go back through the wormhole, back to their own solar system. However, that appears not be possible.

Will they find a way back through the wormhole to the Solar system and eventually set up a colony on Mars as originally intended? Or are they stuck here for good?

They begin exploring the planet knowing that they will have to establish a colony, but almost immediately they run into trouble with the wildlife.

There are enormous wildcats, giant tigers and monstrous snakes… and immediately I was put off because this is a cop-out.

It is extremely unlikely that on another earthlike planet, evolution (a fortuitous set of accidental mutations that led to life as we know it on Earth) is unlikely to have produced the exact same set of circumstances to produce anything that is familiar to us. The author uses the old 19th century idea that life on other worlds would be exactly the same as it was on earth, only larger or smaller, less muscled or denser muscled depending on the gravity, and in the case of this planet that they discovered, because it is slightly smaller than Earth with a subsequently lower gravity, the wildlife would be much larger.

Ideas like that started to be put aside by the 1930s as more scientific knowledge regarding other planets in our solar system became familiar.

Although authors like Captain W E Johns who grew up before the 20th century began still used those outdated ideas, he was an exception in the 1950s. Many other authors wrote of alien worlds in which the life was startlingly different from anything on Earth or what we would be familiar with, and they did this convincingly.

To find a writer who in 2008 can only imagine life on an alien planet in a system 51 light years away from Earth was the same as on Earth but suffering from gigantism, is disappointing.

The explorers are attacked by enormous cats the moment they land, and no matter how well written their problems may be, the circumstances described are not believable. I can't accept that on an alien planet in a far distant star system there will be any kind of life that is even vaguely familiar to what we know, let alone the same only much bigger. Whatever life there is will most likely be vastly different to anything we can imagine.

The colonists quickly decide to set up bases on various islands where there are no mega-fauna, and to search these islands for minerals rather than on the mainland areas.

Since none of this is about Mars, other than the fact that it was where they intended to go, I skimmed through several more chapters and couldn't get interested in what happens to the characters. Skipping through to the end I discovered that it stops abruptly at the end of some action, and when one of the women discovers she is pregnant (producing hope for the future of the colony) whereas before landing, they found that most of the men were infertile. Something in the fruits growing on this planet has counteracted the effects of the radiation or the bad food they had on the ship which turned the men infertile. This will be continued in another book.

That was it as far as I was concerned.

There was no indication at the beginning that this was book one of a series which means a reader may assume this is a stand-alone story. To discover otherwise is disappointing.

Though this book was a free download, presumably to get the reader interested in buying the follow up books, I don't think it is a series I will be interested in following.

Something different...

The Empress of Mars by Kage Baker (2009)

A delightfully picaresque novel set on a Mars that was initially colonized by a private company, The British Arean Company, which as British Luna made a huge profit mining the Moon. Governments can no longer fund space exploration so it is left to private companies which of course operate to make profits for their shareholders. The British Arean Company sets out to terraform Mars to make it habitable. To do so required certain kinds of people, the wild, the non-conformist, the adventurous, the crooks escaping authorities, and all kinds of misfits and dreamers. The Company laid claim to most of Mars and allocated various groups land to transform. The company also controls what comes to Mars and sells at a profit the essentials that the colonists need.

Unfortunately, the Company set up its first colonies in the deep gullies and trenches not knowing that these would concentrate the winds and sand storms with quite devastating effects. Land granted to a Celtic Clan near the higher ground of Tharsis Ridge also fails to be amenable to general agriculture, but the clan manages to survive and develops an enclosed ecology with pigs, sheep and some cattle. They also grow barley and other grains using human and animal wastes as fertilizer. The British Arean Company fails to make the profits anticipated from mining and terraforming and retrenches many of the people who worked for it. Those people are stuck on Mars since none of them have enough redundancy funds to pay for a return trip to Earth.

One of them, a plant biologist named Mary Griffith builds a small community of misfits and dreamers where she brews her own beer (often using barley bought from the Celtic Clan) and sells it to the ice haulers, carbon dioxide miners and other sundry visitors. She has the one and only tavern, bar, restaurant and general meeting place for the independent people left behind after becoming redundant. She calls her tavern The Empress of Mars, and the characters that she meets and is involved with form the basis of a series of interconnected stories that revolve around Mary and her daughters and other misfits who share some of the living space within the tavern.

Unlike some other picaresque novels (set on Mars) this one is more connected and fluid with Mary central to all that happens. It is fast paced, easy to read, and one is always turning the page to see what will happen or how

Mary will cope. That she and her cohorts, through luck (She finds the first huge 'red' diamond on Mars which makes her independently wealthy, inadvertently starting a 'diamond rush' with new people flocking to Mars to make their fortunes.) and clever scheming, eventually outsmart the British Arean Company, bringing about its downfall, and how the potential for human survival on Mars is developed is a total delight, leaving this reader wanting more. I would love to see another story set much further along to see what has transpired as a result of Mary Griffith and her friends' efforts to survive and start the terraforming of Mars.

Martian Legacy by Fred Lane (2009) self-published

There are two expeditions to Mars in the year 2024. The first has Harold T Kane (Harry) trapped in his rover while his partner Dr. Karen Hansen, a micro biologist and physician is back at the lander about 11 kilometres away. Harry had misjudged the angle of descent into a canyon and his rover overturned, an inauspicious beginning for the first day on Mars. The only exit from the rover is via the dome on top which opens up, but the rover is upside down and the exit is blocked. The Lander is too far away for Karen to walk without running out of oxygen before she gets there, and there is nothing the other two members off the expedition in orbit around Mars can do.

The second expedition is still in transit and has yet to reach Mars.

The beginning promises much and certainly encourages the reader to continue.

Harry figures out how to turn the rover over so it ends up back on its treads. He starts rocking it in the direction of the downward tilt and eventually the machine rolls past its balance point and tips over back onto its treads. Once this is achieved, he collects some samples from around the site and returns to the lander where Karin is anxiously waiting. The samples are meticulously stored to prevent contamination from the two humans.

Their next problem is to find the factory ship sent to Mars by NASA before they left Earth. It was somewhere nearby and was supposed to be manufacturing from the water frozen beneath the regolith fuel for their return trip to Earth as well as oxygen for replenishing their supplies. When they find the factory, it is not working because it had fallen over on landing. They manage to right the factory and get it to start its manufacturing processes.

The second expedition carries a geologist and a paleontologist/archaeologist who are tasked to look for signs of ancient life on Mars. Their lander comes down a fair distance away from the site of the first lander. The two members of that expedition immediately get to work on digging out an area in which they are going to look for fossils or other signs of ancient life, especially when they discover what appears to be a stone age tool.

When the time runs out for the first expedition Harry and Karin take off and rendezvous with the return ship in orbit. There is a minor problem with docking in orbit but that is soon solved and they go back to Earth.

The second expedition wastes time excavating a site that yields little so the archaeologist decides to rappel down the side of the canyon which is composed primarily of sedimentary rock in search of a more likely site to excavate. He commences digging in a cave, and soon discovers an impenetrable wall. His companion helps to expand the dig and they find an opening in the wall leading to a small room. While they are making the cave larger a sand storm traps them inside and they can't get out. The small platform they had constructed to allow them access to the cave was blown away and the canyon walls are too steep and crumbly for them to climb out.

But they manage to retrieve their rappel line so they can climb out. The various mishaps that occur ramp up the tension and help keep the reader interested in finding out what will happen.

There is sexual tension and romance between the first two on Mars, Harry and Karin, there is danger from the environment from which the persons involved manage to extricate themselves. The second expedition discovers ancient ruins that are highly advanced buried inside the side of the canyon, which doesn't make sense to them when they compare the primitive tools they discover in later layers of sedimentation. They do a survey using explosives set off in various locations and reading the echoes of the sound waves returned they discover an enormous city that had been buried in the sedimentary rock that forms the side of the Canyon, (Valles Marineris?). It must have taken hundreds of thousands of years for this to occur way back when there was water on the surface of Mars millions of years earlier.

Back on Earth Karin has cultured the soil and discovered what appears to be microbial life that is tough and able to do strange things. Unable to contain it, a flu like pandemic affects practically the whole population of Earth. It doesn't kill anyone but it does lodge in their bones and makes them stronger. It also has the affect of changing people so they become sick around anything technological. A new movement, like a cult where people want to return to nature and have nothing to do with anything even slightly technological, spreads rapidly in the wake of the flu pandemic and Civilization virtually collapses within weeks.

While the new flu is still rampaging across Earth, the second expedition is returning. They have discovered fossilized skeletons of ancient Martians and are bringing them back.

Karin discovers that the Martian virus which takes the form of nanoscopic ovoids connected together with filaments to form complex structures, is composed of Nano machines, not living viruses, which explains why she couldn't culture vaccines against the pandemic. Unfortunately, there is no way they can stop these Nano machines from infecting almost everyone. One of the side effects of the infection is the total reduction of sexual desire. No one is interested anymore, and Karin suspects that within two generations humans and animals on Earth will become extinct. It appears that what is happening to Earth life is what happened millions of years ago to Mars and its inhabitants.

Harry, whom she married on their return to Earth, is affected by the virus while she isn't. He goes off to join the new return-to-nature movement and some months later while leading a group of similar minded people attempting to sabotage a power station supplying electricity to Los Angeles, Harry receives a massive electric shock while climbing an electric fence, which momentarily kills him. CPR is used to bring him back to life and discovers that he is back to what he once was. The Nano machines inhabiting his bone structure and his body have all been neutralized or killed. He realizes there is a cure and he heads back to the research centre where his wife is working. Together with those who are immune they go out and abduct people, subjecting them to electric shock treatments which they now know kills the Nano machines.

The story more or less finishes on a positive note with the two main protagonists thinking that eventually a new expedition will be sent to Mars to excavate the incredible city buried in the side of the canyon.

Somehow, the story doesn't gel. It seems to be a combination of a novel that shows exciting promise, mixed with a fictionalized documentary speculation about what would be discovered on Mars when the first expeditions finally get there. Though well written, there is too much telling and not enough showing, so it seems uneven and lacks overall excitement.

It has all the tropes one expects in a story about Mars: paranoid fear of bringing back an alien microbe to which we have no cure and which could cause a pandemic, discovery of primitive intelligent life, including skeletons and artifacts, and the discovery of an advanced civilization, long gone.

Since there are thousands of photos from Mars showing many aspects of the surface, the descriptions of the landscape do match what has been recently discovered. The dust storm depicted seems pretty real as well, as are the sparse details of the ship in orbit and the journey out from Earth and the return. The author is a physician and an amateur astronomer, which explains why his details regarding culturing vaccines and the scientific way in which the virus is examined are believable.

The story does exactly what it promises in the blurb on the back cover… *it leads the reader expertly down many scientific byways, while at the same time being drawn along by the appealing human story. Martian Legacy combines our best hopes and worst fears as they are played out together.*

It isn't just as exciting as it could have been… but if you are a fan of stories about Mars, it is better than many others, self published or not, and is worth the time to read.

The Victorian Era reborn

As the world progressed from the end of the 19th century into the beginning of the 20th there were many interesting stories that dealt with Mars. The Longer stories mostly covered the journey to Mars and the discovery of highly civilized beings living there, making comparisons with human (European) civilization on Earth. The shorter works had a much narrower focus based around a single event that usually took place on Mars.

There were of course many stories that dealt with exploration of the solar system's planets and moons, but we are primarily interested here in those stories that dealt with Mars. With Mars at its closest in opposition at that time, scientists and astronomers turned their thoughts to what kind of life existed on Mars, — and they had no doubt that life did exist — and there was much studying, speculation and extrapolation of possibilities all based on what was thought to be accurate science. Since Mars was the only close planet the surface of which could be seen in telescopes (Venus is actually closer but the dense cloud cover prevents anything from being seen) it was Mars that everyone speculated about.

Unfortunately, Professor Percival Lowell's belief that he saw canals on Mars, and his drawings that depicted the surface lined with these canals as well as his 'logical' speculation that the canals were constructed by the inhabitants of Mars to save the planet from drying up by bringing water from the polar ice caps, inevitably led to the belief that Mars was inhabited by a superior but dying civilization. Even if Percival Lowell had not published two books dealing with his speculations about Mars, the simple fact of what he had supposedly discovered fired up the imaginations of many writers who couldn't resists extrapolating from Professor Lowell's 'discoveries' regarding Mars.

The few scientists who could find no water vapor in Mars' atmosphere, who claimed the air was over 90 percent carbon dioxide with a surface pressure too low to be breathed even if it contained oxygen (which it didn't), that it was far too cold even in the tropics, were ignored by early novelists as well as the later authors who supplied the growing pulp fiction magazines with endless streams of stories. They didn't want to, or couldn't believe that Mars was uninhabitable as far as humans were concerned.

In spite of growing information regarding Mars, most of this was ignored by writers right up until 1965 when the 21 grainy photos of Mars' desiccated and cratered surface were sent back to Earth. Once the photos had been seen, there was no denying the reality of Mars. It was not what had been thought or imagined. It was vastly different, but astonishingly beautiful as the many subsequent photos from the robotic missions showed.

After several decades of abandonment, writers again returned to the new Mars and much more realistic stories began to appear. But some still preferred the old stories and the risible speculations scientists once made and have crafted new stories which take place at the end of 19th century, and while modern in approach, attempt to capture the feeling and manner of stories that were published in the late 1890s to around 1910 before the advent of the pulp magazines.

One such story is ***The Martian Ambassador*** by Alan K Baker (2011).

It is set in the year 1899 (the year after H G Wells published The War of The Worlds). Six years earlier radio contact had been established with Mars, thanks to a message sent to the planet by Nicola Tesla using his newly invented Magnifying Transmitter in Colorado Springs. Almost immediately the Martians responded and sent a number of Cylinder ships to Earth. (Curiously, the first of the Martian cylinders landed in the same part of the English countryside as did the first one in H G Wells story.) An embassy has been established and a number of Martians work there fostering trade between the two planets. Earth supplies Mars with materials it no longer possesses, while in return Mars allows Earth access to some of its superior technology, which is why we have omnibuses that walk through the city on three legs – Martian walking machines. The machines that wreaked havoc and destruction in H G Wells' story here are used as cross city transport. They are far more efficient and can carry many more people than the ubiquitous hansom cabs.

The story opens with the Martian Ambassador being murdered in a horrible manner and Thomas Blackwood, a special investigator for Her Majesty's Bureau of Clandestine Affairs has been asked to investigate along with Lady Sophia Harrington to assist. She is investigating a series of slasher murders across London. These murders appear to have been committed by a supernatural creature, a masked ghostlike being with incredible strength and the general public are under the impression that the slasher is a Martian.

The Queen and her Clandestine Affairs Bureau want the matter cleared up as soon as possible, since the Martians are threatening to take matters into their own hands if Humans can't deal with it. The Knights Templar who are the police operate from their London Headquarters, New Scotland Temple, where their forensic department has examined the body and determined it was suffocated by mutated flour mites which sucked the oxygen from the Martian's respirator. How the mites were introduced into the respirator remains a mystery because the Martians are extremely fastidious when it comes to making certain their respirators function correctly, but someone had to do it which means there is a traitor in their midst.

The Martians are humanoid but have evolved from something resembling a cross between birds and reptiles. They find Earth's atmosphere too dense, too rich to breathe and always use a respirator when out and about. They also wear a harness that helps them resist Earth's stronger gravity. Their embassy has airlocks to help them maintain Martian atmosphere and pressure within.

Queen Victoria insists that Blackwood solve the mystery as soon as possible because the Martians are threatening to take matters into their own hands if something is done soon. With their superior science and technology, they could easily take over the Earth if they wanted and there would be nothing humans could do about it. The other urgency is that a World Fair is to be opened in a few weeks and Britain and Mars are the main exhibitors. Queen Victoria wants the mystery solved before then.

Complicating matters is the intensity of the random slasher murders has increased and the slasher is screaming out things that imply Martians are involved, which makes witnesses to the murders believe Mars is behind it. A growing movement wants the British Empire to get rid of the Martians. If public opinion continues as it is, a likely war between Earth and Mars could ensue.

Someone also has tried to kill Blackwood by supernatural means via his recently bought cogitator, a computer device that accesses the ether that exists between worlds and permeates all environments, and they almost succeed if it wasn't for Lady Harrington who saves his life by destroying the cogitator.

This is all delightful stuff that almost recreates the time period, except for some modern concerns that seep into the background. Concerns such as the world being polluted by industrial wastes as modernization takes hold. Humans are also developing space blimps that can travel across the ether to other worlds so soon they won't be reliant upon the Martians and their space cylinders for travel between Mars and earth. There is an alternate world where faeries live in a forgotten paradise. They are able to travel between worlds and one of them helps Blackwood and Lady Harrington with their dual investigation.

There are also Venusians and here they are hideous creatures who have destroyed their world by centuries of massive industrialization. This is contrary to what writers and their readers thought in 1899. They all thought Venus, because of its cloud cover, was tropical with abundant rain forests, massive oceans and creatures that resembled dinosaurs or other similar life forms. Having the planet destroyed by runaway industrialization is definitely a modern 21st century idea. The Venusians created a runaway climate warming change that has seen the atmosphere fill with noxious gases and the planet rapidly dry out to become uninhabitable. The remnants of the Venusians live underground, and they want to take over Earth and Mars for themselves but they are not strong enough unless they can provoke a war between the two planets that will destroy them, after which they will come in and take over both.

Eventually, with much action and thrilling near deaths, Blackwood and Harrington solve the mystery of how the Ambassador was murdered, how an evil wealthy human has collaborated with the Venusians to promote a war between Mars and Earth, how he has used the nasty beings that exist within the ether to attempt to kill Blackwood, how the slasher (a Venusian provocateur) obtains a Martian fighting machine which he uses to partially destroy the World Fair Building killing many visitors and almost starting the war between the planets.

It all finishes well as Blackwood destroys the Martian fighting machine and manages to kill the implacable Venusian killer.

The author acknowledges his favorite martian story in a note at the end, mentioning that he named the plain where the Martian Parliament sits as *Yoh-Vombis,* after Clark Ashton Smith's 1932 creepy story T*he Vaults of Yoh-Vombis,* where a team of archaeologists are attacked inside an ancient Martian temple by slug-like creatures that eat away the tops of their heads and their brains to take over their bodies.

I looked up this story and read it, finding it not very remarkable and certainly not as well written as *The Martian Ambassador*... so, well done Mr Baker.

Murder on Mars

A series of 5 novels published between 2011- 2020, by Greg Fowlkes.

In the foreword to the first book in the series ***The Blood Red Sands of Mars,*** the author apologizes for the title and explains that it was written (in the bloom of youth) in 1979, but was not published. He explains that he wrote about a lifeless Mars, demonstrated by the images sent back from the initial rovers and satellites. At this point, many authors abandoned any idea of writing a story set on Mars, since it appeared to be as lifeless and as harsh as the Moon. The idea of finding remnants of ancient civilizations on a dying planet were abandoned absolutely because the Mars as seen by the cameras on the rovers had been unchanged for millions, if not a couple of billion years.

There were no ancient remnants, no known plant life, or any other kind of life. Even though it was the nearest planet to us that could possibly be lived on by humans, it was so different to what anyone had expected over the last few centuries, that writers were stunned and simply couldn't set their stories on this 'new' Mars. Some did try, Lin Carter for example, but his stories were a mixture of old fantasy ideas mixed in with a little bit of what new knowledge had been publicly disseminated. Compared to earlier decades, the 1970s had hardly any stories published that were set on Mars or dealt in some way with this planet. There were a few exceptions, (mentioned in my previous book ***Dreams of Mars***) and Greg Fowlkes was one of those, though he didn't actually publish his first Mars story until 2011. In retrospect he said he wanted to name it ***Murder on Mars***, but his publisher insisted on its original title.

Greg Fowlkes wanted to show how difficult it would be to establish a colony on Mars and what the reasons for doing so could be. He also wanted the story to be a murder mystery.

There are some 200,000 people on the planet, half of them living in the main series of connected habitats called Mars City. The rest are scattered around the planet in smaller camps and habitats operated and run by a number of individual mining corporations. There is no official government on Mars. Those who don't work for a mining corporation are working in one way or another for the UN which oversees what goes on in the main colony. Mars City is partly buried under the regolith to avoid cosmic ray bombardment which because of the extremely thin atmosphere (of carbon dioxide) is a serious threat to any human on the planet. Originally established with temporary inflated habitats that were sprayed with insulation to seal and firm the structure, they were to be abandoned when a new more solid concourse was constructed with fused silica bricks. But once abandoned they were taken over by miners and other workers who preferred some privacy to having to share bunks in the newer area where temporary workers' dormitories are located. There are airlocks to every separate dwelling and business so in case of a catastrophic loss of pressure, most individual places can be sealed off.

Since it costs so much to get anything to Mars from Earth, nothing is wasted. When something is no longer used for its original purpose, it is scavenged and used for something else. Every inhabitant has a pressure suit which must be used outside, or they will be dead within a few seconds, from decompression and subsequent freezing. The atmosphere contains no oxygen and it can't be breathed. Inside the habitats oxygen is at a premium, so every inhabitant has plants growing in their room or rooms, supplementing the habitat's oxygen supply. Mostly what are grown are vegetables and herbs. There is no space for trees or enough water to use on them, so fruit is a rarity and expensive having to be shipped in from Earth. Meat is also unavailable since there is no space to grow enough grass for cattle and sheep to feed on. There are a few chickens, and one enterprising person has a small farm where pigs are fed scraps, so pork, ham and bacon, are available in a very limited amount. This means that the inhabitants are vegetarian, through necessity.

There is no law, since there is no government, and the police force which consists of only twelve people scattered across the whole planet, with four of them stationed in Mars City, is not really a police force but more like a security team that helps keep rambunctious miners who may have had bit too much to drink of the home-made alcohol, from getting into too many fights. Drunks are locked up and usually let free once they sober up. Any serious criminal, is exported back to Earth on the next available ship.

The man in charge of the police force, is called Chief Inspector McKernan, because Chief Inspector is more acceptable to the mixed population than 'Sheriff' (too American) which might offend those who aren't of American origin. The police are employed by the UN and the Chief Inspector has the right to send anyone back to Earth if he thinks they could be a real problem. Naturally, his associates are called constables.

Most people who come to Mars, come because the pay is good and there is nothing much to spend it on, so they can return home reasonably wealthy. They usually stay for a period of three years. If they renew their contract, they are paid an extra bonus as well as higher wages, and some do take this option, but many don't, knowing that after six years, they may not be able to re-adapt back the Earth's higher gravity. So, there is a regular turnover of workers who work for the mining conglomerates, that come and then go after three years.

Usually, those that stayed for a second contract don't go back. Mars is becoming their home. They find various ways to make a living and to survive in the main part of the colony, running bars and bordellos, and other supply businesses. Some become independent prospectors wandering about the surface looking for a strike that could make them wealthy. Some have set up repair shops to re-purpose salvaged items that were abandoned but could be used for something else. A good percentage of the population of Mars City consists of those who decided they would not go back to Earth, and so over time, the population has gradually increased. Along with this increase, and the feeling that Mars is their home rather than Earth, comes a desire to be independent of Earth.

This is a theme that runs through all the stories in the series, coming to a head in the fifth book.

The Blood Red Sands of Mars (Book 1).

The story opens with a miner having been murdered at his claim in a remote area. The body was discovered by another miner who went there to see him. Detective McKernan is informed and asked by the UN Governor to solve the crime. This is the first time anyone had been murdered on Mars, so solving the murder is also a first for the detective. At the same time the Governor introduces McKernan to a reporter, Helga Orlofson, who has come from Earth to do a story or a series of stories on what it is like to live and work on Mars. He asks McKernan to show the reporter around, and since the reporter is a beautiful woman, (of which there are not many on Mars) he reluctantly agrees to take her with him.

This dates the story to the 1970s since the reporter is writing for a newspaper and she takes photos using film cameras. There had not been a hint of digital cameras in the 1970s. There are other things that date the story such as telephones, and the use of walkie-talkies the police use to communicate with each other. These things though, can be ignored because they hardly impact the story in any way.

The first thing the detective does is to take the reporter and have her get a properly fitted pressure suit so that when they go outside onto the surface of Mars, she won't have any problems.

Having the lead character show and explain things to a new person on Mars is a good way for the author to give the reader lots of information about Mars that would normally be obvious info-dumps, but this way, the background information is more unobtrusive and is absorbed by the reader without much notice.

They fly out to the remote claim where the body was discovered, and it is still there waiting for them. He gets Helga to photograph the scene. The miner had been shot through the face mask, and if the bullet hadn't killed him instantly he would have died within seconds anyway as the pressure inside his suit rapidly evacuated. The body is frozen and together they load it onto the plane and take it back to Mars City where a doctor at the hospital can examine the body.

What McKernan (Eric) has to figure out is who killed the miner and why, and how it was possible that a high-powered firearm could have been smuggled onto Mars when such things are not allowed, for the simple reason that bullets fired in a pressurized environment can puncture holes in the habitat allowing air to escape with disastrous consequences. He also discovers the miner's claim has disappeared from the records, and that anyone can now register that claim as their own.

In the process of showing the reporter around, she witnesses him and one of his associates break up a fight in a cheap bar where miners and other workers hang out when they are in town. This kind of thing aids in giving the reader a glimpse of what life in an enclosed habitat could be like on Mars and is well done without detracting from the overall story.

There is a hint of romance between Eric and Helga, but eventually this comes to nothing because she has to return to Earth to file her stories.

There is plenty of action, once the story gets under way, and Eric even has to rescue Helga from the clutches of the murderer as we near the climax. We find out that some of the mining corporations are corrupt and turn a blind eye to some nasty stuff that goes on in what is a very harsh environment on the surface of Mars.

The descriptions of Mars outside of the habitats is realistic and can be verified by looking at photos from Mars which are publicly available. The way the Habitats are constructed seems realistic considering what was know about Mars in 1979. Overall, the story is entertaining with enough excitement, twists and turns to keep a reader enthralled.

I wonder why the author waited until 2011 to publish this story. Did he put it in a drawer while working on other stuff, and then forgot about it? He doesn't say. But he does say that when he wrote the second story in 2012, ***A Death at Station Alpha,*** he tried to keep the same setting originally envisaged all those years ago. There are some minor details that have been updated to give the story more of a present time feel, but these are for the reader to discover.

As the reader can imagine, all the stories in the series are set some 200 plus years in the future when travelling to Mars is a lot faster than it currently is, and when there is a considerable population base on the planet to require a small police force.

A Death at Station Alpha (2012)

Book one was more an adventure/romance during which a murder is solved, where we can get a good impression of the harshness of Mars, but this second story takes a completely different approach. The author uses the traditional British locked room mystery, as the style to emulate, and he does it very well too.

Station Alpha is some 1200 kilometres away from Mars City. It is a scientific research station set on the edge of an escarpment overlooking an incredible vista of the planet. There are 13 scientists based out there. One of these scientists, alone in his lab overnight has been found, in the morning, to have been brutally murdered. There is a pick axe embedded in his forehead. No one had visited or left the station for weeks because a severe dust storm had kept the area totally isolated. Someone inside the station had to be the killer.

McKernan is sent to investigate, and the whole story then takes place inside Station Alpha as McKernan interviews everyone there, all of whom can account for their whereabouts and can verify each other's stories for what they did overnight. On the surface it appears that none of them could have killed the dead scientist without someone being aware of it, yet one of them had done it, because there was no one outside the station who could have come in and then left through the airlock without any of them knowing. It was impossible. McKernan is the first person to visit them since they had been cut off by the sandstorm, and he was there to find a killer.

In this second story, which takes place three years after the events of the first, Eric McKernan has been promoted to Detective Chief Inspector. The structure of the story follows the traditional method. Every suspect is individually interviewed and all their stories of what they saw and heard during the time when the murder took place are clear and concise. It appears at first that none of them could have done it.

The author, in an afterword, states that he left clues for an astute reader to find in order to figure out who the killer was, but I must have missed them. There is a twist at the end that I didn't expect that actually makes sense and satisfactorily concluded this story.

Even though it all takes place inside Station Alpha, the impression of being on Mars is subtle and well maintained throughout. The mystery is intriguing, and there is also a chase, at the end, which reminds readers that the events taking place are on Mars, a place that can kill you in a few seconds if you make a mistake.

A Corpse in Hut Town (2014)

Hut Town is the older part of Mars City, the original habitats that were constructed before the newer mall like main city was developed. All the original companies who operated from the old habitats moved to the new area, abandoning the older buildings which were mostly hardened inflatables. They were supposed to be abandoned but nothing on Mars is ever abandoned, it is simply re-purposed and re-used. Very quickly Hut Town became the location people sought to escape living in dormitories, or when they wanted to start some kind of private business. Ownership is by possession, since there are no official records or titles of ownership, but once someone has claimed ownership or bought it from someone departing to return to Earth, no one else disputes it.

The areas closest to the new Mars City are more respectable while the further away a location is, the less likely it is to be wanted by honest people. The most distant locations in the series of tunnels and habitats are occupied by bars and bordellos catering to miners and other workers taking time off and looking for entertainment. Many of the areas furthest away from the newer Mars City are unoccupied, or occupied only sporadically by people who want to keep their activities private. Some parts of Hut Town are poorly maintained and it is in one of these more remote areas of the complex that a body is found.

At first McKernan thought it was the body of a young girl. It was stuffed in a tunnel under the walkway where service cables and pipes are located. The body was frozen solid since warmth is not supplied to these areas and they remain Martian ambient temperature, which is generally very cold.

McKernan has the body sent to the hospital for an autopsy. It appears at first that she was strangled and dumped where no one would find her, because the last time these service tunnels had been inspected was more than two years earlier. That assessment was correct but the big surprise for McKernan was that the body was that of a young man, dressed as a woman, and that he had been strangled, but that isn't what killed him. While unconscious, and thought to be dead by the killer, he had been stuffed in the service tube and he froze to death.

As McKernan and his team try to find out who the victim was, there were no records of anyone missing over the past two years, they discover another body, this time a female who had been strangled in exactly the same way, and left in a remote tunnel that was barely used. This new murder had occurred only three months before its discovery.

The team now has a serial killer to find, and without any obvious clues, their concern is they may not find the killer soon enough to prevent more murders from happening.

This third novel is more a typical police procedural. The reader follows the police as they search Hut Town for clues that could lead them to the killer. In the process we get to see how Mars and the new Martian population are evolving, how the colony and the mining corporations are set up, and how the people, an increasing number who have opted to stay at the end of their three-year contract, go about making an independent living on Mars.

This third book is the most interesting so far, because of the way the life of the Martians is being revealed to us, but combined with the first two, a fascinating picture of the evolution of the colonists living on Mars, and how they are developing the planet emerges.

The killer strikes again, killing a sex worker who had been willing to talk to the only female police officer in the group. (Elena Ortiz).

While all this is happening, Chief Inspector McKernan has interacted with the female doctor who examined the first body, and the beginnings of a romance appears between them. He takes her to different places for dinner and we get to see even more of the martian way of life in Mars City, which adds more dimension to the story unfolding.

As they eventually discover the identity of the first victim, McKernan is approached by an old friend who is the boss of one of the largest mining corporations operating on Mars, and he asks the Inspector not to reveal the name of the victim, who according to records had been killed in an accident and cremated after his remains were sent back to Earth. This in itself is unusual because shipping anything between Earth and Mars is extraordinarily expensive.

The final part of the story involves identifying the killer, the reasons why he killed, and how McKernan and his team finally confront him to bring the story to a good conclusion.

This is probably the best written book of the three so far, as the author settles into his martian background. It is intriguing, with enough excitement to keep the reader interested in several main characters, all members of the police force and their friends. It also opens the possibilities for other stories in the same setting but featuring some of the other characters.

Murder at the Mars Club (2016)

The Mars Club is an exclusive private club with some residences attached, frequented only by the wealthiest people, which means the bosses of the mining corporations, visiting government officials, or their invited friends. It is modeled on the style of an old English Club, with décor reminiscent of such a place, with wood paneling, carpeted floors, plush lounge suites etc. It is located in the Heart of Mars City in between two luxury hotels catering to wealthy tourists, the only people who can afford to come to Mars who are not contracted workers.

On Friday nights the Club holds a formal dinner, with members and guests having to dress accordingly. One of the attendees, who lives on the premises, but who generally keeps himself apart and doesn't socialize much, has the custom of, after dinner, retiring to the cupola, which is on the roof of the building and the only part exposed to the outside Martian environment, where he smokes a cigar and drinks a glass of port from his private collection held at the club. While the various members who had attended the dinner are enjoying their after-dinner activities, playing cards, billiards, or reading in the lounge and the library, the sole waiter goes up to the cupola to see if the guest there requires anything else, and discovers he is dead.

The man who runs the club, one of the wealthiest people on Mars, Otis McAndrews, McKernan's friend and chief of the biggest mining company operating on Mars, calls the police to come and investigate.

The club is locked down, no one is allowed to leave while the police, Inspector McKernan and one of his junior constables, Ferris, investigate and interview all those present.

The victim had been poisoned with cyanide in his port.

Through the questioning of all those in the Club we find that each one of them could have been able to put the few grams of cyanide needed to kill someone in the glass of port, which had been set on a tray in the bar, for around ten minutes waiting for the waiter to take it up to the 'victim'.

Each member, during those ten minutes had for some reason or other walked individually past the spot on the bar where the drink was waiting. Each one of them had a grievance with the victim that could be a motive. Each one had been observed leaving or passing into the bar on the way to another part of the club by at least one of the others. This makes everyone a suspect, including the Inspector's friend, McAndrews. Each version of their activities over the time from the end of the dinner to the moment when the body was found, corroborates everyone else's version since they all overlap to varying degrees.

But the important question is who had the cyanide in the first place?

Cyanide is something easy to obtain on Mars because it is involved with refining ores and rare earths. Ferris investigates the various mining companies and discovers only one has reported a shortage of cyanide, which is tightly controlled, and that one company belongs to Otis McAndrews. The further they dig into each individual's story of the events over that short time, the more it appears to lead towards McKernan's friend.

But, as in all good murder mysteries, the obvious direction is nearly always not the right one. The clues are there for us to interpret, but usually we are surprised to discover who the real killer is and why he did it. And such is the case with this book. It's logical, but still a surprise.

This is a well thought out story that is easy to read and hard to put down until it's done.

A Body in the Dust. (2020)

The events in this story take place a couple of years after the last, so over the whole five books, some six years have passed. McKernan is involved with his doctor friend who is sharing his accommodation in Hut Town, but who still hasn't made up her mind about whether to return to Earth when her 3-year contract terminates or whether to stay. The hospital could certainly use her expertise and would welcome her as permanent doctor. Much of this depends on McKernan, but he is not truly aware of this so there is an underlying tension between them.

Mars has progressed to the point where the general population wants to be independent of UN control and a general election is looming in which everyone will vote. Two rival political parties have formed, one which wants to see eventual terraforming so future generations can live outside, but which this generation will see no benefit from in the short term, while the other party simply wants to keep everything the same, but with self-control. McKernan is in charge of overseeing the election and maintaining proper control. Meanwhile, a couple of unrelated suicides have occurred, where people have simply opened an airlock and walked outside without bothering to put on a pressure suit. They of course died within seconds. The mystery is why these people who are only too well aware of the dangerous environment Mars presents them, would do such an irrational thing.

Constable Elena Ortiz, who is based at a station called Junction Three, is on her way back from a patrol to Junction Four, an all day drive each way, when she sees an abandoned Buggy by the side of the track. She stops and discovers a body in the dust beside the buggy. The person had opened his face mask, an irrational suicidal act, and had died a horrible death. She immediately radios her boss in Mars City, McKernan, who tells her to secure the body, so it can be brought back to Mars City for forensic examination. She takes some photos of the general scene and of the body for later identification.

Being late, she decides to cover it up with a tarpaulin weighted down with a rock in each corner, and to drive home to where her husband and child are waiting for her. She will come back with him in the morning so he can help her load the body into the buggy and so he can drive back the person's abandoned buggy.

In the morning when they go out to do that, the buggy has gone and there is no body to be seen. Her husband questions her, but she knows they are at the right spot. The four rocks she used to hold the tarpaulin in place are there. She discovers the tarpaulin hidden under sand in a nearby ravine. There are buggy tracks leading away from the main track but there is no way of telling if they are of the missing buggy or whether they had been there for a long time.

As Junction Three Station starts making plans to accommodate the large number of people, independent prospectors mostly from out there in the wild countryside, expected to turn up at the station for the up-coming vote, she begins questioning those arriving to see if they had seen the buggy. She has a photo and its registration number (which turns out to be a fake number with no record), but only one person admits to having seen a buggy with a similar number, and this was a long way away and months ago.

Ortiz decides she will follow the tracks left near where she first saw the body, to see where they lead, and on her next patrol she does that. She follows the tracks for several hundred kilometres into ever more rugged country and reaches a point where a marker had been left beside the road. A few kilometres beyond that as she enters a broad open plain a sudden pop opens a hole in the buggy's windscreen and the air immediately starts to evacuate. She slams it into reverse and backs back away from the open plain.

Fortunately, she is wearing her pressure suit, but not the helmet. It would take too long to put that on so she grabs an emergency patch and slams it over the hole to prevent more air from leaking out. She then puts on her helmet and adds another patch to cover the temporary one. This makes it strong enough to hold so she can drive back to Junction Three. On the way she stops beside the marker on the side of the track and decides to examine it. She digs around it and discovers a body. As she extricates the body, she realizes it is her missing body with the open facemask. She straps this on to the side of the buggy and heads back to Junction Three.

Her husband, and her boss in Mars City are horrified that someone has shot hat her with a high-powered rifle, even more horrified that such a weapon exists on Mars where all such items are prohibited.

In Mars City the body is identified as one of four missing people, whose contract had terminated but who hadn't returned to Earth. One of those four was the son of a man who years before constructed a designer drug that would stimulate memories of the past, allowing a person to relive them with total reality. Unfortunately, too much of the drug cause people to become permanently lost in the memories without ever being able to recover. McKernan is wondering where the son has somehow been making this drug and selling it in Hut Town, where the people who opened an airlock and walked out, probably thought they were back on Earth and simply wanted to go for a walk in the outdoors. Hardly noticing some political friction and fights caused by rival ideas of the two parties in the upcoming election, McKernan organizes a small force to go out and follow the tracks from where Ortiz found her body.

They find a logical location after travelling across a wide area of Mars. They are shot at, but McKernan has come prepared and he is riding on the top of a buggy (outside with his pressure suit on) and he has a repeating rifle which he uses to return fire. That was something the assailant hadn't expected and he is caught off guard.

Ortiz fires her shot gun at a person who appears from a large lava tube in front of which, two buggies are parked, one of them being the missing one she saw at the beginning. He surrenders.

Inside the tube has been walled off with bricks and an airlock is fitted. The police team with their two prisoners enter through the airlock and find the lava tube has been pressurized for several kilometres. Rows of grow-lights are positioned over a long plantation. These lights are needed for earth plants to grow since martian light is only a fourth that of which lands on Earth.

It is confirmed by the prisoners that the four of them pooled their resources when their contract ended and used the money to set up this enormous agricultural farm inside the lava tube. They wanted to grow the plants to extract the memory drug so they could sell it locally and make a good living. McKernan tells them they could have become wealthy simply setting up such an agricultural farm to grow vegetables for the growing martian population. There was no need to produce mind altering drugs.

The fourth man they find at the far end of the lava tube, sitting in a stupor. He had taken a handful of capsules containing the drug and was lost in his past on Earth rather than be captured by the local police.

The loose ends are tied up with the result of the election a few days later, and the decision of McKernan's doctor lover deciding, because she is pregnant, she will stay on Mars with him.

It's an abrupt ending, which in my view leaves the reader hanging because the suspicion is that there will be more stories set on this particular version of Mars.

If that is the case, I look forward to them.

Clearly Different

Martian Sands by Lavie Tidhar (2013)

This Martian story has a bit of everything in it as it mixes aspects of different genre conventions within SF.

There is primarily a Martian colonization by Israelis, who went there after the Second World War, which was cut short and altered through the intervention of time travel, by an Israeli coming back from colonized Mars to change the course of the second world War to prevent the massacre of six million Jews who were rescued and taken to central Africa where thousands of space ships transported them to Mars.

There is inadvertent time travel back to ancient Mars and a truly old civilization.

There is an assassination attempt in a smoking bar, in which some pivotal people are killed, but who later reappear in a variety of alternate time lines both in the past as well as in the present time on Mars (Circa 2051).

If you mixed a punk feeling with Philip K Dick's concepts of Mars, with Edgar Rice Burroughs' Martian civilizations, and a hint of Ray Bradbury's silver locusts, time travel, alternate realities, disembodied beings and AIs, with some ultra-violent terrorist activities you get a story that is fascinating, often incomprehensible, yet weirdly enough, once you get to the end it does make sense. It creates a picture of a very strange future that in reality isn't any stranger than the world and the times we currently live in.

It is a fascinating story.

There were two limited editions published in 2013, one signed by the author, and the other unsigned. I don't think it has appeared yet in a paperback edition, although the author has many other novels in both paperback and hardcover.

The author grew up in a kibbutz in Israel and South Africa and currently lives in London. He is an award winning fantasy author and has been nominated for many SF and Fantasy awards. This story reads like it has been translated into English, but was probably written in English. I find it impossible to categorize , so it stands by itself as a brilliant example of modern story telling. Since it is a limited edition, copies of this book are hard to find.

Memory by Teresa P Mira de Echeverria (2012 Spanish, 2013 English)

Set on Mars in the near future; human colonists have created genetically modified men and women capable of living on Mars unprotected, which are used as slaves to help with the terraforming of the planet. These altered people can live for hundreds of years, but if they reproduce, their offspring will be human. The genetic modifications do not carry on into the next generation. One of them, Ajax, is capable of remembering everything that has happened and everything that will happen to him, but we don't find this out until later in the story.

The story is told from the point of view of a young lonely boy, Jebediah, who yearns to leave his small moribund community but who thinks he never will. He is playing out the front of his home when his elderly neighbour arrives in an ancient pink Bel Air Chevy convertible. Jebediah loves that old car, but what is more exciting is that accompanying his elderly neighbour is a native, the first one he has ever seen. His neighbour gestures for him to join them, and knowing his father wouldn't even notice if he wasn't there, Jebediah joins the occupants of the car and they go for a drive. Jebediah is absolutely fascinated by the Martian. This native tells Jebediah enigmatically that it isn't time yet. Jebediah has no idea what the Martian is talking about, but he is more desperate than ever to leave his small community. In the car they go to the reserve where the natives live and he meets a couple of other boys (Mestizos) who are human offspring of the modified Martians and who have braided their hair to resemble the fine tentacles their parents have instead of hair. It is here that he begins to fall in love with the dignified Martian, Ajax, who kisses him briefly and again tells him it isn't time yet.

All the time they are in the native village Jebediah feels Ajax is watching him, that somewhere in the future there is a secret they share, but he can't imagine what that could be. Returning home Jebediah waits outside while the native Ajax and his elderly neighbour go inside.

Jebediah has no reason to go inside since his father never talks to him, or to anybody. When Ajax comes back outside again, he sees Jebediah and comes over to him. "Don't forget me," he says before leaving. But the boy insists on Ajax being his friend. Ajax takes off a bone necklace he is wearing and gives it to Jebediah, pats him gently on the head and walks away.

Five years later, the natives who lived nearby all moved to the other side of Mars to *Planitia Utopia*. They also started a rebellion against the human colonists where zones of conflict separate communities. The natives don't want to continue terraforming Mars but want to return it to what it once was. As a result of the conflict the nearby mine closes down and the town of Olympic where Jebediah lives loses most of its population, almost becoming a ghost town. When the elderly neighbour dies bequeathing his house and pink Chevy to him, Jebediah now has the opportunity to leave for good. He leaves his town and heads to where the natives have established their own community.

Although the natives are slower to age, and live six times the lifespan of normal humans, Jebediah is astounded to find Ajax hasn't changed since he last saw him. Their reunion is joyful. Ajax is delighted that Jebediah remembers him. Jebediah joins their revolution to discontinue terraforming and to force the majority of humans to relinquish control of Mars.

Up to this point the story has the kind of nostalgic feel one encounters in Bradbury's Martian Chronicles, but from this point on it becomes very different as it explores personal relationships and sex roles, confronting rituals which involve biting off a finger, marriage that involves three people, in this case Jebediah and Ajax — both males — and a young woman called Abacus because she is a genius at maths. It is Ajax's idea because he wants to have a child which genetically combines the uniqueness of them all, which will be Martian and not human. Martian Native men can also carry a child as well as can the women. How they do it isn't explained nor is it necessary. After some months the child is transferred from Ajax to Abacus who carries it to term. When the baby is born, a girl, she is truly Martian and not human at all. She dies shortly after birth but not before Jebediah gazes into her eyes and sees a very different future.

At this point I became confused as the story jumps into the future where Laurel, the first true Martian born is still alive and has become a parent with her triple marriage which is now the normal family grouping. The child born has four eyes and other features that to a human would be horrible, but to a Martian is beautiful.

There is also a flashback a couple of hundred years to when the first modified humans were being worked as slaves, and where Ajax has a vision of his future and all the events that will occur. But not only that, Jebediah is somehow experiencing a different past to the one he had lived in, one that promises a very different future for Mars.

My confusion is whether the whole story is part of the vision Ajax has early on or if the flashback at the end is only to highlight the beginning of the story in order to explain why the modified humans were created. It does explain some early aspects of the story. On the other hand, it could be a way of illuminating different possible futures, all of which are as viable as the one already experienced.

It just seems a little confusing to me. I have to trust that the translation from Spanish to English is accurate, but my feeling is that there should have been more to the story at the end, which would have made it extremely good, rather than just very good. It is certainly a vision of Mars that is strong, enigmatic, almost poetical, full of positivity; different from other contemporary English publications.

Memory is part of a collection of Spanish Science Fiction collected in a volume called *Terra Nova, an anthology of contemporary Spanish science fiction*. Published in 2013.

The only problem with a story translated from another language is, how accurate is the story translated into English? Does it reflect the original or is it only an approximation of the original? Since I can't read this story in its original Spanish I have to trust that the translation is as accurate as possible.

I feel it is good to read stories that have been written in another language because they exhibit a different cultural heritage and viewpoint from what I am used to in English, which is predominantly from an American viewpoint.

Different cultural viewpoints enrich our overall reading experience and should be welcomed.

Email from Mars: Outbound by Lon Grover. (2012)

A tour bus driver and a poet, Lon Grover has written an unusual 'novel' in which the story is told via a series of emails sent to and from the 6-person crew of a space ship in transit to Mars interspersed with some action that takes place on Earth involving an assassination attempt. There is also some poetry.

There have been novels and stories written before in the form of letters, and they have been successful, but this style of story telling vanished more or less half a century ago, when writing letters began to diminish. Having conversations and communicating via emails was also for a time quite prevalent, but these days, this kind of communication is more likely to take place between older people. The younger generation use twitter and other similar platforms.

To tell an engrossing story using emails (or letters) requires considerable skill to present it in a way that is captivating enough to keep a reader interested. I don't think this author has that skill yet.

There are a number of things that turned me off:

Infodumps, where information is presented to explain background details or to explain about Mars, and how a mission to get there would be made, take up considerable parts of the first few chapters.

Listing the characters during countdown, and explaining what each of them does, what their education and background is, does not progress the story. It stops it dead. Perhaps the author wanted to generate tension during the countdown by examining each character as the numbers reduced to lift-off. To me, this information resembles the notes one would make when developing characters, and which would be kept aside for reference as the story progresses, and not be just dumped into the story.

Questions to the astronauts from people and kids back on Earth which the astronauts answered via their emails, are interesting. A lot of factual information is given, but it could have been presented to the reader as material within a number of action sequences rather than simply telling the reader how things would happen. The author tells us the story rather than letting the story evolve through the interaction of the characters involved.

Another thing that put me off was mixing tenses: A paragraph will be written in present tense, and when an astronaut speaks to one of the others it switches to past tense. People do speak in the past tense, but saying she or he said, instead of she or he says, regardless of what they actually say is not consistent with the paragraph before and after which is in the present tense. There is also mixing present and future tense as the author continues to tell us what they astronauts will be doing in the future as regards the mission.

Book presentation is also important. It is a matter of aesthetics, of design. I dislike text where every paragraph is separated by a double space (which is a default format for business documents and reports). That a writer wouldn't reformat the page so that it appears more like what one would find in a standard book is, I feel, being lazy; it's not that hard to do. Reading a story where every paragraph is separated by a double space is jarring, even worse when some paragraphs near the end of a page are split in the middle by a double space. That was probably an error introduced by having it as an eBook which is then printed on demand, rather than a book properly designed for printing. I also think text should be justified both left and right as it gives the book a more professional appearance. In a professional publication, acknowledgments are usually presented at the end of the book, not at the beginning where they are a distraction.

I lost interest at the end of chapter five. I found the emails to the astronaut's family and friends, and from them in return, to be mundane at the least, and didn't progress the story forward. I won't be buying the volume that follows this one, **Email from Mars: Under Martian Law**, or the proposed third volume, **Email from Mars: Inbound**.

No doubt there will be readers out there who will find this book interesting, and will buy it and the subsequent books. I commend the author for actually writing a book and proposing to write more; it's not easy, no matter what the end result. To actually complete and publish a book is an achievement and is something to be proud of.

Cydonia by Scott V Kelly MBA (2013)

Does the author think he has more credibility if he adds MBA, Master of Business Administration, after his name? Having an MBA doesn't guarantee the ability to write and tell a story, and this is amply demonstrated in this book.

Having bought this book because of the title, *Cydonia* and its attractive cover, I was disappointed with the content. The idea of 'the face on Mars' being built by an ancient civilization, or by beings alien to Mars is certainly not new. The Internet is full of conspiracy theories dealing with exactly that, and other authors have also told stories based around that concept. (Alan Steele's *Labyrinth of Night* published in 1992 is one fine example. *See Dreams of Mars page 212*).

Having plodded through the whole book, only because I paid an expensive price for it, I was disappointed. It reads like a first draft with everything the author could think of thrown into the mix. It hasn't been edited for structure, nor has it been line edited. He obviously relied on his word processor's spell-check function which doesn't tell you a word is wrong unless it is spelt wrong. There are so many words used incorrectly, almost on every page, with grammar that is confused, often passive rather than active, that the story becomes difficult to read.

Reading a book should be almost like watching a good movie. One becomes immersed in the flow of the action and the development of the characters to the point of not realizing that a movie is made up of an incredible number of individual images that are projected so fast they blur together into movement. Reading a book that is well written should be similar. One becomes immersed into the story without being aware of individual words or sentences unless there is wrong word or an unfinished sentence that jars the mind to snap the reader back out of the story. That is what happens with this story all the way through. It needs to be proof-read, or line-edited to find correctly spelt words that shouldn't be there, words spelt differently but pronounced the same, or confused grammatical tenses, between passive past tense, active past tense, with present tense.

The first three chapters are the kind of notes and information an author would create as preparation for plotting the story. Information dumped on us in these chapters could have been inserted incrementally within the text and action of the story, rather than given as the first three chapters.

There are twelve people in the crew who land on Mars, and there is not any idea in my mind of how these people look. What their characters are like, and how they interact with each other, and that means I can't identify with any of them, and have no idea of their likes, dislikes, motivations, or relations with the other members of the crew, especially after having spent months travelling from Earth to Mars. They are just names.

The idea of the crew and their set-up on Mars is based on the *Mars One* scenario where, at the time this story was written (in 2012-2013), the final candidates had been narrowed down to 100 potential colonists who would make a one-way trip to Mars. They were to be further narrowed to four groups of four who would begin travelling to Mars after the supply missions had set up equipment and robot-built bases in preparation for the arrival of the first group of colonists, who would then expand the bases with additional modules in readiness for further arrivals of colonists. By 2020 all the supply missions were to have been completed and the manned missions due to begin. The project was to be funded through a TV reality type show which would follow the astronauts through the whole voyage to Mars and their subsequent attempts at colonization. Unfortunately, *Mars One* could not secure sufficient financing and bankruptcy was declared with all future activities canceled from 2018 onwards. This was not known when **Cydonia** was written, and could not be imagined since everything about *Mars One* seemed positive and was proceeding on schedule. The story is extrapolated on the basis that *Mars One* would have continued as planned.

There have also been other novels based on the *Mars One* scenario. **Mars One** by Jonathan Maberry (2017) a young adult novel, beautifully written and published by Simon and Schuster, immediately springs to mind.

With **Cydonia**, the first real indication of action that propels the story forward finally begins with chapter seven. Chris, the TV journalist, with a woman called Heavenly, is heading out to the wall of the crater where the base has been established. She asks him when are they going to look at 'the Face'? She had seen him return from solo exploring but told no-one, so she knows he had discovered something. Reluctant to trust her initially he finally accepts that she is also working for the people on Earth who he works for and together they decide to examine the straight wall, partially buried, that runs from the 'pyramid' to 'the Face'. Using rock penetrating radar, they discover there is a hollow inside, meaning it is artificial, constructed by someone or something far in the past, but they need to come back another day to find an entrance.

They find an underground installation that connects 'the Face' with 'the Pyramid'. They decide to keep this a secret because the leader, Shamus, doesn't believe there could ever be life on Mars, that Earth is the only place life exists. There are childish confrontations between Shamus and Chris that seem pointless. Shamus is a scientist and he doesn't want to share anything with Chris who is a journalist, (who is also religious, and also a member of a society that believes Atlantis set up a colony on Mars). Shamus wants to be the one who is recognized for finding anything they discover on Mars. The mystery is compounded when a skeleton of a sheep is found buried in the sand. This should not be here. The doctor, Olaf, determines the DNA proves the sheep is over 5000 years old and is of Earth origin. When Chris further explores the underground complex beneath 'the Face' he discovers a desiccated human body in a space suit. The body is also more than 5000 years old and is human. On entering the underground complex Chris and Heavenly find many other bodies of the people who built and lived in this ancient complex. The author implies that these people died suddenly when the atmosphere was stripped from the planet by the collision with the meteor.

Up to this point the story, even with bad grammar and obviously misplaced words, promises to be intriguing. Further exploration by the group as a whole after Chris was forced to admit his discovery leads to ridiculous conflict between Chris and Shamus who yell at each other and eventually have a fist fight. Shamus calls Chris in anger, a HYPOCRATE (sic), and it is written with capital letters for emphasis. Later, still on the same page, he calls him with a more controlled tone, a hypocrite, and this time it is spelt correctly. There are examples of words like *from* being written as *form*, confusing *to* and *too*, *its* and *it's*, *hopped* instead of *hoped*, and too many other misspelled words or homonyms used that jar, which kept stopping this reader from processing what the author was trying to say.

But when the author has his characters claiming that scientific evidence proves the Earth is only 7500 years old, and Mars is the same and it had a beautiful climate with oceans and seas just like Earth did 7500 years ago which was all destroyed by a monstrous meteor that crashed into the planet 5000 years ago creating a giant cracked canyon and stripping the atmosphere to turn it into the desiccated world of today, he started to lose me. Even more so when he began claiming that the lost civilization of Atlantis had obtained space flight and had colonized Mars while it was still earthlike before the great flood that Noah experienced which destroyed our world... The ancient language they find in the Martian ruins turns out to be Hebrew implying that the Atlanteans spoke this language and that it was the language spoken by everyone who came from the Garden of Eden. It was only after the world degenerated into wars and the babel of other languages that God flooded the world, destroying Atlantis and its culture, also implying that the meteor that hit Mars and destroyed the Atlantean colony about the same time was also the work of God.

The whole story just falls apart and becomes even more ridiculous when someone on Earth attempts to remotely destroy the colony by detonating an atomic bomb that had been planted before the colonists arrived. Why? So, knowledge that Atlantis had colonized Mars would not be known on Earth?

When a second ship arrives and five more colonists are added to the original colony, whose people start having babies, the story ends. There is a brief mention that tensions on Earth develop into full scale wars which leaves the Martian colonists isolated. The final brief chapter has the colony surviving 100 years into the future with one of the last original colonists looking out over the Martian landscape as she dies.

There is the germ of a story here, and if the author had decided to have a structural edit, it could have been made into something better.

The Ruins of Mars (2013 – 2014) by Dylan James Quarles

At 790 pages the three books that make up **The Ruins of Mars** add up to an epic story.

The story opens with two AIs, Romulus and Remus, having been sent to Mars to make a complete map of the planet from low orbit, discovering an ancient city buried beneath the surface by the edge of the great Valles Marineris.

This discovery fires up Earth people and convinces NASA and the US Government to further explore Mars knowing that it had once been inhabited. It also fires up riots and other nasty episodes as the general population and various religious groups come to terms with the fact that humans are not or were not alone in the universe. Earth is pretty much in decline with resources running out and people clamoring that governments should spend money on feeding people instead of expensive trips to other planets. Most of the planet's activities are controlled or run by a number of AIs. The newest od these called Braun is installed in a starship to take an expedition to Mars to explore the ruins and to establish the base for a colony. The hope is that Mars can be altered in time so humans can live there. One of the people on the Mars mission is a young archaeologist, Harrison Raheem Asad. The crew is multinational. The captain is Russian, the chief pilot is Latin American, the scientists are Chinese, Korean, German and Italian while other crew members are American, French and British.

On the voyage out alliances are formed and pair bonding takes places. This makes for an interesting dynamic as events unfold on Mars. Apart from laying the foundations for a future colony on Mars, the main object of the crew is to examine the ruins to find out what the ancient Martians were like and how if possible, Earth could have been affected by them.

Before the team arrives at Mars, Romulus and Remus having fulfilled their mapping mission during which the ancient buried city was discovered, noticed a series of strange electronic signals emanating from Phobos and decide to investigate. Their beings, their very minds are suddenly drawn away from the satellites in orbit and they find themselves millions of years in the past, on Mars and able to observe how the Martians lived. Whether they are actually in the past or are in a superb reconstruction of the past, a massive computer simulation, is unclear at this point. They find they seem to have humanoid shaped bodies that are invisible to the primitive Martians. They can see each other but to the Martians they are as insubstantial as ghosts. Trapped there in the past, they watch as the Martians evolve and as a number of weird spaceships arrive with tall aliens whom they believe to be gods speak to them telepathically by using one of their own children as a voice. The aliens command them to construct a city, and they bring other Martians in from other parts of the planet to help with the massive construction.

When the expedition arrives on Mars, what had happened to Romulus and Remus is already four years old. To the team, the two satellites are dead and frozen, still in orbit.

A base is set up, and close scanning reveals the massive extent of the ancient buried city. Braun, the AI that runs the ship named after him, also assists with the exploration. The team discover lava tubes and tunnels underneath the city which weren't apparent from orbit, which will give them easy access to most of the city without having to dig down from above. While they have AI controlled diggers working on the surface to uncover the ruins, the team set up a lift that can take them and their equipment down the side of the massive canyon to a lava tube that allows them to enter underneath the city.

There are a number of incidents that take place as the base is being set-up, which gives the reader a reasonably accurate picture of how harsh Mars can be. It also shows us the logic and implacability of Braun, the AI that controls everything on the ship and in the base, and how its logic sometimes contravenes what humans would naturally do. This is interesting because in time, Braun will evolve and develop, just as the human members of the expedition will also change as a result of what they do and encounter on Mars.

The first book finishes on an exciting note as the team discover three statues in a huge globular cave deep under the city. Two 4 metre tall androgynous aliens with three eyes and kneeling before them a small humanoid female bowing towards them.

Marshall, one of the older team members, who saved Harrison's life during an arduous repair in a massive dust storm as they were establishing the base, stares at the statues and says 'It looks like there are – um – two different kinds of people here. Which ones are the Martians?'

Book two is subtitled Waking Titan, and it begins exactly where the first book finished, with the team in the cave with the statues. Braun notices there are emanations of energy that the humans can't see and he suspects something weird is going on.

There are more flashbacks to Romulus and Remus and what they are observing in the ancient past as the Martians and the city they are constructing evolve.

The doctor Elizabeth Kubba, informs Liu the Chinese scientist, that she is pregnant and wants her to abort. Liu doesn't want to do that, Neither of them can understand how this is possible because every crew member had been sterilized before the journey to Mars commenced. They didn't want people having babies in space or on Mars. Kubba who is having mental problems of her own, related to awful shit she'd done in the past, is becoming unstable. She creates a distrust between Harrison and Liu who were lovers almost from the moment they left Earth orbit on their way to Mars. Before this distrust can be resolved, Liu is killed in a violent accident caused by Braun while they were cutting away the statue of the kneeling woman to reveal another tunnel behind her.

Harrison is distraught at the death of his lover. He blames Braun. It takes some time before he begins to see the deceptions Kubba has introduced to them.

In the meantime, Braun has decided to examine the anomalous radio signal emanating from Phobos. Before they can stop him, he is sucked into it and in effect vanishes from the ship and all the devices in the base that he monitors and controls. Without Braun, the ship in orbit can't return to Earth.

Pushing on, the team enter another tunnel behind the kneeling woman and discover, after traversing a long tunnel, a huge domed room in the middle of which is an altar with something on it that glows like the sun. Around the altar are hundreds of skeletons, prostrate, facing towards the centre and the glowing artificial miniature sun.

When Harrison moves through the skeletons to the altar and touched the glowing object floating above it, the object flashes horrible red colours and appears to have a split across it. Everyone instantly falls unconscious. Harrison finds himself in a strange cave where people are using heat laser like devices to melt rock as they reshape the lava tubes. He sees two semi transparent figures which he discovers are Remus and Romulus. They also can see him. He asks them who they are and they tell him.

Meanwhile at the same time, back on Earth the whole world has been shattered by the magnetic pulses that emanated from the sun at the same moment Harrison had touched the device in the cave on Mars. Everyone on Earth under 5 years old, and everyone over 80 years old were instantly killed by the pulses from the sun. Those in between were knocked unconscious and wake up with splitting headaches. Millions killed instantly with untold collateral damage as people in planes flying were knocked out of the sky when their electronics failed. Every AI on Earth was also obliterated.

Harrison begins to get an inkling of what killed the Martians, but why is it happening again?

Meanwhile on the ship orbiting Mars, the captain is informed that a Chinese ship, ostensibly a supply ship, is on its way to help them and will arrive in a week. The ship is full of Chinese special forces soldiers, in hibernation, and they will take over the base. The Chinese originally denied sending a ship, but later admitted they had when it was discovered. The captain has orders to destroy the ship before it can land on Mars and her pilot and one assistant, Julian the ship's designer, make a covert mission to the Chinese ship. They find everyone on board is dead, having been killed by the pulse which also half fried their electronic equipment. They decide to blow up the ship to make it look like it was destroyed while trying to enter Mars' atmosphere, an accident, to avert what could be the start of a major war on the home planet. They also discover on reaching the approaching ship that its outer hull had a dozen killbots attached. These killing machines are super-efficient and there is no stopping them by most means available to the people they go up against. It is imperative the ship be destroyed before it can land on Mars. The killbots must be destroyed. It takes Julian longer than expected to set the explosive charges and as the ship begins to enter the atmosphere there isn't time for him to leave. He sacrifices himself by blowing up the ship manually. Unfortunately, one killbot starts to awaken and ejects itself just as the ship blows. It lands on Mars and begins its mission.

Book three, subtitled the Eye of the Apocalypse begins here. More is revealed that makes sense. The Chinese knew there had been aliens on Earth because they discovered a cave with a device similar to what was found on Mars, and when they knew about Mars, they immediately sent a ship with killbots and marines to capture the device. If anyone got in their way, ie the colonists at Mars base, they were to be eliminated.

Scientists and astronomers have worked out when the next pulse from the sun will arrive. It is when the Earth and Mars are in alignment, in opposition, with the sun. A pulse will be released that will most likely destroy whatever was left of human civilization. There is much more tension in this third part of the story as we countdown to the next devastating pulse. Things are falling apart on Earth as they are on Mars.

Harrison retrieves the mysterious object from the room with the skeletons, and as they go back up in the lift outside the cave entrance they are fired upon from a great distance. It is the killbot. It spotted them and tried to stop them. Harrison and his mate narrowly escape the killbot, and make it to the top of the canyon rim, but the lift is destroyed. Harrison takes the alien device back to the base to see if they can figure out what it does. If anyone can do it, the Korean scientist who created Braun AI will. She has also created a clone of Braun, a female version, and keeping her off-line saved her from destruction during the recent pulse. In time, she finds that the object is a way of opening a wormhole to another place, ancient Mars. Unfortunately, it needs another device to complete the circuit and they believe such a device exists on Phobos, the source of the mysterious radio signals that took Romulus, Remus as well as Braun. They need to activate both ends of the circuit to create the wormhole if they hope to retrieve the missing AIs.

The team try to stop the killbot from advancing but one of them is killed.

On their second attempt they bury it by blowing up two sides of the canyon walls in a narrow spot where the killbot has to pass to get out of the deep canyon. They think they have succeeded in stopping it as many tons of rocky rubble fall on top of it.

Kubba, who has gotten worse, mentally, attacks Yijay Lee and steals the device. She heads outside and walks off into the desert. Harrison discovers what she's done and chases after her. Kubba wants the device to transport her into the past, but what she sees is the killbot digging itself out of the rubble and continuing its advance towards the base. When Harrison catches up with her, she is suddenly remorseful when she hears how much damage she did to Yijay and returns with him to the base to see, as the only doctor, what she can do to help. Yijay loses one eye as a result of the attack. They lock Kubba in her room since she is a danger to all of them.

Knowing the only way to stop the killbot is to disable its electronic brain, they build a grenade that will emit a strong magnetic pulse when it explodes. The only problem is they will have to get close enough to it to lob the grenade right on it. Even though the bot is seriously damaged it still drags itself forward with the only functioning limb it has left. It slowly drags itself forward across the sand getting ever closer and closer. Its weapons are still functioning and that is the danger. The plan is to get close enough to it so one or two of them can distract it allowing the third member of the team to lob the grenade on top of it. This plan works but not the way they planned it. Kubba gets herself involved and it is she who throws herself on top of the killbot with the pulse grenade. She is killed as the grenade explodes; the pulse emitted also killing the killbot.

Back on Earth the US government is evacuating essential people to a deep underground bunker in Alaska in the hope that they will survive the next pulse.

In orbit around Mars, the captain, the shuttle pilot and one of the scientists, head towards Phobos where they hope to activate the second alien device simultaneously with the one on Mars. They want to open a wormhole so they can rescue Braun and the other two AIs. AS a storm is brewing on Mars, the team on Phobos enter the moon and find a huge cavern in which the device is located. AS they approach it the device on Mars makes contact and the device on Phobos and it is activated creating a wormhole between the two locations that leads into the past. The cloned AI is immediately sent in and she rescues Braun and Romulus, one of the two twins. Remus was lost, set free into the void.

But Remus isn't dead, he is rescued by something that turns out to be an artificial construct of the original Alien that watched over the ancient Martians. Yuvee is now an AI with incredible power. It resides in a space ship hidden in the asteroid belt. It is the only one of its kind left after billions of years. Yuvee's people once travelled the stars to observe life as it evolved on a number of planets. They used wormholes connecting suns to travel through. What they didn't know was that each time they went from one star to another it damaged the star causing rifts that emitted magnetic pulses. These pulses eventually wiped out life on the planets around that system. Once they exited our sun, they realized what they had done, so they didn't travel any further. They hid in the asteroid belt, where they eventually died off. Only Yuvee, who was left to watch over the Martians remained, as an artificial being, similar to Remus only far more complex.

By the time we get to this point, the pulse that will wipe out life on Earth and the rest of the solar system is imminent. But Yuvee explains to Remus that it can be repaired. His ship has developed the capacity to do so, but they need to go into the sun as they do it.

The book ends with Yuvee, and Remus in the huge alien ship heading towards the sun to neutralize the pulse that is just about to be emitted.

The book ends on a high note with the Earth, what's left of it, safe for the time being, and our main characters also alive and looking forward more positively.

Overall, a much better story than I thought when I first started to read it. Ancient ruins discovered on Mars is a theme often used in many modern martian stories, and some are better than others. This is one of the better ones.

On the negative side, the weight of the books and the way they have been printed speaks of amateurism and is off-putting to someone who likes a professional looking book.

But don't be deterred by the appearance of these three books. The story and the writing are first class, and there are enough twists and turns to keep you on the edge of your seat from beginning to end.

Chapter Ten

The new Golden Age continues

Young adult fiction is a category that is doing very well for science fiction and fantasy stories, and it seems the stories are generally much better than those produced for adult readers. Perhaps one of the reasons is that the stories are not bloated with additional background material or peripheral action to fill a larger number of pages. They tend to be leaner, straight to the point, resulting in a more compelling read which can be finished in a much shorter time.

Mars Evacuees Sophia McDougall (2014)

I like books that range from 200 to 400 pages and Mars Evacuees comes in at 327 pages in the Egmont paperback. It's a nice-looking book with an eye-catching cover.

Alice Dare is the daughter of a famous space fighter pilot who is part of the defense forces battling the Morrors to regain control of the Earth. The Morrors initially came and announced that they were going to live on the Earth but only at the poles where the temperature suited them, and as a bonus they would stop the Earth's runaway climate change by cooling the planet. Only they didn't stop there. They built mirrors in space that deflected the sun and the Earth began cooling rapidly into an ice age. The Humans tried to stop this and a war began with the Morrors who have invisible space ships which can't be seen but can be detected with heat sensing equipment,. They also wear invisibility cloaks so no one knows what they look like.

Alice is a 12-year-old girl at a private school. She is called to the principal's office and told she is going to be evacuated to Mars, while most of the other girls at her school are being moved further South to escape the encroaching ice.

Alice joins 300 other students who are all being evacuated to Mars. Mars is in the process of being terraformed and it now has areas where the air is almost breathable and where lakes are forming. There are plants, specially modified to survive on Mars and some small wildlife similarly modified.

Beagle Base has been specially built to house the three hundred school children. It has dormitories, eating hall, kitchens, storage areas, a sports field, garages for vehicles and small planes, a hangar for space ships, a number of connected domes for agriculture like wheat growing, soya beans, a tree nursery, science and maintenance areas. It is also designed to train the children to be military personnel when they are of age, so they can continue the ongoing fight against the Morrors. It is thought that the Morrors don't want Mars, and are only interested in Earth, cooling it down to a temperature that suits them but is far too cold for humans to tolerate.

The kids settle in to Beagle Base and their ongoing studies are conducted by pestiferous robots, with little interaction between the kids and the adults apart from the military aspect of their education.

On a field excursion, one of Alice's younger friends sees a strange animal near a newly formed lake. It looks like a large worm with a rotating mouth that eats into the sand and rocks. It flies away but no one else saw it and no one believes him.

Suddenly, all the humans disappear. They take off for the other military base on the planet but don't return. The kids are left to their own devices. Very soon the bigger or older kids form groups that fight each other for limited supplies, that use bullying tactics to get their own way, intimidating the younger kids. Alice and a few friends don't like it, and as hope diminishes for the return of the adults, they decide to steal the only space ship left in the hanger, to go in search of the other military base where they think the adults went. One of the teaching robots that looks like a goldfish attached itself to Alice's group so they could continue their studies, much to the annoyance of the group, but they put up with it because they have no choice. It won't allow them to do anything unless they spend at least one hour a day studying whatever subject it decides they need to learn.

As they travel the 3000 or so miles to the other side of the planet where the military base is, they encounter a swarm of these flying metallic worms. They are diving into the ground and devouring the rock surface throwing up clouds of dust as they proceed. They also attack the ship Alice is flying eating holes right through the metal. One of them is trapped inside and they manage to kill it with a flame thrower. But the ship is damaged and won't fly properly. They are forced to crash land and are then faced with the problem of traversing a large part of Mars to get to the military base, but they have limited oxygen supplies and food to cover the distance.

Alice comes up with the idea of using a large agricultural robot, some of which are working in a nearby valley planting seeds. With the help of the goldfish (teacher robot) they manage to hack into the ag-robot's programming to reprogram it to carry them on its back.

All goes well for a while until Alice sees something weird out of the corner of her eye and the group discovers a Morror wearing an invisibility cloak. She (like her mother) can just barely see them. No one else can. They capture the Morror and are initially disgusted with how it looks but soon get used to it. They are the first people to ever see one. They also discover it is from a crashed space ship and is the only survivor. The other Morrors are dead, lying on the ground covered with a large invisibility cloak. Alice is astonished to see they are all very different from each other, and later after discovering their captive is only a thirteen-year-old child, like themselves, they are somewhat sympathetic towards it. They of course take it with them as their prisoner. It happens that the young Morror can speak English and so they can communicate with each other. During their trek to the military base they find out that the Morrors have five sexes and that three are needed to produce children, which is why they look so different from each other. They were forced to leave their own planet because it was destroyed by an invading alien species. They developed the invisibility cloaks so they couldn't be seen by the aliens and they fled from their part of the galaxy in search of a more suitable planet to live on. Earth was what they found. The Morrors don't like Mars because it has no magnetic field and they cannot find their way around. But they do have a hidden base on Mars.

When the group reaches the human military base, they discover it has been destroyed and there is no sign of anyone there. There is however a small space ship there and the kids commandeer it. The captive Morror decides to show them the way to the hidden base, especially when the area is attacked by the flying worm things. These are the reason the Morrors left their home world. It had been devoured by these metallic monsters, and they had followed them to the solar system and would soon devour Mars, Earth and all the other planets, before moving on to discover another system to consume.

When they find the Morror base they discover the humans from the military base as well as their own teachers are prisoners, but the Morrors have no idea that their implacable enemy has followed them to Mars. They are horrified when they see the dead creature the children have with them.

At this point Alice convinces the Morrors that the only way to defeat the planet eating aliens is to join forces and call off the war. They fly back to Earth to negotiate peace, but the Earth security forces think it is an attacking fleet and sally forth to do battle. Alice manages to contact her mother who is the leader of the defending forces and convinces her not to fire on them because there are humans on board. She finally convinces her mother that the Morrors want to make peace so together they can fight a much worse enemy, an enemy that will eventually destroy the galaxy.

Part of the peace process is for the Morrors to allow more sunlight in so the Earth doesn't become too cold for humans. The Morrors were actually building an invisibility cloak to make the Earth invisible to any observers from outer space, hoping they could hide from the metallic planet eating things, but they are already here. They can easily adjust the shield so it lets sufficient light through to keep the temperature reasonable for both sides. They join forces and fight off (supposedly destroying) all the attacking monsters that had followed the Morrors from Mars. Alice is reunited with her mother and the story ends here on a positive note with humans and Morrors as allies together occupying the Earth.

What I liked about this story is that it is easy to read, has enough tension and action to satisfy the needs of the story, and it does have the sense of wonder I remember getting from similar stories I read fifty to sixty years ago as a teenager myself.

Alice Dare is also a wonderful role model for younger readers who can imagine themselves doing what she does. That the children directly cause the two warring parties to stop and join forces is a positive message to adults that the future belongs to the children and they don't want the world they will inhabit to be ruined by adults who should take more notice of the children.

Hilarious and bloodthirsty

Gestapo Mars by Victor Gischler (2015)
Regardless of the title, nothing takes place on Mars.

Mars is ruled by the Gestapo, and the Reich. Their headquarters a is on Mars, and they occupy over 400 planets throughout the Galaxy. A group of rebels led by the direct descendant of one of the worst of the Nazi rulers on Mars, called The Brass Dragon, is fighting the Reich on many different fronts. At the same time an alien menace, the slug like Coriandon who want to take over Mars, must be stopped at all costs.

Carter Sloan, who has been in cryogenic sleep for over 250 years (on Earth) is woken up and activated. Unlike the newer versions, he is unaugmented and therefore undetectable to electronic surveillance. He is a spy, a womanizer, a fighter capable of creating untold havoc, as well as being the Reich's most able assassin. He is sent on a mission to kill the Brass Dragon's

Daughter, and so begins an unbelievable journey/chase, across interstellar space. This is action adventure at its best with something unexpected happening in every chapter, if not every few pages, as Sloan battles against impossible odds, always just succeeding, to complete his mission.

It's hilarious, and bloodthirsty, full of memorable caricatures that are aptly named for what they do, one for example being Master Sergent Hamfast F Kolostomy, a real bad-ass whose middle name is Fuck All (F). He leads a suicide mission against the Coriandons to blow up one of their ships which closes one of the wormholes leading to the solar system, thus preventing one of the Coriandon's fleets from getting there.

The big showdown at the end is to prevent Mars being attacked by the second Coriandon fleet which used a different wormhole to get there, and Sloan guarantees the Reich's success, by blowing up the sewerage system of the Coriandon's giant battleship which controls the fleet attacking Mars, filling the ship with their own shit, causing them to abandon it and give up the battle.

Knowing his time is up, his work is done, Sloan sneaks off and returns to Earth, partially abandoned, and puts himself back into a cryogenic sleep in the hope that far in the future if he wakes up again, things will be better.

This is great entertainment and fun to read. Although we never actually get onto Mars, the thought of Mars and what it represents to the Reich and the Human race is embedded throughout the whole book.

Closer to reality

Oxygen (2001, 2011,2015)
The Fifth Man (2002,2012,2015)
John B Olsen and Randy Ingermanson

These two novels constitute one long story. The first, *Oxygen*, relates the training and the journey to Mars, while The Fifth Man is about what happens when the crew have arrived and established themselves on the surface. Both were published in 2001 and 2002 respectively, and the background is based on Robert Zubrin's plans for a journey to Mars and the setting up of systems to sustain the first explorers, (delineated in his book *The Case for Mars*). At the time the stories were written it was feasible that an expedition to Mars could be possible, if not almost certain to have occurred by 2014. (Zubrin himself wrote and published a novel also depicting a first expedition to Mars that takes place in 2011, *First Landing*, (2001). (See *Dreams of Mars* page 268).

When it appeared that 2014 was overly optimistic, the authors revised their two novels and changed the dates given throughout, which would have dated the story, to dates commencing with year one, the year the astronauts were selected for the journey. This shifts the story into a non-defined near future, making the story plausible and probable.

Valkerie Jansen, who is tough enough and resourceful enough to survive the imminent eruption of a volcano, initially trained as a doctor but later switched to biology specializing in extremophile bacteria, is famous for having discovered new species of bacteria living in conditions previously thought of as inimical to life of any kind. She is recruited by Steven Perez, director of the Johnson Space Centre. She had applied for a position with NASA and they had accepted her application. She is brought into the program where four astronauts are training for the first trip to Mars. NASA needs someone like her who is a specialist in extremophile bacteria because they hope to find such bacteria somewhere on Mars.

At first the other astronauts resent her because she is an outsider, brought in to train with them, and if she is selected then they know that one of them will be displaced. Bob Kaganovski, one of the astronauts, is immediately smitten with Valkerie, but hides his feelings. She too finds him attractive but keeps her feelings to herself. Bob is the engineer who can fix anything and he thinks if anyone is going to be bumped off the mission it will be him. However, he decides to do all he can to help Valkerie succeed, if that's what it takes for the mission to get underway. He wants the mission to Mars to go ahead whether he is part of it or not. In fact, they all want this to succeed because it will be the only shot they have. Congress is already cutting funding and if this mission doesn't get off the ground there will not be any future manned missions to Mars.

Josh Bennett is a celebrity astronaut and the leader of the team. He always has a stream of women chasing him, and NASA uses him whenever they need publicity to generate public interest. The other two team members are Kennedy Hampton, who is a superb pilot, but a bit of a sleaze bag as regards women, and Alexis Ohta, Lex, a geologist and the only woman on the team.

Valkerie is pushed almost to her limits, forced to train harder and longer than the others in order to catch up, and as the departure date approaches the Head of the mission Nate Harrington invites her to be part of the mission as a specialist (biologist). She is ecstatic at first but suddenly realizes that someone will be displaced if she accepts. She is told that Josh will step down to become Capcom for the mission and that Kennedy will then become Captain. The team now consists of two women and two men, and they'd better get used to each other because once the mission starts, they will be closely confined in the habitat and the rocket taking them to Mars.

Even at this point in the story there is a lot of tension with the remaining Mars crew resenting the change NASA forced upon them. The biggest tension underlying the story is whether Valkerie will find life on Mars, because if they don't, there may be little funding for future missions.

Outside of the training area there are constant protests by radical religious groups about finding life on Mars destroying the credibility of the Bible, and a celebrity author who has written a book about back-contamination. This author insists the astronauts should not be allowed to return home in case they bring with them unknown Martian bacteria that could destroy life on Earth. A lot of protesters maintain the same view.

Taking off is a nail-biting moment because gusting winds throw the rocket slightly off and part of it clips the gantry supporting it, causing some damage to the side of the ship. Still, the mission goes ahead and they exit Earth orbit and start the transit to Mars. Not long into the transit they deploy the solar panels and discover one of them was damaged during the takeoff. Exiting the vehicle to fix it, Bob and Kennedy discover there are strange coloured wires connected to something that shouldn't be there. Josh tells them not to touch the wires, but Bob accidentally touches them with the tool needed to repair the panel and causes an explosion. A split in the side of the hull causes the air to evacuate from the capsule. Valkerie, wearing a space suit as she assisted the other two to exit the ship, manages to find a piece of flat metal which she welds over the rent in the hull to stop any further air from leaking out. She immediately rushes to the control deck and finds Lex in a desperate situation and manages to stuff her into an emergency atmosphere bag. Returning to the airlock she finds Kennedy cowering inside but no sign of Bob. She exits the ship and finds Bob still tethered to the ship and hauls him inside. Sealing the airlock, she releases oxygen from the Lox fuel tanks, since most of the air was lost into space. With Lex in a coma the three remaining crew members evaluate the situation.

Someone tried to sabotage them. Someone doesn't want the mission to succeed. Who could do that? They each suspect the others. No one had access to the ship or the crew training facilities in the last few months other than the four astronauts selected for the trip, and Josh and Nate, back at the Johnson Space Center. None of them would want to sabotage the mission. They had spent years of their lives working on it. Yet someone had. At this point paranoia sets in as each suspects the other. None of them have a motive. But what is worse. They discover there will not be enough oxygen for all of them to get to Mars. There is only enough for one.

As the tension becomes almost unbearable (fort the reader), a solution is found that requires a difficult docking with another supply space ship also on its way to Mars. This doesn't work out as they planned, and although they gain some extra oxygen, only two would be able to continue on to Mars. Eventually it is decided that Valkerie who is the smallest, and would use the least oxygen, would remain awake and that she will put the other two into an artificially induced coma where they would use the least amount of oxygen. They don't particularly like this idea but they have no choice. It is either that, or not survive at all. Lex is already in a coma from the decompression injuries she received when the atmosphere was voided.

With power off, and in darkness, Valkerie manages to stay sane until they reach Mars orbit when she wakes up the two men and Lex. With barely any oxygen left, they manage to land the ship as close as possible to where a robotic base had been established, where there is ample oxygen waiting for them. The only way to get it though is for Kennedy and Bob to suit up and walk the several hundred meters to the waiting habitat where they can access the rover and fresh oxygen supplies. With muscles weakened by months in free-fall they find walking that distance extremely difficult. They almost run out of air in their suits, which means that back on the ship (the Ares 10) there will be no oxygen left for Valkerie and Lex.

The trip back at the fastest speed the rover can manage, a mere 15 mph, is not enough for them to get back before the last of the ship's oxygen has been used up. They dock to rover and race into the Ares to find both women unconscious and with no apparent pulse. Heartbroken Bob brings Valkerie into the rover and Kennedy brings in Lex. They head back to the Mars habitat and go inside. It is only later that Bob goes into the rover and discovers Valkerie is alive, Stunned, he doesn't know what to say as she explains she used what was left of the drugs used to previously induce a coma to put both her and Lex into a coma so they wouldn't use up so much oxygen, so they would have a chance to last long enough for the men to get back with the rover to save them.

As the first book finishes here, Bob blurts out that he would like to marry Valkerie.

Oxygen, the second part of the story begins about 9 months later. They have established themselves in the habitat and are doing geological work as well as attempting to grow vegetables in a greenhouse. Lex and Valkerie are examining salt crystal outcrops inside a deep crevasse when the crystal deposits give way and Valkerie discovers a deep cavern. Pushing her way into the cavern she sees fossilized archaebacteria. The cavern is also warm as steam is being vented up from somewhere underground. Pushing her way further into the cavern to see what she can discover, she accidentally dislodges rock and soil and it collapses onto her, trapping her.

Her calls for help are picked up by Bob who is working outside the habitat with Kennedy. He immediately rushes to the rover and heads for the location where he knows they are to rescue Valkerie.

Later, Kennedy accuses Bob of pushing him over which almost smashed his helmet, scratching the faceplate. Bob says she wasn't anywhere near Kennedy when he fell over, he was already on his way to the Rover. Then they start hearing thumping noises outside the habitat and going out to look they find nothing. Discovering scrapes on the side of the Habitat as well as the rover leads Bob to accuse Kennedy of bad driving which Kennedy vehemently denies. When noises start happening inside the habitat at night, they begin to worry. Are they being paranoid, or is something else really there? Meanwhile, Kennedy is beginning to lose it. He was already unstable, but after months of being cooped up he is getting worse. He begins to believe the other thee are trying to kill him. He also makes a pass at Valkerie which she rebuffs and this infuriates him.

Valkerie has set up a series of petri dishes in her lab to see if the soil recovered from her suit and the clay that got stuck into the joints of her suit while she was inside the cavern harbor bacteria. She discovers live bacteria growing in the cultures made from the clay and is excited, but they decide not to inform NASA about the discovery in case NASA decides to strand them on Mars for fear of bringing home alien bacteria that could devastate humans on Earth. This is especially after two of them get sick with a fever and breathing problems. NASA is threatening to leave them on Mars when Josh comes clean. He planted the explosives on the ship. They were not meant to damage the ship in transit but were to explode when the ship landed, expelling a collection of Antarctic archaebacteria which hopefully Valkerie would find and think there was life on Mars. He wanted the mission to succeed and finding life on Mars would guarantee that. It must have been that bacteria that infected the two astronauts he claims.

But something else is happening. Valkerie hears glass smashing in the middle of the night and rushing down to her laboratory she finds her petrie dishes with the Martian bacteria cultures smashed and lying on the floor. Something pushed her in the legs and knocks her over. They begin to think there is another person on Mars, a fifth person, who doesn't want them to succeed, but how is this possible? There couldn't have been a stowaway on their ship, and as far as they know the Russian Mars probe, which stopped sending signals two thirds pf the way to Mars wasn't a manned mission. Then their radio signals to Earth are being jammed at odd periods.

Back at the Johnson Space Center the technicians are working furiously to decode the jamming and suspect the Russians are doing it through an account set up by Josh on their computers when he was training at Baikonur.

They also discover that Josh's computer had been used to relay stuff, via the Russian computers and the FBI arrests him for sabotage.

It becomes very complex as things go wrong on Mars and accusations of espionage within NASA itself becomes a mystery that has to be solved. The threat of back-contamination has been removed as they believe Josh's story. But they still don't know Valkerie has discovered Martian bacteria and cultured them. Kennedy goes completely bonkers and the other have to restrain him and they lock him up in a storage habitat without a space suit so he can't escape. When the storage unit explodes into flame destroying their food supplies and their fuel for the return vehicle, and presumably killing Kennedy, life on Mars becomes really difficult. Someone activates the return ship in orbit to initiate a burn that would cause it to crash into Mars, but engineers on Earth stop this before the action can happen, so the return ship is safe. But without food for more than a month, how are the astronauts on Mars going to survive for another year before they are due to return to Earth. Without fuel, how can they launch into orbit. Someone drives off with the rover and they have to suspect that there is another person on Mars. There is no other answer. It couldn't possibly be some evil malignant Martian life form that wants them gone. The planet is basically dead, with no other life anywhere, other than the bacteria Valkerie found. Everything started happening after that.

Something is consistently destroying their habitat and their only solution is to get off the planet, and into the return ship in orbit, even though it is too soon. There is plenty of food on that ship and there is no way they could last on Mars more than a few weeks. They are already starving to death.

Whatever is trying to destroy them has also smashed the fuel lines on the MAV (Mars ascent vehicle) needed to get them into orbit and it has drained most of the fuel out. They have to re-manufacture enough and that means going back to the cavern and extracting a ton of ice which they can break down onto oxygen and hydrogen to make the fuel for the MAV. Under pressure and extreme conditions, they get enough ice and have to transport it back to the base. Mysteriously the rover comes back and Bob and Valkerie on their way back with the ice, sneak up and enter it to find out who has been driving it. They discover a mad disheveled Kennedy. He wasn't dead after all. He attacks them and they again subdue him and finally manage to convince him they mean no harm; they want to help him.

They just manage to do this and as they are attempting to refuel the MAV something destroys the base's nuclear power station and they run out of power for the pumps needed to transfer the fuel. Kennedy, in order to redeem himself rushes to the power station and plugs back the power lines but exposes himself to harmful radiation since the shielding has been damaged.

He has to hold the power line in by hand while the pumps are transferring the fuel. The rover, driven remotely returns to attack the MAV and the three remaining astronauts just manage to get inside and launch before the base of the MAV is damaged too much to let them leave.

This story has further surprises and unexpected twists to it that are not foreshadowed, keeping the reader tense and full of expectations.

The two books together are an exciting story that makes sense when you get to the end. In my view it is one of the better stories from the second decade of this new century. The books are cinematic in experience and would make a fantastic film or better still, an extended TV story.

The Colonization of Mars by Larry Richardson (2010 -2011- 2015- 2016)

Originally self-published in 2010, it has apparently been revised several times, which means all the typos and small errors have been eliminated. My copy is the 2016 version. It is a long story with 576 pages.

As expected for a book with almost 600 pages, it is a slow read, but continuously fascinating in the details that build an absorbing picture of Mars as human colonists would be likely to find it. What I found most interesting is that all the colonists sent to Mars, by a private consortium are older or elderly scientists rather than young people. They went to Mars with never having any intention to return to Earth, and this affects their attitude towards the colonization.

But there is more going on than simple scientific exploration of Mars. The human colonists are assisted by a variety of AI robots with various design configurations, such as rover drivers, biological and geological explorer machines, management machines, construction machines among others. These machines are building habitats for a future influx of new colonists.

Most of the colonists, because they are older, don't like to travel or explore much, being content to stay inside the initial habitat to conduct their research, but eventually moving to a new habitat which replicates earthlike conditions constructed inside a massive lava tube under the surface.

Only one person, Sam, one of the less elderly ones, wants to go out and explore the planet, and the story focuses mainly on Sam as he travels across Mars (being continuously video recorded for transmission back to Earth to keep their sponsors happy) exploring the phenomenal landscapes of the planet, with the help of the AI in control of his rover or Rollagon. He gradually develops an empathy with his first Rollagon AI, suggesting there is more to the AIs than the colonists suspect, and which is confirmed with the longer duration voyage around the planet with a second (female) AI Rollagon.

Ultimately it is a sad story when a secret experiment goes wrong and the colonists are infected with a disease they can't control and section by section they succumb to it.

Our traveler Sam is the only survivor, being years away and isolated from the other colonists as he explores the planet. Over that time his relationship with the Rollagon AI, and his friendship with the previous Rollagon AI leads us to believe that within certain constraints the AIs are gradually developing an independence, and individual personalities beyond their initial programming.

When Sam, the explorer finally returns (by this time he is 80 earth years old) he is the last human to survive, and the AIs look towards him for inspiration and direction regarding their future on Mars. There will be no more colonists coming because Earth has degenerated into anarchy and space travel is abandoned. But on Mars there is still hope and the story ends on a surprisingly positive note.

Overall, this is a good story, well written, that draws the reader in, and although not filled with action as many Mars stories are, it is filled with fascinating details and extrapolative speculation that entices you to read on to find out what is going to happen next. This is a book to keep, which is not something I would say about a lot of self-published stories.

Making Mars by Michael Hallett (2016)

Aimed at younger readers, the main protagonist is Dirk a young teenager, who goes to Mars, where his father is already a working member of the established colony. Mars had been in the process of being terraformed for 100 years and the atmosphere has reached the point where it is partially breathable. The general temperature has also risen so in some areas the permafrost is beginning to melt. Dirk is the only kid on Mars, although a couple of his father's friends have had a baby, the first one born on Mars.

Dirk's job is to assist a robot companion collect the parts, being delivered from space via disposable cranes which activate on proximity to the surface, and lower the cargo slowly so it arrives undamaged. The cranes are then left as scrap. But Dirk is an inventive teenager and he salvages the disposed cranes and uses parts not damaged to repair those that are damaged. He also collects the unused fuel and refuels repaired cranes so they can be used as a means of land transport. They are in the process of building a space elevator which will make delivery of essential goods and spare parts so much easier for the colonists. Everyone in the colony works for the company that established the colony, except for two people, one a government representative and the other a policeman, basically exiled to Mars. They have a number of schemes running to benefit themselves, and one of these involves taking blood from the only teenager on Mars, and on-selling it to Earth. They make life difficult for Dirk.

What is good about this story, is that although there is a lot of explanatory detail (e.g., Dirk asks his father and associates many questions about their life on Mars and the answers fill in details which explain how the colony came about and how the terraforming is proceeding) it doesn't drag or slow the story; it makes it more interesting. There is enough action with Dirk and his robot companion (which also evolves more human-like characteristics as a result of its association with Dirk) to keep the story moving forward. Dirk spends what time he can get free, exploring the nearby area and discovers a medium crater sever kilometres away from the base. He comes up with the idea of having the company to get a water or ice comet to impact in the crater to fill it with water so they can go swimming. Having comets impact the surface to release water was one of the ways they have been terraforming the planet, although they don't do that so much now that the atmosphere has thickened a bit.

There is much excitement regarding this comet and Dirk one day goes exploring in the crater where the impact is expected to occur. A dust storm forces him to take shelter in a split in the side of the crater wall. The dust is highly abrasive and could damage his environment suit so much it becomes useless. Waiting out the storm, he sees a cave, enters to find it connects to an ancient lava tube. He enters deeper into the cave, follows it down and discovers what he thinks are animal tracks and photographs them. He believes he has discovered life, but as yet has no proof. This would be momentous and would change everything. He takes the photos back to his father's friend; a biologist, and she can't be certain that the marks were made by an animal. She gives him some cameras, tripods and recording equipment and asks him to set them up in the cave. Two cameras that will take pictures using a motion detector to trigger them, and an infra-red video camera that will record continuously for 24 hours.

With these set up in the cave, they wait. Unfortunately, Dirk can't go back the next day. The government officials want him for medical tests; tests he views with suspicion, but is unable to stop them from happening. As soon as he recovers from the tests he heads back to the crater and the cave deep beneath it to retrieve the cameras. They are astonished to discover several photos of a lizard like creature, but what is more astonishing is the video captured a humanoid female emerging from deeper in the cave to examine the cameras. She takes them off the tripods, looks at them and replaces them unaware that she has been silently videoed by the infra-red camera. The excitement is palpable, but Dirk suddenly remembers the comet. It is due to impact in the crater if a few weeks and there is no way they can stop it. If that happens, whatever life there is under the crater in the lava tubs and caverns will be destroyed. He has to stop it.

At this point they still haven't told anyone of what they have discovered.

The final few chapters are nail-biting, as Dirk and his robot companion and his father and friends devise a way to divert the comet at the last moment so it impacts not in the crater but a few kilometres beyond it.

Unfortunately, the story finishes here. With this reader anxiously waiting to get the next volume of the story to find out what happens.

There is a note from the author to check his website for details regarding the next volume, but the link doesn't find any web-pages or websites regarding this.

It appears the author has not yet written the next part of the story, which I would have expected to be completed since the first part was published in 2016. There may never be a finish to the story, but regardless, it is still worth reading because it is a good story.

Mars 20 — Saving Utopia by Shelby Hiatt (2016)

Lovely cover design which immediately in my mind places this story in the young adult category, without even opening the book. Young adult is a huge category and there are many first-class science fiction stories in this category.

In 2055, on Mars, two teenagers, Kit (18) and her boyfriend Rob (19), are outside dust surfing when a crisis occurs back at the base. Apparently Robs parents had an argument which was serious. The teenagers were called back and on arriving Rob finds his father cradling his mother who seemed distraught. From what his father says Rob realizes that this wasn't their first argument. Later that day, at a baseball game the youngsters were playing outside (wearing their newly developed pressure suits and helmets because the Martian atmosphere is unbreathable being almost all carbon dioxide), the parents watching start arguing over the runs scores and it rapidly degenerates into a brawl. People punching each other, pushing, shoving, and kicking, wrestling each other, but with little damage other than bruises, blood noses and sore egos, because the skin-suits they wear protect them from such physical violence. Not understanding what is going on, the game stops and the teens escort their parents back inside the major habitat. Even Kit's mother seems dazed and unwilling to talk.

To get away from the inexplicable sadness in the habitat, Rob, Kit and another younger sibling head off for what they call a picnic. It's really an excursion outside, away from the adults. They go to the landing site of the UK's Beagle 2 spaceship. Not long there, they are interrupted by the arrival of another buggy with an adult who informs them that Something awful has happened to Rob's dad. Racing back to the habitat they find his dad is dead. He had been trapped outside without his skin-suit. They discover his mother had been trying to commit suicide by going outside without her skin-suit, and Rob's father had tried to drag her back inside. In the process the airlock door had closed and he had been left outside without his skin-suit. It was a terrible accident. Rob's mother was taken to the infirmary where she is in a catatonic state.

There are other parents too, who are affected by the mindless arguments that sometimes become physically violent, and the children come to the conclusion that their parents are homesick for Earth. They spend all their spare time watching old videos, sporting events, musical programs and other such stuff either broadcast from Earth of from the files they brought with them when the original colony was established. Not all the adults are affected, nor are the 2nd generation, the children born on Mars.

Being the oldest of the children born on Mars, Kit and Rob, feel an obligation to solve what is wrong with their parents, but they can't find anything physically wrong. It seems some of the parents are retrogressing into their childhood, or at least they act like spoilt kids, which is incomprehensible to those born on Mars. They have no feeling for Earth at all; Mars is their home.

Things get worse, with some parents attempting to leave the habitat without their skin-suits. They prefer to die rather than to stay on Mars. They've been there for more than 20 years, so their sudden severe bouts of homesickness are inexplicable. Isolating the affected parents, the teenagers come up with a series of games and physical activities to keep the affected parents amused, and this works for a while, until a couple more exit the habitat and commit suicide outside.

After much angst, Kit discovers the reason for the affliction. The only ones affected were those who worked in the dome where they grew their food. Something in the concrete made from Martian regolith was leaching oxygen out of the atmosphere resulting in hypoxia and brain damage to those who worked long hours in the greenhouse. They can't have anyone working in there long-term anymore, and that means food production will be diminished. A big problem, unless they can find running water to channel through the agricultural-dome, and running water is impossible to find on Mars. All the water that exists is deep underground.

They don't have enough stored food to keep the colony going if they can't grow their own. And there is no way they can return to Earth after such a long time in the lesser gravity of Mars. Earth also has its own problems with rising seas due to global warming, mass evacuations to higher ground, and other consequences. They need the Mars colony to succeed, so there will be a place for humanity when Earth is no longer viable.

Kit and Rob take a rover and go in search of water. They head towards the pole and pass close to Olympus Mons. Drilling discovers nothing and they think that what is needed is an asteroid to hit the surface and blow open a deep crater which would help melt the permafrost and elicit a flow of water.

NASA has the ability to nudge dangerous asteroids aside in order to protect Earth and they suggest nudging one and having it collide with Mars, impacting the surface near the pole. They make this happen but from such a great distance they can't be exact and the co-ordinates given them by Kit and Rob don't help.

The asteroid crashes into the top of Olympus Mons and reignites that gigantic ancient volcano. There are mars-quakes, and the volcano starts spewing slow moving lava. It does however melt the permafrost and generates an enormous flow of water which runs down the ancient channels towards the Mars base.

The parents, momentarily happy to have something to do, manage to dig channels around and through the middle of the colony so the water will travel around and through the colony, narrowly averting a washout and a disaster. They also manage to get it to flow through the greenhouse agricultural dome, which they need to grow their food. With the colony saved, it all ends well, even though there is nothing they can do to restore their parent's mental capacities.

The continuing eruption of Olympus Mons will generate enough heat to keep water flowing for the near future. They suggest to NASA that the Earth people should move to the Atacama Desert which is high and dry with a thin atmosphere, where they could acclimate future Mars colonists in preparation for trips to Mars. The underlying message to the readers is that we should have taken better care of Earth so it wouldn't be experiencing global warming and climate change which future generations will be forced to live with.

That this story would appeal to younger readers I have no doubt.

What teenager doesn't want to read a story where their generation saves the world in spite of the mess their parents have made?

I found it entertaining and probably would have enjoyed it much more if I was a young reader, but I'm not young anymore and generally prefer a story that has more complexity to it.

Lost in the Red Hills of Mars by Jackie Hunter (2017)
This is a book to be proud of. It has an eye-catching cover and a lovely interior design, and on top of that it is really good story. It also looks professional. Although written for a young adult audience it is a delightful story for readers of any age. The author says it was inspired by her students and their love of Mars. She worked in school administration as well as teaching science and mathematics to middle school students.

The protagonist is Celine Red Cloud, a thirteen-year-old girl of Cherokee descent, and the only girl born on Mars in the mining colony set up by Mr. Rittenhouse, a wealthy business man.

Rittenhouse and his son Alex are due to arrive as the story opens. Celine is also missing her father who disappeared on an exploratory mission to what is called The Chaos region. His partner's body was found in a canyon, partly gnawed and eaten, presumably by feral wolf-like dogs, descendants of pet dogs that escaped into the wild. Her father's body was never found and he was presumed to be dead. But Celine doesn't believe that.

Her 13th birthday is due in a few days and her mother is insisting that she has an injection they call a Brain Booster, something that Celine is terrified of and doesn't want. It is supposed to help with brain development. Her mother has become engaged to the colony's chief security officer, Morg, who Celine despises and can't understand why her mother would have any interest in him. Morg does come across as a sleazy character with hidden secrets, or at least that's how Celine perceives him. She is convinced Morg doesn't want to find her father, because he wants to marry her mother.

Contacting her grandmother back on Earth Celine is told by her that her father is still alive. Her grandmother is a tribal shaman or something like that. (*I'm not exactly clear about that.*) She has seen Celine's father, her son, lost in a deep cave in The Chaos region. The conversation she has with her grandmother leads the reader to see that Celine has special abilities which are just becoming evident. She sees auras given of by people and other living things and can see how the colors change as the emotions of the person alter. She also begins to be able to modify the auras she sees by controlling her own aura. Knowing that her father is still alive she is determined to go and look for him.

Meanwhile, the ship bringing Rittenhouse and his son Alex and a crew of bodyguards has arrived and the people are in quarantine for a day. Celine is told by Morg that she is to show Alex around the base. Celine is all for it because she thinks Alex is the best-looking guy on Earth, having seen his adventure videos.

At first the two teenagers don't get along. Their personalities clash, and Alex isn't as nice as she thought he was, being self-centered, basically a spoiled brat.

Rittenhouse wants to find the co-ordinates for a large body of ore that Celine's father was supposed to have found. Morg is reluctant to send any expedition to The Chaos region for reason that are not yet clear, and suggests they look in the valley where the other body was found. Meanwhile Celine has convinced Alex that the two of them should go and search for her father. Alex sees it as an adventure he can film for his travel program. When Alex's father decides to send him back to Earth the two teens hastily put together the equipment they need for the search and quietly leave using the excuse that Alex is going to show Celine inside the space ship due to take him back to Earth.

As the two teens head out on foot, we get to see what Mars is like. How cold it gets at night, how suddenly that happens and if the teens don't use a special tent to conserve heat, they would freeze solid as the temperature plunges. The air is thin and not breathable. People need to use oxygen masks, or they take a special pill that oxygenates the blood and makes the lungs dormant. They need to wear an outdoor suit that prevents radiation damage, since Mars is constantly bathed in radiation. They also have gravity-controlled boots which can increase or decrease the effect of gravity, enabling them to maintain muscle strength in case they need to return to Earth. The sky is deep purple shading into pink and red, and the desert is barren, rocky and dangerous. Dust or sand storms can blow up at any time, and dry lightning caused by friction of the dust in the atmosphere can be extremely dangerous.

As soon as it is noticed the kids are missing, a search party is sent out after them, but Celine and Alex have a good start. They survive a storm and the first night out in the open. The next day they descend into a massive crater, trek across it, and climb up the much higher other side. To have gone around it would have added several days, and they don't have enough supplies with them for that. It is here that Celine also discovers she has phenomenal vision, like super vision. She can see small details many miles away which Alex can barely see using his binoculars.

Scientists of the colony have found bacterial life underground, and that they have managed to find sufficient water to almost cover their needs, but life is harsh. The food they eat is all synthesized and the small amount brought by Rittenhouse is truly welcomed.

Somewhere it is mentioned that the trip out from Earth takes three days which jars the reader at first. But it is explained later that some kind of wormhole is produced to allow the ship to get to and from Earth in that time. We also find out later that Celine is part of a secret eugenics program that has over three hundred years begun to produce people with strange and superior powers. It was an ongoing military experiment.

There is also a hidden military base that Morg and Dr Bayley (Morg's boss) know about, where enhanced humans or cyborgs are based, and two of these cyborgs are used by Morg to track down the teenagers with a view to killing them and destroying the cave systems (of lava tubes) under the volcanoes. He doesn't want anyone to know about the underground lava tubes and the fact that they contain rivers of water and are quite warm.

The kids discover this when they enter the caves. They find glowing worm-like things hanging from the ceilings, which Celine sees are affected by the emotions of her and Alex. They can switch off their glow, plunging the caves into utter darkness, and they can discharge electric shocks when feeling threatened.

The kids discover Celine's father who is insane and thinks they are there to steal his food. He cooks and eats the worms. He also can breathe the air because it has a high oxygen content. He refuses to come back with the kids and all of them are trapped inside the caves when two cyborgs detonate explosions that create a flood.

The teens can't escape because the cyborgs block the entrance with a massive rock. Alex succumbs to whatever affected Celine's father and becomes quite irrational. Celine discovers paintings inside a part of the cave that relate to her shamanism and her grandmother.

This I didn't find credible, but it is a small part of what happens while Celine is struggling to survive. She finally manages to exit the cave system and heads back towards the colony, leaving her father and Alex inside. If she can get back, someone can come and rescue them. She has an encounter with wild dogs on the way back and barely escapes. The dogs are starving with hardly anything to eat other than some mole like creature that lives beneath the sand. She finds that while she has been lost, her mother has returned to Earth so she is alone, until her father and Alex can be rescued. Morg has also disappeared and she suspects he is lost in the cave system because she did hear another voice wailing in there somewhere.

There are mysteries implied, but no explanations. There is a hint regarding Cherokee shamanism but this isn't followed through, it's just there in the background. Celine discovers she has been missing for nearly six months even though she knows she has only been in the caves for several days.

While recovering in the medical ward, Celine overhears Dr Bayley talking with another doctor saying it is too late to give Celine her Brain Booster shot to prevent the development of her abilities, because she has already developed beyond expectations.

Her father and Alex are rescued, and it turns out the glow worms give off a toxic substance that permeates the air and affected the minds of whoever breathes it. Celine didn't breathe it because her lungs were dormant while she had been taking the oxygen pills.

Alex and his father return to Earth while Celine and her father remain on Mars. The discovery of water has encouraged Rittenhouse to fund an expansion of the colony, and already a large group are being trained on Earth.

The story concludes with a number of unanswered questions and I suspect there may be another story to follow this where Celine is much older and her powers are fully developed. I think also the ecology of Mars needs further development in order to explain the glimpses of life the author has given us, and possibly this would be part of a further story.

I enjoyed it. It is engaging and at points hard to put down. It has that sense of wonder that many contemporary stories lack so that's a bonus, which is very good for a first novel.

Last Day on Mars (2017)
Kevin Emerson

Subtitled ***Chronicle of the Dark Star***, this book is the first installment of a trilogy full of mystery, strange aliens, mind boggling science and edge of your seat excitement. It is the year 2213 and the story follows two teenagers in particular, Liam Saunders-Chang and his friend Phoebe, as they prepare, along with the last of the human colonists, to leave Mars and the solar system behind. The sun has started to swell and expand. Humans abandoned Earth, before it was burned to a crisp, for Mars where they constructed hundreds of massive starships which will take millions to a distant star where an earthlike planet that needs some terraforming has been discovered.

The children have been born on Mars and they know no other home. They are reluctant to leave everything behind, but know they have no choice because the sun will keep expanding and the solar storms will get worse and within a couple of years Mars will fall out of orbit and burn up in the constantly expanding sun. Not long after that the sun will collapse then explode as a nova wiping out the entire solar system. The humans in their starships want to be well out into interstellar space before that happens.

All the other starships have left, and the last ship is about to leave. The parents of the two protagonists still have some experiments to conclude, while their teenage children are left to their own devices on this very last day that humans are on Mars.

They stay out to watch the arrival of a massive solar storm and the effect it has on the planet, something they had never seen before because everyone retreats underground into shelters when a solar storm arrives. During the storm they observe something strange on Olympus Mons. It appears and disappears intermittently and they are not sure whether they saw anything at all. Later their parents assure them that there is nothing on Olympus Mons other than their science lab deep underground in the lava tubes inside the extinct volcano.

As the moment of departure draws closer the children are the only ones, along with their parents, left on the surface. Everyone else has been ferried up to the last starship in orbit which must leave at a specific time.

As the time draws near, things go wrong, and disaster strikes the lab. The atomic power generators have gone critical and will soon explode. A series of minor explosions destroys the lab where their parents are working, seriously injuring them and it is up to the two teenagers to rescue them. While doing this they discover something momentous, something totally unexpected and alien, which will have a significant bearing on what happens in further volumes of the trilogy.

Rescuing their parents at the last moment is far more difficult than expected and this causes them to miss the starship. It leaves without them. It will travel slowly until it reaches Saturn where another colony of humans in orbit are to be picked up before finally departing the solar system. The two teenagers with their parents in stasis to preserve them until proper medical help can be rendered, have a fast ship and their hope is to catch up with the starship before it departs the solar system forever.

The tension becomes almost unbearable as the resourceful teens with their robot companion desperately try to reach the starship while someone or something wants to prevent that from happening.

I won't say anything more here because what happens in this final part of the book has bearing on what will follow in the next volume, ***The Oceans between Stars.*** I can't wait to read that. Only this first volume of the trilogy is mentioned because it almost entirely takes place on Mars.

The writing is excellent, and the thrills generated by the protagonist's adventures over the last few hours they have on Mars will keep readers entranced regardless of their age.

The concluding volume is ***The shores beyond Time.***

Different and unexpectedly good

Prime Meridian by Silvia Moreno-Garcia (2017)

This is a beautiful novella of life in a near-future Mexico City where a young woman, Amelia, who dreams of Mars, both in the cinema and of the actual colony where she always wanted to go but can't afford it, struggles to make ends meet in the massively over-crowded, heavily polluted city where thieves and street gangs extort anyone they can. Amelia works as a paid companion, but her only steady job is an old film star who once starred in a movie called Pirates of Mars, who likes to reminisce with Amelia about her past life as a B grade actress. Desperate for enough money to survive and to pay her share of expenses, Amelia resorts to regularly selling her blood, which goes to other old people who hope to rejuvenate themselves with transfusions from young people. A broken-off romance from some years earlier is revived when her wealthy ex-boyfriend hires her as a companion. This doesn't go well as he is engaged to one of Amelia's casual friends. Through all her struggles to survive she imagines herself as a heroine in that awful movie Pirates of Mars. When her revived relationship begins to falter, the old film star dies but leaves her the poster from the film, and a sum of money, which she uses to finally buy herself the trip to Mars she always wanted.

The final scene is ambiguous, making it hard to determine whether it is from the old Pirates of Mars movie that Amelia always imagines, or is it in fact, Amelia finally arriving and stepping out onto the surface of Mars.

For anyone who has been to Mexico City in recent years, the impression of how difficult it is to live there is rendered with such reality as to be painful. I lived in Mexico City in 1969 when the population was a touch over 8 million, and again revisited in 1989, twenty years later when the population had more than doubled, and desperate people struggled to live on polluted streets with air that was virtually unbreathable with a visibility of no more than 400 metres. There were armed guards, male and female, standing in front of banks and most major buildings, who glared threateningly at any passer-by who glanced their way. It isn't too hard to believe in the massively overpopulated city of today with more than 20 million inhabitants, and how much worse it will be a few more years into the future. Silvia Moreno-Garcia, has captured this city with sparse details that ring absolutely true. Although no one actually goes to Mars in this story, the vision of Mars and the desire to go there that Amelia has in her mind permeates the story from beginning to end making it even more remarkable.

She is a writer to watch!

Remember Mars One?

In 2016, four years after *Mars One Consortium* was established with the object of sending people to live permanently on Mars without the possibility of returning, a book delineating how this would be done, ***Mars One – Humanity's next great adventure***, was published. The book consisted of scientific articles outlining the organization's intentions, methods of selection of volunteers, and how they would go about training and setting up a colony on Mars. It also included interviews with the final 100 people selected to begin the basic training in which they explained their reasons for applying to go to Mars.

These 100 people were to be whittled down to 6 groups of four. The first of these groups was to be sent to Mars in 2023, with the others following over a ten-year period. Prior to that a number of robotic missions would take place from 2020 to put necessary equipment on the planet so the first group could begin building the colony. It was a bold plan which the organization hoped to finance by filming the training and the establishment of the colony on Mars as a reality TV program. Initially people laughed at the idea of a one-way trip to Mars. Who would volunteer if there was no possibility of returning to Earth?

Strangely enough, more than 200,000 volunteered, and from 2012 until 2016 that number was whittled down to 100.

After a lot of publicity worldwide, a sudden silence followed and nothing much has been heard of them since. It now appears that in January 2019 *Mars One Ventures* has declared bankruptcy in a Swiss court, and the company has been dissolved. In February 2019 it was announced that *Mars One Ventures* was in administration and that as soon as this was sorted *Mars One* would redirect its focus on the execution of the actual voyage to Mars. So, the idea, the company, and the hope of going to Mars was not yet dead, but only if they can secure the necessary hardware and equipment needed to undertake their plans. In reality, there does not seem to be much hope of this happening.

A year after the publication of ***Mars One – Humanity's next great adventure,*** Jonathan Maberry, a multiple Bram Stoker Award winning novelist, produced a best-selling young adult novel called ***Mars One*** (2017). The focus of this story is on one young person Tristan who with his family is on the first mission to colonize Mars. The author has followed the guidelines set out by the Mars One ventures, but has changed the idea of sending groups of four to Mars to establish a colony. He believes that concept wouldn't work, and that the first group should consist of 40 people with a number of them being families rather than individuals. This would give the colonists more incentive to survive any problems that could happen in transit or once they arrive, and allowing for injuries or death, there would still be enough members to continue. With only four, any injury would be a disaster and perhaps none of them would survive, which would put future small missions in doubt.

The story begins a few months prior to departure and follows Tristan and Izzy (Isolde) and his friends until it is time for him to say goodbye.

The story is told from the viewpoint of Tristan, who was twelve years old when his parents were chosen to be in the first group. As the day of departure looms, Tristan is now 16 and has fallen in love with a schoolfriend called Isolde. He has the agonizing duty to bid farewell knowing he will never see his girlfriend or any of his other school friends ever again after leaving for Mars. Complicating this is that he is constantly being followed and monitored by the reality TV crew who are filming everything he does and says for later broadcast. They have paid millions for the rights to do this and there is nothing Tristan can do about it. A lot of this money is used to finance the voyage to Mars and the setting up of the colony. Some of it will go into a trust fund for Isolde and his other friends who will remain on Earth. Not only has the worldwide audience gone mad over Tristan and Izzy, they are also following the others who also have reality shows based around them.

But not everyone agrees with the idea of humanity departing the Earth. A protest group known as the Neo Luddites are constantly protesting the Mars One voyages, and as the departure date gets closer this radical group's protests are becoming more violent. Tristan has been assigned bodyguards to protect him as he alternates going to school with his training regime preparing him as a ship's engineer on the voyage to Mars.

There are three other families also in the first group getting ready to depart, one with another young man, and two with young teenage daughters. The organizers have made sure the numbers are evenly matched with families, married and single people of various ages.

The two transit vessels that will take them to Mars have been built in orbit. Also in orbit around the Earth is a Chinese space station, The Shanghai Wheel, that keeps its activities shrouded in silence. Just before the Mars One shuttles were due to launch to take the colonists up into orbit to rendezvous with their two transit vessels the Chinese announced they had already sent a ship to Mars, the Red Dragon, with a crew of 22. It had been built in secret inside the Shanghai Wheel and was launched two days before the Mars One group was to depart. Tristan and his fellow crew mates were upset at this news as they considered that they would be the first to get to Mars. Then they calm down and decide that they would still get there first because their ships were faster and could take a higher orbit allowing them to pass the Chinese in transit.

The initial pert of the voyage is taken up with routine checks and maintenance and time seems to be passing quite well. Tristan is still in love with Izzy and they constantly *Skype* each other, until the increasing distance creates longer and longer time lags, meaning they can only talk by recording a message, sending it, after which they must wait for a reply. They gradually realize they have less and less to talk about, and must eventually accept they will never be able to be together.

Meanwhile, things on one of the ships goes wrong. There is a malfunction with the sewerage system which flood the ship with human waste. A massive clean up job ensues and Tristan's mother (chief engineer) goes across to the sister ship to help sort out the problem. Half the crew get sick as a result of the breakdown and things are not looking good when escaped water gets inside the walls and causes short circuits with the electronic systems that maintain everything on the ship. When something similar happens on their own ship Tristan suspects sabotage. The problem is they don't believe it is possible. Who would sabotage the ship knowing it would also kill them?

It's at this point that they are told the Chinese ship that left before them was not manned. It was a supply ship carrying fresh supplies for a mission that was sent to Mars two years earlier. There is a Chinese crew already in orbit around Mars, but since their arrival, nothing has been heard from them. It is unknown whether they are still alive. NASA manages to reprogram one of its satellites orbiting Mars so they can see what may have happened to the Chinese ship (Red Dragon). They discover the lander is still attached so no one went down to the surface.

Should the Mars One people attempt a rescue? The adults don't want to compromise their own mission by using extra fuel to rendezvous with the Chinese vessel. The teenagers want to rescue the Chinese crew if it is at all possible. They make a point of saying there are no national boundaries in space and that all humans should stick together to help each other. Mars One headquarters back on Earth vetoes any rescue attempt. But when it is discovered that someone is alive on board the Red Dragon, they ignore the directive from Earth and decide they will rendezvous with the Red Dragon and attempt a rescue.

Another attempt is made to sabotage their ship but this time Tristan catches the saboteur in the act. It is no one he expected and is stunned. The saboteur has killed a security guard by slitting his throat and is attempting to open the airlock to suck all the air out into space. Tristan struggles to stop the airlock from being opened and in the process grabs the saboteur by her hair and her neck is broken. Her companion on their sister ship has succumbed to a viral infection making no further attempts to stop the ship. It is at this point that Tristan realizes in hindsight he should have suspected from the conversations they'd had over the last few months that she was a Neo Luddite as was her companion on the sister ship. How many of them had worked their way into the training system with the object that some of them would be chosen for the actual mission and could sabotage the ships? Tristan now knows the Neo Luddites are not simply a protest group, but are really a terrorist organization.

Finally, with the dead buried by injecting them into space where they will be drawn down into Mars' atmosphere, burning up on entry, the attempt is made to cross over to the Chinese ship to rescue any survivors. This is a nerve-wracking scene and would make a brilliant sequence if ever this story was made into a movie. There is only one survivor on the Chinese ship, and 17-year-old girl called Ting.

The novel finishes here as the rescue is complete, with only a short bit following this showing the landing on Mars and Tristan being chosen to be the first to step onto the surface. Ignoring the prepared speech everyone had learned in case they were chosen to be the first, he simply states for the reality show cameras; "*I am a Martian. And I am Home.*"

Chapter Eleven

The end of the second decade

As we near the end of the second decade of the 2000s we find a surprising number of authors making a living by writing and publishing independently of major publishing houses. The books they produce are usually eBooks with some titles also produced as printed books. The quality of the books as printed products has improved considerably over the last few years, but the stigma of being '*self-published*' or '*independently published* ' still remains in the minds of readers. Rightly so, because there is still a lot of rubbish published that lacks editing and writing skills, and these tend to overwhelm the market so that better quality material is hard to find amongst the millions pf books published.

One of these more recent authors who is producing top quality SF is a self published independent author, Doug Pruden. As far as I am aware, his first published novel was *The Ares Weapon* (2016) featuring a delightful protagonist called Dr. Melanie Destin. I discovered this book in 2018 and after reading it, immediately bought the three follow up books detailing her life and adventures on Mars, and between Mars and the Earth's Moon. I bought them as paperbacks, because I prefer a proper book rather than an electronic one. They are all available as eBooks for those who prefer this format.

The Ares Weapon (book one - 2016)
Set far enough into the future to have Mars sufficiently terraformed for colonies to have been established with a large enough population to want to be independent of Earth or Terran influence, for significant populations to exist in cities on the Moon who also wish to be independent of Earth, and with the hinted possibility of future conflict between the three human occupied bodies, this story is an exciting prelude to a four part series called *Mars Ascendant.*

The Ares Weapon, sets up the situation and introduces the reader to Dr Melanie Destin, as well as a number of subsidiary characters who will no doubt gain more importance as the series progresses.

In this first book, almost none of the action takes place on Mars, (although Mars seems to be a strong influence in the background); it takes place in Space between Mars and the Moon, and between the Moon and Mercury. It finishes with Dr Destin finally arriving and settling on Mars.

There is a short prequel to this series (***Requiem's Run*** *– written two years later in 2018, oddly subtitled book one*). It seems appropriate to mention it here since the events that take place explain why Dr Destin comes to the Moon and what she wishes to achieve. There is also a short story that deals with Melanie as a young teenager using her wits to survive in London devastated by a recent war which fleshes out some details mentioned in passing as background information in *The Ares Weapon.*

Her goal is to work as a doctor and save enough money to enable her to go to Mars. But on arriving she soon discovers she hasn't got a chance at getting any meaningful work because the major Terran and Martian corporations have a closed system where they only hire their people from Earth or Mars and don't hire anyone on the Moon. After the war that enabled the Moon to become independent of the Earth, the Moon is ruled by a dictator called Regis Mundi, who fancies himself as a Roman emperor and lives an opulent lifestyle in a villa modeled after an ancient Roman palace. He calls himself Dominus and his corporation Corpus Rego, controls everything on the Moon. If Melanie can't work as a doctor she will be deported back to Earth and that is something she doesn't want.

She manages to find a job as a doctor in a clinic that helps the poorest people and what she earns is a pittance, barely enough to pay her rent and for some food. She is recruited by a ship's captain to work on his cargo freighter, the Requiem, as the ship's doctor. She accepts the job but doesn't realize until she is on board that they are also smugglers that run contraband between the Moon, Mars, and the outer planets and the Galilean colonies. On this ship she meets her only true friend, the engineer called Schmaltz, and she does develop a companionable working relationship with the Captain.

The setting is far enough in the future to have advanced technology like artificial gravity that is used to keep earth standard gravity inside the domed cities on the moon to prevent medical complications from bone loss and muscle atrophy which would occur after prolonged periods of lesser gravity. The space freighters also operate at near earth gravity for the same reasons. People also have cortical implants to enable better communication, as well as allowing authorities to track their whereabouts.

The Ares Weapon begins sometime later after the end of *Requiem's Run.*

Some of the ship's crew have changed and there is a new captain with whom she doesn't get along. When the Requiem returns back to the Moon, she takes shore leave but soon discovers she has been fired.

Suddenly, her life as a spaceship doctor and resident of the Moon is falling apart. With no money and no means of getting a job she reverts to an attempt to be a prostitute, something she once did on Earth before a benefactor sponsored her and paid for her medical education. She gets trapped by the *Morality Police* and is arrested. After some forced medical intervention, she is manipulated to take a position as the ship's doctor on a mysterious venture in a stolen military space cruiser. The ship, stolen by Dominus Regis Mundi's people, once belonged to the Earth's military forces so it has up to date weaponry.

Earlier in her life Melanie Destin was a specialist in nano medicine, and the people on this mysterious ship need someone like her to assist them with a virulent nano disease pathogen which Mars wants to use as a threat to control Earth, or to prevent Earth from having any control over Mars, but which other people from Earth (Terra) also want as a bio-weapon. It works within minutes to kill anyone infected and as far as is known, there is no antidote or cure. It appears that a ship carrying samples of this nano bio-weapon has been deliberately abandoned on Mercury, its crew all killed by the nano pathogen, and the ship she is coerced to join is going to retrieve this abandoned ship and whatever it contains. Regis Mundi in particular wants the *Ares weapon* to further his ambitions to control Earth. He doesn't want the Martians or the Terrans to have this weapon and is using this stolen ship to recover the nano virus. The Earth forces as well as the Martians have also sent ships to recover the virus from the abandoned ship on Mercury, but it is Melanie in the stolen ship controlled by Regis Mundi that gets there first.

There are betrayals, interesting friendships and alliances formed, and a developing romance between Melanie and the guard (Dylan) employed to watch over her. He is a secret agent working for the Martians against Regis Mundi. There is enough political skulduggery with plenty of page turning action and excitement to keep a reader from putting down this book until it is finished. The ultimate confrontation between the various forces to obtain the nano bio-weapon takes place near Mercury and the Sun and how Melanie manages to outwit them, discover she is immune to the virus, and destroys or disables the weapon is the culmination of the story. She saves her guard's life when he is infected by the Ares virus by administering a transfusion of her blood, and through him she also gains her longtime ambition of being able to settle on Mars, bringing back to Mars the contained nano virus from the abandoned ship on Mercury.

As a story, it is complete in itself, finishing satisfactorily enough to be set aside if the reader doesn't want to follow what happens later, but it also leaves enough possibilities open to encourage the reader to follow what happens to Melanie Destin over the course of the next three books.

A very good beginning to what promises to be an excellent series.

Mother Mars (book two, 2017) has Melanie settled in the huge Martian orbital habitat, Olympia, where the wealthier people of Mars live. She has recurring nightmares that seem to be gaining in intensity every day… always the same, which upon awakening she only remembers certain words or concepts; *aggressive, purge, abomination*. She is seeing a psychiatrist (JR) but doesn't trust him as he seems to know things about her that she hasn't told him. Her live-in partner (and lover) is the bodyguard Dylan, from the first book, whose life she saved when he was inadvertently infected by the nano virus known as the *Ares Weapon*. Dylan is also the Head of Security on Olympia as well as Mars down below.

Melanie works on Olympia treating the wealthy and their pseudo illnesses and minor problems, but she wishes she could do the real medicine she trained for on Earth. Her assistant Dani, is a nurse who once was an asteroid miner who also has a hidden past which is slowly revealed as the story progresses.

Regis Mundi and his entourage which includes his assistant Felix (one of only two artificial humans, the other assists Talus Varr, leader of the ruling triumvirate of Mars), arrive at the orbital habitat, and this sets in motion a revenge plan. Regis Mundi has to discredit Talus Varr. Mundi wants to rule Mars as he once did before being deposed by Talaus Varr and the other two members of the ruling council.

Talus Varr, who went by the name of Walter Bickel on Earth years before, was Melanie's sponsor who saw potential in her and paid for her medical education, asks Melanie to take on a new job. It appears the Ares virus has lost its potential, dying and becoming ineffective once a container is opened. He also suggests that the nanites in Melanie's bloodstream that protect her from diseases, (which have also died and disappeared from her system) were not the reason she managed to defeat contamination by the virus in the ship abandoned on Mercury. She is naturally immune.

She doesn't believe him and she takes on the job to research the nanites to see why they are dying and also to see if Talus Varr is correct. Late one night she enters the Lab and injects herself with a live sample of the virus, which almost immediately is neutralized by her auto immune system. She repeats the experiment two more times with the same result and then tries to hide the empty containers knowing she will have to come up with an explanation for the missing nanites. She finds out from Talus Varr that she was part of an experiment and that she was genetically altered before birth to be immune to the virus and any other viruses. (She has never been sick ever in her life.) This pisses her off as she realizes that she has been manipulated all her life by Varr or Walter, whatever his real name is.

She tells Dani her nurse what she has done and Dani hacks into the computer system to try and cover up the video of her in the Lab alone at night, but the video has been altered, and it shows her stealing the nano virus and leaving which she didn't do. But not only that, Dani is unable to delete or alter the already altered video no matter what she tries. One of Dani's talents is hacking into and altering complex computer systems. When they find out that one of the ruling triumvirate has been murdered deliberately infected and killed by the Ares virus. Melanie is blamed and by implication the man who had hired her, Talus Varr.

Suddenly she finds herself on the run with Dani and Talus Varr. The police are after her and leading the chase is her lover and partner Dylan. Dylan doesn't believe she is guilty even though the evidence points directly to her, and tries his best to stall the investigation to give her time to get away.

They use Talus' personal space yacht to leave the orbital habitat and head down to the surface where they hope to disappear into the crowded mining camps, and terraforming habitats. Pursued by the police as well as by Felix on behalf of Regis Mundi, Talus explains to Melanie that Mundi was once one of the rulers but he advocated using the Ares virus (*something that wasn't developed on Mars but was found in a distant location beside a crashed space ship 40 years earlier*) to eliminate humans on Earth so Martians could return to their home planet. When told the virus would eliminate every living thing, all animals and plants, anything alive, leaving the planet a barren waste like Mars, he didn't care.

Mundi was deposed and expelled from Mars. He went to the Moon and set up a business there which eventually controlled the Moon and fought off domination by Earth. Now he wants to come back to Mars and become the supreme ruler of the whole solar system. It was he who setup the murder of the other council member making sure Talus and Melanie would be blamed. Now he is back on the Council and in control. He has sent his assistant Felix Altius to chase after Melanie and to push the police to act faster.

Talus Varr believes Melanie can deactivate the Ares virus, and he takes her to the original site where it was discovered. With the police close behind them, they use Talus' space yacht to head across Mars to the remote crater where the nano virus was first discovered. By this time Melanie has concluded that the virus in not made up of individual nanites but that each of them communicates with each other and with whatever is at the original site; in effect, they are a single organism, and collectively highly intelligent.

At the site Melanie discovers there is an ancient space ship that has been there for 4 billion years and that the nanites are swarming over the whole crater. They allow her to enter and here she finds the source of her nightly dreams, they have been trying to gain contact with her ever since she defeated the infection in the ship on Mercury. She is welcomed into the ship and all the nanites swarming over the crater come back and reform into a much larger space ship which immediately takes off. Talus and Dani with Felix follow in their ship but have trouble keeping up. They only catch up when the alien ship lands on an asteroid. It turns out the asteroid is the mother ship. All of it is made of nanites and was built billions of years ago by other vastly more advanced beings. It was this mother ship that seeded the four planets with life and that when the fifth planet was accidentally eradicated, things started to go wrong. The object of the nanite organism now is to eradicate life on Earth and Mars and anywhere else humans have gone on the solar system, and to start again with a new set of creatures. Melanie is not the only human immune to them and they want to collect the others and use them as seed stock to start a new cycle of life once everything else has been eliminated.

But Melanie has other plans. She manages to gain some control which enables her to draw the ship with Talus Dani and Felix in to the mother ship so she can be rescued. She also manages to take control of the mother ship and escapes by returning to the ship that brought up to the mother ship. She causes this ship to head towards Mars where she has it crash into Olympus Mons. The enormous crash activates the ancient volcano along with several others and they begin spewing lava and gases into the atmosphere, speeding up the terraforming of Mars by thousands of years. And since the ship was composed of billions of nanobots, she alters their programming so that once they are inside Mars, they begin revitalizing the planet's core, bringing Mars back to life.

The government and the whole of Mars thinks that she crashed into Olympus Mons with the alien ship and that she is dead. They call her *The Mother of Mars* and she has become a legend to the millions who live and work on the planet.

Felix discovers he is more human than he thinks as he has feelings for Dani, but he goes back to work for Regis Mundi, while making plans to eventually escape to be with Dani. Talus Varr is still on the run. Dani has gone back to Jupiter hoping that one day that Felix will be able to join her. Melanie has taken on a new identity and is working on Mars as a doctor where she actually gets to practice medicine with people who need her help since there are no other doctors there, and for the moment she is happy.

The Child of Mars (book three, 2017).

Ten years have gone by and Melanie is thinner and older and has altered her identity. She has also disabled the identity implant in her brain so she can't be found or tracked. Her new name is Dr Corrine Ross. Arriving at one of the settlements she regularly visits she is followed by a stranger who has identified her and wants to capture her for the reward posted. Regis Mundi doesn't believe she died in the crash that activated Olympus Mons and a hundred other smaller volcanoes. He wants her for her genetic makeup that allows her to control the Ares virus. There are people all over Mars looking for Melanie, for the reward.

When Dylan kills the bounty hunter, they realize that there are too many rumors that Melanie still exists, which enables the Security forces to ascertain she is still alive and roughly where she might be. Melanie and Dylan must again go into hiding. This last clinic she visits will be the final one. Regis Mundi also wants to eliminate Talus Varr, his old rival, who with a few rebels is hiding somewhere near the North Polar ice cap, but isn't too concerned because they are a spent force after Regis Mundi dropped asteroids from out of space onto the locations where potential rebels lived. Regis Mundi also has an experiment running with cloned children, based on the genetic makeup of Melanie Destin, combined with artificial human DNA. These children are in a hidden base on Mars and all of them have died but one. He desperately wants to regain the last clone and will turn Mars upside down to get her back.

Carlos Montoya, (who has always worked for Talus Varr), who was once Melanie's lover and whom she thought had been killed, reappears and rescues the last child left. He seeks out Melanie, who is stunned to find him still alive, and begs her to take the rescued 8-year-old girl, as he has no one else to turn to. Melanie is reluctant to have children of her own, never having experienced a normal life which makes her think she is unfit to be a mother. But she agrees to take Adrianna the young rescued girl. From the moment they meet Adrianna and Melanie rub each other the wrong way. Adrianna however makes a connection with Dylan and Dani which strangely enough causes Melanie to feel jealous.

Heading across Mars to where the rebels have control, they are pursued by the security forces of Regis Mundi who wants all of them. He is sick and is terminal. His object is to transfer his mind into the body of Felix, his previous advisor who is an artificial human who is stronger and faster than humans and who also doesn't age. His experiments with Adrianna the 647th clone and the only one so far to survive, are attempting to use her to control the nanites that were once called the Ares virus. She has limited control. He wants to use her as the ultimate weapon to switch on and off the Ares virus whenever he needs to.

The bulk of the story is about the chase across Mars while the security forces attempt to capture them. At the same time there is much development of the main characters as they are forced to rely on each other to survive. Finally, Melanie discovers what there is about Adrianna that put her off; she is exactly what she herself was when she was a child on Earth and had to fend for herself. It was obvious to Dani and Dylan and Felix, but not so to Melanie. Adrianna is a clone of Melanie and is therefore her little sister.

When the security forces capture Dylan and Felix and Adrianna during a skirmish, Dylan is killed and Adrianna and Felix are taken back to the centre where she had been cloned. Regis Mundi is on his way. Preparations are being made to use Adrianna once again to control the nanites held there in stasis. Preparations are also being made to Transfer the seriously ill Regis Mundi's mind to Felix.

Knowing that the rebels are on their way to rescue the captives Mundi is expecting to recapture Melanie as well. He wants the secrets embedded in her DNA that allows her to control the alien nanites. A trap is set to capture them and then to destroy the complex.

It doesn't work out that way though, tables are turned, a traitor is revealed and dealt with, Melanie and Adrianna discover their true relationship and work together to destroy Regis Mundi using the nanites he so wants as a weapon. The survivors manage to escape before the whole complex is turned into nuclear slag.

With Regis Mundi and his cohorts out of the way Talus Varr manages to convince Melanie not to leave Mars with Felix, Dani and Adrianna. He wants her to stay as the nominal head of a new government. Everyone reveres her as *The Mother of Mars*, and this is the title she takes for her position. She is the only one who can hold together the various groups that have trouble agreeing with each other.

The book finishes with Melanie accepting a four-year term as the figurehead of the new Martian Government

The Legacy of Mars (2018) is the fourth book in the series. It begins four years after the previous book finishes, with Melanie going to visit Talus Varr to tell him her time is up and she wants to leave, to join her friends in the Galilean system. They just happen to be on Mars for a gladiatorial game in which Adrianna is participating. Adrianna who is now a bit over 8 years old appears physically to be 16. There is something wrong with her genes and she is suffering from accelerated ageing. All of the clones in the experiment were genetically altered to age rapidly so their development could be monitored over a short period. Adrianna was the last of them and the only survivor. On Olympia, Melanie wants Adrianna to stay so she can undergo a series of tests to determine how her condition can be altered to prevent the rapid aging.

The focus now shifts to Earth where after years of fighting, the various national factions have been reluctantly united under a ruthless dictator, Apollonia Ryder, who wants to shift the majority of the Earth's population to the rapidly terraforming Mars. Earth's resources have been depleted, the climate is gradually freezing and the planet is becoming uninhabitable. At the moment they have a delegation on Olympia trying to negotiate a trade deal for desperately needed resources.

There is a third force at play in this volume: the nanite space vehicle that is hidden in the asteroid belt. The communal mind of the nanites has formed into an avatar of Melanie who had been captured by them in the previous volume and whom they had tried to absorb into their collective consciousness without success. She took control of their smaller ship (lost on Mars for millennia), deliberately crashed it into Olympus Mons and reconfigured the nanites so they would rapidly increase the rate of the terraforming. The mind of the mother-ship still wants to complete its mission of eliminating all life on the planets in the solar system in preparation for re-seeding with the altered DNA of Melanie and Adrianna. It also wants to absorb these two. This alien being disturbs an asteroid and sends it towards Earth. The Terrans destroy it, but blame Mars and call off the trade negotiations. Apollonia leads an armed fleet to attack Mars, to wipe out the Martians so Terrans can immigrate and live there.

On Olympia Adrianna sees what she thinks is Dylan and tries to find him. What she saw was a golem that has taken on the form of Dylan whose body is no longer in the grave Melanie dug during a skirmish on Mars in which he was killed. This golem can also alter at will its appearance. It is malfunctioning, having had access to the memories of Dylan in the body recovered by the nanites. The nanite collective also sends another asteroid towards Earth but this time it is shielded so it can't be detected. This time the asteroid breaks up and practically wipes out the entire population. The Martians through Talus Varr offer to rescue the remnants of the population and bring them to Mars, but the fleet is now determined to take revenge and destroy all of Mars.

On Olympia, Adrianna has been captured by the golem and transferred to a life pod in which the nanites can invade her and take over her consciousness. Melanie is desperately searching for Adrianna and finds her and the golem who wants to capture her for the collective. The Terran fleet is coming within weapons range and a battle begins. Felix configures the geosynchronous satellites around Mars used to create an artificial magnetic field to deflect damaging radiation from the sun, into a weapon that uses magnetic pulses to strip atoms apart. He sets it up to be triggered when the invading Terran fleet is within missile range of Mars.

With most of the Martian fleet destroyed, including the flagship with Talus Varr on board, (he regrets he will never be able to tell Melanie that she is his daughter), the Terran fleet begin to unleash missiles to destroy the domed habitats on Mars. Felix has to trigger the magnetic atom stripping weapon by hand and is injured by radiation from the explosion. The bulk of the Terran fleet is vaporized into its component atoms and the few remaining ships surrender. The War is over. Melanie meanwhile convinces the nanite alien being that they are the result of the original seeding of the planets and that life shouldn't be destroyed and started again. It should be accepted for what it is. Adrianna and Melanie return to Olympia in time to escape before rubble from the battle impacts and destroys it.

Back on the surface of Mars which now has a breathable atmosphere, thanks to the rapid terraforming of the altered nanites within the planet, Melanie takes over the residence of Talus Varr. Felix is healed with Varr's medical equipment and they discover Adrianna has been cured (while being partially absorbed on the nanite mother-ship) of the deliberate aging modification, and that it appears she may well live without ageing for thousands of years. Melanie finally concludes that Mars is where she really wants to be. She now wants to stay rather than go to the Galilean system with Felix and Dani and Adrianna. She has been voted by the Martian populace to be their leader with the honorary position of *Mother of Mars*.

All in all, a satisfactory ending. This last book was a fast read because it was well-paced with enough tension and surprises to keep a reader enthralled. In fact, all three previous books would not allow this reader to put them aside until finished. The four books are basically one long novel totaling over 800 pages. They could very well be published as one book rather than four, (after all there are quite a few Science Fiction authors whose books always contain that many pages and they sell well) and if picked up by a major publisher, I'm sure it would also sell well.

Mars Ascendant is for anyone who likes a fast, action story with enough character development and mystery to be intriguing. The science seems reasonably believable, with the whole story being reminiscent of those from the Golden Age of SF when a sense of wonder enveloped the reader's experience.

Subsequent to having read those four books, plus the prequel **Requiem's Run**, D M Pruden went on to start another series of books set in the solar system called the **Shattered Empire** before returning to write more novels about Dr Melanie Destin that take place before the **Mars Ascendant** series of books. There are five of them and together with the **Mars Ascendant** books, there are 9 in all plus the prequel, which I am not sure how that novella fits in since I have yet to read the 5 earlier adventures of Melanie Destin. They are only available as eBooks either individually or as a boxed set.

However you look at it, this set of stories is a monumental effort, that from what I've read so far, is nail biting with tension and full of believable characters and situations. No lover of science fiction 'space opera' or hard SF, however you want to label them, should miss reading these Melanie Destin stories.

The Unknown by Angel Wedge (2018)
Another self-published novella that looks attractive.

Lovely cover, although why someone is walking on the surface of Mars without wearing a helmet needs to be explained. The interior design is less attractive with no indents at the beginning of each paragraph, and a double space between them. This might be acceptable for an eBook, but to print it like that as a paperback makes it unattractive, in my eyes. Without a slight indent at the beginning of each paragraph, it is harder to read.

Intriguingly the text on the cover says: *We reached Mars. We weren't the first.*

That immediately made me think; *aliens on Mars*, but I was wrong.

At least a hundred years after the first Moon landing, and after a journey that took years, a huge ship arrives and sets down on the surface. Not far away is a mountain range. Due to the cost of fuel and the sheer size of the ship it is a one-way trip. This first ship contains a crew of hundreds; scientists, engineers, geologists, doctors, planetologists, biologists, psychologists, adventurers and explorers who all know they will not return to Earth.

They don't mind being alone. They all have their jobs and ambitions and are happy to have arrived safely. They can't wait to begin exploring. Their job is to establish a base, a small city in which the people on several other equally huge ships that are following them will be able to occupy. The colonists are privately funded and answer to their companies back on Earth.

On the 6th day after landing, Elle has set out to explore the edges of the overhanging cliffs while her friend Jasper is exploring around the base looking for hazards that should be removed to make the area safe. Elle arrives at the cliff face in her buggy and steps out to collect rock samples. She looks down, and is stunned to see footprints other than her own and wheel tracks from a buggy. The tracks are narrower than her buggy and the footprints are definitely not hers. The wheel tracks continue along the base of the cliff face and would be hidden from observing satellites above. She freaks out, yelling and screaming. Nearby Jasper hears her incoherent voice and thinking she is in trouble, races to help her. When he gets there, she shows him the tracks, and he understands why she panicked. At first, they think maybe they had a stowaway on the ship who has come out here to play a joke on them, but on consideration that seems too ridiculous. They get into their buggy and follow the tracks to see where they lead. The tracks lead into a large cave and inside they discover a huge airlock door.

They now know for sure they were not the first to reach Mars.

Jasper recalls that the technology to get to Mars existed back in the 2020s, so it is possible someone came here all that time ago.

Elle remembers the old stories and conspiracies about a crazy guy called Emmanuelle Wallace, who was convinced humans were destroying the planet and needed to get off it in order to survive, and who was supposed to have left for Mars with a number of followers, but most people considered them folk tales, and silly stories. Wallace disappeared and no one ever heard of him again. There are no records of other ships taking off for Mars, unless it had been suppressed. Maybe he and his many followers did make it to Mars. That would piss off their expedition leader who had given up so much to be the first person to step onto Mars' surface. Anyway, not knowing what they might find or even if the airlock door would open, Elle pulls the release catch and some dim lights come on. Jasper is surprised that such old technology still works. They wait for the air to recycle and then the door begins to open. Elle is staring into the space behind the door, still not visible to Jasper. As the door finally opens Jasper too stares at an astronaut who is in the airlock and who salutes them.

The Mars astronaut joins them and they head back to the base where inside everyone is absolutely stunned. Immediately the military members of the expedition want to know if the Martians are hostile. The Martian, a young woman, is friendly and excited. She explains that they are descended from Wallace, and that they have a city built inside the mountain, several cities in fact. They have interesting technology from that which existed fifty years earlier, which evolved along a different line from the more modern technology of the newly arrived ship.

As Jasper and Elle get to know the Martian Boudica, or Boo, they are invited to visit the Martian city. The Earthers want them to spy for them, to see what weapons they have, to find out if they are a threat to the new arrivals. Jasper and Elle are reluctant to do this but agree because it makes sense. In the Martian city Jasper is introduced to Bose who is an engineer and he takes him on a tour of the city while Elle gets to know Boo on a more intimate level. Both Jasper and Elle are convinced the Martians are not a threat, but there is something they are reluctant to talk about, a hidden hollow beneath the city that no one has access to. When asked about it, the Martian elders refuse to say anything.

The paranoid Earthers back on the ship and their new base think the Martians are hiding a weapon. They don't trust them, and the more military members want to storm the place and find out. This becomes more urgent when the second ship arrives and lands near the new base. A third ship is imminent as well and the captain of that ship is a die-hard militarist. He would have no hesitation in attacking the Martians.

Elle and Jasper concoct a scheme with Boo and Bose, to enter the restricted area. Elle is a computer whiz and can override the computers that control access to the area, and soon they are on their way to find out what is hidden beneath the city. The Martian elders are monitoring the area and immediately know that they can't stop the group. So, with the Earther leader they follow the youngsters and are right behind them when the finally enter to hidden space.

There is no weapon there, but there is a huge stone orrery that is actually functioning. It is hundreds of meters wide and made of polished granite, and it still functions using stone gears built underneath it. The ball representing the outermost planet is more than two hundred meters from the ball representing the sun. When the Earthers ask what it is, the Martians say it is a clue as to where Emmanuelle Wallace and his devout followers went. There is a plaque which states that Wallace and his crew went in search of what was waiting for them. Why they would want to keep that a secret, even from their own people, is not explained.

The story ends here with, presumably, the imminent possible conflict no longer a problem. Elle and Boo are in awe of the fact that those people were willing to spend years and years of their life in space in search of the unknown.

Parts of the story are interesting, the parts that Elle is allowed to see, and how she compares it with life on Earth, but overall there isn't enough action and a bit too much telling rather than showing.

I was disappointed with the ambiguous ending. It was too abrupt. It promised much, but fell flat. Maybe there will be another book to continue the story... that would be interesting.

Some thoughts...

It has got to the point where I approach reading a POD book with trep-idation, thinking that most self-published stories have not been edited or formatted to make them easy to read.

They often have the appearance that the author, having completed the first draft, rushed to get the book out, without correcting mistakes, polish-ing, editing and formatting the text so the story looks and reads better. What may look good as an eBook, hardly ever looks good when it is printed unless it has been reformatted as a print book. Usually they aren't, which is always a disappointment when I pay sometimes considerable money (including post-age) to have a printed copy sent to me. I am becoming reluctant to buy these books now, and even less interested in having them as eBooks.

But 2018 was also a good year for well-known publishers and smaller independents publishing numerous Mars stories.

UMO by K Patrick Donaghue (2018) *eBook*
A short prequel to the ***Skywave*** series of *eBooks*.
UMO stands for **U**nidentified **M**agnetic **O**bjects. These things swarm around Earth and Mars in the ionized upper layers of the atmosphere and in near space. Astronauts have often seen them and NASA maintains they are nothing more than light reflecting off frozen particles that have condensed on rockets passing through the atmosphere which later fall off when the rocket goes into orbit.

The author of this story suggests they are living electromagnetic enti-ties. As the story opens two Russian missions to Mars have been destroyed by swarms of these UMOs that clustered around the satellites as they went into orbit around Mars. A third probe sent images of the destroyed Russian probes back to NASA.

The American military considers these UMO to be dangerous and wants them destroyed. A manned mission is sent to Mars to investigate, and this mission carries three probes; one to examine spectroscopically what could have caused the destruction of the probes, one to take X-ray images of the in-ternal aspects of the rubble left in orbit, and the third which contains electro magnetic pulse missiles to destroy the UMOs by disrupting their magnet-ic emanations. The military considers the three astronauts are expendable. They want the mission to be a success and they don't care what happens to the three astronauts. Capcom at NASA control does care about them and does his best to help them when they get into difficulties.

As the story opens, the manned mission is entering Mars orbit, searching for the debris of the destroyed probes. Testing their equipment, they find they can't deploy the probe with the missiles which they want to release first before using the other two probes to examine the wreckage in orbit.

One of them has to go outside to manually release the EMP missile probe before releasing the others that can examine via X-ray spectroscopy the wrecked Russian probes. While he is outside a small swarm of UMO appear and float around him. They give off a violent magnetic or electrical charge and all the electronic equipment in the ship goes dead. Not only that, the ship is put into an uncontrolled spin which takes it out of the low Mars orbit they had attained. Then the UMOs vanish in an instant. The two left inside the ship initially panic but quickly revert to their training and while the captain prepares to don his space suit and exit the ship to rescue his crew-mate, the other one checks the circuit breakers throughout the ships and manages to switch back on all the electronic components. Getting ready for the EVA takes almost two hours, but before that can begin, they need to stabilize the ship, which ends up in an orbit much further out.

The captain finally gets to the stranded crew-mate who is still breathing but unconscious. He brings him inside and the slow process to get back in begins. Once they are inside and have resumed contact with Capcom, NASA's monitoring tells them that their crew-mate is brain dead. They are told put him in a space suit, switch off the oxygen and eject him from the ship.

Back on Earth the Military has over-ridden NASA's control and they want the mission to destroy the UMO to go ahead. But the two remaining astronauts want to find out more about the UMO first. One of them, a biologist, believes they are swarming in much the same way bees do and they are attracted to the X-ray pulses emitted by their equipment. The military wants them to switch on the X-ray equipment to attract the UMO then when they cluster around the X-ray source, to destroy them with the EMP missiles.

The astronauts don't want to do this. They don't believe the UMO are dangerous and put forth the theory that like bees that come from an over-crowded hive they are searching for a queen to start a new hive. They think the magnetic pulses given off by the X-ray equipment are the same as the emanations that come from a new queen, but when the UMO find no queen they destroy the source of the emanations and go in search of another source. They don't believe the UMO are dangerous.

However, the military takes over and remotely controls the space ship, forcing it to release the probes that emit X-rays and wait for the UMO to swarm so they can be destroyed (they hope) with the EMP missiles. The astronauts can't stop the ship from functioning and the probes are released. As the UMO swarm over them there is a serious electrical and magnetic disturbance which throws the space ship out of orbit around Mars and sends it careening off into deep space. We don't find out whether the EMP missiles worked as planned or not.

An afterword lets us know that the two astronauts have survived and are somewhere near Calisto and Jupiter, and that we should now read Skywave, the first of the books in the **Rorschach Explorer Missions**.

This is a well written, exciting e-novella and is worth reading even if you don't follow up with Skywave or the other books that follow. The doomed astronauts are displayed with considerable sympathy and as a reader you will care about what happens to them as well as cringe at the unpleasant way in which the American Military is portrayed

The Mars Experiment by Brian Edward Hurst (2018) *eBook*.

Although it seems promising, I found it disappointing. The biggest put-off for me is that the characters are simply mouthpieces for the author to express his ideas of how a Mars Colony could operate.

He does this by having a group of new colonists arrive on Mars and these new people are shown around the facilities and everything is explained to them by older colonists who have been on Mars from the establishment of the colony. To generate reader-interest the author throws in old ideas such as fossils being found deep down in caves proving life once existed on Mars, and running water deep beneath the surface. This constant explaining of how things work by various 'old hands' takes up a considerable portion of the book. It is like the way stories were told at the end of the 19th century into beginning of the 20th century. By the 1940s, 1950s and on, very few authors told stories this way. They allowed background and historical details to emerge as part of the action or character interaction, not page after page of explanations about how things function with the only action being a group of people being shown around an established base.

One of the new arrivals sees something odd while being shown around; he spots a couple of strange looking children who quickly vanish into deep and dark recesses of the base. He was under the belief that no children existed on Mars. The boss of the colony shortly after explains that he used to work at Area 51 in the US dealing with Aliens and UFOs, and he and his wife took part in experiments to merge human DNA with that of the small spindly aliens to produce offspring that could survive on earth and the two children the new arrival saw deep down in the base are actually their own children who are adapted to live in the lower gravity of Mars. There are many other alien human hybrids who exhibit heightened intelligence on Earth as well but the general public doesn't know about them. None of the Martian settlers have seen these two children (which I find odd since the base can't be that large) and if the new arrivals saw them how come no one else has. The children are telepathic and can communicate with many other aliens in space ships in the solar system. The aliens have discovered that a disaster will befall the Earth in about 100 years' time when the Sun changes its output. On top of that the Earth's atmosphere is being polluted to the point of making it unbreathable around the same time as the Sun's increased output.

The aliens see the planet Mars as a haven for both Humans and themselves, but human cruelty towards animals must end first. There are all kinds of crude messages thrown into the text regarding pollution, extreme weather, all caused by human activities, radiation from cellphones causing brain tumors and other similar ideas. Another obvious message is when a newly arrived Indian character, comments about humans all being different, British, American, Indian, Chinese, Japanese, Philippine, and who knows whatever else in the mixture all seem to be working happily together on Mars, obviously implying why this doesn't happen on Earth.

The colonists are developing a mine deep down in Valles Marineris and they open up a cavern filled with crystal plants that are glowing. It is an artificial garden, an alien garden that appears to be growing wild, as if no longer maintained. They find human skeleton in the garden, a skeleton that is seven feet tall. They also find a metal disc engraved with something resembling hieroglyphics, at which point they are attacked by a monstrous alligator like reptile. They flee in panic. The lizard thing can't get through the small opening the human miners made when accessing the garden. It tries, forcing its way into the mine only to retreat because the lesser atmosphere is too cold and not dense enough to breathe. (see page 100) Back in the base thy hybrid human alien girl wants to make telepathic contact with the lizard creature to see what it thinks.

At this point the aliens in the space ships out in the solar system contact the human alien hybrid girl (telepathically) and explain to her that the tall alien they found in the garden was their enemy, and these giant beings forced the small spindly aliens to move off planet and live in space. The giants once came to Earth but the heavy gravity was too much for them and primitive humans attacked and killed them so they set up a colony deep beneath the surface of Mars. The small aliens eventually came to Earth where they contacted humans (at Area 51) with the object of creating human alien hybrids, because they can't reproduce living in space. They have been reasonably successful to this point...

And it is here that I thought reading any more of this would be a waste of time. There are still a couple of hundred pages to go. I couldn't be bothered to find out what else the author throws in regarding conspiracy theories or how the story finishes. He has obviously tried to include as much as possible in this story to attract those people who believe in alien conspiracies, flying saucers and other UFOs, and that many important people are alien (lizard) human hybrids who will eventually take control of the Earth.

I'm not one of those people so this story is not for me. But I'm sure there will be many 'out there' who will love this book.

I think the author needs to work more on how to structure a story dramatically, to show the excitement the newcomers feel on seeing the Mars base for the first time, rather than telling the reader all about it.

Micromium - Clean Energy from Mars, by David Gittlin (2018)

Not a title that stands out and I would have bypassed it until I saw that it was an illustrated novella. There was no listing of who the artist was, but David Moratto is listed as interior designer. The author worked marketing and business communications which led me to suspect he was also the illustrator as well as the author of the story. The greyscale drawings appear to be computer generated and may have originally been rendered in colour but are printed in greyscale on crème paper which gives them a rather endearing aspect.

The story seems a bit labored at the start, but quickly becomes hard to put down. A team of auditors has been sent to Mars to monitor the activities of a private mining corporation as it mines, and refines this unusually radioactive material (not found anywhere else) into fuel rods which it ships to Earth with the promise of it being able to generate massive amounts of clean energy. This is exactly what the Earth needs to overcome the use of fossil fuel and to prevent further catastrophic degeneration of the climate. The company as a result stands to make billions of dollars in profit.

On Mars, millions of years ago a massive crater was formed either by volcanic activity or from the impact of a massive meteor impact. Siloe Patera is the crater in which the unusually radioactive mineral was found, and is the location of the mining colony. Unfortunately, there have been accidents with the power generators using micromium fuel rods and the WEC (World Energy Commission) wants to know how it is produced and what can be done to safeguard the use of it so accidents don't occur.

The Martian mining colony also reported an accident in which it claims two geologists were killed in a micro-meteorite shower, and they are short staffed. They do not want the auditing team to be there and they don't have the personnel to assist them.

When the audit team arrives, they find they can't get access to certain areas of the mining operation, and are prevented from entering by human-oid robots that are supposed to do much of the mining, but to the audit team, seem more like guards. Even though they have authorization from the WEC, the mining company claims it has intellectual rights that involve the processes of the production that they do not want people to see. It also won't allow them into storage areas where the ore is being processed, claiming the process is delicate and entering would upset it and cause delays, and the company depends on sending a regular shipment of fuel pellets to Earth. They do not want this to be disrupted.

The audit team proceeds to check the surrounding crater for signs of Mi-cromium, but hardly finds any, which makes them think the deposits have been used up, and unless the company can find more on Mars, its contract will be terminated. An accidental fall injures one of the audit team and she is hospitalized and confined to bed. The other three in the team begin to think something is not right, that the mining colony is hiding something.

At this point it is beginning to be intriguing. Two of the miners using a rover head off to the far extremity of the Siloe Patera crater having moni-tored a strong signal that suggests the presence of micromium. At first, they think this is a false signal, an anomaly, but coming around some mountain-ous debris near the edge of the crater wall they are stunned to discover a huge alien ship sitting there.

Now I was hooked. There's nothing better I like than a story in which aliens are discovered, especially on Mars.

Getting close to the ship one of them exits the rover to examine the ship up close and immediately it triggers something. A door opens and a huge robot rolls out with lights flashing. Terrified, the miner retreats back to the rover but stops when he realizes the flashing lights are an SOS signal. He approaches the robot and follows it inside and up into the enormous ship. He is told by the robot telepathically that it has been damaged in its flight from a nearby double star, and unless it can repair the stasis pods where some of the crew are sleeping, they will die. It needs his help. The ship, which is intelligent also requests his help in reviving the surviving crew members. He doesn't know what to do, but feeling good he agrees to help. He discovers the crew are very human in appearance except for their size. They are two thirds bigger than humans, and have 6 fingers and toes instead of five as we have. They come from a much heavier planet in their star system and are bigger and stronger than Earth Humans. He agrees and together with the robot they repair one of the pods and revive its occupant, a stunning woman who tells him (also telepathically) that her name is Silena. She is the captain of the ship and after reviving the other two, another female and a male, she explains they are on Mars to rescue a previous expedition in which the ships crashed. They want to know what caused them to crash and to see what they can recover from them. Their other reason is that they have brought with them machinery that can terraform Mars and make it more habitable. Their home world is about to be destroyed by their sun which is collapsing and will explode. They were surprised to find a colony of humans on Mars and are willing to work with them. They do not want to disrupt whatever the colony is doing.

Meanwhile the auditing team knows nothing of the alien ship and is trying to get access to the storeroom and processing areas. They have a court order from the WEC but the mining chief refuses to acknowledge it. On Earth the mining corporation boss tells them to not let the audit team see anything. And reveals to the reader that they found two alien ships that had crashed and were trying to obtain advanced technology from them, ostensibly for the benefit of mankind rather than personal profit.

The miner who discovered the alien ship and helped revive the crew, as not allowed to go anywhere near it, but he sneaks out in a rover and heads back to the alien ship. He is almost there when he discovers he is being followed. It is by his partner who has orders to kill him so he won't reveal anything. He gets into the ship but his partner also gets in. There is something however, in the ship that removes murderous thoughts and after a brief skirmish the man following him decides he doesn't really want to kill him after all. The two humans stay on the ship while the two female aliens take a fast shuttle and fly to the mining camp where they ask the mining boss to allow them to recover their two lost ships. He claims possession because he found them and has them in storage and doesn't want to give them back. The aliens insist that all they want to do is examine them to determine what went wrong and why they crashed. An agreement is reached.

Meanwhile, the WEC has compelled the Corporation boss to get the miners to allow the audit team access to the storage and processing areas.

When the audit team finally gets to the storage area they discover two giant aliens are already there ready to open the airlock. After a bit of misapprehension, the two groups enter together and discover, piles of ingots of micromium. The aliens explain that this refined metal is the fuel from their interstellar space ships. It has been affected by cosmic radiation over the prolonged journey from their home system and it causes malfunctions in their ships machines causing the ships to crash. It almost happened to their own larger ship, but this ship had back-up systems installed which saved them. Micromium comes from their home world and is not found on Mars. The audit team then realize that the mining corporation is perpetrating a massive fraud. It seed the mine with small amounts of micromium to give the idea it was mining it, whereas in reality it took the fuel ingots from the crashed ships, along with other equipment, and while grinding the ingots up and producing the fuel rods it sends the Earth, the corporation is also trying to find ways of utilizing the alien equipment it recovered from the ships.

The aliens find that among the stasis pods taken from the crashed ships, one of them has a survivor in it. He is not yet dead while all the others are. They want to take the pod back to their larger ship to revive the occupant. The audit team need to send a report back to WEC headquarters explaining the massive fraud that's going on. Suddenly power cuts off and none of them can leave the storage area. The mining boss has locked them in. They are meant to die there when their oxygen runs out. They have seen too much.

The aliens have weapons with them and they blast the airlock door open so they can all leave. They accompany the aliens back to their large ship and convince them to take them to a relay station where they can send a message back to Earth to report on what was happening on Mars. Blasting their way into the station they are about to send their message and report when the relay station is attacked by a group of miners and robots. The aliens are still in their ship and escape whereas the audit team is captured and rendered unconscious. When they wake up, they are strapped inside their own small space ship that is about to take off. The takeoff is automated and they know something awful is going to happen unless they can stop it. Even though there is robot accompanying them to make sure they don't do anything, they manage to disable it and switch off the automatic systems to abort the takeoff.

They barely get outside when the ship blows up. But there are several rovers there and the miners see them escape. As they run towards a rocky outcrop the miners attack, but suddenly the alien shuttle appears and blows up two of the miner's rovers. The last one immediately turns tail and runs. Rescuing the audit team, the aliens head back to the mother ship which is threatened by a massive storm that is heading towards them and the mining camp. There has never been a storm like this on Mars and the team are barely inside the mother ship when it hits. They manage to get up and out into orbit from where they see the mining camp obliterated. Once in orbit the team is told that the alien Sirena had created the storm artificially but it had got out of control. They then tell them it had been reported on Earth that the team had died in the ship which exploded on takeoff, they also tell them that they will take them back to Earth, before abandoning Mars altogether.

Back on Earth they are stunned to find the audit team is alive and that it is accompanied by a giant female alien. They want to interrogate her but she explains she is there to vindicate the audit team so that their stories of what happened will be believed. She refuses to answer any of their questions and tells them that if they try to stop her, she will destroy the Earth completely.

Her ship in orbit has that power. She is escorted back to her shuttle while the audit team are invited to talk to the president, before facing their superiors at the World Energy Commission.

The story basically finishes here. There is an epilogue that explains what happened after meeting the WEC, but it all ends well.

I found the story entertaining, well written, well worth the time taken to read it; but then I always like stories about encounters with aliens, whether benign, as they are here, or otherwise.

Apart from that it is a good looking book inside and out.

Finding Life on Mars – *a novel of isolation* by Jason Dias. (2018)
The title is suggestive in a couple of ways.

The basic set up is there is a colony on Mars that has been established for a long time; long enough for the original colonists to have children who have grown to adulthood. These children are different in many ways from their parents, almost autistic is many cases. They don't like to be touched. They are hypersensitive to the emotions expressed by the original colonists, their now almost elderly parents. They have phenomenal memories and ways of communicating between themselves that even the slightest gesture contains many nuances of information, (which their Lander parents cannot see or understand). They do not think of themselves as humans, which is how they refer to their parents. They think of themselves as the Trueborn and their parents are the Landers. This comes up a number of times at which moments their parents remind them that whatever they may think, they are still human.

The last information received from Earth was that the climatic and ecological situation had deteriorated so much that the remnants of the humans had retreated into bio-domes for survival, and that these bio-domes are failing. Temperatures are reaching the 150 Celsius mark across most of the surface and once the bio-domes fail there will be no one left. The Martian colonists will be the last humans left alive in the universe. The Landers are having trouble reconciling the fact they are the last humans left alive while the Trueborn children are unable to understand their parent's emotions.

One of the elderly colonists continually monitors the radio frequencies for a hint of intelligent life elsewhere in the universe. He also sends a daily radio message to Earth, hoping that someone one day will respond. This is becoming more a forlorn hope as time progresses. Finally believing that Earth is truly dead they discuss ways in which they can mourn the passing of the home planet, a symbolic funeral service is suggested. The Trueborn find this idea incomprehensible.

The colony itself is failing. They do not have the capacity to replace technology that breaks down. There are no spare parts, and anything that breaks down is scavenged for parts that could be useful elsewhere. They mostly live underground in a huge space created by detonating two atomic bombs to form caverns which they can seal off from the outside Martian environment. They live in one area while in the other they grow corn under artificial lights, old neon tubes that can't last much longer. Some have already failed and the crop is becoming less. They also grow mushrooms in the darker caverns, and the only meat they obtain is from rats they imported originally that also live in the darker caverns feeding on the mushrooms. They have old technology but can't repair it. Chairs and beds are made from the remnants of the sails and ropes that helped lower the original landing vehicles. The only spare space suits for use outside on the surface are from those who have previously died. They can't fix the suits or replace them. Everything is like that, all scavenged from the original landing ships. They can produce water by extracting it from the frozen regolith, and they can split water into its various components for oxygen and fuel needed, but basically —as the author states; they are like Neanderthals living in an environment designed for modern Humans.

On a scavenging expedition to the site of a crashed landing vehicle several miles away in a crater they discover a fungal life form growing nearby which seems to be producing small amounts of oxygen from the iron in the regolith. This was something bio-engineered on earth to assist with the terraforming of Mars, but because it had crashed most of what it contained was destroyed on impact. The two Trueborns discover that the spores from this mushroom had spread across the crater and up along the other side masses of mushroom like growths are extending across the plain above the crater. (This is the first instance of finding life on Mars.) Some of the growths are large enough for the two Trueborn to cut open and scrape out what was inside the giant stem. They hollow out enough space the create a small room. Putting back the piece they cut away to get inside they discover that the fungus produces enough oxygen as a byproduct that they can remove their helmets and breathe.

They keep their find a secret when they return to the home cavern. But this is not their only secret. Some of the Trueborn have had children of their own, which of course are grandchildren of the original colonists. They keep this secret from their parents for the simple reason that they believe they are no longer human and their children likewise can't be human, in the way the Landers are. (This I think is the second example of finding life on Mars.) But unknown to them, their parents have known about the grandchildren but do not want to say anything. They are waiting for their children (the

Trueborn) to tell them and this eventually happens when the colony comes under threat.

One of the Trueborn suggested to the Landers that a radio message would be suitable as a eulogy; a radio message beamed into space will go on forever and at some distant future time somewhere else in the universe, an intelligent being may hear the message and understand that they are not alone, that others had existed before them.

In the process of broadcasting this eulogy they receive a sudden message from Earth. There is one person left; a madman who likes the fact that he is the last human left alive in the universe. He threatens to destroy the colony using the third atomic bomb still floating in orbit around Mars, but he gives them time to say their last words first.

This gives the author an opportunity to show the destruction of the Earth through the eyes of the remaining original colonists who broadcast their stories of how they ended up on Mars and what the Earth was like during that time, as ecological disasters and petty wars ruined the planet.

Meanwhile because the colony is threatened by imminent destruction, the Trueborn are forced to reveal the existence of their children, and are surprised to find out their parents had known for years about them but said nothing.

They all evacuate to the crater where the giant mushroom forest exists and take refuge by hollowing out spaces inside the stems.

At the same time a couple of the Landers have decided they will retaliate by scavenging one of the rocket engines from the defunct lander vehicle and convert this into a bomb that they will send to Earth to destroy the lone mad survivor who is threatening them with destruction. They work out the coordinates from the radio signal they received from Earth. This is glossed over so the reader hardly notices. Knowing that the rocket/missile they send to Earth will take seven to ten months to get there, which means that at any time the mad earthman could send a radio signal to activate the atomic bomb in orbit long before their missile gets to Earth.

Up to this point the story is well written and quite acceptable, although I did think the stories each of the Landers told of their experiences on Earth were too long and distracted from the tension building up in the Mars colony, but the end of the story for me was a letdown.

The evacuated colonists and the grandchildren after a few days return to the home base. The rocket missile to Earth has been launched, and a couple of the original colonists finally die (of old age), and the reader is left wondering, what is going to happen next? How is all this going to be resolved? Did the signal get sent to activate the bomb in orbit? Will the colony eventually survive?

Personally, I think if another book is to follow that concludes or continues the story, this should have been stated on the publishing page or the title page, i.e. *Book One (of two or three)*. The impression given is that this story is complete and this is a stand-alone book.

Unfortunately, the reader is left hanging which I found disappointing. I like to know in advance whether the book I read is part of a duology or a trilogy before I invest time in reading it. If I knew in advance, I would probably have waited for the following books to be published before reading the set as a single long novel.

Apart from that, the story is well written, the feeling of isolation is an underlying theme and isn't intrusive, but as a reader you can feel it, and the characters are engaging and believable for the most part, which is a lot more than can be said for many other self-published books.

The Lady Astronaut books by Mary Robinette Howal (2018)
From Tor Books.
The Calculating Stars (2018) and *The Fated Sky* (2018) are prequels to the novella *The Lady Astronaut of Mars* (2014) eBook. *(See **Dreams of Mars** page 308.)* There was so much history and backstory implied in this novella that it seemed inevitable that Mary Robinette Kowal would have to write all of that, and she has, beginning with *The Fated Sky*. These books combined present an impressive alternate history of the of the US and of the 'conquest of space' across the years from 1952 to 1963.

Prior to the story's beginning Kowal says she had Dewey defeat Truman as President because she wanted a President who would start the space program earlier.

The story begins with the destruction of the eastern seaboard of the USA by a massive meteor that smashes into Washington and destroys the government, the city of Washington DC, New York and all other major cities along that coastline, with tidal waves killing further millions as the sea inundates much of the low-lying coastlines. With the US government destroyed a new government is formed in the new capital of Kansas City where the nascent space program is underway.

Apart from the dust and smoke and water vapor thrust into the atmosphere, the resultant greenhouse gases are going to warm the whole planet to the point where within less than a century the oceans will become so hot, they will start to boil, by which time every living thing will be dead. The only hope for humankind this extinction event is to establish a colony initially on the Moon, and then send people to live on Mars. Unfortunately, most of the surviving population does not believe this because the mass of debris ejected by the meteor impact has caused temporary cooling that will last a couple of years before the inevitable heating commences.

At the start of the story some satellites had been launched and only one or two people had actually gone into space. The **N**ational **A**dvisory **C**ommittee for **A**eronautics (NACA) is the space agency responsible for activities in space and Elma York is a computer, who with a number of other women, calculates the mathematics needed for the launches. She is taking a break with her husband Nathaniel, a rocket scientist and lead engineer working on the launching of satellites, inland in the mountains at their family log cabin when the meteor strikes. They think at first that it is a nuclear launch made by the Russians against the US. This is 1952 and the Cold War is omnipresent in everyone's lives.

Elma, during the Second World War was a pilot who flew supplies and delivered troops to where they were needed. She didn't fly combat missions, but she did fly jets as well as propeller driven planes. She was not the only woman who did this (there actually was a female squadron of pilots during the war) and a number of ex-pilots are working with her as computers for NACA. As in the real world, these women were essential for determining the orbits and trajectories of the rockets launched. They were brilliant at calculating and rarely made mistakes. IBM computers were gigantic, slow in calculating, and had to be fed with punched cards that often were incorrect because programmers made mistakes punching the cards. The rocket engineers relied on the women who were the computers.

In this alternate world many of the prejudices that existed quite strongly in our world similarly exist here, and this is shown in the way the characters react together; the disinclination to have 'black' people in positions of importance, the relegation of women to domestic roles, the dislike of 'Orientals' and so on.

The Calculating Stars covers the story of how some of the women computers, and one in particular, Elma York, became astronauts and why it was essential to have one of these computers on each space mission both orbital (where a space station is established) and on journeys to the Moon where a small base is being established. The head of the facility didn't want women to go into space, the lead astronauts didn't want women in space; they all claimed it was too dangerous, but Elma points out: you cannot start a colony without women, so there should be female astronauts. She has an intense desire to be the first female astronaut, and constantly pushes her superiors into accepting her. She also convinces them that if they want to make the general public believe that it is safe to go into space, then they need to have women in space as well.

To demonstrate their skills, the women who work as computers and who are also members of women's aeronautics clubs, decide to put on an air show. This generates a lot of good publicity, especially when Elma's plane hits a flock of birds and she is forced to make an emergency landing. When asked to go on a children's television show that tries to make science interesting, she is billed as the Lady Astronaut, and the name sticks, to the chagrin of the male dominated astronaut corps. The head of NACA then decides to use her for publicity, to help generate the funds they need to keep the space program operational. At this point there is the beginnings of cooperation between NACA and the broader international space community The International Aerospace Coalition (IAC). Together they can raise enough funds to keep the program operational.

There is some technical stuff relating to getting rockets into orbit, getting rockets to the moon and other related material, all blended neatly into the background. The main focus however is the animosity between the lead astronaut and Elma York, now named the Lady Astronaut. There is a compelling reason for this apart from misunderstanding between the two, but they are forced to work together especially as good publicity is needed to keep the space program alive, against people who are demanding more should be done to rehabilitate the damaged parts of the country. Elma is instrumental in getting children around the country to form clubs, whose members all want to be lady astronauts when they grow up. These children obviously convince their parents that going into space is a good thing and that living on Mars would also be good.

No one yet believes that the world is heating up and will heat up to a point where it becomes uninhabitable in another 50 years. Prejudice against African Americans is slowly being overcome as they are accepted into the astronaut corps as pilots and engineers, for the men, as well as computers, for the women who are pilots. Other countries such as South Africa contribute funds as well as at least one pilot astronaut to the program.

As the story evolves Elma York is instrumental in getting NACA to accept women for astronaut training. Many of the computers apply as well as the pilots from the aeroclub, and some are accepted. The training is rigorous, and many don't pass or are not accepted because they don't have the requisite hours of flying time on jets. There is some resentment firstly because it seems although open to everyone, too many black women pilots are rejected, and secondly, because Elma makes it through and the other women think it's only because they need her for publicity to keep congress interested enough to continue funding. She has an uphill battle convincing everyone that she is there on her merits and not just because they need her for publicity.

The las two chapters have the women astronauts being accepted and right at the end Elma, the first Lady Astronaut, is finally on her way to the Moon. It is now 1958 and the first trip to the Moon is taking place.

This story and the subsequent one is told from the viewpoint of Elma York. What happens to her, how she reacts to male prejudice and the prevailing ideas of what a woman's place should be in the 1950s, and how hard she had to work to change those 1950s conventions, is a gentle reminder of how far we have come today in regard to black rights, women's rights and other such matters, while still letting us know how far we have still to go.

The Fated Sky begins three years later in 1961 with Elma working as a space ferry pilot bringing people down to the newly established IAC moon base or ferrying them around to different locations on the Moon where scientific research is taking place. She rotates living on the Moon for a few months with returning to Earth.

Returning to Earth with a shuttle carrying passengers, there is a mishap and the shuttle goes off course and almost crash lands in a remote field hundreds of miles away from where it should have landed. A group of Earth First Protesters, mostly African American, appear on the scene and when they recognize the Lady Astronaut, Elma York, they decide to use her to gain better conditions for themselves and the people most white Americans seemed to have forgotten. There is a standoff which ends badly for the protesters being shot and wounded. This brings the FBI into the picture as they believe there is a connection between the Black pilot of the shuttle who was seen talking to the Earth First Protesters occupying the ship before they noticed the Lady Astronaut

Back at the base in Kansas City the FBI want to interrogate all the African American astronauts on the automatic assumption that they must be involved with the growing protests around the country. The FBI wants to get rid of all African American astronauts, which is why to prevent this, further training of the Mars astronauts takes place in orbit, where the FBI has no jurisdiction.

People are beginning to realize that the ever increasing and destructive stormy weather is a direct result of the meteor impact nine years earlier, and that things are only going to get worse. They want the money being spent on the preparations for the trip to Mars to be spent on improving conditions on Earth. Like the politicians, they don't believe the Earth is doomed, and that all that talk is just to scare congress and other world governments into spending money for the first trip to Mars which will lay the foundations for a colony.

The Mars expedition has been selected and all the astronauts are men. When the unreliability of the clumsy mechanical computers is realized the IAC reluctantly agrees they will need the living computers to calculate the course corrections needed to be certain of getting to Mars. All the computers are women and so they have no choice in the matter. The crews will have to be mixed.

And here again we have prejudice and race cropping up… one ship is all white, while the other has a mixed-race crew, with African American, Latino, Brazilian and so on. Elma's old astronaut foe is commander of the expedition and he is aboard the mixed race-crewed ship. When the IAC head selects Elma to replace one of the female Mars crew members (*because of the good publicity this will generate*) the crews of both ships are incensed. There is nothing they can do about it and eventually have to accept her. To Elma's astonishment, the leader of the expedition, her old foe from the Second World War, Colonel Stetson Parker, insists that she be his co-pilot. Both ships have a crew of seven, while the third ship is loaded with supplies for the first base on Mars and will run automatically in tandem with the other two.

It is a three-year journey to Mars and back. The idea is they will get there, land and set up a base for future colonists to occupy, then return to Earth.

The bulk of the book covers the journey to Mars.

There is much that goes wrong. The women complain that they are relegated to cooking and laundry duty which NACA headquarters maintains it is their area of expertise. One ship is infected with food poisoning well into the trip and two of the crew from Elma's ship have to go over to render aid since the doctor died. (The doctor didn't have to die, but NACA insisted they not go across to render assistance). Ignoring NACA's demands Elma and the doctor from her ship go across to help. There are body wastes and diarrhea floating about all over the ship which has to be vacuumed up. The remaining crew are in the gym part of the ship where slight gravity helps make it easier to treat them.

Not long after leaving Earth orbit and heading out to Mars Elma figured out a way to send private messages to her husband Nathaniel using a code hidden in the garbage that constitutes part of the wavelength the message is broadcast on. (They are using teletype machines.) But one of the other women in her ship figures this out and accuses Elma of spying on them and sending this info back to Earth, when all she wanted was to have some private conversations with her husband.

Other things happen and, in a spacewalk to fix a leaking ammonia problem, one of the astronauts is accidentally killed. His partner blames himself. Instead of pulverizing the frozen body and compressing the result into a cube for returning to Earth, (they had a bad experience doing this with the doctor who died on the other ship), they decide to eject the body into space. Unfortunately, the drifting body impacts with their communications antenna and that needs to be repaired.

Isolation begins to take its toll and odd relationships are unexpectedly formed, especially between Elma and Parker who has great respect for her as a pilot. Communications between the ships and Earth is cut off, and they don't know if it is their fault or if something happened back on Earth. It takes a couple of months before they regain contact, and the reason was the protesters had attacked the NACA headquarters and destroyed power to the whole city.

Suddenly Parker is distraught and confesses privately to Elma that his wife (previously a taboo subject) who has been in an iron lung because of late polio infection, had died when the power to Kansas City had been cut off by the protesters. By this time however they have arrived close enough to Mars to require maneuvering for orbital insertion. The computers are kept busy and once orbit is achieved the crew, apart from Stetson and Elma who must remain on the ship to make preparations for the return journey, head down to the surface to set up the base for the future colonists. NACA won't allow Elma down in case something happens to her because she is needed to calculate the math for the return trip.

Ironically, the first person to step onto the surface of Mars in 1963 is the African American astronaut who was Elma's shuttle pilot and who was under FBI investigation for a suspected link to the Earth First Terrorists.

This is where the story ends.

There is however a short epilogue which has the first colonists arriving on Mars three years later and amongst them are Elma York and her Husband Nathanial thus setting the scene for the novella which takes place many years later when both Elma and Nathanial are respected elders of the colony.

I would hope there is one more book to come which details the establishment and development of the colony on Mars as well as telling us what happens to Earth when it heats up too much to be livable. It would then tie in nicely with *The Lady Astronaut of Mars*.

But regardless, the two novels forming the prequel are really one magnificent story that leads into the final original story from 2014. They were a joy to read and should be on every Mars-story-aficionado's list of favorite books.

There was a follow up novel about the establishment of the lunar base with the other astronauts, **The Relentless Moon.**

The **Calculating Stars** won in 2019, the *Nebula Award* for best novel, *The Locus Award* for best SF novel, and the *Hugo Award* for best novel.

Do not miss reading these books...

Post Apocalyptic Mars

Denver Moon — The Minds of Mars Warren Hammond and Joshua Viola (2018)

This is a modern, post-apocalyptic grungy Mars. It has overtones and influences from Noir detective fiction, Cyberpunk futures, and imagery that reminds a reader of movies like *Total Recall* —the original and not the re-make— and *Blade Runner.*

Earth is uninhabitable and humanity has settled on Mars which is being terraformed, the end result of which won't happen for centuries. Most citizens live underground in what can only be considered as warrens with only the wealthy living near the surface where domes protect the city from exposure to the Martian elements. There are mines, and commerce and brothels, and androids that are as intelligent as humans, that look human in every respect, and who also have feelings like humans.

Denver Moon makes her living as a private investigator, her first case being the investigation of a series of murders of android prostitutes that have had various body parts removed. On Mars Robocide is a felony and in the story prequel *Metamorphosis*, Denver is trying to solve why someone would mutilate and kill three robot (android) prostitutes.

Is it really murder if the victim isn't a human? This story is available separately both as a short story and as an illustrated comic book. It is also included in *The Minds of Mars* as an extra. There are also 3 comics; *Murder on Mars, Rafe's Revenge, and Transformations.*

Sometimes violent murders are carried out by sudden victims of a disease called red fever. Not everyone is afflicted with this disease, but it seems to be spreading and getting worse. Denver is colour blind and it seems everyone born with the inherited gene for colour blindness is not affected by the *feve* (red fever). When the couple who brought Denver up as their own daughter are violently murdered by someone suffering from red fever, she begins an investigation into its causes that leads her to the Church of Mars which believes it has the cure by using faith and prayer as the answer to control the *feve*. She also receives, via her AI implant, a message from her dead, or presumed dead grandfather, which suggests he isn't dead and that the Church of Mars holds the key to what the *feve* really is.

During her investigation the Monks from the Church try to kill her, but she escapes. The leader of the Church of Mars also doesn't want her investigating because of secrets he implies she is better off not knowing about, which only makes her more determined to search for the truth of what the Church did with her grandfather, whom she now believes is not dead but imprisoned somewhere on the surface of Mars. The Church leader Hennessey warns Denver that her grandfather (Ojiisan) Tatsuo is not who she thinks she is, and she is better off thinking he is dead. She refuses to accept this and goes in search of him and finds him only she is too late. He is rescued and captured by an excommunicated member of the Church of Mars who now runs a huge mining corporation. They also capture her because they need her AI who has the memories of her grandfather inside of him. Her grandfather's mind had been erased before he was kept prisoner and isolated on the surface in a remote bunker on the other side of Mars from Mars City and they want to extract the AI's memories and re-implant them in her grandfather.

Denver discovers Hennessy was right and her grandfather Tatsuo was not to be trusted after all. There are aliens disguised as humans who are in control of the terraforming, and that they are the cause of the red fever due to experiments they make on human minds in an attempt to control them. She discovers that her grandfather was in cahoots with these aliens that are bug-like but can shapeshift so they appear to be human. They have taken control of nearby inhabited star systems and the solar system is their next acquisition except they are having trouble taking control of human minds and red fever is the result of failures. Tatsuo has been breeding human clones —to supply the aliens with fresh minds to study— on a spaceship that had circled out from Mars to the far reaches of the solar system before returning. Denver with the help of her shuttle pilot friend and her AI gets on board this ship and attempts to destroy it by having it burn up and crash into Olympus Mons.

Although it sounds implausible it all fits together in an exciting, visual, almost cinematic nail-biting story the modern reader can't put down. Destroying the ship doesn't end the story, it restores a balance. The aliens are still there on Mars and they have to be rooted out or humans will never fulfill their own destiny.

Denver Moon Book Two. The Saint of Mars (2019)

Six months after the alien ship with its human victims, experiments in transferring human minds into the alien shape shifters, crashed into Olympus Mons, Denver is back on the job looking for a suspect who is responsible for the disappearance of several people in the Red Tunnel. The aliens who appear as humans are in control of the terraforming of Mars. Their long-term object is to make the planet suitable for them and the human race which they intend to enslave. They have conquered and enslaved hundreds of other races in different parts of the galaxy, but are having trouble getting control of humans. Very few Martian colonists know there are aliens amongst them, who in all appearances are indistinguishable from humans. Denver, because she is colour blind, can sometimes see a glint in the eyes which betray the fact that the human she sees is an alien. The red Fever has disappeared because this was a failed attempt by the alien insectoid shape shifters to infect the human brain to make it subservient. Human brains do not respond. They can't be controlled.

After two months of searching Denver has finally discovered a suspect which she and her companion AI weapon (Smith) are following. She doesn't know who hired her, but it doesn't matter. If the money is there, she will take the job. Following her suspect into an ally, he disappears. No one she asks will tell her that they saw this person enter the ally except for a beggar girl who indicates a door to a workshop operated robotically.

Entering the workshop Denver finds a hidden door which opens into another space where she finds the missing humans strung up on hooks. Some of them have had their heads removed. Before she can react, the door opens again and the beggar girl comes in and changes in front of her into one of the aliens. It shoots her with a stun gun and she loses consciousness.

She wakes to find herself hanging by her tied wrists from a hook. Her AI weapon, Smith, is laying on a bench while the alien explains it is going to remove her brain and transplant it into itself. Previous methods to gain control have not worked and now they are trying to find a more direct way to do it. Communicating with her AI she tries to distract the alien while Smith attempts to reposition on the bench in able to shoot the alien. It manages to do this, and after a brief struggle she manages to get herself unhooked and releases her wrists. She sends a message to Hennessey, the leader of the Martian Church, who has also been fighting the aliens and their infection for years. He doesn't respond.

Leaving the hidden workshop with the bodies of the lost humans and the carcass of the alien bug shape-shifter, she takes on another job from Jard, an old associate who runs a whorehouse using androids, that she has had problems with before. He wants her to assassinate the new leader of the church who claims that Hennessey is ill and dying. There are android monks picketing his place which is causing him to lose business and he wants it stopped. It appears that the new church leader has been recruiting androids to become his close followers. He rescues them and reprograms them to work as monks. He also wants to get rid of the shape-shifters from Mars, but he has a deeper ambition. He wants to get rid of humans altogether and replace them with androids. He has himself over the years gradually replaced every part of his own body with android parts, so is in effect an android. His ambition is to live forever as ruler of Mars where the remnants of the human population at present live because Earth has been made unlivable, (presumably by pollution etc.). Mars is the last bastion for the human race in the solar system. But humans destroy everything and need to be replaced, not by shape-shifting aliens but by humanoid androids.

Unfortunately, Denver is outwitted by the new Church leader and by her own grandfather (*Ojiisan*) Tatsuo who has been working with the aliens for years. But there is a reconciliation of sorts when she is seriously injured trying to escape the android monks who are after her. He grandfather who has told her she will inherit everything (which she doesn't want) has brought in the shape-shifting doctor in charge of terraforming Mars to heal her broken bones, ribs and concussion. He also has with him a shape-shifting woman who is to accompany Denver to a hidden place where the new Church leader is supposedly meditating as part of the takeover of the Church from the old leader (Hennessey), and their job is to assassinate this new leader.

Making their way through a warren of hidden tunnels, built secretly by Tatsuo, her grandfather, she and the alien assassin enter a massive chamber, built by the Church, and there is a final confrontation between the new leader and Denver. Hennessey is barely alive but he helps Denver to defeat the new leader (which she discovers at this point is a rogue android).

Like the previous book, this is fast paced and highly entertaining no matter how improbable the plot and the twists in the events are. It all seems to fit together and make sense when you get to the end. The background environment is also highly evocative and convincing in a grungy believable way. There is a final moment where after things settle down the Church of Mars has to come up with a story to convince its followers that they have been saved. They want to make Denver the first Saint of Mars, which after some convincing, she reluctantly accepts. The final scene has her returning home and something is off. She sees what looks like her table in the rubbish piled up in the alley near her place and on entering her apartment, she sees the same table where it was supposed to be. She immediately pulls out her weapon, Smith, and fires at the table, which turns out to be the shape-shifting assassin whose final act was to kill Denver.

We now know the story will continue because Denver has yet to finally deal with the aliens who are still intent on taking over the human race. Besides that, the last page has a note which simply says **Denver will return**.

And return she does, in book three, **The Thirteen of Mars**. (2022)

It is 2 years after the end of the previous book (and two years it took for this to be written and published). It opens with Denver and her grandfather Ojiisan approaching a hidden laboratory in one of the terraforming plants isolated in difficult terrain, hoping to find Dr Werner, the shapeshifting bug scientist who had been trying to control human minds (unsuccessfully) which resulted in the red death that killed so many after driving them crazy. They enter his lab but discover he isn't there, but they find nurseries where millions of bug eggs are hatching. Having given up on trying to control humans mentally, the bugs that control a third of the galaxy with subjugated races and hive minds have decided that extermination of humans is the only answer. All the terraforming plants around Mars are being used as nurseries to grow and hatch bugs to take over the planet.

Denver discovers that Dr Werner is also wanted by his own kind as a traitor because he didn't follow orders to exterminate humans, but keeps trying to control their minds, mechanically now rather than genetically, but he is no longer on Mars. He has gone to Earth to continue his experiments.

Fighting their way out of the hidden laboratory they are attacked by thousands of tiny bugs that eat holes in their space suits and as they struggle to get back to their ship Ojiisan loses too much air and succumbs from the effects of oxygen loss. Denver manages to get him back on board their ship, but his mind is gone (again), only this time it wasn't a memory wipe as before, but his brain has ceased functioning having died from oxygen starvation. His body is still alive and nanobots inserted into his blood stream have managed to work their way into his brain where they keep him breathing although he remains in a deep coma with no brain activity.

Upset because she'd only just got him back after 20 years of not knowing him or where he was, she is determined to have the memories of him that she downloaded into her personal weapon (Smith) uploaded into his empty brain in the hope that he can be revived. Everyone tells her it is a lost cause. He is dead, only his body is still functioning albeit artificially because of the nanobots. Smith is also playing up because he thinks he is Ojiisan as well as Smith, which creates problems for Denver. Although Denver wants to kill Dr Werner, she knows he is the only one capable of transferring Smith's intelligence from the weapon into the brain of her grandfather. She must take Ojiisan to Earth for Dr Werner to operate and transfer the weapon's intelligence.

Getting together a crew and a ship she hires from her longtime friend who also comes along as the pilot, she heads to a devastated Earth. There is trouble at the spaceport as the bugs try to stop her and the crew from leaving but they get away. She takes with her, the Botsie (Android) friend she freed from servitude. He, with others of his kind, have evolved as independent intelligent beings. They can communicate with each other over long distances, although not as far as Earth. Together they can maintain contact mentally with each other as a group collective, in effect an artificial hive mind. Their ship is followed by someone who claims to be from the asteroids who turns out to be a bounty hunter looking for Dr Werner on behalf of the bugs hoping to conquer or exterminate humans. On Earth he helps them get into the laboratory where Dr Werner is using survivors from the devastation of Earth to further his experiments on human mind control.

A complex situation develops on Earth at the only place where humans managed to survive, near Japan, and she is trapped by DR Werner who wants to experiment on her brain. He doesn't get a chance as she is rescued by the bounty hunter in collaboration with her weapon (Smith). They manage to capture Dr Werner and head off into the solar system to where a gate leads them to enemy territory. It's during this part of the journey she discovers that the bounty hunter is a shape shifter, a bug, but he is on her side. It's the only place they can go to have the operation done. The bounty hunter also wants to convince his superiors that the Botsies are an artificial intelligent hive, and if they can do this they could save humans and Mars from extermination.

While the transfer is taking place, the bounty hunter is trying to convince the ruling committee of hive minds that the Botsies and humans are and can be a hive mind and should be left alone, but with only one Botsie there, they are unconvinced.

Meanwhile the mind transfer is successful, but Dr Werner once again betrays Denver and escapes leaving them trapped with an army of fighting bugs attacking them. They are rescued by her friend the pilot who blasts a hole in the side of the habitat where they are trapped. They manage to get back on board the ship. Unfortunately, her friend is killed as this happens. They get through the wormhole and back to their own solar system but are followed by a group of faster bug ships that will destroy them when they catch up.

All seems lost but at the last moment another ship appears with the other Botsies and they clearly demonstrate to the attacking bugs that they are a hive mind and should be left alone.

There is an epilogue that takes place forty years later when Denver and Ghost (the bug who joined her crew, the ex-bounty hunter) are relaxing on Mars that now has breathable air, when a message is sent to them that Dr Werner has returned to Mars and is obviously up to no good. They find him and although he tries to trick d Denver with an improved means of mind control, it doesn't work, and she finally manages to kill the bastard and get revenge for all the evil he had perpetrated on Mars and its humans.

Thin Air Richard K Morgan (2018)

This blockbuster story is set in the same universe as his Takeshi Kovaks novels (***Altered Carbon, Broken Angels*** and ***Woken Furies***) but perhaps not quite so far in the future. Mars has been colonized for centuries and there is a large population living in The Gash, or The Valley, (Valles Marineris) which has been roofed over with a strange clear barrier that allows light through but contains partially terraformed atmosphere at a suitable pressure for breathing without aids. Several lager craters have also been modified for human settlement.

The bulk of the population live and work in many cities scattered along the length of the Valley, over three thousand kilometres, and they are connected by fast trains as well as air transport. Businesses are run by large corporations, some based on earth, others on Mars, so there is rivalry between them, and added to this is rivalry between a Chinese established community in one of the terraformed craters, miners, and an independence movement that wants nothing to do with Earth in any form at all. As in any industrialized urban environments there are slums, and rough areas where sensible people do not frequent, where there are the clubs, brothels, bars and cheap accommodation used by working class laborers, places that are often frequented by thieves, rival gangs, and insalubrious people one would rather not encounter.

Hakan Veil, an ex-enforcer who was once part of the military lives in this rundown area. He is still equipped with military body-tech that makes him a living weapon in exactly the same way that military force members are equipped to make them more invincible as soldiers and marines. He is no longer part of the military but he is still equipped with their body technology which was implanted in him at a young age and allowed to grow as he also grew. It hasn't been updated because he is no longer part of the military, but is nevertheless formidable. He works as a fixer, a problem solver, the person you go to when you want something nasty done, or someone eliminated for whatever reasons.

When he was drummed out of the military he was exiled on Mars and he has had enough of the place after eight Martian years there. He wants to go home, but the cost is impossible. Momentarily in jail because he was involved in a vicious murder on behalf of the Chinese, although the police can't prove it, he is released when a delegation of people from Earth Oversight come to do an audit of Mars. He is given the job on behalf of the police of body-guarding one of the delegates, Madison Madekwe, who doesn't want someone shadowing her every move and who turns out to be much more important than anyone would have thought. When she starts to investigate the disappearance of someone who supposedly won in a lottery a free trip to Earth, all kinds of murder and mayhem ensue.

She dismisses Veil early the first morning saying she will be auditing a company and will find her way home Veil insists that he will be there when she finishes and goes off to take care of some other private business. He is attacked with an extreme naval weapon, a tactical bomb, but he escapes.

Unknown to him Madekwe left the company audit early with a group of company bodyguards. She is kidnapped and her five bodyguards are vanquished before they knew what had happened. Veil blames himself for her kidnapping and his momentary lapse of attention. He sets out to find her and bring her safely back. At the same time, he begins making inquiries regarding the missing lottery winner and things go from bad to worse as buried secrets, and corruption at all levels surface, and at every turn there is someone who wants to eliminate Veil for reasons of their own.

This is one of the most violent stories set on Mars that has been written. Yet the violence and corruption in context of the story and the imagined future is all too convincing and has a feeling of reality about it. There are unexpected twists and turns, setbacks and betrayals, all logical within the context of the story which leaves a reader breathless, yet at no time does the reader imagine that it is taking place anywhere else but on Mars.

This is a brilliant extrapolation of the kind of gritty noir Mars stories that were written in the early 1950s such as Lester del Rey's ***Police your Planet*** or Cyril Judd's ***Mars Child***, (originally ***Outpost Mars***)

It is dense with sharp detail and very much updated for the 21st century.

A spectacular Space opera

Lunar Dust, Martian Sands by Tom Chmielewski (2018)
Subtitled: **Book One of the Martian Sands** Series.

The reader's attention is immediately captured as the story begins with a cargo shuttle ship pilot landing at the major Moon base, Tranquility Centre, to unload his cargo from Mars and the asteroids. Ed, the pilot of the 'tug' *Cydonia Zach*, is part of a family company that carries products and raw materials from Mars and the Asteroids to Luna for on-shipping to Earth and returns with manufactured goods and other products needed on Mars and the Asteroids. His aunt runs a tourist shop that sells Martian products to visitors up from Earth while at the same time acting as a shipping agent for goods and raw materials like rare mineral ores brought from Mars to sell to Earth and vice versa. Caught up in the swirl of human activity Ed is, as always, impressed by the colors of the clothes the people from Earth wear, and in general the activity and the noise of so many people crowded together at Tranquility Base. It's always quiet, and drab inside his tug on the stretches between Mars and the Moon, and it takes him a while to adjust to the noise and activity around him as he heads towards his aunt's tourist shop.

In the first paragraph the author hints at unease on Earth as people down there are tired of space travel and colonies on the Moon, Mars, and elsewhere. This is brought further into focus as he heads through the crowded walkways to his aunt's shop, where he needs to report to see what cargo she has arranged for him to ship back to Mars. She informs him she has a special package she wants him to take to Mars, a woman.

He doesn't run passengers, there is a ship leaving about the same time as him the next morning that takes tourists to Mars. Why doesn't she go on that?

The woman informs him she had a passage booked, but canceled it and replaced it with a return flight to Earth. She wants whoever is tracking her or following her to think she is returning to Earth. This is to throw off people who want to harm her or worse still silence her completely. There is something seriously political going on but neither his aunt, nor the mysterious woman are willing to talk about it. His aunt wants him to smuggle the woman on board and take her to Mars when he goes back. In the meantime, his ship is already being loaded with cargo. Ed is not happy about this, but his aunt insists.

Pretending that the woman is a helper they head to the cargo bay and she takes some packages into the ship but doesn't come out. They hope no one is monitoring the video feeds of the loading bay, or that they won't notice there is one person less after the ship has been loaded.

The ship won't take off for several hours but that is okay since Ed needs to do preflight checks to be sure everything is functioning as it should.

Having implied at the very start of the story that there is possible conflict between Earth, the Moon, Mars and the Asteroid colonies, the reader is drawn into the story with the promise of several mysteries evolving that will have to be solved.

Takeoff is routine and the *Cydonia Zach* heads to the L1 point where a cargo module from Earth is waiting to be attached for transport on to Mars. Also, at this Lagrange point the passenger ship *New Brunswick*, is about to load its additional fuel and connect its fusion drive engine which it will use to take it to Mars. Ed will do the same with his *Cydonia Zach*, and will follow one hour behind the New Brunswick.

There are a number of shipping companies and they all rent the fusion drives, powered by Helium-3 which is mined on the Moon, from one company that developed them. They own the patents and the rights and won't allow any other organization to develop a rival fusion drive.

The fusion drive has allowed the solar system to be opened up to exploration and colonization by cutting down the travel times to the various planets, moons, and asteroids. When the Mars Earth window is open, travel time between the Moon and Mars is only a month whereas with chemical drives it took as long as 7 to 9 months, depending on the orbit taken to reach Mars.

Once on Mars with the window closed. It is another two years until the two planets are close enough to make the journey short and profitable. That two-month window is the tourist season for Mars and many Earth people visit for a short stay before returning. But there is a rumor going around that a certain physicist has developed a means of increasing the power of the fusion drive to the point where a trip to Mars will take two weeks instead of a month. Every shipping company wants to get such a drive as it would help open outer space and the asteroid belt for further development and exploitation. There are many other asteroids other than Ceres which could be developed.

The mysterious woman Ed has smuggled on board his Tug is called Faizah, Swahili for she who is victorious, and she is going to Mars to work with his uncle who runs the agricultural enterprises on the planet as well as a shipping company called 4th Orbit. Ed is one of 4 O's pilots. There is also some confusion as the ships are about to depart the Moon because certain cargo hasn't arrived and other cargo is substituted. They can't wait for stuff that hasn't arrived because there is a strict timetable for launch and departure that must be precise.

It is common practice for two ships to travel from one location to another an hour apart, in case something goes wrong with one of the ships, the other is not far away and can help. Ed is one hour behind the *New Brunswick*, and they have just reached the turn-around or midway point where the ships turn and use the fusion drive to decelerate when the *New Brunswick* explodes.

The luggage module has been shattered and debris is scattered, the fusion drive is badly damaged and is adrift, and the passenger module is partially damaged and spinning wildly. The crew has been killed and some passengers injured. Ed immediately informs Mars and tells them he will attempt to rescue and tow the passenger module to Mars. This is a nail-biting episode as Ed comes to the rescue. Again, he has only a certain time to affect the rescue before he too must turn and decelerate for Mars orbital insertion.

In the middle of the rescue attempt a shipping company contacts him by radio asking him to rescue the cargo module in which certain crates are stored. It is drifting wildly and will head towards the far reaches beyond the asteroid belt. They offer him a huge sum of money but he refuses. His concern is to rescue the passengers. He knows many are still alive since he has been in contact with the stewardess in charge of them.

Finally, making Mars Orbit, Ed returns to the surface and finds that a bomb was the cause of the ship exploding, so it was deliberate sabotage.

Was it aimed at Faizah? Was this the reason she wanted to get to Mars secretly and was smuggled onto the *Zydonia Zach*?

Or was the explosion meant to destroy the cargo in which the supposed prototype of a new faster fusion drive was being shipped to Mars, and on to Ceres? The developer of this new drive was also on board the ship and died in the explosion. It later turns out he didn't die but was murdered, and the murderer was a passenger on the ship as well.

Ed's uncle on Mars was also a co-sponsor of the scientist developing the new faster fusion drive. 4th Orbit would like to break the monopoly of the company leasing the fusion drives since they control space travel. They of course would do anything to prevent the development of a faster drive causing them to lose their monopoly. A number of groups on Earth are claiming responsibility for the explosion; these are the groups that want space exploration and travel closed down. The presidential candidate also wants to curb further development and is calling for a moratorium on money spent on space exploration and expansion. If he is elected, he will stop further funding and will bring those living on Mars and elsewhere back to Earth. (None of them want to go back.)

Even two hundred years into the future the author assumes that the USA will be the one spending the most money in space. There is no hint or mention of Russia, or China or the European Consortium who could all be developing activities in space, especially China who I see as the main rival in space to the USA. It is all very American with the government and various private companies providing the funding and controlling the assets.

The first complication arises when the FBI accuse Ed the pilot who rescued the travelers from the exploded ship, as being responsible or at least a co-conspirator in the sabotage. Then shortly later when he is having dinner with the stewardess from the rescued passenger module, the dome enclosing the smaller city where the agricultural farm is located is sabotaged. The air lock blows out and there is a desperate struggle to contain the air, but the crops are lost, and numbers injured but no deaths. Again, because he was there when it happened, the FBI are blaming him as a conspirator. Ed has his suspicions about who could have been responsible because he sees one of the rescued passengers who had helped him to dock the module to his tug, is also there and is helping with the work needed to rescue people and to close off the breach. He claims he was on the first train in to help but Ed knows that train only had medical staff so he immediately suspects this guy had something to do with it. Then there is the mysterious Faizah, who seems to be in the middle of everything that is going on, and his uncle, whom she works for, is also hiding something from him. Even the stewardess is acting suspiciously.

The policeman investigating the case knows Ed is unlikely to be involved, but he had to investigate on the request of the FBI. The reader also knows, and this develops tension within the reader because what is obvious to the reader is not obvious to the characters involved.

Meanwhile, the *Cydonia Zach* is being prepared to take cargo and a new passenger module where many of the surviving passengers from the exploded ship are to travel on to Ceres. The FBI asks Lenowitz, the policeman to drop the investigation. They are now saying it is a terrorist organization on Earth that it responsible, but no one believes it. Lenowitz is taken off the case and is made Captain of another ship, the *Grissom*, which is to follow the *Cydonia Zach* to Ceres. While this has been going on a distant ship from an asteroid mining community has managed to track down the cargo module, which contains the prototype fast fusion drive, as it drifted out into space, and is bringing it to Ceres. All the suspects and all the protagonists are in one way or another heading for Ceres, which is where the murdered inventor of the new fusion drive was heading for. He had a partner, a physicist who has become a monk and with whom he wanted to share his invention.

It gets more complicated as so many protagonists are involved in trying to outwit each other.

When the cargo module is unloaded and the supposed crate containing the fast fusion drive prototype is being taken through Ceres to the docks where one of the main competing space ship competitors is waiting, Faizah and Ed manage to steal it from the crew transporting it and take it into the laboratory space occupied by the Monk. On examining the machine, it is discovered to be a fake. It doesn't and couldn't work. The whole thing is a scam, with people being blown up and murdered for something that doesn't work.

Meanwhile the police are outside and can't get in, while the actual murderer, who is finally revealed, manages to get in through an outside airlock and is threatening to kill them. They talk him out of it and explain that the machine is a hoax. But Ed knows there is a hidden disc (a quantum disc) somewhere, and the real details of the improved super-fast fusion drive are on this disc. The stewardess carries the clue to the answer in a book she was asked to deliver to the Monk, by the inventor of the drive. Once all the protagonists are taken care of with each getting what they deserve in the eyes of the reader, the story satisfactorily concludes with the promise that the solar system will soon be opened to further exploration, development, and of course, political and business shenanigans.

The stranglehold by the company that owned the rights to the fusion drive which everyone had to lease from them is broken. Nothing will be the same after this... or will it?

The novel is full of detail that creates an in-depth picture of a complex civilization that includes space travel and planetary colonization, government bureaucracy, big business corruption, shifting popular beliefs, and ordinary people who just want life to be better, but none of this intrudes into the action or the problems the characters are experiencing, it enhances it. They are obviously influenced by the world they live in, but their actions and responses are perfectly natural in context, and are quite believable as far as the reader (*this reader*) is concerned.

This is as complex a work as any of the massively long books produced by other better-known popular authors, but it is all contained within 267 pages rather than 8 or 9 hundred. Though complete as a stand-alone novel, it is further enhanced by two more books that extend the story to show us a superbly complex society where large colonies on the Moon and Mars, and asteroids like Ceres, are inhabited and developed with regular trade and travel between them, along with the shenanigans that come with big business and politics.

The two books that follow are, ***Rings of Fire and Ice***, set out near Saturn, and ***The Silent Siege of Mars***, which returns us to Mars.

Rings of Fire and Ice (2018) begins with a short prologue regarding the crash of a ship called *Rings of Fire,* that is exploring Saturn's moon Enceladus. Suddenly its close orbit starts decaying with chaotic movements and the incoming telemetry is garbled. The out of control ship crashes onto the surface with apparently no one surviving. A small escape pod did manage to get away from the Rings of Fire, but there would not have been enough supplies on board to sustain its occupant for more than a short time. What actually happened to cause the crash is a mystery that has never been solved.

Fifteen years later, and only a couple of months after the end of the events depicted in the first book in this series, Ed Ferald is preparing to take the *Cydonia Zach* which has now been fitted with the prototype Averink Drive that will get them to Saturn in about a week instead of the usual several months it takes with the slower fusion drives in common use. 4th Orbit, the Martian company owned by Ed's uncle has to prove they can get to Saturn Station to bring back the scientific team before the US government cuts off funding and strands the team there, where they would have to stay for a further 8 months before a suitable window opens again to make a transit to Saturn and return to Earth or the inner part of the system possible. The Averink Drive if it works as predicted will open up the solar system to exploration and development, with transit times to most places in the inner system only a matter of days and to the outer system weeks instead of months.

Jeff Haroldson, an investigative reporter for the leading Mars news syndicate is to accompany the *Zach* on the trip to Saturn to rescue the crew. He is to write a story on the rescue attempt, but he also wants to dig into the mystery of what happened to the *Rings of Fire* and the reason it crashed. He also wants to explore Ed's backstory because Ed was also stationed at Saturn Station during the time of the crash and had been involved with one of the pilots of that lost ship.

With only two days before departure, an injunction to prevent both Ed and Faizah from leaving Mars has been issued. Ed and Faizah secretly depart Mars in the middle of the night, hours earlier than necessary to get to Phobos station where they will attach the Averink Drive for the trip out to Saturn, to avoid receiving the injunction. If the *Zach c*an be delayed for two days, 4th Orbit's contract will be void and Asteroid Technologies will have the rescue contract. They have a ship ready to depart from Phobos. However, Ed and Faizah get there, attach the drive and depart.

OSAR, **O**rbital **S**earch and **R**escue are in charge of the mission and Ed's friend and former policeman Lenowitz is in charge. OSAR seems like a cross between the Martian Police, and the Martian equivalent of the FBI. They handle all kinds of stuff relating to the security of Mars and its inhabitants in the various colonies scattered across the planet. They have stopped, with Ed's help, a terrorist attack on one of the established cities. This terrorist group wants to close down Mars so the money spent there will be spent on Earth to combat the ravages of pollution and climate change. The new President of the US (and by extension of Earth itself) is backward looking and wants to close down all space exploration and development, and use the money being spent on returning Earth to the way it once was. Neither he, nor the groups he funds, can see the long-term benefits to all if space exploration, and mining continues. They only see it as a drain on money that could be spent to improve Earth.

The *Zach* departs on time and hurtles toward Saturn at 1.5g constant acceleration. It could go faster, but in experiments where the drive was pushed to a higher acceleration it has failed. 1.5gs is safe, and they have no problems until they reach the turnover point a few days later. The ship is turned and the drive switched on again to decelerate to a speed that can allow insertion into orbit around the Saturn system. Suddenly everything goes haywire, with the screens screaming that the drive will self-destruct and it is automatically switched off. They are stranded halfway to Saturn and if they can't slow down enough for orbital insertion the *Zack* will sail on past Saturn and out of the solar system. Ed uses the tug's rocket engines to slow them slightly and sends out a mayday call for rescue. There is not enough fuel in the rockets to slow them enough. It could be enough to be rescued if another ship was somewhere nearby.

Usually ships travel in pairs, with one following the other an hour apart, so if anything happens to one of them, the other is able to rescue the people on board. This time, since the Averink Drive was experimental, there are no other ships capable of keeping up with it, so they are alone, stranded halfway between Mars and Saturn.

Ed and his screw desperately try to find a way to fix the drive, and just as they are about to jettison the Averink Drive, and use the rest of their fuel to slow the Zach a bit more, they receive a radio call to say a ship, the *Ceres Charlene*, a dubious ship operated by a smuggler, is on its way to rescue them. Ed thinks there is something suspicious about this, and on checking the Ceres Charlene's departure time and its timetable, he discovers they had already changed course to come and rescue them days earlier, so they knew in advance that Ed would have trouble with the drive. They knew the drive was going to be sabotaged.

Faizah's independent computer analysis of the drive doesn't show any anomalies. She convinces Ed that the Zach's computers are showing the wrong information. OSAR is informed and Lenowitz conducts an investigation into who was working on preparing the *Zach* for departure and finds a technician who inserted malignant software to falsify info from the drive and to shut it down. Someone wants to steal the Averink Drive and the so-called rescue ship would have picked it up and brought it back along with the crew and passengers on board the *Zach*.

Ed has also received mysterious messages from someone called ROI, who warns him of attempts to stop or to sabotage his trip out. No one can figure out who ROI is and all they know is that this person is working (from afar) with the guys on Ceres who helped develop the Averink Drive. Once they start the drive, while ignoring the false telemetry they finish the trip to Saturn. It's at this point that Ed realizes the messages from ROI originate from the Saturn System, because the delay in receiving is non-existent. ROI is in the Saturn System.

On arriving at Saturn Base on Titan, nothing is what it seems and the scientists are covering up something. Jeff and Ed soon discover that Roi is an acronym for *Rings of Ice,* which is what the pilot Syeira renamed the shuttle. She was a former lover of Ed when he was stationed and training as a pilot on Titan. Now they wonder if she made it back to Titan and is still alive somewhere.

What they discover is that the crew of the *Rings of Fire* were infected by a kind of virus, ejected from Enceladus in the geysers that periodically erupt, and that this virus turned the crew into crazy unthinking maniacs that killed themselves and caused the ship to crash. The only survivor was Syeira who ejected in an escape pod. It turns out she was immune to the virus, having previously been exposed to it on an expedition to Enceladus. At that time, she was with Ed, and he too is immune, although he doesn't know it yet. She has enclosed herself in an isolated base, and no one at Saturn Base wants to talk about her, and most believe she is dead, having starved to death inside the escape pod.

As the base is closed down Faizah discovers hidden files in their computer system that indicates Syeira is alive and she and Ed go in search of the place where she is isolated. They find her, and the doctor who is working with her to discover a cure. The great fear is that if this virus ever got loose on Mars or Earth it would turn everyone into crazed maniacs who would systematically kill each other.

Now the problem is, if the Saturn base is closed down, who will stay to look after Syeira who is secretly in isolation at a remote science base that everyone thinks has been closed and abandoned years before. Some people decide to stay, while others who are working for the US Government or for IDS (**I**nterplanetary **D**rive **S**ystems) who supply most of the fusion drives and who would go out of business if the Averink Drive was successful) and ASTECH (**A**steroid **T**echnologies), or the Terrorist group sponsored by the US President, try to prevent Ed and Faizah from finding Syeira and whatever research into the virus they had been conducting. The doctor decides to stay because he is close to finding a cure. Most of the others want to leave

This story finishes with a successful return to Mars and the true story behind the loss of the *Rings of Fire* finally known to the whole system.

But this, as exciting as it is with many unexpected twists and turns, is only half of the story. The other half is ***The Silent Siege of Mars*** (2019).

The Silent Siege of Mars opens with the return of the Titan Eleven scientists arriving, coming through Martian Customs and Security, to a cheering welcome from a large crowd filling the terminal. But there is someone in the crowd who is not who he seems. He is particularly interested in the Titan Eleven as they are escorted to a secure location by OSAR officers. This man, known as Ryan, is trying to listen to the conversation between Ed Ferald the *Cydonia Zach* pilot and Peter Lenowitz, head of the Criminal Investigation Branch of Orbital Search and Rescue as they discuss the forthcoming trial of the Titan Eleven for obstructing the investigation of the *Rings of Fire* crash, for lying during the investigation years before, and covering up what they knew. The Martian population consider the eleven to be heroes and the trial results will be a foregone conclusion, with all of them let off.

OSAR is however concerned at the increased threats of terrorism that have been occurring with Earth-Firsters demanding that the Averink Drive not be developed or that it be delayed for 10 years to allow Earth time to recover from climatic devastation of the last few centuries. The Martians and those who inhabit the Asteroid Belt want independence from Earth control and they see the Averink Drive as the means of setting up profitable (for everyone including Earthers) enterprises throughout the solar system, as well as the expansion of colonization. On Earth they fear that the smartest scientists, and businessmen will be lured off-planet.

Once everything has settled down Ed makes another quick round-trip to Titan to bring back Syeira and Dr Latas who has married her and who is searching for an antidote, a vaccine to the virus that sends people crazy and homicidal. A partial vaccine has been developed and both he and Syeira can come out of quarantine. Ed who was with her on Enceladus and who also contracted the benign form of the virus, is immune and because of his romantic relationship with Faizah, she too is immune. So is his uncle Carl, head of 4 O for whom they both work. The virus, called the Maniae Prion, works incredibly fast and can infect people in a few hours and spreads extremely rapidly. It is soon discovered that three vials of this Maniae Prion were smuggled back to Mars from Titan. Two of the vials are on Mars while the third is on Ceres. The rest of the story concerns the search for these three vials of deadly virus, on Mars, Ceres and Phobos, with attempts to release the virus being thwarted by Ed and Faizah, with help from their journalist friend along with OZAR's head of security as well as the captain of the *Ceres Charlene,* whose ship has also been fitted with the Averink Drive. They also team up with an ex-Russian spy called Jósef, whose trade skills match those of Faizah who once worked for MI6.

A quick trip to Ceres to search for the vial takes place and they find this one is a fake with the captain of the *Ceres Charlene* risking his life to save the others searching for the virus. His actions to save them make him a hero.

The two big rival companies on Earth, ASTECH (**A**steroid **T**echnologies) IDS (**I**nterplanetary **D**rive **S**ystems) and 4the Orbit (4- O) from Mars, form a conglomerate to produce the Averink Drive on Mars as well as on the Moon. They don't want to miss a stake in the profits to be made by not getting access to the Averink Drive since their fusion drives are all too slow in comparison. The First-Earthers, backed by the US President, are more determined to hold Mars and the Spacers to ransom by threatening to release the Maniae Prion where it will do the most harm. They don't care if they destroy Mars's population, or Ceres or the Moon's, as long as Earth is safe. But not even Earth is safe from the Maniae Prion if it gets loose there.

The story moves along at breakneck speed while the reader gains an understanding of the complexity of life on Mars and the outer solar system, as well as the dirty politics Earth uses to gain what it wants. There are many minor characters that are vividly brought to life and are integral to the story no matter how small a part they play.

The focus in all three books is on the characters and the parts they play as they interact with each other. There are lighter moments that release the developing tension and these are deftly woven into the action. Background details bring to life the environment and the locales where the action takes place, whether on the Moon, in Space or on Mars, Ceres and Titan, are woven into the story with such skill as to be unobtrusive, but they are there and they establish where the story takes place, making the action and interplay of characters believable.

A superb quartet

The NewCon Press quartet of Martian novellas.
A matching set of novellas with attractive cover art by Jim Burns.
The four titles are: ***The Martian Job*** by Jaine Fenn (2017), ***The Martian Simulacra*** by Eric Brown 2018), ***Phosphorous: A Winterstrike Story*** by Liz Williams (2018), and ***The Greatest Story Ever Told*** by Una McCormack (2018).

None of the stories have any link with each other than being stories set on Mars. *NewCon Press* publishes quality science fiction, fantasy and horror, and in 2010 they won the Best Publisher Award from the European Science Fiction Society. They consistently produce beautiful small books that are a delight to hold and to read.

Starting off the quartet is ***The Martian Job*** by Jaine Fenn, a wild non-stop action story about stealing a valuable artifact from a Martian Corporation's headquarters where security is extreme.

In this future the US doesn't exist, having been wiped out by an AI developed by the US military. The world is run by large corporations and business conglomerates, the biggest of which is the Everlight Corporation, a Chinese company. On Mars, Everlight is the biggest player and basically runs the whole planet. Deimos has been hollowed out and the remnants of the US settlers on Mars live there. When Lizzie, who works for Everlight receives a message from her brother on Mars to tell her if she gets this message, he will be dead. She dismisses it as a joke. But then she gets a long-distance call from her mother who is still in prison on the Moon. Her mother wants her to buy out the rest of her sentence for a crime committed 10 years earlier in which her father was killed. She wants her to do this with the money left by her dead brother. Lizzie used to be a con-artist working with her mother, but for the last 10 years she has been straight while working for Everlight Corporation. She wants nothing to do with her mother or her brother.

Called in to see her boss at work, she is informed that her position is under scrutiny because she never declared on her application forms that she had a criminal history. The history is on her mother's side, but this reflects badly on her in the eyes of the Chinese. Impulsively she asks to take some unpaid leave while her boss and his superiors consider her position. She books a trip to Mars on the cheapest flight so she can find out what happened to her brother.

His death had been reported as an accident. He was outside using a flyer when it crashed and he was killed. Lizzie doesn't accept this for one second as she knows her brother was an experienced flyer. She wants to examine his body, but is told by officials that it had been recycled since no one had claimed it. Approaching his last known associate, Lizzie finds out about the job he was hired to do and wants to talk to the person who hired him.

After doing this she decides to take on the job her brother promised to do, that is to steal a valuable artifact, a giant pearl on display at Everlight's Martian Headquarters. It is displayed in their private museum and is surrounded by incredibly complex computer-generated security measures. She wants to do the job to stick it to Everlight, who she knows will fire her. She wants them to lose face since this artifact is so important to them.

To do the job she will need assistance and she sets out to hire a pilot for their escape, a computer expert who can bypass the various security measures, and another person to help with whatever else needs doing; the same people as were hired by her brother. There is a fourth person with whom she isn't happy about because she only meets her online and can't see her. But this person, presumably on Deimos is essential to her plan. The plan is to enter the secure facility via the air ducts, steal the artifact, escape by using the abandoned tunnels, and fly high up beside Mount Olympus where the escape vehicle can be scooped up from Deimos.

Everything goes according to plan until she gets the artifact at which moment her computer expert turns on her. She has been working with Everlight to prevent just such a theft from occurring. There is a brief fight and Lizzie escapes with the artifact. Joining the other two they use different vehicles and escape using various tunnels to confuse whoever will be following them.

Outside on the surface they get together again at the flyer and take off. There is another flyer in pursuit of them but they manage to avoid it by using the thermals that rise up off Mount Olympus, and gliding high after they ditch their engines. One of the others turns on her as they escape from the pursuing flyer, and in a scuffle, he accidentally shoots the pilot who Lizzie is very fond of. He tries to take control of the flyer but the pilot had locked the controls so no one else could pilot it. One of the shots had penetrated the screen and air is escaping, and the last thing Lizzie remembers as she passes out from lack of oxygen is their craft being grappled and hauled up into orbit to be taken to Deimos.

She wakes up in a hospital room on Deimos to be informed that she had died in the flyer but they had brought her back to life. They are happy to pay her for the artifact and take her to see it. She also discovers that the giant pearl is really an AI. No wonder Everlight did everything it could to prevent her from stealing it. Her immediate concern is that all hell will be unleashed by the AI. But she is reassured that this one is different. It is a Chinese developed AI and as such it has a different set of values built in. It isn't warlike as the US AI was. It is delighted to be free from the constraints put upon it by Everlight Corporation which used it to run their solar system wide businesses. It wants to see the universe.

Lizzie discovers that Deimos wasn't just a hollowed-out habitat; it had been converted into a giant space ship and was leaving Mars' orbit, heading to Proxima. Lizzie is given the option to go with them or to return to Earth. Thinking about it, she realizes there is nowhere in the solar system where she would be safe from Everlight Corporation and she decides to go with them if they transfer her payment to her mother in prison on the Moon so she can buy her way out of the sentence, with the balance to be donated to a charity on the Moon. She won't need money on the voyage to Proxima.

And the story finishes here, having not let up for one moment from start to finish. It is a good old-fashioned kind of pulp story, the kind that fascinated me when I was a young teenage reader more than fifty years ago. But the difference between the stories from now is that they usually have strong female protagonists whereas back in the 1940s through to the 1960s all the protagonists were male. Having a female protagonist adds depth and character to the story, and this makes it so much better.

I love these kinds of stories and this one by Jaine Fenn is a beautiful example.

The Martian Simulacra is a *Sherlock Holmes* story and is set in the year 1907. Ten years after the initial Martian invasion which was of course defeated by bacteria the Martians had no immunity to, there is a second arrival of Martians. They have developed a vaccine that gives them immunity from Earth's bacteria, and this time they come in peace. They claim that the first invasion was launched by a dissident and violent group of Martians that had caused trouble on their home planet but who had now been vanquished, and this 'new invasion' was to develop peaceful relations and trade between the two planets and their peoples.

The Martians have set up a space port in London and their ships are constantly arriving and departing. The trip to Mars only takes one week and to travel there, passengers need to be sedated and encased in a special fluid that takes care of their bodily needs as well as protecting them against the massive acceleration occurring during the voyage to and from Mars.

Sometimes I wonder if this kind of second invasion where the Martians take over the Earth through economic reasons rather than fighting a war, was a trend started by Arkady and Boris Strugatsky who wrote a story called *The Second Invasion from Mars,* translated into English from Russian in 1979. (*See page 46 Dreams of Mars.*) A more recent example is the novel *The Martian Ambassador* by Alan K Baker (2011) set in 1899 where the Martians have an embassy in London to represent their negotiations for trading with Earth. It involves a murder mystery where the detectives are asked to solve a gruesome murder of a Martian official. The description of England during the 1890's is evocative and delightful, exactly like this story set in 1907 which has Sherlock Holmes and his companion Dr. Watson being asked to go to Mars to solve the murder of a famous Martian philosopher.

Holmes is dubious about the reasons for going to Mars, and being the genius that he is has already learnt the Martian language. He cannot find any reference to this famous Philosopher in the Martian Encyclopedia or in any of the translated Martian literature in the public library. However, he is curious and he decides to go with Watson to Mars. Watson in the meantime has met a delightful young lady who supports the protests against trading with Mars. There are three-legged war machines positioned all over the city which in her mind represents a threat. She warns Watson and Holmes about going to Mars. At the spaceport prior to departure they also run into Professor Challenger, who has been invited to Mars to give a lecture regarding his adventures. Holmes also thinks this is odd. Why would the Martians be interested in those kinds of adventures? But Challenger is so excited about the trip he takes no notice of Holmes' suspicions.

Watson is surprised to discover as he is put asleep for the journey that the girl he met is also working as a stewardess on the Martian space ship. She slips something into his jacket pocket.

When he wakes up on arrival at Mars, he finds the message in his pocket is a warning to be careful, and to meet her at a certain place at a specific time in the afternoon. She also warns them to be aware that they will be followed. The Martians are not what they seem.

The Martian ambassador who accompanied them on the trip to Mars tells them he will collect them in the morning and they will undergo a brain scan. Meanwhile, the two travelers go for a roundabout walk on their way to meet the mysterious girl. They soon are aware that they are being followed but there is an altercation and those following are held up. At the meeting place the girl is disguised as a Martian which is almost good enough to fool them. She warns them that the Martians are not what they seem and that they are going to conquer the Earth in a way no one expects. But before she can explain more, she rushes off because the Martians who had been following Holmes and Watson arrive.

Back at their hotel they catch up with Professor Challenger and for some reason Holmes thinks there is something odd about him. He seems too ebullient and keeps talking about how great the Martians are.

In the morning they are picked up by the ambassador who tries to question them about what had happened in the street when they went for their walk, talking about terrorists from the north who want to do nothing but cause trouble. Neither man admits that anything untoward had occurred and the ambassador seems satisfied. At the science centre he takes them through a large museum where the history of Mars and its people are on display. Finally, he takes them to a place where a small space ship is on display and asks them to enter it. Once inside he locks them in and they are gassed into unconsciousness. On waking, they find themselves in a prison cell in a remote desert location. There is no way out. They can do nothing but wait disconsolately to find out what will happen.

After several hours a small flying vehicle lands outside the prison, but no one exits. They wait, and wait, for several more hours before another vehicle lands and out of this vehicle comes the girl who had warned them. She breaks them out of the prison and they fly to a remote location in the north where the other race of Martians, what's left of them, live in a city partially destroyed by the Martians who had invaded the Earth.

The girl explains that the equatorial Martians had destroyed the city of the northern Martians and had invaded Earth. They are invading again but are using a different method. Once they had established diplomatic relations with Earth and were flying regularly back and forth from their spaceport in London, they had invited many of Earths leaders and prominent people to visit Mars as guests. Once there they make brain scans and using the information extracted from the brains of those scanned, they create simulacra which are indistinguishable from the real person. These simulacra are sent back to Earth to replace the persons copied, who are murdered. Watson, Holmes and Challenger are the latest to be invited and copied. Holmes and Watson were locked away in a remote prison as a trap to entice rebels out into the open.

Flying back to the equatorial city Watson and Holmes see copies of themselves about to board the space ship on its return journey to Earth. The girl gives them a special electric gun which will disable the simulacra and as Holmes and Watson try to prevent their simulacra from boarding the ships she is shot and seemingly killed in an altercation with Martian forces. The Martians on the ship don't know that the real Watson and Holmes have not boarded and they return to Earth with the simulacra.

Watson and Holmes are then taken to a location where the northerners have a small ship ready to take them back to Earth. Arriving back on Earth they disguise themselves as chimney sweeps and ring the bell of their residence. Mrs. Hudson answers and is astounded to find that Watson and Holmes are there. She tells them she just saw them enter earlier.

Entering their residence, they carefully approach the drawing room where they discover Holmes and Watson simulacra seated bone still and appearing to be dead. As they approach the simulacra they spring to life and try to kill the originals. Watson manages to fire the electric gun at his copy, rendering it immobile and dead, and then shoots the copy of Holmes which is trying to strangle the great detective. Having killed the simulacra, they can now relax and truly be themselves again. The story finishes here with the suggestion that they will face a stern struggle to unmask the Martians already ensconced in positions of power on the Earth.

There is after that a brief Coda:

Watson is still upset about the girl he liked. Holmes explains that the person he had encountered on the outbound voyage as well as on Mars was actually a simulacrum. The rebels too have access to the same technology as the equatorial Martians. Holmes then brings the girl into their rooms and Watson is ecstatic that she is alive and he regales her with what had happened to them on their trip to Mars.

The reader can presume that this second invasion doesn't go ahead now that Earth is aware of it and that Holmes and Watson will root out the dastardly villains trying to take over the Earth by stealth.

A very enjoyable romp, not to be missed by Mars aficionados.

I found *Phosphorus —A Winterstrike story* by Liz Williams hard to place in context since at this moment I have yet to read the two novels *Banner of Souls,* and *Winterstrike*, from which this story has evolved.

Suffice to say that initially it reads as a simple story of a young girl who is taken on a journey from her home in a city under siege during a continuing war, to a remote Martian city, long abandoned, that seems to have been constructed not by humans but by something else.

The society to which she belongs is all female, and there is the odd mention of 'men remnants' running wild in the deserts, but this comes to nothing in this story. It is there probably to add background and to remind readers of the previous story in those two earlier novels. There is also a mysterious reference to a ghostlike being who influences the young 14-year-old protagonist, who discovers some answers to mysteries suggested in the text as she wanders about the abandoned city and the surrounding desert. There is also an intriguing alien presence, ferocious hunters who travel between the stars and the dimensions searching for prey to hunt. These hunters crashed onto Mars centuries or millennia earlier and remnants of them and their damaged ship still remain.

The young girl, through her dreams, and her curiosity, searches for and discovers the ancient ship, and the story ends abruptly after she has had a transformation (hinted at earlier in her dreams) to become something other than human. The depiction of the hunter insect-like aliens is convincing and their story intersects with the story of the girl although their timelines are millennia apart. I suspect this story would make more sense if I had read the other two novels, which I will do as soon as I can get them. Apart from that, Liz Williams writes evocatively and the story is quite enjoyable.

The Greatest Story Ever Told, by Una McCormack, a best-selling author famous for her TV tie-in novels.

I find it hard to picture this story taking place on Mars as the only clue to its setting is the mention of canals a few times in passing. It seems that it could have taken place at some unknown time in the past in a place like the Gobi Desert or some other such cold desert place. But I am assuming, because of the mention of canals, and not because it is one of the four novellas packaged as **The Martian Quartet**, that we are on an ancient Mars when it did have a breathable atmosphere with water and shallow seas dividing continents and islands.

It is a beautifully delineated story of a slave rebellion against their masters who are determined to slaughter every one of them for the audacity of wanting to be free. There is no mention anywhere of men. Every character is a woman. There are adults, warriors, kitchen hands, general workers, and children, all female, who leave their places of enslavement and embark or a journey to freedom. They are attacked by their masters who want them dead but who are unexpectedly beaten by the slaves, called Hands. The masters assume the Hands are ignorant because they are nothing more than indentured workers, but they make everything the masters use and need. And they can think for themselves which the masters do not believe they can do. Initially this is the masters' undoing. The soldiers they send to kill the rebellious Hands are ambushed and defeated.

The Hands decide to take the fight to the masters and so they trek towards the city occupied by the masters, defeating every force sent to stop them, until they arrive at the city. It is here they change their tactics to wanting to negotiate instead of fight, and this is their undoing. The masters send massive numbers of troops out and also attack them from the air in flying machines called Birds. The rebellious Hands are pushed away and their retreat back south is cut off, forcing them onto a peninsula beyond which is the ocean and scattered distant islands. The story peters out with a few of the children being ferried across to the islands along with the young Hand, Iss, who is the narrator of the story. She survives and 50 years later tells this

The end of the second decade

story. The world is a much different place by that time and she has gained her freedom.

What I found fascinating about this story was each that chapter is sep-arated with a folklore tale told by the young kitchen hand Iss to entertain the others around their campfires. The stories she tells create a fascinating history of the culture and beliefs of the people going back centuries and millennia, so as readers we gain a broader picture of the world and its history that ties in with the action taking place as the Hands trek and fight their way to freedom.

It's an unusual story, but worthwhile taking time to experience it.

All up, the four stories, each very different from the other, are well worth adding to your collection of stories about Mars.

Of these four novellas, only one was written by a man, and even though his main protagonists are Sherlock Holmes and Dr Watson, the female char-acter who interacts with them stands out to the degree that without her, there would not be a story, or it would be a very different and less interesting story.

What is interesting about today's harking back to the pulp era of half a century ago, is that the lead characters are often strong women, and they are generally written by women rather than men. Half a century ago this was almost never the case. The stories were dominated by male protagonists and females hardly received a mention. Even if a story was written by a woman writer, for example Leigh Brackett, who wrote beautiful stories set on Mars, always her featured protagonist was male. That's what was marketable to the general reading public back then and that's what publishers sought.

How things have changed since then!

Today's stories feature women as well as men, and the women are often the better characters with men coming off second best. There is also much more character development and insight into how people think and feel, whereas that never happened in the early pulp stories. They were generally all action and involved solving some kind of technical problem.

The deeper emotional influence female writers bring makes the genre much better. The characters have empathy, and emotions that no character exhibited in the male dominated pulp era. The new stories are not all action; even if action is the primary focus; they have a greater depth of character that captures and makes readers feel more involved with the story than they otherwise would be. This also makes them remember the story for a much longer time.

Male writers today are realizing that females make up half the population and that their choices of stories to read is important. Generally today, more women read books than do men, so now the reverse is happening. Men are writing stories with predominantly female lead protagonists, just as women once wrote stories with predominantly male protagonists (40 or 50 years ago), and these female characters exhibit all the qualities male protagonists once had, but they also have more emotional depth than did those male characters, which gives these newer stories a completely different feel.

Obviously, some writers are more successful with their depiction of female leads than are others, but this depends on the subconscious perspective of readers both male and female. No two people will agree on how successful the writer is.

For those who are wavering might i suggest reading the *Melanie Destin* stories by D. M. Pruden, or the *Denver Moon* stories by Warren Hammond and Joshua Viola. Although these are written by men, their lead characters are strong women, which clearly reflect the changing attitudes towards women and their position in society as equal rather than subservient beings.

On top of that, they are good stories anyway.

Strong female protagonists

Body Suit (2nd edition 2018)
Nebulus (2018) a sequel to ***Body Suit.***
By Suzanne Hagelin.
The author says she is hard at work on a third book due for completion mid-2019, however, there was no sign of this book in 2020 and as of January 2021 it still hadn't made an appearance.

A sub-theme throughout the two books is how artificial intelligence can be affected by who creates it and how it is used, since the AI is dependent on who creates its value system. The author believes a lack of humanity in an AI is a failure of the programmer. She is fascinated by the possibilities of Artificial Intelligence and is pursuing this theme in the proposed third book.

No doubt, robots, human-like or otherwise, will be essential as humans expand into space and set up colonies on Mars. The story opens with Sil, Silvariah Frandelle, a beautiful young business woman, once wealthy, but somehow framed for mismanagement and corruption, forced into bankruptcy, and to avoid spending years in jail, she has agreed to become an indentured miner for a corporation working to extract valuable minerals on Mars. At the fulfillment of her working contract, she will be a free woman free of debt, but the problem is, very few people on Mars ever live long enough to expunge their debts.

She uses what is left of her credit to buy an off-world body suit. These suits are incredibly complex, like space suits, but more than that, they are environment suits, capable of regulating the body chemistry of their wearer, and maintaining an ideal environment within the suit for the wearer.

They are puncture proof, bullet resistant, flexible, able to self-repair, and can be used as hibernating suits if necessary, and the young salesman assures her it is their '*anti assassin*' model, the most expensive one on the market. They can also change their appearance so to an observer she could appear to be wearing something other than the suit. It's just what Sil needs when she is on Mars.

She can't afford it, but she convinces Walter, the salesman, to do a deal with her becoming a representative of the company who could be testing the suit under extreme conditions. She also promises to send Walter market tips which will enable him to buy stocks that could increase in value to eventually make him wealthy. He agrees, and she leaves with the most expensive and complex suit.

The suit also contains an AI to maintain its functionality. But what Sil doesn't realize is that she is part of a greater experiment in cloning and development of special humans, as well as intrusive AIs that spy on her every move and try to affect her decisions and actions. There is something secret going on in the Mars colonies apart from the mining activities of which she is an indentured laborer.

As time goes on her interactions with the intrusive AI called *Companion* —it not only monitors her and tries to affect her actions, it also helps run the entire Mars colony and interacts with many other people — changes the way *Companion* thinks, and gradually it becomes more human-like and less programmed and robotic, until it actually becomes an independent thinking being, who decides to help Sil rather than to hinder her. It also helps everyone else when a disaster strikes the colony and many are killed.

There is a lot going on and Sil eventually discovers her father is behind most of her problems and is the direct cause of why she is on Mars. One of the secret projects he is running on Mars is the development of a new breed of humans, grown artificially.

One of the people who went to Mars with Sil is in charge of this project and when most of the workers opt to return to Earth she stays to look after these babies. When the station's working robots are ordered to kill the babies Sil manages to rescue one and hiding her in her body suit which adjusts to accommodate the baby, she manages to get off the planet and into orbit where she encounters the nasty programmer who had originally programmed *Companion* and used it to spy on her. He has built another version of Companion and this AI reflects the nasty nature of its programmer.

When they try to kill the baby Sil has, she escapes in a pod and heads back to Earth, where she encounters Walter, who is now very wealthy and who can't wait to help Sil. He has fallen in love with her. Together they evade the machinations of her father who is trying to claim the baby as his property, and who is trying to do everything he can to make life miserable for Sil.

The descriptions, and imagery of Mars, and its environment, and the difficulties entailed in working there, both in an enclosed habitat as well as outside, are convincing enough to be believable and in many ways affect how Sil and the other characters react and do things.

Nebulus, the second book, follows Sil on Earth as she fights her father's lawsuits and attempts to capture or hinder her. He wants possession of her and of the baby girl she brought with her from Mars. He claims they are his property. He delights in disrupting her life and that of Walter who she has now married. They fight him to get the baby girl recognized by Earth authorities as a human being and not something produced in a lab which would be property.

During these activities, we get to see how different Earth is in the near future and how difficult life is for those without money or means to provide a suitable life.

It also inter-cuts with the people left on Mars in the damaged habitat where *Companion* is struggling to help them to survive, but he has been damaged and can't find much of his memories. He has hidden copies in different places but it is difficult to get these together to make him whole again.

Sil is unaware that many of her friends survived the disaster on Mars that destroyed the main habitat and their greenhouse. Her main concern is protecting the baby and herself from her nasty father.

That they succeed in the end is expected, but the author keeps the reader on tenterhooks while the story progresses in unexpected directions, which makes it hard to put the book down.

It is as good as the first book.

The Denser Plain (2021) concludes what is now called ***The Sylvarian trilogy***.

Eight years after the events on Mars and later on earth where Sil foiled attempts by her father to get guardianship (i.e. control or ownership of Scarlett) he resorts to other means. As the story opens they are on the run from hunters hired by her father to kidnap Scarlett, whom he considers to be his property. Hiding in South America, when a kidnap attempt almost succeeds, they decide to head to Guam, an orbiting city where they will stay before heading to the Moon, where Penn (Sil's father) has a hidden base, to confront him and solve their differences forever.

While slow going at the start, I did enjoy the interaction between the AI humanoid beings and other less sentient robots and androids. The author has carefully thought how these artificial beings could relate to humans in general as a well as to the humans who programmed and educated them. Her belief is that any AI being created will reflect the prejudices and concepts regarding right and wrong, good and bad, that exist within the programmer, and so will be an important part in the consciousness they are creating once it has evolved into sentience, demonstrated with the various AI beings the family encounters in Guam and on the Moon.

The scenes on the Moon are full of action and are a fascination picture of how the Moon could be developed. The way Sil, Walter, Scarlett and a couple of AIs are evolving is engrossing. The action scenes are convincing, and in my mind – cinematic.

There is not much reference to Mars except in passing with their personal AI, Daisey who decides to go to Mars in search of a missing AI partly damaged during the events that took place on Mars. There is a small group of adults and children surviving there of whom we get glimpses throughout the latter part of the book until finally they become important at the end.

What ultimately disappointed me was the character of Penn, Sil's megalomaniac father and his efforts to control her, and her family. He has been reduced to an overblown caricature who is simply unbelievable.

The insertion of weird aliens that inhabit a multi-dimensional realm where a tear in the fabric of the universe threatening to upset time and reality, which they are fighting to repair, and anchor, is uninteresting and distracting, and I suspect only inserted as a means of getting Scarlett to Mars after she was eventually kidnapped.

The story would be as good if not better without those few segments added in, although the author would have needed a more prosaic means of getting Scarlett to Mars near the end of the story. Whatever the aliens are doing seems to have little relevance (or clarity) regarding the events occurring throughout the story, and my tendency initially was to skip those early chapters entirely so as not to lose the flow of the main story, but then I thought they must be there for a reason, and read them, only to discover later I might as well have skipped them anyway. The place they come from has given the title to the book which itself seems to have no relevance to the two previous titles.

I think the first two books made a fantastic story, and the final book for me adds nothing to the overall story arc, apart from tying up a few speculative ends while expanding on human AI interaction. There are a few mentions about Mars to link it to the other books, and a few scenes on Mars with those who survived the events earlier told as well as a the final scenes, with an epilogue to explain what happened after the story ends.

The Music of Mars by George G Moore (2018)

There are several lead protagonists but the most important one is Gretchen Blake, an archaeologist black-banned from working because she disagreed with her boss on an archaeological dig. She also is recovering from the shock of her husband terminating their marriage contract.

The Earth in the future (in this story) is a different place than we know today. Europe consists of a collective of socialist republics, while America is a dystopian state where individual lives are controlled completely by government or by big business corporations. If Gretchen can't find work, she will lose her apartment and be transferred to the grubby barely inhabitable apartments available to the poor. She accepts a job that will take her to Mars for a short time; to decipher a collection of symbols found on a sealed door in a cave.

Her Martian employer, MarsVantage has discovered a remote cave in which there is a door sealing off a hidden area. Inside through scanning they see thousands of stalagmites and stalactites of a new mineral that when wet with water releases enormous amounts of electricity. They only have a few fragments and with what they think is in the sealed cave they would be able to generate more than enough power to become self-sufficient, and be able to export the mineral to Earth at a profit.

Interplanetary, a huge company had once established itself on Mars but due to a serious accident involving an airlock, in which several people were killed, the company split up and MarsVantage took over activities on Mars. The boss of Interplanetary has never forgotten the embarrassment of the airlock disaster and is determined to regain control of MarsVantage by instigating sabotage and other activities to try an make it appear incompetent so the board will eventually agree to a buyout, enabling Interplanetary to regain complete control. They have spies inside MarsVantage and they are tasked with finding out what is going on, what secrets are being hidden, and especially why MarsVantage would hire an archaeologist.

There are some employees who long to return to Earth and these people have been approached by Interplanetary infiltrators to act as sources of information. Frank Brentford, who employed Gretchen, along with his boss Chuck are the only two who know about the door in the cave, and they don't want anyone to find out in case information is passed on to Interplanetary. They have applied for the mineral rights to whatever is in the cave, and this too is a secret because if Interplanetary found out they would claim it as theirs since they were the first to establish the colony on Mars. While Gretchen is being familiarized with life on Mars Frank and Chuck are also involved in trying to find the spies within their midst.

Up to this point the story is slow going and the characters are not outstanding. They only come alive once Gretchen is taken to the cave and her work to decipher the symbols by the sealed door begins. Interplanetary's attempts to find out what is going on also ramp up and there is sabotage, an attempt on the lives of Gretchen and Frank, and both of these, who initially were frosty towards each other, begin to warm up as Gretchen proves herself to be more resourceful than expected for someone newly arrived from Earth.

The interesting thing is no character talks about aliens or ancient Martians while to the reader it is obvious that the door and the symbols etched into it are alien. No one other than Chuck, Frank and Gretchen even know they exist. They don't want MarsVantage to be seen as a bunch of crackpots. They especially don't want Interplanetary's spies to find out about it and report back to their company CEO. Everyone on Earth thinks those who believe in aliens are either crackpots or part of a conspiracy. Of course, Gretchen knows the symbols are alien and is excited to begin work deciphering them. Finding alien technology would be a highlight of her career, and so far, studying images of the symbols has led to no clues whatsoever. They don't relate to anything earthly at all.

After a day's delay to confuse any Interplanetary spies who might be waiting to follow them, they finally depart for the secret cave. But one guy knows where they are going and has headed out ahead of them. He sets up a camp on the opposite side of the valley where the cave is so they won't see him and waits for them to arrive. His instructions are to get whatever they find in the cave and if necessary, to kill them so they won't talk.

Frank has brought along spare oxygen vests and also a portable airlock which they use to seal the entrance of the cave so they can work inside without having to wear spacesuits. They also set up sleeping gear inside. After two days of fruitless work Gretchen because she plays guitar and reads music finally thinks the symbols that are circular set on lines represent musical tones. She begins experimenting with the notes the symbols represent played back in different scales. No results. She decides that perhaps she is playing the tones too slow or perhaps too fast, so she begins repeating the sequences again at various speeds. At the fastest speed her computer is capable of producing, there is a corresponding sound from the door, and it slides up and open.

Inside the cave they discover hundreds of rows of what seem to be stalagmites and stalactites, but they are not natural, being arranged in sets, and conclude that the cave is a super battery. All it needs is water to be running through it. What does the battery power? That is what Gretchen wants to know.

At this point, since we now know the cave is of alien construction, and the reader meets the caretaker, an electronic being that resides in the central control room of an ancient, buried city. The caretaker's job is to preserve the city and the knowledge it contains for the eventual return of its inhabitants. It makes repairs when something breaks down, by downloading itself into a massive robot so it can physically fix things. The caretaker leaves a message for the visitors to its defunct battery. There are other batteries still function- ing elsewhere which it uses to maintain the city. Those who created it came from another star system when their star died, and Mars was one of several planets in various star systems that it 'terraformed' to enable its people to survive. It wasn't successful even though they tried for millennia, and as the planet began dying again, they set of in search of another star with planets promising to return after 1000 orbits. It has been more than 200,000 orbits and they are still absent. The caretaker is lonely and wants to go in search of its people, but it can't manufacture an interstellar ship because it manufac- turing plant has been damaged. Seeing that the two beings had entered the defunct battery the caretaker leaves a holographic message for them.

Gretchen finds the message and has trouble downloading it because it is a huge file, a video running at super high speed with words under the images.

Exiting the cave through their portable airlock they are about to head back to the settlement when they discover their rover (tractor) had been sab- otaged. All the computer controls had been fused and burnt-out. Gretchen makes a fake call for help, knowing that the saboteur would hear it. Frank calls a friend on a private radio frequency and asks that she pilot a ship to recuse them. She wants to come immediately, but he tells her to wait until morning. As far as they are aware the saboteur doesn't know that they have extra oxygen vests inside the cave and could stay there for several days. The saboteur thinks they will run out of breathable oxygen after another 8 or 9 hours. They retreat back into the cave and wait for the saboteur. He will want whatever they found and will also want to make sure they are both dead, so it can be reported as an accident. Just as the night is almost over the saboteur enters the cave through the airlock and is captured by Gretchen and Frank. He will be sent back to Earth for trial for attempted murder. He is someone they all know, an employee of Interplanetary. But Frank knows there are others, and they still have to be wary.

On the trip out to the cave Frank explained to Gretchen that originally an expedition from Socialist Germany had set up on Mars and when a sec- ond expedition arrived with additional supplies, they couldn't find anyone there. Everyone was missing as well as one of their rovers. That was 50 years before Interplanetary arrived on Mars. No one goes near the abandoned dome because they think it is haunted.

When Gretchen finally deciphers part of the message it explains where the city is and that the caretaker will be waiting for them. Gretchen creates a reply with images and English words, takes it back to the cave and plays it using an endless loop, in the hope that the caretaker will see it and understand. Frank and Gretchen find when they go to the location indicated, nothing but an endless expanse of desert. The city has been buried under sand. But an opening had been excavated and the caretaker robot is waiting for them. And of course, by this time the caretaker has learnt the English words Gretchen put in her message and it very quickly leans to speak more English as they converse. It takes them into the city and explains what it needs. It shows them the damaged manufacturing plant and they discover what happened to the German expedition. The rover crashed through the dome protecting the city and fell into the manufacturing plant damaging it. The people in the rover were all killed. The caretaker thought the city was under attack and when the other members of the German team came to rescue their compatriots the caretaker killed them to protect the city. But now it needs their help.

It wants them to repair the manufacturing unit so it can construct a spaceship in which it will go in search of its lost people. Frank offers the caretaker a deal in which they give him an old spaceship to convert, if in turn they can have some of the technology in the city. The caretaker agrees.

A full-scale expedition is sent to the city, and one of the members is also an undercover worker for Interplanetary. The boss back on Earth wants to know what MarsVantage has found and wants it for himself. He doesn't care what must be done to get it. His plan backfires and he is caught in the act by Frank and Gretchen. Finally, MarsVantage comes out on top with the possibility of an expanding colony, and a future fortune to be made from using the advanced technology in the city.

The agreement with the caretaker was that Frank and Gretchen would become the new caretakers of the city, its technology and cultural archives in exchange for the old spaceship they gave it. It took several months but it installed an interstellar drive in the old ship and the story ends as Frank and Gretchen (now the head of the archeology department on Mars) watch the ship depart for the stars through wormhole it creates as it takes off.

Although predictable, (that human explorers will find evidence of a prior extinct civilization or evidence of an alien technology or civilization on Mars — possibly far more common than new writers think) it is still an entertaining story once you get past the first several slow-moving chapters.

Something More traditional

Peter Cawdron rarely writes a sequel to a novel already written since each of his novels stands alone, usually with the underlying theme of '*First Contact*' with an alien intelligence, or something alien whether intelligent or not, and how humans deal with it. They are some of the best first contact stories you will find.

However **Reentry** is a sequel to his novel **Mars Endeavour** (2016) later retitled **Retrograde** and published in a superb hardcover edition. (*This book is discussed in* **Dreams of Mars** *page 311.*)

Reentry by Peter Cawdron (2019)

This is a tense, nail-biting novel that has Liz Anderson returning to Earth, not as a hero but as a suspect because she brings with her on several hard drives, the remnants of the AI she defeated on Mars.

The war started by the AIs on Earth which initially decided to eliminate humanity from the planet is over. A stalemate has been reached, or is it simply a pause in hostilities?

Liz is confined and a mysterious helper is on her side, not to mention the AIs that remain hidden and part of every computer and electronic network on the planet. Are they trying to help her? Are there other humans who realize that the war stopped because the AIs decided they didn't want it to continue, but could if they choose totally destroy humanity at any time?

Liz is interrogated by Congress which believes she is collaborating with the AI entities but can't prove it. Protesting groups want to eliminate her believing she is responsible for the war with the AIs that has decimated the planet. There are confrontations between the rebels and the army, the AIs help Liz to escape and resurrect her dead lover whose mind they uploaded on Mars. They find a suitable body on Earth and download his electronic consciousness into it.

Is it her lover or something else entirely?

The evolution of Artificial Intelligence, and more than one of them, is a good part of the background of this story. The realization that almost everything on this planet is linked electronically, and the possibility of Artificial Intelligence evolving is logical and frightening. The author suggests that for all to survive, there needs to be communication and understanding between the two disparate intelligences. The story concludes with an incredible chase sequence that is extremely cinematic, with the two protagonists, Liz, and her revived lover, Jianyu, making it to a launch facility in French Guiana and eventually returning to Mars.

I suspect that there could be another novel exploring the theme of mutual cooperation between Humans and AI entities that will play out on Mars after Liz and Jianyu have returned to the struggling colony.

If that is the case, I look forward to it enthusiastically. Peter Cawdron is a writer to watch and respect, but I suspect this will not happen as there are many other aspects of 'First Contact' that he wants to explore.

However, both these books, **Retrograde** (**Mars Endevour**) and **Reentry** make up one long story dealing with the first real contact with human developed **Artificial Intelligence**. (*And both are available in hardcover editions.*) The ultimate consequences for humans do not appear to be good, but this is left for readers to speculate about.

Losing Mars (2018)
Peter Cawdron

This is quite different from his earlier Mars novel, **Mars Endeavour** – later retitled **Retrograde** (2016) in which a multinational colony had to deal with a nuclear war destroying Earth as well as their own political and cultural allegiances until they finally come to grips with their real enemy, the computers that control their entire environment and thus their survival on Mars.

In this story the colony established on the surface is small, consisting of three couples, two husband and wife couples and one lesbian couple. They are all American, not multinational. In the background there is a hint of rivalry with the Chinese having a four-man mission exploring the moon Phobos. They know they are there but there is no contact between them.

The story opens with one husband and wife team exploring the edge of a massive canyon system when an accident occurs. The man slips on frozen regolith and falls over the edge where he is partially buried in falling rocks on the first of a series of ledges that extend far down into the canyon.

He is alive, but not conscious, and there is the possibility that his suit may be compromised. This can be monitored from the base. His partner is incapable of rescuing him and calls for help. The only other person ready for the long, involved process of preparing to go outside, is the other male member of the expedition. He is already suited up for exterior work because he was working in their greenhouse. The remaining marsnauts in the base don't want the only other man to go out and attempt a rescue but time is of the essence. He takes a rover and heads out to the canyon where the accident occurred while his wife, the expedition's doctor, and the other two women are monitoring all activities from the base control centre.

At the canyon's edge he winches down to the ledge where the victim lies partially buried. He begins to clear away the rubble burying the injured marsnaut but he can't be seen from the rim of the canyon by the man's frantic partner. The other three back in the base dispatch a large remote-controlled balloon type vehicle from which they can oversee what's happening on the ledge. It floats over the canyon. As the two are about to be winched back up by the injured man's partner, they slip on the frozen regolith and slide off the edge and drop down towards the next of a series of ledges that extend kilometres down to the bottom of the canyon. Dangling precariously, they can't be hauled back up because they are stuck beneath an overhanging ledge. The person above can't see this and continues to try and winch them back up. This will damage the protective suit, so the rescuer cuts the winch cable and both of them drop down to the next lower ledge. The only course of action left is for them to jump onto the balloon vehicle if the women back at the base can remotely control it with enough precision to get right to the canyon wall so the barely conscious injured man and his rescuer can somehow jump onto it and hold on.

The tension is ratcheted up and the reader is breathless while the two dangling men somehow manage to climb on board the floating vehicle, which them immediately flies back to the base, a trip of ten minutes as against the 30-minute drive back in the rovers.

While this rescue attempt in underway, something disastrous happens to the Chinese taikonauts exploring Phobos. Two of them are killed and the other two remain alive but unconscious. Their condition is being monitored back on Earth by the Chinese, who reluctantly notify NASA that there was an accident. NASA notifies the marsnauts but tells them there is nothing they can do.

At this point we are a third of the way through the book, and the tension is beginning to mount.

Feeling helpless the six marsnauts suspect NASA and the Chinese are holding back crucial information. They would also like to attempt a rescue but to do that there are problems. Their lander has only enough fuel to get into orbit where it would rendezvous with their return vehicle orbiting Mars. It only has space for six. To rescue the Chinese taikonauts orbiting Phobos means at least two of them would have to stay behind on Mars. Once in orbit the lander would be unable to land back on Mars and would have to rendezvous with the return vehicle in orbit and they would then have to return to Earth. Those left on Mars would have to wait, stranded until another expedition is sent from Earth before they could come home. Half of the Marsnauts want to make a rescue attempt while the other half don't.

The longer they wait the less likely it will be for the taikonauts to survive.

As more information is relayed from the Chinese via NASA the marsnauts finally come to a decision. Two of them, the husband of the medical officer who is a pilot, and the wife of the lesbian couple who is a doctor, will try to rescue the Chinese while the other four will remain on Mars.

In orbit they rendezvous with their return vehicle and use it to maneuver into close proximity to the Chinese ship. While the pilot remains in the ship the doctor spacewalks across to the Chinese ship. The airlock is open so there is no atmosphere inside. Entering the ship, the doctor sees something very strange which the taikonauts must have brought up from Phobos. It glitters and has a weird effect on her mind. Although the heartbeats of the two surviving taikonauts are still being registered on monitors, they are not in the ship. The doctor seems to be in a trance, hallucinating, and doesn't come back out. The pilot repositions the ship and spacewalks across to get his partner out of the Chinese ship. He too is affected by whatever is in the Chinese ship.

All their movements are being watched, listened to and monitored from the Mars base, and also by NASA and the Chinese back on Earth, but there is no help they can give because any communication takes forty minutes either way so is relatively useless. The astronauts are on their own.

After some very strange events that take place in the past as well as the future the pilot manages to extricate himself from the Chinese ship. The intensity increases as the pilot almost gets himself lost in space but manages to recover and finally gets his partner out from the Chinese ship. They decide they need to take a closer look at Phobos and make an attempt at a close flyby which becomes ineffective and the ship soft crashes into the Stickney crater. It is here that everything unwinds. They hallucinate, remember false memories, discover the moon is partly hollow and there are some very alien constructs inside. The pilot realizes that something is trying to communicate with them, but it makes no sense to them at all.

Eventually, the marsnauts manage to escape the weirdness of Phobos and get their ship off the surface of the moon. They return to Earth knowing that both NASA and the Chinese are already covering up their discovery. They do not want the world to know what was discovered on Phobos. They will of course secretly send more missions to the moon in the future, but that will be another story. (*Perhaps?*) This one finishes a few years later with all the original marsnauts back on Earth.

It is also a 'First Contact' story, unrelated to his other two Mars stories.

The science in the story regarding Mars and what it would be like exploring the surface, the possible dangers, the beauty of the strange landscapes that seem so familiar but are truly dangerous, the orbital mechanics and other information in the background all are, I think, scientifically accurate. At least it rings true. The depth of the characters is also well delineated, and overall this makes the story much deeper than simply an action adventure with the familiar trope of discovering ancient alien structures on, not Mars this time, but on Mars' moon Phobos.

Peter Cawdron is certainly an author to watch.

Hard hitting and violent

No Way by S J Morden (2019)

No Way is a sequel to *One Way* (*see* **Dreams of Mars** *page 329*) and continues exactly from the point where this first book finishes.

If anything, it is more tense and nail-biting than *One Way*.

In the first book the team of 8 astronauts which consisted of 7 prisoners serving life sentences, who were trained in the various construction trades needed to build a permanent base, and one supervisor Brack, who kept them in line. The company, XO Enterprises, took a contract from NASA to build a base in anticipation of a NASA team being sent to Mars.

They were supposed to build the base using robots, but the dust destroyed that possibility, so they opted to send 7 prisoners who in their view were disposable. They didn't have to pay them anything other than keep them alive while the base was built. A lot of money was made because they never told NASA what they were doing. None of the original prisoner astronauts expected to go home, but they were told they could live their sentence out on Mars while they maintained the base.

Brack, the supervisor, was an ex-special forces mercenary soldier and his job was to eliminate the prisoners once their work was completed, making their deaths look accidental. He was supposed to clean up after each was dead to leave no trace. But although Mars was a harsh place, there seemed to be too many accidents, making everyone suspicious of everyone else, and because it was Frank (the viewpoint character) who discovered the bodies, the other prisoner astronauts suspected he was killing them off.

The bodies were stored in the return capsule that Brack lived in while the base was being constructed. He never stayed in the base as the others did. The plan was that once this was done the ship would take off and XO would remotely control it, altering its orbit so it would fall into the sun, destroying all evidence. As far as NASA was concerned, the base they would occupy had been built by robots. Brack was to stay on Mars and meet the NASA astronauts and return to Earth with them once their mission was complete. The final confrontation at the end of the book has Frank being shot by Brack after a fight between the last two astronauts alive. But Frank isn't killed. He survives and manages to kill Brack instead. He is the last one left alive.

No Way begins with Frank disposing of the bodies of his co-worker and of Brack. He takes them back to the return ship and stores them. He contacts XO and tells them he will expose them if they don't allow him to return with the NASA team due to arrive in a few months. XO tells him to clean up the mess to make it appear nothing had happened, and when the astronauts who are on their way arrive, tell them the robots that supposedly built the base were sent back in a remote-controlled ship for evaluation. Frank has to pretend to be Brack.

Meanwhile Frank is out scavenging supplies XO sent that landed scattered across a wide area. They tell him that they are additional supplies for the base. At a very remote location, at the edge of the distance he can safely go before having to turn back or run out of oxygen, he discovers someone else in a rover and wearing the same kind of XO space suit is also looking for supplies. Stunned, he confronts the man and finds out he is from another base on the other side of the volcano from where the first base is established. This second base (also XO funded) is in trouble. Their ship was damaged on landing, and their communications were destroyed. They can't contact XO nor can the use radio beacons to find their supplies, some of which Frank has already scavenged thinking they were for Mars Base One. The guys in the second base are starving.

Back at his base, XO tells Frank not to mention the second base to the NASA astronauts when they arrive, or they won't let him come home. The second base was meant to be a secret, funded by the money NASA paid XO for establishing a robot built base. They won't tell him why the other base was built.

When the NASA team arrives, Frank finds it hard to integrate into the team and tends to keep away from them as much as possible. They begin a series of experiments and one of them is to set up seismic stations in a line extending up the nearby volcano. They also build a small staging base on the volcano to stay overnight so they don't always have to return to the main base every time they go there. The summit of the volcano is at the limit of the distance they can travel before having to return so they won't run out of oxygen. But the summit of the volcano is also within range of the other second base that only Frank knows about.

Not long after setting up the seismic stations one of them goes offline and Frank heads out to see what the problem is. He can't find the station. It isn't there, and he knows the guys from the second base had scavenged it for spare parts. They want to build a radio so they can contact XO back on Earth. The other astronauts think perhaps the seismic station disappeared into a sink hole above an old lava tube, but Frank knows better. He doesn't say anything though.

Frank and three other astronauts are up on the base when a sandstorm begins to make doing anything difficult. Frank and his partner return to the base, but the two others don't come back. Only one does, and she says that her partner wandered off to look at something and disappeared. She suspects he may have fallen off the edge of a cliff and they all go in search for him. They find no trace of him and reluctantly have to call off the search when they start to run out of oxygen. No one will admit defeat but they must return to the main base.

Once back there, Frank sneaks out again and takes a rover. He wants to see what is going on at the hidden XO base on the other side of the volcano as he suspects their team mate may have encountered one of the other secret team members and was taken prisoner.

Driving all night, he arrives on the other side of the volcano just before dawn. He sees the damaged return ship partially tipped over and slowly drives towards it. He sees the inflatable base under an overhang so it is hidden from satellite cameras. As he gets out of his rover to walk over to the damaged ship someone comes out of the base. He thinks it is his missing team member but when he gets close it turns out to be the scruffy astronaut he had encountered out on the plain scavenging supplies. Touching helmets together so they can talk, (The radios don't work) he asks where the other man is and the scruffy one tells him nothing. He hits Frank on the helmet with a large wrench and Frank staggers back. He manages to grab the space suit and rips off the name badge while they scuffle. He also breaks the other person's ankle causing him to collapse which enables Frank to get away. Suddenly other guys in suits come rushing out of the base and Frank retreats to his rover and takes off. The other astronauts follow him in two small rovers. They catch up and Frank manages to ram one of the rovers, tipping it over. He escapes when the second rover stops to help the fallen one.

Back at the base one Frank comes clean and tells the astronauts who he really is, what Brack had done for XO, that there is another base on the other side of the volcano and that their associate is a prisoner. He shows them the name badge he ripped off during the scuffle. They don't believe his story.

After contacting XO to relay their message to NASA, XO informs them that Brack is a homicidal maniac who thinks he is Frank Kittridge. They should be very wary of him. Frank can't prove his story since all the evidence has been sent into space and left to fall into the sun. He tells them there is one piece of evidence, the gun Brack brought with him to Mars; Frank had buried it outside under a small cairn of stones. They retrieve it, but they still are unsure Frank is telling the truth. They lock him in the medical bay while they decide what to do. Before they can come to a decision the base is attacked by a group of desperate men from the secret base. They grab one of the girls outside and storm into the base hoping to kill everyone. Frank kills one in the medical bay and takes another prisoner. He foils their action in the main part of the base and they escape in their rovers.

Questioning the prisoner, the NASA team finds out the rogue team from the secret base had been starving to death and they have eaten the man they took prisoner.

Finally, they believe Frank's story. They set off to rescue their other comrade recently taken prisoner. And their object is to destroy the other base entirely. They do this in a tense confrontation where they blow a projectile through the wall of the hidden base deflating it. They race in with a spare space suit for their comrade only to find she isn't in there. She is in the ship with the leader of the group. Heading back out to the damaged ship they hook up their rovers with a cable to the leg of the space ship and try to topple it over.

When this doesn't work Frank rams the legs of the ship with his rover enough times to topple it. As the airlock bursts open and the air gushes out, they rush in to grab their companion and fit her into a space suit before she freezes and her blood starts to boil. The leader of the group is wearing a space suit and he attacks Frank with a heavy hammer. Frank manages to shield himself but his arm gets shattered in the process. He is knocked to the ground and the rogue astronaut is about to smash in his faceplate when the NASA leader shoots the pistol that Brack had brought to Mars, blowing a hole in the faceplate of the attacking astronaut killing him instantly.

On their way back to their base they come within 500 metres when all the telemetry of their space suits cuts out. If they can't reset them, they will suffocate within a few minutes. The rover stalls. Frank understands that a kill switch had been set by XO remotely to trigger the cut off whenever anyone came within a certain distance. The same kill switch also floods the base with carbon dioxide in case anyone is inside without a space suit on. They don't want anyone alive to testify about what happened on Mars. But Frank is a survivor, and he manages to get into the base and resets the computer so the kill switch is deactivated.

Their problem now is how to contact NASA and the authorities when all their radio goes through XO Mission control. It takes them a few days but they manage to build a radio that can use the deep space system NASA has for monitoring distant satellites and probes, so they tell their story. But XO people vanish. Their control centre is deserted with everything useful destroyed. A few minor people give evidence to the authorities about what XO was doing, so the whole world knows what has happened. NASA wants to bring back its people, but they won't go unless Frank can come with them.

Frank is reluctant because he will end up back in Jail where he was to begin with, while a couple of the others also want to stay so they can continue their experiments and research on Mars. They know if they go back, cutting the mission short, they will never return again.

The decision is ultimately up to Frank. They won't go back without him, but if he wants to stay, they will stay as well.

Frank decides to stay.

The story ends here. Finally, the reader can take a deep breath and relax. This would have to be one of the most 'edge-of-your-seat' thrillers set on Mars in recent years. The tension, the violence and the action doesn't let up for a moment, but constantly builds right to the end.

While the story is satisfactorily finished (*across the two books which make one long story*) it is still open enough to allow for a possible continuation.

I for one would be happy to see another story showing us what happens to Frank and those on Mars as the base becomes an established habitat and more people arrive, but this may never happen...

Cycler ships, an idea from 1985 by Buzz Aldrin

The Last Dance by Martin L. Shoemaker (2019)

An odd title for a book about travelling to Mars, but it hides layers of meaning which become clear as the story concludes, at which point it seems apt.

Portions of this novel have appeared in *Analog Science Fiction and Fact* as far back as 2012, but as a novel it doesn't read like a fix-up novel, it is complete and engrossing although not structured in a linear way.

The *Aldrin Express* is a cycler ship, travelling in a permanent orbit between Earth and Mars, using gravity slingshots around each planet to redirect it on its way. It requires minimal thrust for minor course corrections to maintain this orbit and can thus be quite a large ship. The idea of cycler ships to transport people and goods between Earth and Mars was first suggested in 1985 by Buzz Aldrin (the second man to walk on the Moon) as an economical way to establish and maintain a colony on Mars. All that is needed is a shuttle or space taxi to lift up goods and people from earth, to match orbits with the cycler and to transfer them to the larger ship. When it reaches Mars, a similar craft transfers those same goods and people down to the surface of the planet. The reverse process occurs when people and goods are sent up from Mars for the return trip to earth. The idea of the cycler ships is to enable commerce and travel to occur at a reasonable cost making it possible for private investors to make money, which is not something government projects can do.

The *Aldrin Express* is a very large ship, and one that gets new additions that are built in space near the Moon which are then ferried out to meet the cycler as it passes. The new additions are attached and during the months out to Mars, finished and made habitable by the crew of the *Aldrin*. The crew are fanatically loyal to their captain, and although most would say they hate or dislike him intensely, they trust him implicitly. He often pushes them beyond their limits, some to their breaking points, but they won't hear a bad word about him, and because they trust him, he also trusts them.

On this current voyage two new large habitable rings were attached to the ship. They came with another crew who were members of the Space professionals (which is part of the System Initiative – a conglomerate made up of the space agencies of various nations) and who simply didn't have the experience for this kind of construction. The *Aldrin's* crew had to fix the problems this crew made which generated friction between the ship's crew and the Space Professionals' crew who were led by an old rival of the captain. Then on the return from Mars, another two rings were added, the first to be manufactured in Mars orbit. The crew worked flat-out to make these two additions habitable, and when the ship finally arrived back to slingshot around Earth the Captain Nick Aames, his second in command, Anson Carver, and his entire crew are charged with mutiny because the captain refuses to add another two rings to the ship knowing it would be impossible for them to do the additional construction work. The crew stand behind him. Because Captain Aames also refuses to let another Space Professionals crew come aboard for the construction, The System Initiative wants to stop them and is willing to destroy the ship. But there is more going on behind the scenes. The *Aldrin* is a privately owned ship, and there are rivals who have now constructed faster cycler ships that want to take the bulk of the trade and the profits, and they have corrupted the System Initiative. The owner of these new faster ships wants the captain court martialed and the crew returned to Earth. They refuse to leave the ship. They believe the Captain was right to refuse the orders given.

When it becomes clear that their ship could be destroyed Captain Aames capitulates. An inspector from the Inspector General's Office, who has plenary powers to decide on the matter is sent on board to investigate and decide what to do with the captain.

The story opens with Inspector General Park Yerim and her assistant coming on board, and they are not particularly welcome. Her job is to find out what happened and whether the captain and the crew should be charged with mutiny for disobeying orders. Captain Aames has locked himself in his quarters and Yerim occupies his office. She invites various crew members in to talk about the Captain and what happened but they refuse at first. She convinces them to tell their stories and in various first-person narratives we begin to understand the relationship between the Captain and the crew and the reasons why they trust him so much and will stand with him no matter what. We also find out why there is so much animosity between the Captain and certain people in the Space Professionals which goes back to a failed earlier Mars Mission where Captain Aames was in charge. He saved the mission but couldn't prevent some deaths and injuries, so it was considered a disaster. He was taken out of active service and worked a desk for the Space Initiative for some years before accepting the Captain's position on the newly constructed *Aldrin Express*.

With the various personal narratives jumping back into the past at different moments where that particular person's life interacts with the Captain, the reader begins to form a picture of the complex character that is Captain Nickolau Aames, and how being a perfectionist caused friction with his colleagues but also helped him build a loyal crew. Yerim is put under pressure from the Space Initiative to find in their favor. She is also threatened by the owner of the new faster cyclers to find in their favor but she resists both of these threats and is supported by the head of the General Inspector's department. She finally comes up with a solution that suits the Captain and the Crew and the Inspector General's Department, but not the Space Initiative. Unfortunately for them, they have to live with Yerim's solution because it is legally binding.

The story is emotional, the characters utterly believable, a superb example of conflicting loyalties, and the action and the technology in the story is understated and doesn't intrude. We don't need to understand the technology of the cycler ship any more than we would need to understand the technology in a passenger cruise ship, or a massive modern plane or a huge international train. We know it's there, and that it keeps the vehicle operating, but it's the passengers and their interactions that make the story. It's the same with *The Last Dance;* it's the passengers, the crew and the Captain that make this story memorable.

The Last Campaign (2020)

Martin L Shoemaker has come back with a cracking continuation of his story about the habitation of Mars. We jump a number of years into the future from where *The Last Dance* finished: the ex- Captain of the *Aldrin*, Nicolau (Nico) Aames, is now living on Mars with his wife, the former Admiral Rosalia Morais (whose backstory forms a compelling part of *The Last Dance)*, and they both work as insurance inspectors in Maxwell City, the largest settlement on Mars with a population of over 50,000. Aames is regarded by the Martian population as being a founder and is respected with reverence, as is his wife because she is the wife of a founder. The Mayor of Maxwell city also came to Mars on the *Aldrin*. It was his father who owned the ship, but he is a different person now than he was at the beginning of the previous story. Nico and Rosalia are brilliant detectives and help solve many different kinds of insurance claims, but because the crime rate is increasing the Mayor wants to create a police force and he asks Rosalia to be the Police Chief. She is reluctant to even think about it at first, but when she realizes how much petty crime is happening, she accepts the position, much to the annoyance of her husband Nico, who wants her to continue working with him.

The mayor is involved in a political campaign to be re-elected. He is up against a local woman who has a strong following and who in particular is favored by a certain journalist who goes out of her way to annoy or embarrass the mayor and his new Police Chief. Hardly having had the time to form her squads of police, she is called on to solve a murder, a leading industrialist's body is found in a burnt laboratory which was arson and not an accident and that makes the body a murder victim.

The story only gets more complicated as Police Chief Morais has to uncover a spy within her new force who keeps informing a particular female journalist of everything that is going on, and it seems this journalist delights in verbally attacking the Mayor and his new Police Chief.

Chief Morais has to root out systemic graft and corruption within her new police force to make them more honest and efficient, while at the same time having personal problems with her husband as well as her ex-fiancé who is now the coroner in Maxwell city. Another murder happens and the story takes off at this point. There is politics involved, with people who want Mars to be free of Earth control, others who want Mars to be left alone in case life is discovered somewhere, (it hasn't at this point), and others who want Mars to be free, but not yet because they don't think it is ready. The Mayor is concerned he is loosing the political battle, while the Police Chief and her new squads are trying to solve two murders as well as other petty crimes that come back to some of the earlier investigations Morais and Aames did for the insurance company with many false claims which were paid out, but in retrospect seem to be far too many to be the result of natural causes.

When a former officer of the *Aldrin* is accused of dealing with stolen goods, Nico acts on his behalf and we find out that the insurance frauds are involved with people who are working on a secret base that most Martians in Maxwell city know nothing about. It involves rich business entrepreneurs and they want to keep it hidden so they can profit when Mars becomes independent.

There is a lot of interesting background woven in to this story that helps build a picture of Maxwell city, of Mars, of how everything functions politically and economically, of how Earth is involved, with a Space-military, base as well as the independent settlements scattered around the planet.

None of this background material gets in the way of the story, it enhances it, makes it believable.

There is a lot of tension as Aames' and Morais' relationship begins to unravel, as more mayhem and murders take place, as the political strategy of the mayor unravels, as System Initiative Space Force becomes involved and assists the police; all resulting in a fine story that keeps the reader interested right to the last page when the real instigator behind much of what has been happening is revealed.

Beautifully realized and intensely engrossing!

I would love to see another story with these same people a bit further in the future when Mars begins to realize its independence.

A mixed bag of stories to take us into 2020 and beyond

Stephen Baxter returns with another long story called ***World Engines - Destroyer*** which is part of a two book cycle, ***World Engines - Creator*** being the second volume. Two of the lead characters in this long story have previously appeared in four previous books in ***The Manifold*** series (*Time, Space< Origin,* and *Phase Space*); Reid Malenfant and Emma Stoney. The evnts that begin this new story are set in the year 2469 where global warming has raised ocean levels so much that England is a series of tropical islands and the population lives a bucolic life. Malenfant has been in cold sleep on the Moon cared for by robots and AIs and is awakened after four centuries because a message had been received from Phobos. It is from Emma Stoney whom everyone thought was dead for 400 years, since she was lost during the exploration of Mars' moon Phobos. She is asking for Malenfant to come and rescue her.

After coming to terms with the very different world of 2469 and with the help of a young girl Deidre, and his medic, an artificial human called Bartholomew, he is asked by the AIs to help save them and the world as it is in 2469.

To do that an expedition to Phobos, to rescue Emma is undertaken. As part of the process of familiarizing himself with the future world he has woken up into he begins to be aware that their history doesn't match his memories of his own early history.

In this world Armstrong has a heart attack during the landing on the Moon and Aldrin eventually takes him outside and speaks the words Armstrong had spoken in Malenfant's world. From that point on history has changed. The story is further complicated when they arrive at Phobos and discover the moon is hollow and filled with enigmatic machinery and they discover inside it a Russian cosmonaut who has a very different memory of history including the events that proceed from the time of the Moon landings. He believes it is 2004, while Emma thinks it is 2006. Emma is also not the same Emma that Malenfant had once been married to, and with whom he had a son, Michael. She never married and never had a son and is surprised that Malenfant is in his 60s and is not the young man she remembers. Further encounters on Phobos bring to light a British space ship (atomic powered) whose commander claims that the British were the first to land on the Moon and that England dominates activities in space.

It takes a while for the people from various alternate histories are able to accept that they are all in the 25th century and not the 21st. The British team have discovered, as Malenfant suspected, that the machinery inside Phobos is a means of interconnecting various timelines and parallel universes of the Manifold where history and points of divergence are quite different. Who or what built the machinery and the artificial moon Phobos is a mystery they are unable to solve at this point.

The first third of the book takes place on Earth where Malenfant has to come to terms with a strange future world.

The second third takes place after they arrive at Phobos and make their astounding discoveries.

The last third sees Malenfant, Emma, Diedre and Bartholomew, join the British expedition which is heading out to a massive super Earth called Persephone where the British has established a scientific base to examine a series of massively tall towers that have been built (like fence) all round the world. The towers are hollow, 100 metres in diameter, 20 kilometres in height, and there are 65,000 lined up all around the world on the equator. The British have discovered the towers are hollow and beneath them are massive machines, engines of some kind. Malenfant suspects they are rocket engines that use nuclear fusion and that Persephone has originally formed inside the orbits of Mars and Jupiter and that it had been moved outside of the Oort cloud some 4 billion years ago.

In the first part of the book the human population was well aware that in 1000 years a rogue planet called Shiva would impact their world and destroy it, but they push that to the back of their minds.

However, Deidre and Malenfant wonder if they can activate the world engines and shift Persephone out into a different orbit that would intersect with Shiva in 500 years as it comes into the edge of the solar system. With the help of the British they start the process by dropping and detonating an atomic bomb down inside one of the tower-exhausts. One by one, a second apart, tower after tower activates and blasts its exhaust into space, until 2600 are firing. As the planet rotates the first tower switches off and the next in line around the horizon activates, so that the push from the rocket exhausts in always in the same direction and always with the same number of engines operating.

Persephone begins to shift, but after one rotation when it gets back to the engine they started with, it doesn't fire, nor does the one after. As another rotation happens and they decide to see if it can be reactivated by dropping a second atomic bomb into it. This fails and the exhaust tower topples over starting a chain reaction that causes the other towers to topple like dominoes. Still, while they had worked Persephone was shoved out of orbit into a higher one that would intersect with that of Shiva as it approaches the solar system.

The British expedition with Malenfant, Diedre, Emma and Bartholomew head back to Phobos where they are going to enter the weird machinery inside in an attempt to go back in time to when the beings who built the machinery were there.

In a short afterword we discover that Shiva impacts with Neptune and the resultant combined massive burning planet dives deep into the solar system, disrupting Earth, not destroying it but pushing it into an orbit inside that of Venus where it is too hot for any life to survive. The children of humanity have been put into cold sleep on the Moon, (now a small planet in its own right still roughly in the same orbit as Earth once occupied), where they are looked after by the resident AIs.

Stephen Baxter is very good at writing convincing alternate histories and there are several that intersect in this novel and all of them seem plausible.

To find out what happened to Malenfant and his group, we will have to read the next book *World Engines - Creator,* but since this has nothing to do with Mars or Phobos once they travel through it, I won't go into it here.

Baxter is a superb creator of technological futures on a massive scale and while some find this fascinating, there are many who are bored with the incredible detail he exhibits in his stories. I must admit, I have found some of his books to be *unputdownable*, while others tend to make me yawn and fall asleep. I thought the *World Engines* sequence was enjoyable. His official sequel to *War of the Worlds* though, *The Massacre of Mankind,* (2017) was for me sleep-inducing to the point where I couldn't finish reading it.

War of the Worlds Battleground Australia (2019)
Edited by Steve Proposch, Christopher Sequeira and Bryce Stevens.
Introduction by Alex Proyas.

With *War of the Worlds Global Dispatches* edited by Kevin J Anderson (1996) (*See Dreams of Mars, pages 47-48*) the Martian invasion is seen through other eyes than the observer who narrated H G Wells original story set in England near London. The dispatches received from various places around the world apart from England, build a more complete picture of a world-wide invasion hinted at in Wells' original.

War of the Worlds Battleground Australia (2019) does the same, only it shows what happened in Australia rather than elsewhere in the world.

The stories in this volume are divided into three sections, *The Past, The Present,* and *The Future,* the shortest section with only three stories.

By far the longest section is *Part one - The Past* with each story set in the same year Wells had his Martians invading the world, circa 1898. I found this to be the most fascinating section especially the first two stories that take place in Melbourne, Footscray and Williamstown.

I grew up and lived in this area for 55 years. I was born in Williamstown, lived there as well as in Yarraville, worked for most of my working life in Williamstown and knew all of the places, the streets and suburbs mentioned as intimately as one could know any place. I'd attended concerts at the Athenaeum Theatre mentioned in Jack Dann's story, and was familiar with the fact that the original name for the Maribyrnong River was The Saltwater, mentioned in Lindy Cameron and Kerry Greenwood's story.

Each story resonated with me and I could picture in exact detail the locations and what might have been happening there. The stories by Jack Dann, Janeen Webb and Lucy Sussex whom I have met on several occasions, and Lindy Cameron and Kerry Greenwood, are absolute standouts for me. Closely following them are other stories in other parts of Australia that I also am familiar with, making these stories come to life in unexpected ways.

Where else but in Australia, would a part of the Martian invasion be wiped out by a bush-fire?

Who, other than an Australian could imagine such a scenario?

Brilliant stuff. In Particular, the two stories by Jack Dann, and Lindy Cameron and Kerry Greenwood, I feel, captured the style of voice used by writers who worked towards the end of the 19th century, whereas the others in *Part One* seemed a little more modern even though their stories were set during the time of Wells' invasion.

The stories don't connect as chapters in a novel would, yet strangely enough they do form a fascinating alternative collective view of the Martian invasion to the point that they do connect on levels other than the obvious, and can almost be read as a novel with a variety of different and fascinating characters.

But not all the Martians who invaded Australia are wiped out, some do survive. *Part Two - The Present* wherein we see how the Martians have managed to survive and how this has changed the country is also fascinating. These are not connected as much as those in part one. Each is a story involving some, or one Martian survivor, and how this affects modern Australians in more remote places is unexpected and often weird. Carmel Bird and Bill Congreve are the only two authors' names familiar to me in this section, but the others are all as equally as good.

Part three - The Future contains three stories, but each presents a strange and unusual alternative future of Australia learning to live with a large Martian population. They show how ordinary people in extraordinary circumstances will cope and will find a way to maintain their heritage no matter how suppressed it could become. The last story by Sean Williams ties up the whole book with an unusual twist.

This is a book every Mars aficionado should read and have in their collection.

Big Red by Damien Larkin (2019)

I am not a fan of military SF but this one was strange enough to grab my attention and intriguing enough to hold my interest until the end. It finishes with a hint that there is more to come.

A first novel, and quite well written except for one glaring misuse of a word; *Parameter*. He uses it several times instead of using *Perimeter* which means a line defining a boundary that is maintained. I wonder how many people mix these two words up? Someone should have corrected this at the proof-reading stage. *Parameter* is a word that defines the qualities of something, and does not mean, in any variation, a line defining an enclosed area.

A team of special soldiers are sent to Mars to fight horrible insectoid creatures that are threatening to destroy the colonies set up there. The soldiers are hired by Marscorp, a ruthless company that is out to control everything that happens on Mars.

Once they get to Mars which was originally colonized by the German Third Reich, they begin to realize something is not what it seems. They discover they are in the past, in the 1970s before some of them were born, and that Mars had been occupied for years. When their term of employment is up, those in control refuse to let them return to Earth, saying the compression machine or whatever it is that sends them to Mars is not functioning and they can't come back. This machine is also a kind of time machine, and it doesn't send them anywhere, it only sends their minds and places them into newly cloned versions of themselves on Mars. The original bodies are still on Earth.

The story is convoluted because it is told both in flashback as a particular soldier waking up on Earth is remembering what has happened, as well as seeing the events that occur on Mars to the same soldier and his comrades as they fight alien insectoids as well as fourth Reich rebels who want to get rid of Marscorp and its mercenaries. Marscop wants to get rid of a small native population of Martians that resemble humans in many ways, and who live underground, and whom they are consistently killing or murdering whenever they see them. There is evidence of ancient civilization on Mars which was destroyed a very long time ago and Marscorp has discovered artifacts and science that has yet to be understood. The ability to transfer minds across time and space to be implanted in cloned bodies is the result of one of the technologies discovered on Mars.

Other settlers came in space ships, it's only the soldiers sent to Mars that arrived via mind transfer into cloned bodies.

Because this is a military SF story, there are more than enough battles and long descriptions of them, but what makes this one different is the way the events of the story are presented in which the soldier at the centre of the events finally begins to understand what has been happening and plans a long-term revenge along with a means of returning to Earth and putting things right for his particular group of recruits. It only makes sense when you read to the end where unexpected surprises occur.

Military SF fans would love this story because of all the battle action involved.

Red Tide
Life on the Martian Frontier, by Jim Grebey (2019)

Credit where it's due: it is a handsome looking book, much better than other self-published books. The premise is good and promises much; A marine biologist working for NASA is suddenly reassigned to a Mars expedition with the purpose of searching for the fossilized remains of ancient Martian life. No life has yet been found, but the geologists working on Mars believe that if the remains of life are to be found, they will be in sedimentary rocks laid down when Mars once had a thicker atmosphere and oceans that could perhaps support the formation of life.

She isn't too happy with the reassignment, but is under contract with NASA and has to go regardless of what she feels.

Mars has been colonized for 60 years and has around 5000 inhabitants living in one major colony. Her immediate boss was the first human born on Mars, and recently elected to be its first governor. He is also the leader of the expedition in search of ancient Mars life, if it can be found.

Mars is run by a private company, a mining company, and her boss is also a major shareholder with that company and very wealthy as well. She really doesn't want to be on Mars but gradually warms to the company she has to keep, and inevitably falls in love with her boss.

The expedition that she takes part in once she has arrived on Mars is beset with problems, due to the harshness of the terrain they are exploring, and is caught in a massive sand, dust storm which almost wrecks the whole expedition, but they survive to discover something unexpected. The very end is left open with the lead character not saying whether she will return to Earth or stay on Mars. Even a brief epilogue doesn't quite tell us what she decided, but it does illuminate what happens to the whole team after their discovery.

The author has thought deeply about how a possible colony on Mars would look like and operate considering another 66 years of scientific development has taken place from the present time.

He has thought about every thing including how travel between Mars and Earth's Moon is a continuous cycle with two ships travelling in a large orbit between the two places. (*An idea first worked out and proposed by Buzz Aldrin, the second man to walk on the Moon*). Passengers in transit to Mars are boarded as the ship circles the Moon after the cargo has been taken off and the ship loaded with supplies and other stuff for the colony. Arriving at Mars the ship orbits the planet while it is unloaded and then reloaded with cargo before the passengers are allowed down the surface. All this has to be done precisely since the ships do not stay in orbit but only circle the planet or the Moon once in their continuous transit between Mars and Earth space. While one ship is at Mars, the other is at the Moon. The Moon has a thriving colony and a huge tourist industry having been established for half a century.

The story follows the lead character's departure from Earth after being reassigned, her travel to the Moon, and her subsequent trans-shipment to Mars. We then follow the preparations for the expedition to travel across the surface of Mars and the events that occur during this period.

Jim Grebey writes well, and most of what he writes here is fascinating or at the very least interesting, but he has not written a novel. He tells us the story. He uses the marine biologist to ask questions which the other lead characters answer in great detail. Instead of showing us how the marine biologist reacts to what she sees and discovers throughout her trip to Mars and while there, which would be very interesting and would certainly illuminate how things are on Mars, he just tells us, and in such detail as to give the impression this is a pseudo-documentary using characters as mouthpieces to explain what he wants to tell us, that is when he isn't actually telling us all the technical details of how this works and why people do certain things given the conditions on Mars. Except for the first chapter, a couple of moments around two thirds of the way through with the banter between the newcomer and when she meets the expedition members, and the final chapter where they almost don't survive a massive storm, the book simply doesn't come alive.

I don't know if it a peculiar American way, but the use of sediment rocks, meaning sedimentary rocks, biologic instead of biological and geologic instead of geological, was jarring to me, and it seems an obscure way of using the word to describe something. He also mixes up plural 's' and possessive 's' referring several times to *sedgeway's* as plural for *sedgeway* which should have been *sedgeways*, and talking about the planet Mars having something, he uses *the planets,* meaning more than one planet when it's clear he is only talking about Mars and should have written *the planet's...*

There are a couple of other minor glitches which were missed during proof-reading, if indeed proof-reading had been done to find mistakes and other odds and ends before setting up for publishing. These little things while not much in themselves, tend to interrupt the flow of the story, at least in this reader's mind which is what makes them stand out.

My feeling is that if he had let the story unfold through the characters actions and reactions to each other and to the events they encounter, with minimal chunks of info being inserted except where absolutely necessary, it would have been a brilliant story. As it is, it is okay, if not rather old fashioned in the way it is told.

The Sirens of Mars, by Sarah Stewart Johnson (2020) non-fiction
Searching for Life on Another World
This is a beautifully written book that is the autobiography (in part) of a young student who becomes a planetary scientist, and astrobiologist while simultaneously being involved with the scientists and engineers who are building the rovers and exploring Mars in search of life and clues to how our own planet evolved. She is now a professor at Georgetown University teaching Astrobiology, and is also serving on the science team for NASA's Curiosity Mars Rover.

It is also the history of Mars exploration by NASA through the eyes of one of its own scientists. Her excitement and enthusiasm for the research being undertaken and the possible consequences of finding traces of life on another planet, specifically Mars, is boundless, and colors the whole book. Flashbacks to a few pivotal moments in the early exploration of Mars and what some of those early explorers speculated and thought emphasizing how for centuries the human race has been captivated by Mars, are woven into the general flow of her story which enhances her own life and work as well as that of the other scientists similarly engaged in Mars exploration.

There is enough excitement, and even tension, within her story to keep any reader engaged throughout. Her writing is poetic and lucid, making this a very readable book for those who are not scientists. And for those who wish to explore further, there are 60 pages of notes citing the references used in her research, and a 10-page index.

This is her first book. One can only wait with bated breath to see what more she will produce in the future, especially if life or the remnants of life is discovered on Mars.

Some shorts from Ben Bova.

Ben Bova has written five novels about Mars from 1992 to well into the 2000s. (*See* **Dreams of Mars** *(2018) on pages 222 to 229 and pages 277 to 280.*) In a recent collection of short stories simply titled **Ben Bova - My Favorites** (2020), there are three short stories related to Mars, written at various times over his long career as an editor and writer. There are no copyright or publication dates given for any of the stories so they could have been written at any time over the last fifty years.

Sadly Ben Bova died from Covid complications in 2020 and this was one of his final books published.

The first is **Muzhestvo**. This was possibly written in the 1990s around the time of the first Mars novel featuring Jamie Waterman who is a pivotal character in the three novels that make a loose trilogy, **Mars**, **Return to Mars**, and **Mars Life**.

This is a short episode in Jamie's life before he was selected to be part of the 16-person crew going to Mars. He is in training with 200 other potential Mars crew members and is on an individual training trip to Kazakhstan in Russia where he encounters four Russian counterparts. They take him up on a flight which is a test to see if he has the courage to go to Mars. They themselves have been eliminated and are acting as trainers, but if Jamie fails their tests, they will make sure he doesn't go to Mars so he cannot endanger their compatriots who have been chosen as part of the crew.

This is a lovely short story that would fit nicely as prelude or as an introduction in a new edition of the novel **Mars**, and as such would help make that novel more complete.

The Great Moon Hoax, or, ***A Princess of Mars,*** is a delightfully funny story that pays homage to other earlier writers and their ideas of what Mars was like before we saw those photos sent back by the Mariner probes, as well as explaining the various conspiracy theories that have been prevalent since around the 1940s, the supposed flying saucer crash at Roswell, alien abductions, the Moon landings, Amelia Earhart and Howard Hughes, President Kennedy and Marylin Monroe, and Bova does it all in a short story. This is one you absolutely have to read.

Mars Farts. Now that's a title to attract a reader.

One would expect something funny, because of the title, but this story is straight-forward. A group of three explorer-scientists are working at a remote location, drilling down through the Martian permafrost to take core samples that they hope would show Martian life in the form of anaerobic bacteria deep inside the planet. They are searching for a source of the periodic methane emissions that have been detected.

Disaster strikes in the form of a swarm of meteorites that bombard the surface and one of the meteorites punctures their hydrogen fuel cell, rendering it useless. They radio back to base (3000 kilometers away) and are told it will take 5 days for them to be rescued. They have battery power gained through the use of solar cells, but with the minus 100-degree temperatures during the nights, it is doubtful that their batteries will be recharged enough to allow them to survive until they can be rescued.

To take their minds off their impending demise, they continue working, and actually discover anaerobic bacteria in the deeper layers of the core samples. They also discover that methane is leaking up through the hole they drilled to take the samples. Methane they assume is produced by anaerobic bacteria, *bug farts*, as one of the characters calls it. They fix the fuel tank by welding a piece of metal over the meteorite puncture, collect methane from the drill site in weather balloons they were supposed to release into the atmosphere, and using a battery powered laser they split the methane into hydrogen and carbon dioxide, collecting enough hydrogen to fill their fuel cell so they can use that to generate heat at night rather than relying on the diminishing battery charges. This helps them to survive the five freezing Martian nights until they can be rescued.

This is typical science fiction in that the science and the discovery of anaerobic bacteria (likely) on Mars is a plausible scenario in which science is used to solve the difficulties they have encountered. There is humor, and enough tension to keep a reader interested to find out how they are going to solve their problem, and when that happens, there is a satisfying release of the tension building up in the reader. This is a good story and it's easy to see why Bova would consider it one of his favorites.

A brilliant story from China

Vagabonds by Hao Jingfang (2020)
Translated from Chinese by Ken Liu *Published in Chinese in 2016.*

Hao Jingfang is the first Chinese woman to win a Hugo award for a novelette, **Folding Beijing**, in 2016. She has a PhD in economics and works as a researcher with the China Development Research Foundation in Beijing.

Ken Liu is an author as well as a translator. He has won Nebula, Hugo, World Fantasy, Locus Sidewise and Science Fiction and Fantasy Translation Awards. His translation of Cixin Liu's **Three Body Problem,** was the first translated work to ever win a Hugo award.

Hao Jingfang's **Vagabonds**, an evocative and beautifully delineated novel, is a credit to her ability to write and her translator's ability to conceive it in English. It is not marketed as science fiction but is presented as a mainstream novel which will give it a wider audience than it would otherwise have if marketed as SF.

It is set 200 years into the future (2201) when there are some 20 million inhabitants living on Mars in a huge enclosed city. This futuristic city is built of glass and steel, since iron for steel and sand for glass-making are the two most common things found on Mars. To the eyes of someone from Earth this city is strange and alien and we do see it through the eyes a visitor who is there to make a documentary film.

This future Martian society is extrapolated from the ideal of a Chinese Communist Utopia and is compared against the avaricious and greedy profit-at-all-costs philosophy of Western societies. Although the people on Mars are not all Chinese in origin, the bulk of them are and how they see their world is definitely different to other 'Western' stories set on Mars. Life on Mars is the epitome of Chinese evolution and is compared to Earth which is the ultimate extrapolation of how (I think) the Mainland Chinese tend to see American 'free' society or Western society in general.

On Mars, everything is free, everyone works together for the common good, everyone is a member of an Atelier chosen when they come of age, and to which they belong for the remainder of their lives, everyone pursues artistic merit in whatever they do, and there are competitions, but no monetary prizes; whatever is developed is used for the benefit of the whole Martian society. Prize winners do have a certain amount of prestige, but this only lasts until the next year's competitions resulting in new winners.

One hundred years before this story begins the Martian colonies declared independence from Earth control and a war was fought. Mars cut off contact with Earth and evolved into a very different society to what it was initially. One hundred years have passed since that war with almost no contact between the two worlds until a group of Martian students were sent to Earth as goodwill ambassadors. They stayed and studied on Earth for five years, and as the story opens, they are returning to Mars. They are accompanied by an Earth delegation who hope to establish new trading and cultural ties but this may not be possible as the two planets have long been on diverging developmental and philosophical paths.

However, those students who went to Earth are no longer the same as they were before —Earth has changed their perspectives on life— and they have problems readjusting to the Martian way. Luoying is one of the returning students and she has changed so much she no longer sees Martian society as ideal, but rather, she sees it as stultifying and retrogressive. She is supposed to select an Atelier, but does not wish to become a member of any of them. She discovers that the death of her parents, who were punished for not doing something expected of them and sent to a mining asteroid where they died accidentally, was caused by her grandfather who is the current leader of the Martians. Her grandfather was a survivor of the brief war between Earth and Mars that resulted in the Republic of Mars becoming independent.

Luoying is a dancer and she accidentally breaks her ankle during her first performance after returning from Earth and finds herself in hospital. During her recovery she begins to delve into the history of her parents and those before. The more she immerses herself into the archives, the more she becomes disillusioned with Martian society as a whole. There are lies told on both sides of the conflict that have not been resolved for the last hundred years, and she needs to bring this into the open. She also needs to find out exactly what part her grandfather played in those historic events; things he has kept hidden from her. She also discovers that political intrigue is ongoing and that she and her fellow students who had been sent to Earth as goodwill ambassadors were actually hostages used by Earth to gain leverage to set up trading negotiations, and that the Martian leaders were aware of the hostage situation and played along with it.

None of the students returned from their five year stay on Earth want to join an Atelier which would determine what they can and can't do for the rest of their lives. They quietly plan to rebel against the current stagnation (as they see it) of Martian society and they begin this by presenting a play that criticizes Mars and its way of life. The play is not well received by the older Martian population.

Her brother Rudy who is a member of the Martian military tells her that they are preparing a preemptive attack on the Moon, to take control of Earth's facilities there to prevent an invasion fleet from leaving Earth space to attack Mars. He is not in favor of this and joins with Luoying and the other returned students who are willing to rebel against the current regime in order to change the Martian way of life, (just as their grandparents did in the past). Rudy also has a romantic interest with one of these students which more than convinces him to join with them. The dissident students also go on an unapproved expedition to a mountainous region where a mine used by the earlier settlers had been abandoned for almost a century. They discover something here that they were not supposed to know about and on their return are punished by being ordered into isolation for one month.

The general population, all 20 million of them live in the one huge city made of glass and steel, Few people are allowed outside into the true Martian environment without permission from the ruling body of elders, but there are plans for a new city to be built into caves drilled into the sides of a huge crater in which they hope to re-create a more Earthlike atmosphere with gardens and forest, lakes and running water. Once completed, everyone is expected to move there.

This is a massive terraforming project, but not everyone is happy about the idea. There are many who do not want to abandon their spacious glass city to live beneath the surface even if they can walk about in the open inside the giant terraformed crater. As a meeting is held to decide what should be the future course of Martian society there are protests outside the meeting hall which Luoying manages to dispel. Her grandfather resigns from his position as consul.

Two Terrans (presumably from the delegation that accompanied the returning students) had stolen a vehicle in which they hoped would take them into orbit where they could rendezvous with the *Maerth* (the ship that cycles between Earth and Mars), but unable to fly it they crash as a sandstorm is beginning. The leader of those wanting to start another war decides not to rescue them, wanting to use them as an excuse to attack Earth's defenses on the Moon by claiming the two Terrans had stolen secrets from Mars. Anka, who Luoying is falling in love with, developed a personal flying suit and goes to rescue the two people. No Martian leaves someone to die in a sandstorm. He is killed accidentally in the storm after rescuing the two Terrans and his act of heroism stops the war from happening by forestalling the event that would have been used as an excuse to start it.

The two Terrans decide to help Mars instead of Earth. Finally, the majority of the population decides that they will move to the new city to be developed inside a massive crater where they can walk freely in the open. So, life on Mars will change and develop a viable and independent society set on a different path to Earth, both physically and philosophically.

The book is divided into three parts with the first two parts seen from the viewpoint of Luoying, although there are some changes of viewpoint to the other members of the student group. The third part alternates between the viewpoints of the main participants in the events leading up to the decision to move while each of the students comes to terms with living again on Mars, not willing to accept their earlier way of life but willing to compromise to create a better future.

Vagabonds is not the usual kind of science fiction story about Mars that one would expect. It is not labeled as SF either. Even the title doesn't hint that it is SF if you see it on a shelf in a bookshop, but it is a profound story that deals with the emotional development of the students returning from Earth and how they each manage to reconcile their feelings and their discoveries of their Martian history and how they evolve as persons who find a way to reconcile their existence and their future.

It is at times a slow read as there isn't as much physical action as one generally finds in a more traditional SF story, but it is a very rewarding story and beautifully written (translated) in English by Ken Liu.

It is time that more SF from other countries is made available for English readers and it seems China has a lot of hugely interesting writers working in the field, who are now beginning to be exposed to the wider world's reading population. We can only benefit as a whole from seeing this other aspect of the world we all live on.

Discovery, Incursion, Relic (2019, 2020) **Resilience** ((2021)
Paul Rix. (4 novels telling a long story.) (**The Martian Frontier** series.)
Discovery,
Two ships each with 12 people on board, plus two unmanned ships loaded with supplies. They are to set up a colony over the two years they expect to be there. This is a NASA controlled mission. Close behind them, during transit to Mars, is a joint Russian/Chinese expedition with the same object, setting up a colony and searching for valuable minerals.

Rix has utilized familiar tropes for his Martian story: *something happens en-route to necessitate a space walk and make repairs.* This time it wasn't a meteor storm but a solar storm which catches one of the crew causing severe radiation sickness.

Difficulty in setting up a base of operations inside a crater that is about to be bombarded by a meteor strike. This makes them rush to set up the base in a lava tube to avoid meteor damage as well as avoid the constant bombardment of radiation upon the surface.

A disgruntled member sabotaging the project. One member of the expedition is spying for the Russian/Chinese mission still to arrive. This person tries to disrupt the cohesion of the group as a way of seeking revenge for the loss of his wife who was a pilot on the first failed expedition to Mars a year earlier. (There is a prequel that tells this story, ***Deception***.)

Discovering that they are being watched and monitored by a pair of aliens. When Georgia has an accident and breaks a leg at one of the supply ships, she sees an alien. Her suit is pierced, and she is about to die a horrible death before the terminal cancer induced by the solar storm earlier can kill her... She wakes up in an advanced medical facility on board the alien's ship, which not only repairs her broken leg, but also removes all of the cancerous cells that are inside her body. The aliens explain that they have been watching humans for 5000 years. They never interfere, but simply monitor and report human progress. They are also watching other advancing civilizations in other star systems throughout the galaxy. They return her to one of the supply ships, not the one where she fell because her crew-mates are there looking for her. But before returning her, they wipe her memory of her encounter with them. Her rapid recovery from cancer (thanks to the aliens) has her beginning to remember her encounter with them.

Betrayal of trust when the crew members find out about the aliens watching them. The spy reports this to the Russian/Chinese expedition due to land in a few days, and they order him to capture the alien ship.

Disaster as a meteor breaks up and smashes into the landing site damaging their ships. One fragment strikes the crater wall causing an avalanche which blocks the lava tube where the base has been established. As they manage to get out, the traitor causes a disturbance to distract them while he grabs Georgia and using her as a captive, forces her to show him where the alien space ship, normally invisible, is located. He thinks because they saved her life, they will let him in if she's with him. He has been ordered by the incoming Russian/Chinese ship to take over the alien ship, because they want its superior technology. Nothing goes to plan and there are disastrous consequences at the end.

Even though all the above is not dissimilar to many other stories set on Mars, the author manages to give us a fresh look at them and has generated enough tension to keep the reader enthralled.

The title ***Discovery*** immediately implies that something momentous or unexpected is to be discovered on Mars, and he doesn't let us down. The story moves along at a good pace, barely giving the reader time to breathe.

Book two, **Incursion**, begins with only four of the original settlers left at Alpha Base, waiting the arrival of another two ships bringing 20 people. There is tension with the new people fitting in and Georgia is relieved that she is no longer commander after her boss was murdered at the close of the first book. Georgia and Joe Mancuso think there is something wrong when Joe is asked to assist with unloading 'mining' equipment from the newly arrived supply ship instead of much needed food and tools to repair broken equipment at the base, since no mining has been scheduled.

Georgia has been demoted to second in command because of her experience, so she confronts the new leader and asks what's going on. He reluctantly informs her that they have brought a newly developed particle beam weapon to test on Mars, ostensibly to destroy asteroids that might threaten the planet, but obviously to use against their enemies, the Russians and the Chinese, who are also bringing similar weapons to test on Mars.

The Russians landed a few days after the American (NASA) expedition and are busy unpacking and setting up their own particle beam weapon. The Chinese have arrived and are in orbit. They have been ordered to set up a base near the pole before testing their particle beam weapon. But a rogue Chinese general on board leads a mutiny that kills the captain, cuts communication with Beijing, and decides to take Mars in the name of China by using their particle beam weapon from orbit to destroy the Russian and the American bases.

Redmayne the traitor and former spy has been taken in by the Russians (*after the events that concluded Discovery*). Although despised by the Russians, they think he could be useful when the new crew arrives to set up their weapons. He is told to help and he is the only one outside, connecting power lines to the new weapon from an external generator when the Chinese in orbit destroy the Russian base with their particle beam weapon. None of the Russians survive the explosive loss of air when the Chinese particle beam hits their base, except for one scientist who happened to be next to an airlock and jumped in and sealed it as air pressure dropped. Redmayne rescues her.

Redmayne and the sole Russian scientist were both about to launch themselves into orbit where an unmanned Russian ship was stationed that could take them back to Earth when they receive a message from Alpha base to tell them they'd been attacked from orbit but the Chinese only destroyed the ships not knowing that the base itself was inside a lava tube. Their particle beam weapon had been untouched since it was some distance away from the ships that were destroyed. Redmayne and the Russian scientist agree to fly over to Alpha base and help the Americans set up their weapon so they can retaliate against the Chinese when the ship is again in a position to continue their attack on the American base.

Unable to repair or set up the American weapon they come up with an alternative plan. They want to send the Russian shuttle which they used to get to the American base up into orbit where they will blow it up in such a way that the debris from the explosion will destroy the orbiting Chinese ship and their particle beam weapon at the same time.

Georgia agrees to help with this plan and there is a climactic finale in which the Chinese ship is destroyed and everyone good and bad gets what's coming to them. Back on Earth imminent war between Russia, America and China is averted as the truth of what happened on Mars is learnt.

Relic is the third book. In the two years since the end of the first book Grant, one of the original crew, was so seriously injured that he was practically dead. Georgia asked one of the sentinels if they could help fix him as they had done to her. He was beyond what their medical suite on board could do so they took him to their home world (*73 light years away*) where better technology could rebuild him, resulting with him becoming an enhanced human with extraordinary abilities. The first third of the book details Grant's recovery and experiences on the Sentinel's home world.

It then continues with Georgia and the others at Alpha base two months after the disastrous events perpetrated by the Chinese rogues and their particle beam weapon. Her DNA had been altered when the sentinels cured her of cancer and her body now repairs itself rapidly when any injury occurs, and it does this without leaving any scar tissue. Georgia's brother, who had arrived with the American ships that brought the weapon, is a geologist and on a survey to a remote part of Mars (*isn't everywhere remote on Mars?*) discovers an area of highly concentrated rare minerals. This could pay back the money invested by mining companies in the missions. But he also discovers an alien probe that could have been there for thousands of years.

Georgia goes with him to see this probe and as she gets close to it and touches it, something is activated ands an alien presence enters her mind. There is a mental discourse which leads her to believe the alien probe is benign, but she inadvertently gives away information regarding the confederation of worlds that the sentinels are part of. She thinks all aliens are benevolent. But when the probe alien suddenly changes and demands more info regarding the confederation of worlds she realizes she had made a mistake.

NASA's new military boss, Colonel Byrne, demotes her and tells her and her friends to stay away from the probe, but it is too late. The probe entity has entered the minds of the others. It now threatens to destroy Earth or to enslave its inhabitants while it plunders whatever it can get from the solar system.

Meanwhile Grant and Falmas, one of the sentinels, detect the signal from the probe and warn the humans on Mars that within 20 hours, the message from the probe will arrive at the probe's home planet and then they will be able to locate the solar systems. The probe's self-defense system causes the sentinel ship to crash as it approaches. The probe is almost indestructible.

The Russian scientist who survived the Chinese attack on her base suggests they use the Russian particle beam weapon to melt the probe since it hadn't been destroyed in the attack. They go to collect it and take it to where the probe is located and start setting it up. The probe entity fights back by trying to control them mentally, but somehow Georgia, who had been slowly changing after she had been healed with the sentinel's nanotechnology, resists being controlled by the probe entity and manages to ramp up the power output from the particle beam weapon which finally destroys the probe, just in time to prevent the not so benevolent aliens from finding the solar system's location. The story ends with the confederation of worlds of the sentinels having something planned for Georgia.

Resilience is book four of the ***Martian Frontier*** series and commences a few months after the finish of the previous book ***Relic***. Georgia Pike and Jo Mancuso are returning from a remote location back to the main base and discussing the perceived hatred the Man in charge, Colonel Byrne back at NASA headquarters, has for her. He's a bully and nobody likes him but being military and running the base on Mars as an extension of his military command has bought conflict between Georgia and him, because she does not follow orders and is considered a rebel. Her ideas for the future of Mars colonization is at odds with his ideas. She is returning to face disciplinary actions for the events she was involved with in the previous book, ***Relic***. That she saved the world from being discovered by inimical aliens that threaten the Confederation, of which the Sentinels observing life on Earth and on Mars are a part of, is irrelevant to Colonel Byrne. He's pissed off because Georgia always defies him. He wants to confine her to the base and not let her have any outside activities because she disappears irregularly as she meets with the Sentinels who want her to do something special. Georgia is different, since they healed her of the cancer she got from radiation exposure during her journey out to Mars.

Her fiend who is the base's doctor is monitoring her health and is amazed at the changes, which at first worry Georgia. Colonel Byrne orders her to be sent back to Earth on the next resupply mission in 18 months, so the doctors at NASA headquarters can examine her. Naturally she doesn't want to go back. A day or two later when she is heading outside to do an inspection she is contacted by Grant, who is now a sentinel working with Falmas. Grant tells her a special investigator, Jillnap, has been sent by the confederation to specifically meet with her, and he takes her on board the sentinel ship and they go to Deimos where Jillnap is waiting.

He explains that she is special, because of what was done to her medically after her accident, and that Jillnap wants to put her through a series of tests to see if she is the one they've been looking for who can help the Confederation defeat the enemies threatening to destroy them, and ultimately Earth and all its inhabitants as well. Those enemies are not sure where Earth is because Georgia had managed to sabotage their probe left on Mars.

Georgia is hoping that Jillnap can tell her what is happening to her body, but he gives her 24 hours to decide whether to take the tests or not, then sends her back to Mars.

While she was away, there was an accident that killed one of the most popular team members and the rest of them blame Georgia although she had nothing to do with it. Because people were searching for her, and could have saved their teammate, which was unlikely, they blamed her.

This time because she disappeared and disrupted work at the base she is confined to her quarters and her space suit and equipment needed to go outside has been taken and hidden from her. No amount of desperate pleading will get the Base commander to allow to go outside again. But she has to go because the alien sentinels are expecting her. She has decided that she would rather undergo the Alien tests rather than return to Earth for the doctors there to experiment on her. Joe Mancuso helps her to leave in the middle of the night, and she is taken up to Jillnap's ship on Deimos, where he puts her through a series of ever more dangerous tests, explaining enigmatically that everyone he's tested has either passed or failed, and failure means death.

A good portion of the story details the tests she undergoes and her reluctance to participate, even though she goes through with them, and ultimately survives all of them. She is special, but she doesn't feel like she can save the galactic confederation. The story also alternates with Colonel Byrne and his attempts to discredit Georgia, to obfuscate the stories of the aliens on Mars by filling social media with conspiracy theories about aliens, while he attempts to find out who has been feeding the press with NASA secrets.

As the book closes, we find out what Georgia's unique ability is and how Jillnap thinks it can be used to save the confederation from a looming war. Georgia doesn't believe it until she uses it to save the life of her brother who is trapped in a sinkhole back on Mars. The story ends with her momentarily returning to Earth with Jillnap in his ship, to confront Byrne who she believes is the only one able to convince the world that they are in danger from an imminent alien invasion. He finally believes her after seeing the alien Jillnap for himself. The book closes with Georgia leaving with Jillnap to head off to the confederation to see how she can help them

That story will continue in another book, which at this moment has yet to be written.

These four books (*so far*) are engaging, full of thrills, and hard to put down once you start reading them. They certainly reminded me of the kinds of stories I loved reading when I was a teenager back in the 1950s, stories that got me hooked into reading science fiction.

Chapter Twelve

The third decade begins well

We are closer than ever to making a trip to Mars and landing people there, but will it happen this decade as we have been promised so many times?

Or will the dream of going to and being on Mars be pushed further into the future?

Only time will tell, but I am hopeful I will see it happen sooner rather than later.

And helping to keep the dream alive, a few good books have already appeared in the first year of the new decade...

Although book one of **The Halo Trilogy** appeared in 2020 I didn't see it until the end of that year and it was closely followed by the second volume in 2021, and a year later the third book appeared.

Gates of Mars
Book 1 of the **Halo Trilogy**
McFall and Hayes (2020 2021)
The background is in the year 2187 the Earth is heavily polluted and the planet is basically a toxic dump. The air is sometimes unbreathable, and the population mostly lives in extreme poverty. There is a constant struggle and often violence as people try to survive in a society managed totally by a computer system called Halo. Governments are non-existent, having been displaced by huge business conglomerates which over a number of years fought each other for control of the planet and its resources, finishing up with 5 ruling families, whose members all live on Mars. On Mars there are a series of huge domes where ideal earthlike conditions and environments have been established.

Crucial Larsen, is a cop, a veteran of the Consolidation wars, but now a Labor Cop, since all police of whatever kind actually work for the ruling conglomerates, constantly monitored by Halo. The whole population is wired into Halo so it knows where everyone is and what they are doing. Occasionally individuals are transported to Mars where they work for the one of the five families. Crucial's ex-girlfriend works on Mars as a biologist helping develop plants that will assist in terraforming the planet as well as special plants and animals to help populate the massive domes under which the Martian population lives.

When Crucial's sister Essential was on Mars working in one of the pleasure domes where members of the elite go to pass time with special hostesses. She sends him a strange message, and shortly after disappears. Disappearing is something that shouldn't happen because everyone is constantly monitored by Halo. But she has disappeared. Crucial is brought to Mars by the family his sister worked for to investigate her disappearance, but nothing goes right. He encounters his ex who is engaged to a high-ranking police officer, targeted with finding out what happened to Essential. She assists Crucial at the start but when things start going wrong, and bodies pile up, she wants to arrest Crucial and send him back to Earth. They all believe his sister is dead, since no one can disappear from the system monitored by Halo. That's what they believe, but there are rebels who don't want to be constantly monitored and controlled, who are rebelling against the system. They have a way of becoming invisible to Halo. Even the five families have a means of switching off or covering up the surveillance by Halo so things are even more sinister. Are the families responsible for Crucial's sister's disappearance? Are they hindering his investigation? What has Essential discovered that warrants the family she worked for wanting to find her?

But out outside the domes, is the real Mars; freezing, desolate, frighteningly beautiful, with no atmosphere to speak of let alone breathe since what is there is mostly carbon dioxide. Somewhere out there, a rebel base exists and this is where those fighting the system hide out, and this base and the rebels are what Crucial needs to find to discover what happened to his sister, and what he finds is not what he expects. It is worse, and far more complicated than he imagined.

This first part of the trilogy is full of riveting action, setbacks, and unexpected surprises. Crucial is like-able but flawed, in much the same way the detectives in the noir novels from fifty years ago were, only updated into a future scenario and mostly set on Mars. The amount of detail relating to both Mars and Earth is woven into the story in a way that is unobtrusive and enhances the reader's belief in the two worlds depicted; a devastated future Earth and a believable future Mars.

A very enjoyable story which solves what Crucial sets out to do but also establishes the premise for the next book in the series. There are still many things to be resolved and many questions to answer.

I liked this story. It's one of the better Mars books to come out in 2020. And the next book is even better...

Scorched Earth (2021) is the second book in the *Halo trilogy*, and it begins with Crucial once again back on Earth where he is happy enough despite the awful conditions that prevail all over the planet. Earth Sucks, as Crucial says, but he prefers to be on a planet where you can breathe the atmosphere. You can't do that on Mars. There is something odd going on in the sunbelt, the abandoned part of Earth that is almost impossible for normal humans to live in. However, life exists there; life that was genetically altered, humans changed so they could survive the ever-increasing heat and the harshness of a large part of the planet that makes the rest of the polluted environment look good. Attacks on patrols, attacks on people all supposedly done by the rebels. But Crucial knows this is not the case. He is in contact with his sister on Mars, Essential, who is the second in charge of the rebel forces, and she assures him that they have nothing to do with the attacks that have occurred in the sunbelt.

On patrol in the sunbelt to find out what happened to a previous patrol, his group is attacked, and taken prisoner by a Saurian, one of the genetically altered humans adapting to the extremes of the sunbelt. Derogatively called Blizzards, these saurians are still human, but they have lizard genes in the genome which allows them to adapt to the extreme heat and dryness. Over time these modified humans are becoming a new species of human.

Crucial's grandmother was one of the first humans to be genetically altered. The five families gave up on trying to modify humans to suit the ruined environment on Earth and abandoned the whole planet, moving to Mars where they set up their domed cities with controlled environments. They generally use Earth as a dumping ground for toxic waste generated by their efforts on Mars.

Crucial wonders what happened to his grandmother, and when he is taken into an underground complex where the Saurians live, they treat him with respect. He learns his grandmother died many years ago. He also discovers the Saurians are not cannibals and they do not prey on normal humans for food or anything else. They just want to be left alone. But in the area where they live, there is an extinct volcano and a group of strange humans are mining there. And they keep everyone away, killing anyone Saurian or Human who comes near the place. Crucial and his team go and investigate the extinct volcano and there is an altercation between them and the mine's security forces, which results in a ship taking off for space to escape. He realizes the people at the mine were Martians.

Barely back from the patrol. He is called by a woman he met on Mars who works for the Singaroy family who previously hired him when Essential went missing. She is on Earth doing some research involving the sunbelt and wants to meet with him. Before he can say yes, he is interrupted by a call from his previous lover Mel, whom he still loves, but lost when she moved to Mars to continue her genetic research there. She wants him to come to Mars as a special investigator to find out why her fiancé Jynks, the head of Mars security, has been charged with murdering a senior member of one of the five families. She is isolated in a prison out in the choke, which is what anywhere outside a domed city or residence is called, because apart from freezing almost instantly, you would choke to death on the tenuous carbon dioxide atmosphere.

No matter how much he hates Mars, Crucial instantly agrees to be the special investigator, and once again he is on a quantum rocket heading for Mars.

Immediately all hell breaks loose. He is again assigned an assistant, the same AI human robot who helped him before, and who is slowly evolving into a more independent being despite his programming, and together they uncover a conspiracy being perpetrated by one of the younger members of the ruling five families. Jynks is innocent even though a video of her murdering the high-ranking family member exists as evidence of her guilt. She has also pleaded guilty, Crucial knows she didn't do it and sets out to find the one who did do it. This brings him into conflict with the other ruling families as well as the rebels, and the whole situation on Mars becomes extremely dangerous and unpredictable. Meanwhile, his sister's search for the servers that house Halo which monitors and controls all human activity on Earth and Mars, continues unabated and with more desperation as the story progresses.

When Crucial finally, after numerous setbacks, discovers where the servers are located and who the murderer of the high-ranking family member was, the story draws to a dramatic, explosive end which only solves a few things and leaves much yet to be finished.

Again, this second installment is a nail-biting thrill ride on both Earth and Mars that is even more complex than the first part and promises that the third and final part will be even more exciting and nerve-wracking.

Mars Adrift (2022) The third book of the **Halo trilogy**.
Crucial and Jynks are about to leave Mars. Accompanying them is Sanders, the cybernetic being who has become Crucial's friend. They are ready

to board the space elevator to take them into orbit where they will take a fast ship back to Earth when a series of meteors crashed down. The meteors smash into the orbital platform at the top of the elevator and it all comes crashing down. They have less than a minute to find somewhere safe to be before the cables and the elevator itself hits the ground where they are waiting. Not only that, more meteors are crashing into the various domes and major habitats around the planet. Mars is under attack. Some mysterious force is directing the meteor strikes, and targeting every major installation on the planet. The five controlling families are now in the same situation as everyone else.

Crucial, Jynks and Sanders make it underground beneath the base of the elevator and survive. At least the two humans survive. Sanders simply drops down and becomes inert, when a meteor hits Phobos where Halo's servers are located. Everything stops. There is no electronic activity of any kind. No connectivity which every single human has had since birth. They are on their own and few know how to cope.

Crucial and Jynks emerge from under the wreckage. Crucial is dragging Sanders behind him on a floating gurney. He will not leave his friend behind. When some form of electronic activity can start again, he will reboot Sanders. Crucial is worried about his sister, Essential, who was on Phobos trying to insert an empathy patch into the servers Halo uses to run everything on the planet. But there is nothing he can do about her while he is stuck on Mars.

They decide they need to find Crucial's and Jynks' lover Mel. They are both worried about her. She lives in Jezero which is 3000 kilometres away, so they need to find some kind of transport to get them there. There is nothing that works, except for what is called a Gonzo Truck — Garbage and Sanitation Overland Conveyance transports. These massive trucks are used to collect garbage and waste from all the domes and settlements, which they compact into balls that are then thrown into orbit to be collected by waste barges. These giant trucks have a hundred wheels and are automatic. They are not connected to Halo, the AI that runs everything on Mars and Earth. They can go almost anywhere, over any kind of terrain. After an altercation with a few people who had loaded a Gonzo with supplies, food and water, which they are going to take to Jezero and sell, hoping to profit from this disaster. Crucial commandeers the Gonzo and they set off for Jezero.

The first act the invaders make is to put a bounty on Crucial and the missing scientist, Melinda Hopwire, Crucial's ex-lover, and Jynks' present lover. Crucial believes that he will find clues in Jezero as to what happened to Mel and where she went. Mel is the only person who knows where the back-up servers for Halo are and the invaders need her so they can get control of

Halo. The invaders are a sixth family that had been exiled after the war on Earth that gave the present five families control of Earth and Mars. They have patiently waited in the far reaches of the solar system and have returned at last for revenge and to take over everything.

Some of the present families' survivors decide they will do a deal with the invading family and work with them. Even a small percentage of the profits expected is better than none, than being like all the indented workers they once used. Everyone is now after Crucial and his friends.

There is no letting up on the action and this part of the Halo trilogy is an absolute page turner, with setback after setback narrowly escaped or avoided. Eventually the three are captured but Crucial and Sanders escape in a pod while being transported to the Moon. They rescue his sister who is on Deimos having got there in a ship that is damaged and she is running out of air.

They return to Mars and trying to stay undercover they again look for clues to lead them to Mel. Just managing to keep ahead of the security forces and the warriors of the invading family they eventually find Mel and her cat. Mel finally reveals that Sanders is the back-up server for Halo and that once he is activated as such simply holder her pet cat (which has the empathy module embedded, will transfer the patch and the AI known as Halo will work for the benefit of all humans and not just the ruling families, which hopefully will no longer exist in the future.

It all ends with Crucial and Melinda taking a fast ship to catch three ships loaded with a horrible brain wasting disease which the invading family was going to infect the whole planet with so they could then sell people the cure, to make themselves enormous profits. Crucial and Mel fire two missiles that destroy two of the ships before they can enter Earth orbit, but the only way to take out the third ship is to ram it. There are three possible ends to this; they are destroyed along with the ship they ram, if they get the correct angle they can push it out of orbit and on into space saving themselves, or they will be shifted in time or into another dimension as the core of the invading ship explodes. It is a suicide mission, and Crucial finally accepts that as does Melinda. Of course, they opt for the second possibility, and the story finishes with them accelerating towards the ship they are about to destroy with Crucial, for the first time in his life, feeling happy.

This is one of the best of the modern trilogies with a Martian setting that I have read over the last few years. There is simply so much in it, the settings, the future Earth and Mars, the human situation, extrapolated from present day trends and detailed to such an extent, it is mesmerizing.

Hover
Mark Wayne McGinnis
(2021)

Set in the year 2049, when a miraculous life-enhancing microbe has been discovered on Mars…

Reading that part of the blurb on the back cover gives the impression this is a Mars story, but in fact the only action that takes place on Mars happens in the last 60 or so pages out of 415.

First up it is a delight to read and is certainly entertaining. It is however, in my view, a glorious soap opera where a scientist has become the legal guardian of his best friend's five children after both parents were killed in a plane crash in Switzerland. Most of the book deals with the trials and problems pertaining to looking after five extraordinary kids, one of whom is seriously ill. At the same time, the scientist guardian has a small collider where he is running a series of experiments which lead to the development of anti-gravity, as means of propulsion. To add to the soap opera quality, there is a nasty, evil, billionaire who is determined to have the anti-gravity propulsion for his own efforts to get to Mars so he can lay claim on the part of the planet that contains the miraculous life enhancing microbe. This character is so evil, so nasty, and abhorrent that he borders on being an extreme caricature, but it fits with the nature of the story.

Just like an old Saturday serial at the movies, the story is full of cliff-hangers that entice you to keep reading to see how the main character, Jack Harding, will get over the obstacles in his way. Initially forced to work for the billionaire who steals his computer programs, to further develop his anti-gravity drive, he finally makes plans to out with the nasty guy, to beat him to Mars so he can claim the life enhancing microbes which he needs to restore the health of one of his five children.

The final 60 pages takes place on Mars and not much real impression is given of how the planet may be, as a number of prospectors race each other to lay claims on areas with mineral deposits, while Jack heads straight for the location of the microbes near the south pole with the nasty billionaire in hot pursuit.

As with most soap operas, all's well that ends well.

It is an enjoyable romp.

Because it does have a Mars setting or the intention to go to Mars, it's worth mentioning here.

Mars Awakening 2021
Brett Mahar.
This has the potential to be a good novel, as well as a long one, but it reads more like a very long synopsis (*335 pages long*) rather than a novel.

It has suspense, unexpected twists and turns, plenty of characters who interact in various ways, but what author hasn't done is to let the characters, especially the several main characters show us their story. They don't inhabit the story. The author does; telling us what they do, what they see, what they say. The author is very much present, and this spoils what could have been a good novel. Only in a few places do the individual characters begin to emerge, and these few spots are the best moments.

I found it interesting enough to read all the way through, but ultimately disappointing because the potential story doesn't emerge. It is left open for a sequel, but I doubt I would be interested if it continues in the same way.

The cover is very attractive, but the interior, though better than some self-published books, is a printed version of an eBook which simply isn't pleasant to read. Printed books have a charm and character different from an eBook, and to not design the book for both formats is just laziness.

The Lion of Mars (2021)
Jennifer L. Holm
Jennifer Holm is a writer of children's books and a best selling one at that. This short novel is her first for what is now known as middle grade readers. It is a beautifully written story that is an absolute delight to read. It has been many years since I read a book like this, and it brought back a feeling of nostalgia for the time when I first discovered science fiction as an eleven-year-old, in 1951, and how excited I was to read stories set on Mars or other planets in the solar system. Most of the authors back then were young as well and as they grew older and more experienced so too did their stories, and the readers of those stories.

The Lion of Mars is about children on Mars. They have never known Earth, having arrived on Mars as babies or very young children. Bell and his friends are around eleven years old, with a couple of them turning into teenagers, whose behavior they find strange. Bell loves cats, especially the larger kind like lions who live in family groups called a Pride. A lion rejected by its pride generally doesn't survive long. Bell has a pet cat, the last of several, and he adores it.

Bell worries about why the adults of the Americana colony don't have contact with the other colonies on Mars. They did at one time because they built an underground railway that connects the various colonies via a tunnel. There is a French colony, a Finnish Colony, a Russian colony, and a Chinese colony. All of them are mostly underground, built into lava tubes to escape the high radiation bombarding the surface.

At one stage they all helped each other, and interacted as one large family, but for some reason the United States colony cut itself off from all contact with the others, and none of the children know why, and none of the adults will tell them. All their leader Sai tells them is that there are hostilities on Earth over minerals in Antarctica, and that the French and the others are the enemy. Bell and his friends would love to meet the children of the other colonies.

The children don't know any better, but their habitat is slowly falling apart as things break down and can't be repaired. They never get enough stuff supplied from Earth and anything urgent would take 8 months to get there anyway.

One of the older kids convinces Bell and a couple of others to take one of the two rovers belonging to the US colony for a trip to visit the French colony. They manage to get there, but get frightened when they see a group of adults with long metallic sticks come towards them. Thinking they are being attacked by the enemy, they panic and race off in the rover. There is an accident as the rover runs over the edge of a crater, and rolls down into it. Bell is injured, breaking his collar bone, while the others are battered and bruised. But they are trapped.

It takes a while before they are rescued by the adults using the other rover. Their punishment is extra chores. But there is disagreement between the adults about whether they should regain contact with the other colonies. Whatever troubles there are on Earth between the various nations should be irrelevant for the people living on Mars, but Sai is adamant that there should be no contact between the Mars colonies.

After the supply ship arrives with some extra food and some of the things they need to repair broken equipment, the adults all become sick with a potentially deadly virus. The children are not affected, and in desperation they decide to go and seek help from the other colonies.

They can't take the only rover left, because the planet is undergoing one of its massive planet-wide dust storms and visibility on the surface is zero, so they decide to take the underground train. The storm has lasted for weeks and is still ongoing, and power has been reduced to whatever they have stored in batteries since there is hardly any sunshine for the solar cells to generate electricity. The train runs on batteries, but what Bell and his friend don't know is that all of the batteries, but one, have been taken out and are being used to power essential things in the colony.

The two boys set off in the train and head towards the nearest colony, the Finnish one, but find it deserted. They wander through the brightly painted rooms and see no one. It looks as if they stopped whatever they were doing and simply left. With no one there to help, and unable to comprehend why the whole colony is deserted, they go back to the train and head towards the next colony, the French one, but the train runs out of power along the tunnel and the two boys are stranded in total darkness. They can't get out of the train because there is insufficient space on either side of the train in the tunnel to allow the doors to open.

They are trapped, and there is no one to rescue them since their adults are all very sick. Bell finds a small hatch in the floor under a seat and he is small enough to get out, his friend is too big and must stay in the train while Bell goes for help. Terrified that he might bump into something weird in the blackness of the tunnel he forces himself to keep going. He only has a glow stick to provide a bit of light but that is fading rapidly.

He sees a pair of glowing eyes and is terrified. However, when he hears a meow, he realizes that it is his cat. It has followed him. He picks it up and continues on to the French colony, where he discovers everyone missing from the Finnish colony is there and they are having as party. They are delighted to meet Bell. Apparently, his cat has been visiting the French colony for some time and they feed it. Bell is overwhelmed by the hospitality of the other colonists and can't understand why his adults are so against them.

There are also people from the Russian and the Chinese colony there. When he tells them what has happened they immediately rush over to help and in no time the American adults are on the mend. The reason they were infected is discovered and remedied. The broken equipment is repaired by the other colonists who have tons of spare parts. Plants and other food the Americans have never seen, are offered, and everyone seems very friendly, which puzzles Bell. The children of the colonies exchange music and the girls talk about fashion and other stuff teenagers are into, and all seems to be going very well, until Sai says the contact must stop.

If they are so friendly why does Sai insist that they are enemies and they should not have contact with them? This is the problem that confronts Bell and the other children.

Bell, being incredibly curious, confronts Sai and tells him he saw photos in the French colony of Sai and the other adults at a party with the French people. Eventually Sai is coerced into telling the reason they have no contact and it is not what Bell or any of the other children would have expected.

It goes back to a terrible accident in which the Americans, and Sai in particular, believed that one of their people was abandoned by the French and Russian accompanying her, who survived while she didn't.

It is a misunderstanding between the adults who when finally confronted with the truth of what happened years ago, gradually realize the futility of trying to keep themselves isolated from the others on Mars.

It dawns on them that without each of the colonies co-operating, none of them would be able to survive. Earth was too far away to be of any help; they had to rely on each other.

The analogy in Bell's mind is that together they were the *Pride of Mars*. One sentence in a book he read about lions on Earth was that Lions who are rejected by their pride do not survive long. He knew instinctively that by isolating themselves from the other colonies would not allow them to survive, and they almost didn't. Things could only get better now they were once again united.

The message is simple, and uplifting.

It highlights how the prejudices and misunderstandings of adults can make children suffer, and that if it wasn't for the innocence of the children and how they reunited the separate colonies on Mars the American one would not be able to survive on its own.

It is a message that should apply to every country here on Earth, but will anyone take any notice?

I'm sure this will be a very popular book, and deservedly so.

How to Mars (2021)
David Ebenbach.

This odd novel is hard to categorize because it is both a short novel as well as a collection of individual pieces, that are not quite short stories, even though several of them were published as such while the book was being written. Could it be known as what is now called a *Flash Novel?*

The author thought the idea of *Mars One* which intended to send volunteers on a one-way trip to Mars to establish a permanent colony there, was insane.

Who would want to go to Mars with the knowledge that they could never return to Earth again? That they would have to live there for the rest of their lives?

Well, 200,000 people applied to go. Amazingly enough these were whittled down to around 200. Elaborate plans were made and published including a timetable of when the various aspects of the scheme would occur, then suddenly, a big silence. No more about the reality TV show that was going to sponsor it, no more about who was going and when they were to begin leaving, no word about who was going to build the spaceships to take them there, nothing in the media anywhere. The *Mars One* project went bankrupt. A couple of novels had been written with this concept as the basis of the story, notably **Mars One** by Jonathon Mayberry (2017).

Playing around with the idea of an eccentric billionaire (*guess who could have been the model*) who financed the colonization attempt, assisted by a reality TV series to help pay for it and to generate public interest in such an undertaking, the author wrote a couple of short stories that were published in SF and literary magazines. He continued developing the ideas and though each subsequent chapter of the book oscillates between an info dump in the form of a manual or a guide written by the billionaire who finances the expedition and the establishment of the colony, and different aspects of how six colonists are coping on Mars with their isolation from humankind and having to rely on each other for support to stay alive.

How they deal with the boredom of being forced to live in a tiny, enclosed space because to step outside without using a space suit would kill them within minutes, dealing with unexpected equipment failures, dealing with deteriorating mental stability, while knowing they can never return to Earth, is shown from the from the various perspectives of the six scientists, three males and three females of different nationalities that comprise the small group.

The book opens with one of the women discovering she is pregnant, which generates varying reactions withing the group, good and bad, because this wasn't supposed to happen. All of them had been sterilized before embarking on the voyage to Mars, but apparently the process didn't work in the case of the two people concerned. There is a hint of mental breakdown with one of the men who has acted violently towards another of the team, and who isolates himself for a while from the others, but they need him because he is their main engineer and the only one able to fix electrical problems that begin to plague them.

As the pregnancy develops the moods and feelings of the colonists alter.

There is a hint of an alien presence, invisible to them, but whether this is nothing more than an internal view of one person's mental instability or whether there is an actual alien presence is not resolved, but left hanging, as the group of six come together with the birth of the first baby on Mars.

Each chapter or story segment overlaps to create a coherent whole rather than appear as a fix up novel of short pieces.

Each chapter is told from the viewpoint of one of the six scientists in the group, so the reader gets a broad perspective of how the whole group is coping with being on Mars, and never being able, at this point, to return to Earth.

They are stuck there, and they have to deal with it, to learn to live with each other or they will all perish. With the arrival of the baby, a girl, they all come together to form a family, and as a family, they will survive.

I don't think enough was made of the supposed invisible alien presence, when it was made clear that no living thing no matter how small had yet been discovered, much to the disappointment and disenchantment of the team biologist.

It is overall an odd story that reads easily and is captivating enough.

This story falls into the category of both science fiction, obviously, but also real or speculative literary fiction because we are living in a time when expeditions to Mars are being planned by various nations and groups so how it will be done and how the people involved will react is more speculative reality rather than science fiction. That's my view.

It is also a book worth reading when you come across it. The writing is beautiful, and once you start reading it, you will find it hard not to keep going until the end.

The first edition copy of this book has a very attractive cover that will stand out on bookshop shelves, so if you see it, don't miss it.

Terraforming Mars:
Book 1, In the shadow of Deimos. (2021)
By Jane Killick.

Based on a computer game, this novel has genuine tension and setbacks for the lead character in a believable Martian setting.

Several big corporations have set up colonies on Mars in which they use indentured labor.

There is also a public funded group from the UN there to begin terraforming the planet. The UN group believes by increasing the greenhouse gases they will eventually raise the atmospheric pressure and the oxygen levels to the equivalent of what is found in high mountainous areas on Earth.

One of the corporations believes that by crashing asteroids into the Martian surface they will raise the planet's temperature and increase atmospheric pressure more rapidly than just by pumping greenhouse gases into it.

Another is working with bio-labs to genetically alter certain earth plants so they can grow on Mars using the Martian carbon dioxide atmosphere to have the plants growing on the surface to produce oxygen. This group also runs the greenhouses where food for local consumption is being grown.

Each of the rival corporations have their own agenda, so there is tension and occasionally conflict between them as their aims intersect, but sometimes they do work together in order to maximize profits.

There is a lot more to the background than the above which focuses on the workers brought up from Earth and how they live in the different corporate colonies.

The story opens (in 2316) with the arrival of a group of 40 indentured workers who are to build a city in Noctis Labrynithus, (Noctis City). A rival corporation has a small biological research facility located in the base of this canyon. They are to be ferried from the landing site near the canyon to Tharsis City, the major city on Mars when an asteroid, coming in on an incorrect trajectory, smashes into the other side of the canyon destroying the bio-lab research facility and almost killing the newly arrived workers. It was supposed to land in an uninhabited area but it started to break up on entry and a large piece is what causes the damage. None of the new group would have survived if the whole asteroid had crashed there instead of just a small part of it.

It was later discovered during an investigation into the event that one person was killed, a computer expert who was in the bio-lab attempting to fix computer glitches. The rest of the staff had been sent back to Tharsis City. It was also discovered that it wasn't an accident, the lab was the target and no one was supposed to be there. Someone working in the corporation that was bringing the asteroids down onto Mars as part of their terraforming attempt had been paid to hide a smaller asteroid behind the larger legitimate one, and that the bio-lab was the target for the small asteroid.

Things get more complicated as conspiracies and jealousies between corporate managements arise. One of those newly arrived 40 workers, Luka, was a computer expert and he is sent to examine the files and the computers used to control the asteroid bombardments and he discovers that the computer worker sent to the bio-lab before it was destroyed was sent there deliberately, so he could be killed in the 'accident' because he had discovered something he should not have.

Luka, who is working for the UN World Government, investigates the lead up to the incident and discovers a conspiracy where multiple motives could lead to corruption and a bad situation for all Martian colonists. Those responsible try to stop him in a number of ways but he survives to finally unmask those responsible for all that has happened. The story's climax is with the corporation that is bringing asteroids down onto Mars brings down Deimos as their final attempt to increase the warming and the atmospheric pressure. Deimos crashes into Mars forming a gigantic crater.

A truly spectacular ending…

The story is complete, but the reader knows there will be more.

This is a good story with intriguing characters, good and nasty, and the style of writing is clear and easy to read. It's one of those hard to put down books.

Terraforming Mars:
Book two, The edge of catastrophe. (2022)
By Jane Killick.

200 years later in the 26th century, Mars is a very different place to what it was in the first book. Colonies have thrived and expanded. There is a constant influx of immigrants from Earth and a huge population of Martian born citizens. There is rivalry of course between the Martian born and the Earth born immigrants.

Ecoline conglomerate is the leading corporation dealing with genetically altering food crops like potatoes to become higher in fibre with less starch, and for the stems and leaves to not have any poison in them so they too can be consumed instead of wasted. Mel Erdan (the biologist) is working not only to alter potatoes genetically for them to be more nutritious, but also to be faster growing so crop turnarounds can be quicker, in order to help feed the burgeoning population.

The central city is beneath a gigantic dome that covers the crater formed when Deimos crashed into Mars 200 years earlier.

The underlying theme is that the native-born Martians want to be independent from Earth, and with mining and food production high, the income earned from mining should stay on Mars rather than going back to Earth. A group of dissidents is causing trouble in Deimos City, and they are relentlessly chased by the Security forces.

When Mel's experimental fast-growing crop succumbs to a massive viral infection, with all the potatoes turning rotten and foul smelling practically overnight, she is devastated. Potatoes are the main staple on Mars. But what makes it worse is that several large farms that used potato seed stock supplied by Mel's lab also succumb to the same viral infection that turns the crops into rotting sludge. She is taken in for questioning by the security police and is blamed for deliberately sabotaging the Martian food supply. They refuse to listen to her when she tells them it was impossible for any virus to spread from her sealed lab, and that being an expert on the matter she is the one who should be able to find a solution.

Meanwhile, the dissident group is stirring up the population and causing food hoarding and subsequent shortages. The ruling Martian governing body issues statements trying to calm the population down, but this only inflames them and rioting begins with looting and people hoarding food.

Rationing is introduced. But wealthy corporations and those higher ranked people who control them are having vital food supplies shipped to their various corporation headquarters, while the general population is having their food rationed.

Mel is officially arrested for sabotaging the food crops no matter how much she pleads innocent. She is to be taken to Noctis City for trial. She is put on a special carriage with a small security detail. This carriage is part of a freight train carrying grain and cereal foods to be used by corporation heavies. While the train is automated, the only carriage with people on board is the one with Mel and the security detail. The trains run on overhead rails between the larger cities.

This train is attacked by a small group of dissidents who blow up the line as the train reaches the spot they chose. With the train partially derailed and carriages hanging off the overhead rail lines they climb on board to steal the food being transported. Mel takes this opportunity to escape from her Security detail and manages to hide on the truck being used to transport the stolen food. It heads back to Deimos City where she disappears into the crowd that forms when the dissidents start to give the stolen food to the people. It turns into a riot as frantic citizens try to get as much food as they can.

The whole economy is falling apart, people don't have enough food to survive on, and the security forces are not helping with their heavy handed tactics. They are also looking for Mel whom they blame for all of it.

Mel's only hope is to find what happened to her potatoes, why and how other crops in isolated greenhouses were infected with the same virus, and who actually caused it to happen. A hopeless situation with the security on the lookout and nowhere for her to go.

But she manages and does find out what had happened and who had done it, and how the seed potatoes from her lab got into other greenhouses. She also, with the help of an old friend in a remote lab, finds a solution. They are almost prevented from revealing the truth, but in the end, they prevail, and the culprits are brought to justice.

Mars and its new colonies will survive, and the planet continues to be terraformed with new technologies emerging to increase the speed of how it will happen.

Another thrilling, fast-paced, hard to put down book that gives us an all too credible vision of what living on Mars may possibly be like.

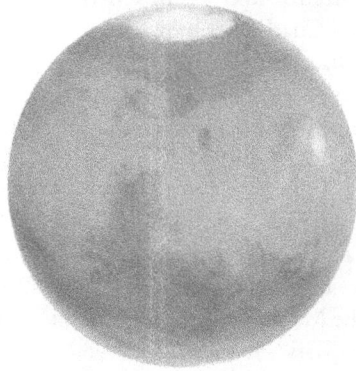

Afterword:

I might finish by mentioning that there are many books about Mars that I haven't yet read, some because they seem to be endless fantasies that go on book after book, (not my cup of tea) as well as a continuing output of eBooks, some of which I have, but many which I probably won't acquire. There are also some books that I started to read but simply couldn't get into them, so they are sitting on a shelf with the possibility to be read, or not, at a later date, all too late to be included in this volume.

And the stories keep coming...

Acknowledgments:

All photos here in this book are credited to **NASA/JPL-Caltechh/MSSS**

It's wonderful they allow the general public to see as well as use these photos.

I would also like to thank all of the authors for producing and writing these Martian Stories. They have allowed me, and many others, to dream of Mars in so many different ways.

I have found the **SFE Encyclopedia of Science Fiction** to be a fantastic source of information regarding long dead authors (as well as those still living and writing) and would recommend any SF fan to look at their website if they want to know anything about their favourite author as well as what they have published over the years.

They state: Our aim is to provide a comprehensive, scholarly, and critical guide to science fiction in all its forms... and they certainly do. To the editors of this encyclopedia, my deepest thanks for the lifetime of work they have dedicated to keeping us fans informed.

John Litchen.

Books and stories mentioned — in Chronological order:

1876 - A trip to Mars - Charles K Landis - 15
1880 - Across the Zodiac - Percy Greg - 20
1901 - Honeymoon in Space - 31
1903 - The Certainty od a future life in Mars - L P Gratacap - 38
1903 - The Great Sacrifice - George C Wallis - 37
1905 - Gulliver of Mars - Edward L Arnold - 41
1907 - Is Mars Habitable? - Alfred Russel Wallace - 63
1909 - Zarlah the Martian - R. Norman Grisewood - 50
1910 - Through Space to Mars/The longest Journey on Record - Roy Lockwood - 55
1911 - To Mars via the Moon: An astronomical story - Mark Wicks - 59
1927 - The Retreat to Mars - Cecil B White - 80
1928 - The Return of the Martians - Cecil B White - 82
1915 - Baron Munchhausen's Scientific Adventures - Hugo Gernsback - 70
1922 - The Planet Mars and its Inhabitants - 90
1927 - The fate of the Poseidonia - F C Harris - 75
1930 - The Ambassador from Mars - Harl Vincent - 86
1931 - Vandals of The Void - James Morgan A Walsh - 91
1932 - Thia of the Drlands - Harl Vincent - 89
1932 - The Lost Machine - John B Harris - 92
1934 - Valley of Dreams - Stanly G Weinbaum - 96
1936 - The Brain Stealers of Mars - John W Campbell Jr - 98
1937 - Star Begotten - H G Wells - 99
1939 - Nonstop to Mars - Jack Williamson - 100
1940 - Westpoint 3000 A.D. - Stanto A Coblentz - 103
1940 - The Red Death of Mars - Robert Moore Williams - 111
1941 - Death Desert - Robert Moore Williams - 112
1941 - The Teacher from Mars - Eando Binder - 105
1941 - The Secret Sense - Isaac Asimov - 106
1941 - The Martians are Coming - Robert W Lowndes - 107
1942 - Holy City of Mars - Ralph Milne Farley /Al R Nelson - 109
1943 - The Cave - P Schuyler Miller - 109
1950 - City of the Dead - G M Martin - 129
1951 - Martian Nightmare - Bryce Walton - 122
1954 - The Crystal Crypt - Philip K Dick - 124
1954 - Kings of Space - Captain W E Johns - 126
1955 - Return to Mars - Captain W E Johns - 129
1955 - Mission to Mars - Sir Patric Moore - 142
1956 - Artifact - Chad Oliver - 135
1956 - Now to The Stars - Captain W E Johns - 133
1956 - The Domes of Mars - Sir Patric Moore - 148
1957 - The Voices of Mars - Sir Patrick Moore - 152
1958 - Peril on Mars - Sir Patrick Moore - 158
1958 - Planet of Exile - Edmond Hamilton - 137
1959 - Raiders of Mars - Sir Patrick Moore - 161

2022 - Terraforming Mars - The Edge of Catastrophe - Jane Killick - 399
2022 - Mars Adrift - McFall and Hayes - 388
2022 - Denver Moon - The Thirteen of Mars - 324

Mars eBooks
Waiting to be read on my Kindle Cloud space.
Deception - by Paul Rix.
Mars Nation - Trilogy by Brandon Q Morris
The Mars One Incident - by Kelly Curtis
Waves on Mars - by D R Swann
The Coming Storm - by D R Swann
Artifact - by D R Swann
Wasting Time on Mars - by A M K Taylor
Colony 5 - by Gerald M Kilby
Mars, The Machine War - by Joseph R Lewis
Mars Colony Chronicles - by Brandon Ellis
(Martian Plague, Martian Ark, Martian Insurrection)
Daughter of Mars trilogy - by Mathew Cox
Back Door to Mars - by Joseph Hunter
Martian Dreams - by Linda Naughton
Dreams of Mars - by Jenni Thornby
Red Horizon, the truth of discovery - by Salvador Mercer
The alliance - by Jason Letts
And because of my reluctance to read novels on a computer, it could be some time before I get to read these eBooks; far too late for me to say anything about them here.

Also recommended is a superb collection of shorter Martian stories in a volume called ***The 2020 Look at Mars Fiction Book,*** edited by Alan Kaster.

It features stories by John Barnes, Stephen Baxter, Paul McAuley, Will McCarthy, Ian McDonald, Linda Nagata, and Alan M Steele, among many others, and is, I think, one of the best representative collections of Martian stories from leading writers in recent years.

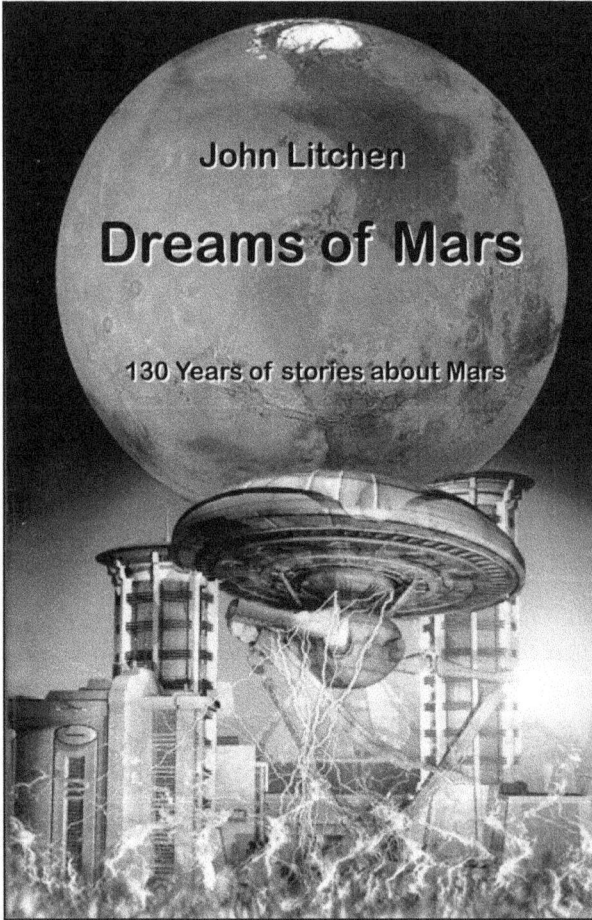

*The cover of my first book of stories about Mars
still available from all the usual sources.*

Thank you for taking the time to read this book.

More Dreams of Mars

www.ingramcontent.com/pod-product-compliance
Lightning Source LLC
Chambersburg PA
CBHW020601270326
41927CB00005B/123